EDGAR ALLAN POE

BOOKS BY JEFFREY MEYERS

BIOGRAPHY
A Fever at the Core: The Idealist in Politics
Married to Genius
Katherine Mansfield
The Enemy: A Biography of Wyndham Lewis
Hemingway
Manic Power: Robert Lowell and His Circle
D. H. Lawrence
Joseph Conrad
Edgar Allan Poe: His Life and Legacy

CRITICISM
Fiction and the Colonial Experience
The Wounded Spirit: T. E. Lawrence's Seven Pillars of Wisdom
A Reader's Guide to George Orwell
Painting and the Novel
Homosexuality and Literature
D. H. Lawrence and the Experience of Italy
Disease and the Novel
The Spirit of Biography

BIBLIOGRAPHY
T. E. Lawrence: A Bibliography
Catalogue of the Library of the Late Siegfried Sassoon
George Orwell: An Annotated Bibliography of Criticism

EDITED COLLECTIONS
George Orwell: The Critical Heritage
Ernest Hemingway: The Critical Heritage
Robert Lowell: Interviews and Memoirs

EDITED ORIGINAL ESSAYS
Wyndham Lewis by Roy Campbell
Wyndham Lewis: A Revaluation
D. H. Lawrence and Tradition
The Legacy of D. H. Lawrence
The Craft of Literary Biography
The Biographer's Art
T. E. Lawrence: Soldier, Writer, Legend
Graham Greene: A Revaluation

EDGAR ALLAN POE
HIS LIFE AND LEGACY

JEFFREY MEYERS

CHARLES SCRIBNER'S SONS • NEW YORK
MAXWELL MACMILLAN CANADA • TORONTO
MAXWELL MACMILLAN INTERNATIONAL
New York • Oxford • Singapore • Sydney

Charles Scribner's Sons
Macmillan Publishing Company
866 Third Avenue
New York, NY 10022

Maxwell Macmillan Canada, Inc.
1200 Eglinton Avenue East
Suite 200
Don Mills, Ontario M3C 3N1

Macmillan Publishing Company is part of the Maxwell Communication
Group of Companies.

Meyers, Jeffrey.
  Edgar Allan Poe : his life and legacy / Jeffrey Meyers.
    p. cm.
  Includes bibliographical references and index.
  ISBN 0-684-19370-1 :
    1. Poe, Edgar Allan, 1809–1849. 2. Authors, American—19th
century—Biography. I. Title.
  PS2631.M48 1992
  818'.309—dc20
  [B]   92-17890
                         CIP

Macmillan Books are available at special discounts for bulk
purchases for sales promotions, premiums, fund-raising, or
educational use. For details, contact:

        Special Sales Director
        Macmillan Publishing Company
        866 Third Avenue
        New York, NY 10022

                10 9 8 7 6 5 4 3 2 1

        Printed in the United States of America

For Tom McGuane

Contents

"In biography the truth is everything," Poe wrote, "and in autobiography it is especially so." Yet he left a trail of misleading evidence behind him and tried to hide his years as a common soldier with a fantastic though circumstantial account of a trip to Greece and Russia. An obituary published two days after his death emphasized the tempestuous career of the strangest and saddest figure in American literature, and rightly said: "His life has been an eventful and stormy one, and if any one shall be found to write its history, we venture to say that its simple truths will be of more thrilling interest than most romances."

Poe's best works are as interesting as his life. Whenever I told people I was writing a life of Poe, they would immediately start to recite "The Raven" ("Once upon a midnight dreary . . ."), which they had learned in childhood and still remembered. T. S. Eliot suggested that Poe's memorable poetry had filtered deeply into popular consciousness by observing: "it goes throbbing in your head [and] you begin to suspect that perhaps you will never forget it." As I became absorbed in this biography and thought about why Poe's imaginative works have appealed to so many readers, I discovered that many of his most weird and bizarre stories—not only "William Wilson" but also "Loss of Breath," *The Narrative of Arthur Gordon Pym*, "The Fall of the House of Usher," "Eleonora," "The Murders in the Rue Morgue," "The Black Cat," "The Facts in the Case of M. Valdemar," "The Cask of Amontillado" and "Hop-Frog"—were extremely autobiographical (though distorted and exaggerated) and could be illuminated by relating them to the events of his life. I also realized that though Poe died almost a century and a half ago, his life, ideas and themes seem astonishingly modern. I have, throughout the book, compared Poe to twentieth-century writers—many of whom (as the last chapter shows) were strongly influenced by him.

Since the quality of Poe's poems, stories and criticism—much of it hastily produced to fend off starvation—varies enormously, I have concentrated on his best work and ignored the rest. While exploring Poe's character and narrating his life, I have tried to follow the advice he gave when reviewing Thomas Carlyle's *Life of Friedrich Schiller* in December 1845: "Biography is not merely a sketch of the poet's life. . . . It is a gradual development of his heart and mind, of his nature as a poet and a man, that endears him more to us, while it enables us more thoroughly to comprehend him."

=== *Acknowledgments*

I am grateful to many people and institutions for help with this book. I corresponded with and interviewed Edgar Allan Poe III, Margaret Woods (a descendant of Frances Allan), Lael and William Wertenbaker (a descendant of his namesake and Poe's college friend). For other assistance I thank my good friends Morris Brownell, Dr. Sheldon Cooperman, Valerie Hemingway, Francis King, Timothy Materer, Ellen Nims and Thomas Pinney. Robert Merrill and a number of Poe scholars have also been helpful: Richard Kopley, Burton Pollin, Edward Wagenknecht and Richard Wilbur.

The custodians of the Poe rooms, houses and museums in Fordham, Philadelphia, Baltimore, Richmond and Charlottesville, and the librarians at Berkeley, Stanford, Harvard, the Enoch Pratt Free Library (Baltimore), the National Library of Medicine and the Alderman Library at the University of Virginia were extremely accommodating. I also received useful material from the Archives Department of the London Borough of Hackney, the National Association of Funeral Directors and the United States Military Archives. As always, my wife Valerie carefully read each chapter and compiled the index.

Edgar: "Some villain hath done me wrong."

Edgar: "[I] am bethought
          To take the basest and most poorest shape
          That ever penury, in contempt of man,
          Brought near to beast."

King Lear

EDGAR ALLAN POE

AN INAUSPICIOUS BIRTH, 1809-1811

Edgar Poe's ancestors were agriculturists and artisans on one side, actors on the other; and the paternal branch of the family had some claim to military distinction. Poe's great-great-grandfather, David Poe, was a Protestant tenant-farmer amidst the endless bogs and stony fields of Dring, Co. Cavan, Ireland, about seventy-five miles northwest of Dublin. His son John, after marrying the sister of an admiral, emigrated in about 1750 to Lancaster County, Pennsylvania. John's eldest son, David, who was seven years old when the family left for America, moved in 1775 to Baltimore, where he made spinning wheels and clock reels, and later owned a drygoods store.

David Poe, a member of Captain John McClellan's Company of Baltimore troops in 1778–79, was appointed Assistant Deputy Quartermaster and authorized to purchase supplies for the American army. When General Lafayette returned to tumultuous acclaim in Baltimore in 1824, he inquired about his old friend (who had died eight years earlier) and paid tribute to his generosity during the war: "I have not seen among these my friendly and patriotic commissary, Mr. David Poe, who resided in Baltimore when I was here, and of his own very limited means supplied me with five hundred dollars to aid in clothing my troops, and whose wife, with her own hands, cut out five hundred pairs of pantaloons and superintended the making of them for the use of my men."[1] Lafayette visited Poe's grave and observed: "*Ici repose un coeur noble."* David Poe had spent forty thousand dollars of his own money on the Revolutionary cause and, though holding the rank of major, was given a courtesy title and always known as "General" Poe. Edgar, with characteristic exaggeration, later promoted his grandfather to Quartermaster General of the whole United States Army during the Revolutionary War.

Poe's maternal grandparents were married in London in May 1784. Henry Arnold remains a shadowy figure; but his wife, Elizabeth, first appeared on stage at the Theatre Royal, Covent Garden, in February 1791 and made her last appearance in London in June 1795. Elizabeth, by then apparently a widow, took a winter passage to Boston, aboard the *Outram*, with her daughter, Eliza, arriving in January 1796. Later that year she married the actor, singer and pianist, Charles Tubbs. She disappeared from theatrical records in 1798 and may have died soon afterwards.

The exceptionally precocious and talented Eliza Arnold (Edgar's mother) made her theatrical debut in Boston, three months after her arrival, at the age of nine. In November 1796 the Portland *Eastern Herald* praised her as the coquettish Biddy Bellair in David Garrick's farce, *Miss in Her Teens*: "Miss Arnold, in Miss Biddy, exceeded all praise. Although a Miss of only nine years old, her powers as an Actress will do credit to any of her sex of maturer age."[2] The following month, another critic was delighted by "the powers of Miss Arnold to astonish us. Add to these her youth, her beauty, her innocence, and a character is composed which has not, and perhaps will not ever again be found in any Theatre."[3]

Eliza, whose mother had died, married Charles Hopkins, an actor, in the summer of 1802, when she was fifteen. An oval miniature, the only known portrait of the petite Eliza, portrays her round childlike face, long dangling curls, unusually large doe-like eyes and cupid's-bow mouth. Seated, and looking straight out of the portrait, she wears a beribboned bonnet, dangling earrings and a low-cut dress, with long sleeves and a high sash under the bodice, which reveals her full figure.

In the course of her extraordinary theatrical career the charming Eliza played—apart from choral, vocal and dancing roles—nearly three hundred parts. These included Shakespeare's Juliet, Ophelia and Cordelia; Lydia Languish and Lady Teazel in Sheridan's *The Rivals* and *The School for Scandal*; and numerous heroines in then popular and now forgotten comedies, farces and tragedies. The year after her marriage, another critic commended the veteran sixteen-year-old's appearance, ability and voice: "Mrs. Hopkins' interesting figure, her *correct* performance, and the accuracy with which she always commits her part, together with her sweetly melodious voice when she charms us with a song, have deservedly raised her to that respectable rank which she indisputably holds in the public favor."[4]

Poe's father, David Poe Jr., three years older than Eliza, was born in Baltimore in 1784. Though destined for the law, he joined the Thespian Club in Baltimore, where young men read and performed plays. While on a business trip to Norfolk, Virginia, he saw Eliza perform onstage, fell in love with the young English actress and eventually joined her troupe. In 1806, only six months after the death of her first husband, David married Eliza in Richmond. The nineteen-year-old widowed actress had been in an extremely vulnerable position, and may have married David Poe (and perhaps Charles Hopkins) for protection as much as for love. Their first child, Henry, was born nine months later in January 1807 and from the age of two was cared for by friends of the family in Baltimore. "General" Poe had been furious when his son abandoned a promising law career for the stage and then married an actress (in those days a profession of dubious reputation and social status). But he was reconciled with the young couple when their first son was born.

David Poe had an attractive face and figure, suitable for juvenile parts and romantic heroes. During his six-year career he played 137 different roles, 19 of them Shakespearean. But all the critics seemed to agree that the experienced, versatile Eliza was a much better actor than David. A notice of 1806 condemned his performance and severely remarked that "the lady was young and pretty, and evinced talent both as singer and actress; the gentleman was literally nothing."[5] In two other reviews, written a few years later, Eliza was highly commended while David was harshly criticized. The first critic wrote: "From an actress who possesses so eminently the faculty of pleasing, whose powers are so general and whose exertions are so ready, it would be unjust to withhold the tribute of applause."[6] But the second said: "a more wretched Alonzo have we never witnessed. This man was never destined for the high walks of the drama;—a footman is the extent of what he ought to attempt. . . . His person, voice, and non-expression of countenance, all combine to stamp him—*poh!*"[7]

Sensitive and perhaps vain about his acting ability, the hot-tempered, hard-drinking David found it difficult to swallow not only these insults but also the execrable puns on his name and allusions to chamber pots. (Such puns would later plague Edgar during his fierce literary disputes.) On more than one occasion David threatened to thrash critics who had ridiculed his wife's costume and endangered his own livelihood.

At the beginning of the nineteenth century (when Richmond, for example, had a population of only 4,000) most American cities were too small to support a permanent theater company and actors were forced to travel the circuit in various towns up and down the East Coast. Eliza acted in Richmond, Baltimore, Philadelphia, New York and Boston, the same cities in which Edgar later lived and worked. Driven by the need to earn money and burdened by a feckless husband, she performed on the Boston stage only a week before Edgar's birth and reappeared one month later.

Edgar was born in a humble lodging house near Carver Street, south of the Boston Common, on January 19, 1809. Mendelssohn, Darwin, Tennyson, Gladstone, Lincoln and Oliver Wendell Holmes were also born in 1809 and all but the composer outlived Poe. In that year Tom Paine died, Washington Irving published *A History of New York* and in Europe Byron brought out *English Bards and Scotch Reviewers*, Goethe *The Elective Affinities* and Schlegel *On Dramatic Art and Literature*. James Madison was president of the United States, Metternich was prime minister of Austria and Napoleon won a brilliant victory, near Vienna, in the Battle of Wagram.

On the back of a watercolor sketch of Boston Harbor, which Poe treasured, his mother had written: "For my little son Edgar, who should ever love Boston, the place of his birth, and where his mother found her best, and most sympathetic friends."[8] In adult life, however, Poe nourished a strong dislike for the city of his birth. He hated its ruling literary class—their stuffy morality, vague Transcendental philosophy, Abolitionist movement and sterile domination of the American literary scene.

Edgar's birth sparked a financial crisis and emotional upheaval in the Poe family. Desperate for money but unwilling to ask his father, David Poe traveled south to Stockertown, fifty miles north of Philadelphia, to the house of his cousin George Poe. Arriving at night, he called George to the door, told George that the most awful moment of his life had come, pleaded for an urgent meeting the next day, insisted he had not come to beg and strode off in a tragic manner. George kept his appointment the following day but failed to find David, who then sent him an "impertinent note." The only surviving letter by David Poe, written on February 23, 1809, sounds like many that were later written by his son. There is the unbalanced, recriminatory tone, arrogant and humiliating demand for money, dubious assurance of repayment, pathetic explanation of distress, testing of

friendship and favor, plea of impulsive youth, justification of a career
that led to destitution, appeal to honor, desperation of extreme poverty, haughty insistence on help—and hopeless ineffectuality:

> *You* promised *me* on your honor to meet me at the Mansion
> house of the 23d—*I* promise *you* on *my* word of honor that
> if you will lend me 30, 20, 15 or even 10$ I will *remit* it to
> you *immediately* on my arrival in Baltimore. Be assured I will
> keep *my* promise at least as well as you did yours, and that
> nothing but extreem distress would have *forc'd* me to make
> this application.—Your answer by the bearer will prove
> whether I have yet "favor in your eyes" or whether I am to
> be despised by (as I understand) a rich relation because when
> a *wild boy* I join'd a profession which I then thought and now
> think an honorable one. But which I would most willingly
> quit tomorrow if it gave satisfaction to your family provided
> I could do *any thing* else that would give bread to mine.—
> Your politeness will no doubt enduce you to answer this
> note.[9]

In late February, after this emotional plea had failed, the Poes left
the five-week-old Edgar in Baltimore with his paternal grandparents,
"General" David and Elizabeth Poe, and continued their theatrical
tour. They returned to fetch him in late August, when the season was
over, placing Edgar and (later) his sister Rosalie in the care of an old
nursemaid. A friend reported that the two children "were thin and
pale and very fretful. To quiet them their old nurse . . . took them
upon her lap and fed them liberally with bread soaked in gin, when
they soon fell asleep. . . . [She acknowledged] that she had, from the
very birth of the girl [in December 1810], freely administered to them
gin and other spirituous liquors, with sometimes laudanum [opium
dissolved in alcohol], 'to make them strong and healthy,' or to put
them to sleep when restless."[10] The etiology of Poe's alcoholism
began in infancy.

David Poe made his last stage appearance in October 1809; by July
1811—when Edgar was two and a half years old—he had deserted
his wife and children and vanished forever. We can only speculate
about the the reasons for David's disappearance. Eliza had a successful
career; David, after many mediocre performances and harsh reviews,
was discouraged, frustrated and professionally jealous. Known for his
heavy drinking, both onstage and off, David may have been dismissed
for incompetence. There may have been recriminations about their

impetuous marriage and his inability to take responsibility for three small and perhaps unwanted children. Illness and poverty certainly intensified the couple's problems and undermined their relationship. Five months later, on about December 11, 1811, David seems to have died, alone, in Norfolk.

From his father Edgar inherited family pride, incongruous gentility, histrionic habits, a volatile temperament, sensitivity to criticism, self-pity, instability, a perverse self-destructive tendency and an Irish weakness for drink. David Poe had lost caste and alienated his family by abandoning law for the stage as Edgar later would do by abandoning his university education to become a common soldier and, when plunging into the uncertain waters of literature, by giving up his career as a West Point cadet to join the destitute writers of Grub Street.

The desertion of her husband, the arduous demands of her profession, the constant movement from one cheap lodging house to another, the sole responsibility for her young children, her life of hardship and poverty, undoubtedly contributed to the early death of Eliza Poe. She made her last appearance onstage on October 11, 1811. Three weeks later a Richmond neighbor told his sister that Eliza was being patronized by Richmond Society: "Mrs. Poe, who you know is a very handsome woman, happens to be very sick, and (having quarreled and parted with her husband) is destitute. The most fashionable place of resort now is—her chamber—and the skill of cooks and nurses is exerted to procure her delicacies."[11]

On November 29 the managers of the Richmond Theater, encouraged by the most respectable families of the city, announced a benefit performance for Eliza, who had been suffering from a long and serious illness. That same day the *Enquirer* reported her hopeless condition and asked for urgent help: "On this night, *Mrs. Poe*, lingering on the bed of disease and surrounded by her children, asks your assistance and *asks it perhaps for the last time*."[12] After a rapid decline, Eliza died of tuberculosis, at the age of twenty-four, on December 8. Her obituary notice observed that "the stage has been deprived of one of its chief ornaments; and to say the least of her, she was an interesting actress, and never failed to catch the applause and command the admiration of the beholder."[13] In her brief life Eliza had married twice, had three children and established a solid reputation as a charming and versatile actress.

Mr. and Mrs. Luke Usher (who gave their name to Poe's most famous story), older, actor friends, who had been Eliza's protectors after the death of her mother, took care of Edgar and Rosalie during

Eliza's last illness. Poe later said that he had never known his mother nor enjoyed the affection of his father, for they had died within three days of each other. The desertion of his father and death of his mother must have had considerable emotional impact on the nearly three-year-old child. Closeted with his mother in their cramped quarters, he must have remembered something of the melancholy atmosphere, poignant silence and hopeless despair as the attendants passed in and out of the sickroom; he surely retained some memory of the racking coughs, the spitting of blood, the sudden crimson hemorrhages and the pallid figure extended on her deathbed.

Poe later emphasized his artistic heritage and exclaimed: "The writer of this article is himself the son of an actress—has invariably made it his boast—and no earl was ever prouder of his earldom than he of his descent from a woman who, although well-born, hesitated not to consecrate to the drama her brief career of genius and of beauty."[14] Besides the inscribed watercolor of Boston harbor, Poe inherited his mother's precocity, talent, imagination, dedication to art and courage in adversity as well as the indelible image of a beautiful dying young woman. He would also share her itinerant way of life, her impoverished existence and her dreary death.

According to Edgar, "General" Poe—who never recovered the money he had spent during the Revolutionary War—had lost his wealth, had been reduced to poverty at the time of his daughter-in-law's death and had been unable to accept responsibility for his grandchildren. Just after Eliza died, Rosalie was taken into the care of the Richmond merchant, William Mackenzie. John and Frances Allan, who had no children of their own, took Edgar into their home—above the store of Ellis & Allan, general merchants, on the corner of Main and Thirteenth streets—and into an entirely different world. Two weeks after Eliza's death, on December 26, 1811, seventy-two people were burned to death during a disastrous fire at the Richmond Theater and the entire city joined the small orphan in mourning.

Chapter 2

CHILDHOOD:
JOHN ALLAN AND ENGLAND,
1812–1825

I ===

John Allan, Poe's foster father, had also been an orphan. Born in Irvine, Ayrshire (southwest of Glasgow) in 1779, he emigrated to Richmond in January 1795 and became the partner of Charles Ellis in November 1800. In Richmond, the merchants, along with the planters and professional men, comprised the three most important social classes. Ellis & Allan exported Virginia tobacco to the rollers of big cigars and "in addition to the wide assortment of cloths and ready-made clothing, the hardware, paints and oils, the firm dealt in wheat, maize, corn meal, grains, fine teas and coffees, wines and liquors. They supplied plantations with agricultural implements, nails and hardware, chartered ships and coastwise schooners; imported tomb-stones—and as a side issue were not above trading in horses, Kentucky swine from the settlements, and old slaves [half the population of the city was black] whom they hired out at the coal pits till they died." In April 1811, toward the end of the Napoleonic Wars and shortly before taking Edgar Poe into his household, the industrious Allan had taken a business trip to Lisbon.

A shrewd, good-looking man, with dark curly hair, high forehead, small widely spaced eyes, blunt Roman nose, sensual mouth and firm chin, Allan was described by a Richmond contemporary as "impulsive and quick-tempered . . . rather rough and uncultured in mind and manner."[1] In February 1803 he had married Frances Valentine, an attractive eighteen-year-old woman with long curls, large eyes, an oval face and dainty features. But her poor health and nervous disposition encouraged Allan to seek sexual pleasure with other women; and one of his illegitimate sons, Edward Collier, who was a few years older than Edgar, also attended school in Richmond. Frances and her sister Nancy, who lived with the Allans, were devoted to Edgar and lavished affection on the attractive, delightful child. Poe later recorded a Proustian memory of his foster mother: "Whenever the bureau drawers in her room were opened there came from them a whiff of orris root, and ever since when I smell it I go back to the time when I was a little boy."

Though Edgar Poe was never actually adopted, his foster parents parted his name and put Allan in the middle. Brought up as an Episcopalian, he was baptized in 1812 and confirmed in 1825. But he soon lost his religious belief and, as he explained in "The Domain of Arnheim," "Some peculiarities, either in his early education, or in the [sceptical] nature of his intellect, had tinged with what is termed materialism all his ethical speculations." He wrote, as the poet Allen Tate observed, as though Christianity had never been invented.

The Allans dressed Edgar like a young prince and took him each summer to White Sulphur Springs and other fashionable resorts. At the age of three he was "a lovely little fellow, with dark curls and brilliant eyes . . . charming every one by his childish grace, vivacity, and cleverness."[2] His parents were fond of exhibiting his precocious talents to their evening guests; and Edgar's retentive memory and musical ear enabled him to learn and recite the most moving and beautiful passages of English poetry. He was encouraged to stand on the dining-room table in his stockinged feet and toast the health of the ladies with a glass of sweetened wine.

Allan, a poor disciplinarian, confused the child by alternately spoiling and scolding him. Edgar was sent to the finest schools, taught every proper accomplishment and brought up with the habits of elegant society. When the mistress of his dame school punished the disobedient boy by hanging a vegetable around his neck and sending him home in disgrace, the proud father condemned the teacher and threatened to withdraw his son from the school.

II ===

America's war with Britain from June 1812 until January 1815 had prevented Allan from conducting business with his native country. But after hostilities had ceased and Wellington had defeated Napoleon at Waterloo, England attempted, after a quarter century of disastrous wars from Lisbon to Moscow, to resume normal commerce. On June 23, 1815 the Allans, with Nancy and Edgar, embarked on an uncomfortable thirty-four-day voyage from Norfolk to Liverpool aboard the *Lothair*. Allan complained that he had to sleep on the floor of the cabin and that his family was denied the use of a fire to broil their bacon. At the end of July, after an absence of more than twenty years, he arrived in Britain to open a London branch of "Allan & Ellis" (the names now reversed). Poe (in his first authentic voice) urged Allan, when writing home, to recognize and confirm his bravery: "Edgar says Pa say something for me say I was not afraid of coming across the Sea."

During August and September, the Allan family visited Scottish relatives in Irvine and Kilmarnock (where Robert Burns had published his poems in 1796); and in October took lodgings at 47 Southampton Row, Russell Square, in Bloomsbury. The following April Edgar, "thin as a razor," entered the boarding school of the Misses Dubourg (whose name he later used for the laundress-witness in "The Murders in the Rue Morgue") at 146 Sloane Street in Chelsea. There he had a "separate bed" and studied spelling, history and geography. In September 1817 Allan rented more comfortable quarters at 39 Southampton Row, the address of the narrator in Poe's trivial story, "Why the Little Frenchman Wears His Hand in a Sling."

In 1818 the nine-year-old Edgar entered the Reverend John Bransby's Manor House boarding school in the country village of Stoke Newington, four miles north of London. That Dissenting community had a rich literary tradition. Daniel Defoe had been educated at its Nonconformist Academy and had lived in the village, where he wrote *Robinson Crusoe* (1719), from 1709 until his death in 1731. Isaac Watts followed Defoe in the Academy and wrote hymns in Stoke Newington; the poet Samuel Rogers was born and grew up there; and Mary Wollstonecraft (who later married William Godwin) opened a school in the village in 1783. Poe, who adopted Defoe's use of realistic details to make his fantastic stories credible, later remembered his first joyous reading of *Robinson Crusoe* and praised Defoe's powers of imagination:

How fondly do we recur, in memory, to those enchanted days of our boyhood when we first learned to grow serious over *Robinson Crusoe!*—when we first found the spirit of wild adventure enkindling within us; as by the dim fire light, we labored out, line by line, the marvelous import of those pages, and hung breathless and trembling with eagerness over their absorbing—over their enchaining interest! . . . The author of *Crusoe* must have possessed, above all other faculties, what has been termed the faculty of *identification*—that dominion exercised by volition over imagination which enables the mind to lose its own, in a fictitious, individuality.[3]

A historian of education has emphasized the mechanical rote learning that prevailed in English schools of that time: "There was, then, no genuine teaching, no conception of the processes of education, of learning; nothing but continuous memorising of a series of classical texts whose content was rarely expounded or understood." And a biographer has described a school, similar to Poe's, at Enfield, six miles north of Stoke Newington, which Keats attended in 1803, when he was eight years old. The basis of the curriculum was Latin, French and mathematics; the atmosphere less cruel and more congenial than in the older and more famous schools:

The small academy at Enfield, with almost seventy-five students, was not thought of as a preparatory school for scholars any more than for sons of the aristocracy. The intention was to offer a fairly liberal education to students whose families were in trade or in the less affluent professions, and who were not necessarily looking forward to entering a university. . . . Some mathematics and science were taught; and the grounding in Latin was good. . . . Greek was probably not taught. . . . French was taught, and Keats learned to read it fluently. If Enfield lacked the advantages of the great Public Schools, it had compensations. There was no fagging. There even seems to have been little or no physical punishment. The school was small enough so that the enlightened influence of [the headmaster] was constantly felt.[4]

Many of Poe's weird stories reflect his own experience and, like "Why the Little Frenchman," take place in towns where he had lived: "A Tale of the Ragged Mountains" in Charlottesville; "The Gold-

Bug" in Fort Moultrie, South Carolina; "Landor's Cottage" in Fordham; and "William Wilson" (whose narrator, like Arthur Gordon Pym, shares Poe's birthday) in Stoke Newington. In this story, Poe transforms the quite ordinary early eighteenth century square, two-story building, with high sash windows and a covered doorway, into "a large, rambling, Elizabethan house," a veritable "palace of enchantment! There was really no end to its windings—to its incomprehensible subdivisions."

The American boy, whose country had recently been at war with England, may have received a cool reception from his schoolmates and found it difficult to endure a second separation from his parents. In "William Wilson" Poe expands the circumscribed grounds and emphasizes the claustrophobic atmosphere as well as the dreary diurnal routine:

> The grounds were extensive, and a high and solid brick wall, topped with a bed of mortar and broken glass, encompassed the whole. This prison-like rampart formed the limit of our domain; beyond it we saw but thrice a week—once every Saturday afternoon, when, attended by two ushers, we were permitted to take brief walks in a body through some of the neighboring fields—and twice during Sunday, when we were paraded in the same formal manner to the morning and evening service in the one church of the village. . . .
>
> The morning's awakening, the nightly summons to bed; the connings, the recitations; the periodical half-holidays, and perambulations; the play-ground, with its broils, its pastimes, its intrigues [created a dismal atmosphere].

"Dr." Bransby, vividly and satirically mentioned (to his considerable annoyance) by name in "William Wilson," was a bald man with white side-whiskers, who wore clerical bands and a short eighteenth-century wig: "This reverend man, with countenance so demurely benign, with robes so glossy and so clerically flowing, with wig so minutely powdered, so rigid and so vast,—could this be he who, of late, with sour image, and in snuffy habiliments, administered, ferule in hand, the Draconian Laws of the academy?"

Bransby (who was not a "Doctor") was born in Suffolk in 1784, earned his bachelor's degree at St. John's, Cambridge, in 1805, married that year and was ordained as an Anglican priest two years later. He taught from 1806 until 1825 in Stoke Newington, where he lived with his kind, motherly wife, two sons and four highly educated daughters. He was headmaster of King's Lynn Grammar School from 1825 until seven years before his death, in 1857. William Hunter, who later attended Poe's school, characterized Bransby as a strict disciplinarian, "a portly and venerable gentleman, with the reputation of being a thorough scholar, very apt at quotation, especially from Shakespeare and Horace, and passionately fond of horticulture."

Hunter also described the quality of Edgar's education in England, his precocious poetry, Bransby's opinion of his character and—what is most interesting, in connection with Allan's later meanness with money—Bransby's belief that his most famous pupil had been spoiled by his foster father's extravagance:

> When he left it he was able to speak the French language, construe any easy Latin author, and was far better acquainted with history and literature than many boys of a more advanced age who had had greater advantages than he had had. I spoke to Dr. Bransby about him two or three times during my school days, having then, as now, a deep admiration for his poems, a copy of which I had received as a prize for an effort in English verse. Dr. Bransby seemed rather to shun the topic, I suppose from some feelings with regard to his name being used distastefully in the story of "William Wilson." In answer to my questions on one occasion, he said "Edgar Allan" (the name Poe was known by at school) "was a quick and clever boy and would have been a very good boy if he had not been spoilt by his parents," meaning the Allans; "but they spoilt him, and allowed him an extravagant amount of pocket-money, which enabled him to get into all manner of mischief—still I liked the boy—poor fellow, his parents spoilt him!" At another time he said, "Allan was intelligent, wayward, and wilful."

Well pleased by Edgar's exemplary achievement, attitude and learning, Allan felt his educational investment had paid off and praised the bright boy in three letters to Richmond in 1818 and 1819: "Edgar is a fine Boy and I have no reason to complain of his progress. . . . Edgar is growing wonderfully, & enjoys a good reputation and is both able & willing to receive instruction. . . . Edgar is in the Country at School, he is a verry fine Boy & a good scholar."[5]

III ══

Frances Allan had been in poor health throughout her stay in England and, though eager to return to Richmond, dreaded the rough sea voyage home. John Allan's business ventures had not, in those difficult times, been very successful. So on June 20, 1820, they finally left Liverpool on the *Martha* for a thirty-one-day voyage to New York, arriving home on August 2.

After two ocean voyages and five years in England, Edgar was more sophisticated and cosmopolitan, and far better educated, than his provincial schoolmates in Richmond. And the relative freedom of the American schools must have been welcome after the rigorous constrictions of English education. In the fall of 1820 he entered the school of Joseph Clarke, a hot-tempered and pedantic Irish bachelor. During the next three years this first-rate classical scholar instructed Edgar in mathematics and taught him to read Cicero, Caesar, Virgil, Horace and Ovid in Latin as well as Homer and Xenophon in Greek.

Master Clarke left a very favorable estimate of the generous character, enthusiastic ardor, intellectual capacity and poetic power of his unusually talented pupil:

> As to Edgar's disposition and character as a boy, though playful as most boys, his general deportment differed in some respects from others. He was remarkable for self-respect, without haughtiness, strictly just and correct in his demeanor with his fellow playmates, which rendered him a favorite even with those above his years. His natural and predominate passion seemed to me, to be an enthusiastic ardor in every-thing he undertook; in his difference of opinion with his fellow students, he was very tenacious, and would not yield till his judgment was convinced. As a scholar he was ambitious to excel, and tho' not conspicuously studious always acquitted himself well in his classes. His imaginative powers seemed to take precedence of all his other faculties, he gave proof of this, in some of his juvenile compositions addressed to his young female friends. He had a sensitive and tender heart, and would strain every nerve to oblige a friend.

Clarke also called Edgar a born artist who wrote genuine poetry while other boys cranked out mechanical verse. When Edgar was eleven years old, Allan showed Clarke a manuscript volume of his poems, which the ambitious boy wanted to have published. But Clarke, thinking this would flatter Edgar's inordinate vanity, advised against publication and the project was dropped. In April 1823 the fourteen-year-old Edgar entered William Burke's school where, during the next two years, he studied Greek and Latin, French and Italian, Geography and Grammar.

The Allans spent the first year, after returning to Richmond, in the home of his partner, Charles Ellis, at the corner of Franklin and Second streets. John Mackenzie, a boyhood friend whose parents had adopted Rosalie Poe, recalled that Edgar liked masquerades, practical jokes and raiding orchards. And Edgar made a tremendous impression on another playmate, Thomas Ellis, the son of Allan's partner. He reported that Edgar had teased Ellis' sister Jane with a hideous imitation snake until it "almost ran her crazy." But he was dazzled by Edgar's skill at sports and reckless adventures:

> No boy ever had a greater influence over me than he had. He was, indeed, a leader among boys; but my admiration for him scarcely knew bounds; the consequence was, he led me to do many a forbidden thing, for which I was punished. The only whipping I ever knew Mr. Allan to give him was for carrying me out into the fields and woods beyond Belvidere, one Saturday, and keeping me there all day and until after dark, without anybody at home knowing where we were, and for shooting a lot of domestic fowls. . . . He taught me to shoot, to swim, and to skate, to play bandy [a form of tennis]; and I ought to mention that he once saved me from drowning—for having thrown me into the falls headlong, that I might strike out for myself, he presently found it necessary to come to my help, or it would have been too late.

Edgar later boasted of his proudest, well-authenticated boyhood deed, and compared it to Byron's imitating Leander by swimming from Abydos to Sestos in Turkey: "Any swimmer 'in the falls' in my days, would have swum the Hellespont, and thought nothing of the matter. I swam from Ludlam's wharf to Warwick, (six miles) in a hot June sun [in 1824], against one of the strongest tides ever known in the [James] river. It would have been a feat comparatively easy to swim twenty miles in still water. I would not think much of attempting to swim the British Channel from Dover to Calais."[6] Edgar, who had undertaken this feat as a wager, did not seem at all fatigued and capped his achievement by walking all the way back to Richmond.

It is rather surprising—in view of the hermetic, neurasthenic and morbid character of Poe's works—to find that young Edgar was a good athlete and liked to roam around the countryside. Colonel James Preston, a classmate at Clarke's school, offered a harsher view of Edgar's character. In that genteel society, Preston explained, Poe was oppressed by the social stigma of his parents' profession: "[Poe] was a swift runner, a wonderful leaper, and what was more rare, a boxer, with some slight training. . . . [He] was self-willed, capricious, inclined to be imperious, and though of generous impulses, not steadily kind or even amiable. . . . Of Edgar Poe it was known that his parents were players, and that he was dependent upon the bounty that is bestowed upon an adopted son. All this had the effect of making the boys decline his leadership; and on looking back on it since, I fancy it gave him a fierceness he would otherwise not have had."[7]

Another friend revealed that Edgar, who later got into fistfights at the university and with an irascible editor, once used a peculiar strategy to defeat his opponent. In April 1823, just after entering Burke's school, he got into a fight with a heavier boy and was vigorously beaten for some time, before turning the tables and giving him a sound whipping. When asked why he had allowed the boy to beat his head for so long, Edgar explained that he was waiting for him to lose his breath before administering the final defeat! As always, Edgar offered an ingenious explanation of his strange behavior.

As he grew older, Edgar's retiring disposition and unsociable manner made him unpopular with his schoolmates, and he never asked any of them to come home with him after class. His traumatic infancy, lack of social status and ambiguous position with the Allans, his unusual travel and education, artistic temperament and nascent poetic powers made him feel—and actually be—an exceptional, isolated individual. In "Alone," an introspective and analytical poem about his youth, he emphasized the difference between his feelings and those of others, and his pessimistic tendency to see, "When the rest of Heaven was blue/. . . a demon in my view":

> From childhood's hour I have not been
> As others were—I have not seen
> As others saw—I could not bring
> My passions from a common spring—
> From the same source I have not taken
> My sorrow—I could not awaken
> My heart to joy at the same tone—
> And all I lov'd—*I* lov'd alone.

In October 1824, during his second year at Burke's school, Edgar—who already knew how to shoot a gun and later became a soldier and a cadet—had his first military experience. General Lafayette had played a prominent role in the Virginia campaign during the American Revolution and was given a grateful welcome when he returned to Richmond that year. Dressed in a rifleman's uniform, Edgar joined the voluntary company that Lafayette had chosen as his bodyguard and paraded in front of the marquee that had been erected in Capitol Square for the reception of the old general.

IV ══

During his years at Burke's school Edgar "lov'd alone" for the first time. He met Jane Stanard, the mother of his friend Robert, and gave her all the affectionate devotion of a son. Whenever he was unhappy at home, he sought her sympathy and always found comfort and consolation. Deeply despondent when Jane died insane at the age of twenty-eight in April 1824, he often visited her grave with her son.

After Jane's death, the future creator of horror stories described the apparitions that appeared in his nightmares: "the most horrible thing he could imagine as a boy was to feel an ice-cold hand laid upon his face in a pitch dark room when alone at night; or to awaken in semi-darkness and see an evil face gazing close into his own; and these fancies had so haunted him that he would often keep his head under the bed covering until nearly suffocated." The superstitious sceptic, who could be terrified by his own imagination, later confessed to the editor George Graham that "he disliked the dark, and was rarely out at night. On one occasion he said to me, 'I believe that demons take advantage of the night to mislead the unwary—although, you know,' he added, 'I don't believe in them.' "[8]

Jane Stanard, "the first, purely ideal love of my soul," inspired Poe's most beautiful elegiac love lyric. Changing Jane to the more poetic "Helen" and addressing her with his favorite woman's name (variants of which appear in the later "To Helen," in "Eleonora" and in "Lenore"), he compares, in sensual rhythm, her sustaining loveliness, which symbolizes a visionary classical ideal, to ancient triremes that carry an exhausted but victorious Greek warrior home from the fragrant coast of Asia Minor. The poem contains, at the end of the second stanza, two of Poe's finest and most famous lines; and portrays the older, maternal, unattainable Jane, as he gazed at her from afar, as the statuesque soul who embodies Hellenic perfection:

Helen, thy beauty is to me
  Like those Nicéan barks of yore,
That gently, o'er a perfumed sea,
  The weary, way-worn wanderer bore
  To his own native shore.

On desperate seas long wont to roam,
  Thy hyacinth hair, thy classic face,
Thy Naiad airs have brought me home
  To the glory that was Greece,
And the grandeur that was Rome.

Lo! in yon brilliant window-niche
  How statue-like I see thee stand,
  The agate lamp within thy hand!
Ah, Psyche, from the regions which
  Are Holy-Land![9]

In 1825, the year after Jane Stanard's death, Edgar fell in love with and became secretly engaged to Elmira Royster, the fifteen-year-old daughter of his neighbor. Elmira later described his melancholy yet ardent character and attempted to defend her father's behavior. But her father's motive for interfering was less noble than she suggests, and the poor orphan was probably considered unsuitable for social and financial reasons.

He was a beautiful boy.—Not very talkative. When he did talk though he was pleasant but his general manner was sad.— He was devoted to the first Mrs. Allan and she to him. We lived opposite to Poe on 5th. I made his acquaintance so. Our acquaintance was kept up until he left to go to the University, and during the time he was at the University he wrote to me frequently, but my father intercepted the letters because we were too young—no other reason. . . . [Poe] was very generous. . . . He had strong prejudices. Hated anything coarse and unrefined. Never spoke of his [real] parents. He was kind to his [backward] sister as far as in his power. He was warm and zealous in any cause he was interested in, very enthusiastic and impulsive.

Elmira inspired Poe's "Song": "I saw thee on thy bridal day," in which her "burning blush," in the midst of her happiness, caused him pain and suggested that she still loved him though she had married another. Elmira was to reappear and revive Poe's love shortly before his death.

In November 1824—between the death of Jane Stanard and the "engagement" to Elmira Royster—the commonsensical Allan clashed with the melancholy and Romantic Edgar, and their cordial relations quite suddenly came to an end. Though Allan had inquired about publishing Poe's poems, recognized that "Edgar is wayward and impulsive . . . for he has genius" and predicted "he will some day fill the world with his fame," Edgar felt his foster father had not encouraged his poetic ambitions. Later, in a self-reflective review of William Cullen Bryant's poems, Poe obliquely criticized Allan by praising Bryant's father: "This precocious dallying with the Muse was rather abetted than discouraged by the father of our poet. . . . [He] scrupled not to foster the errant genius of his son, and to act for him in capacity of guide."[10]

John Mackenzie, whose family had adopted Rosalie Poe, shrewdly observed that Allan's sharp-edged, irascible character failed to arouse Edgar's affection and that his parent was capable of severity, even cruelty, when he lost his hot temper: "Mr. Allan was a good man in his way, but Edgar was not fond of him. He was sharp and exacting, and with his long, hooked nose, and small keen eyes looking from under his shaggy eyebrows, he always reminded me of a hawk. I know that often when angry with Edgar he threatened to turn him adrift, and that he never allowed him to lose sight of his dependence upon his charity."

The mood of John Allan, the very incarnation of the materialistic instinct, became darker when the land and cotton booms collapsed in 1819. The period of deep economic depression that followed the bust lasted until 1824 and forced him that year to dissolve his partnership. His bitterly angry letter of November 1, 1824 to Edgar's older brother, Henry, presents a striking contrast to his warm praise of Edgar's scholarly progress during the years in England. Allan now seemed puzzled by Edgar's moody behavior, by his teenage attempt to define his identity and assert his independence. He criticized Poe's character and condemned his lack of gratitude, while emphasizing his own patience and tolerance:

> I have just seen your letter of the 25th ult. to Edgar and am much afflicted, that he has not written you. He has had little else to do for me, he does nothing & seems quite miserable, sulky & ill-tempered to all the Family. How we have acted to produce this is beyond my conception—why I have put

up so long with his conduct is a little less wonderful. The boy possesses not a Spark of affection for us, not a particle of gratitude for all my care and kindness towards him. I have given him a much superior Education than ever I received myself. If Rosalie has to relie on any affection from him, God in his mercy preserve her.—I fear his associates have led him to adopt a line of thinking & acting very contrary to what he possessed when in England. . . . Had I done my duty as faithfully to my God as I have to Edgar, then Death, come when he will, had no terrors for me.[11]

Allan's bitter, self-righteous letter marked their first estrangement and led to a crucial turning point in Edgar's life. Edgar's grief and gloom after the death of Jane Stanard; Allan's habitual vacillation between indulgence and severity; the inevitable clash of antithetical temperaments; severe economic difficulties; the natural adolescent rebellion of the fifteen-year-old boy; his uneasy awareness of his ambiguous and insecure position; Allan's resentment of his increasing maturity and independence; Edgar's refusal or inability to reiterate his gratitude and affection; the possibility that Edgar had sided with his invalid foster mother when she discovered Allan's sexual infidelities (which had resulted in the birth of an illegitimate son); and the yearning for love that led to Edgar's secret engagement to Elmira Royster, all influenced his sudden transformation from a darling child to an ungrateful son.

Four months after he wrote this letter, Allan's fortunes changed even more dramatically than Edgar's had after his mother's tragic death in 1811. Allan's uncle William Galt, one of the richest men in Virginia, died in March 1825, leaving Allan a vast fortune of several hundred thousand dollars. Soon afterwards Allan bought a luxurious $15,000 house, at the corner of Fifth and Main streets, with two lofty stories, wide porches and high ceilings. It now appeared that Edgar might one day inherit Allan's money—if he could remain on good terms with his foster father. But his difficulties with Allan grew even worse when he entered the university.

Chapter 3

THE UNIVERSITY OF VIRGINIA, 1826

I ===

When Poe entered the University of Virginia at Charlottesville in February 1826, it was the most idealistic and most dissolute college in America. Its attractive setting, its Palladian style, its Rotunda modeled on the Roman Pantheon, its ten pavilions and 109 dormitory rooms extending along the East and West Range, made it one of the most impressive architectural creations in the country. Thomas Jefferson, the first rector, had conceived the idea of the university, chosen the site, designed the buildings, hired the accomplished professors (most of them English), planned the curriculum and the schedule of classes, and written the regulations that governed the students. He had opened its doors the previous year, he said, echoing the principles of the Enlightenment, "to develop the reasoning faculties of our youth, enlarge their minds, cultivate their morals, and instill into them the precepts of virtue and order—and generally, to form them to habits of reflection and correct action, rendering them examples of virtue to others, and of happiness within themselves."

Oxford and Cambridge were Anglican, Harvard Unitarian, Princeton Presbyterian; but the University of Virginia was nonsectarian. There was no chair of theology, no required attendance at chapel, no church on campus. The absence of religion may have encouraged Poe to abandon the beliefs of his childhood. The lack of structure and discipline was also reflected in other aspects of university life. At Virginia, unlike most colleges of the time, the students were free to elect their own subjects of instruction, to make their own boarding arrangements with the "hotels" that were leased to private individuals and to regulate the university by a unique system of student self-government. Every Sunday Mr. Jefferson regularly invited some of the students to dine with him at Monticello, and Poe must have met him on several social and academic occasions. Jefferson died at the age of eighty-three on July 4, 1826, while Poe was at the university.

The college rules were quite severe but generally ignored. Tobacco, wine, liquor, servants, horses, dogs and guns were strictly forbidden and frequently enjoyed. One rich young buck arrived with a team of thoroughbred horses, a servant, a fowling piece and two pointers. Gambling and dueling were both prohibited and commonplace, and the "hotel" keepers often gamed with the students. Jefferson mistakenly thought that student self-government would propagate virtue and prevent disorder. "Provision was made for a board of censors, chosen by the faculty from the most 'discreet' students, which would deal with minor offences and make recommendations to the faculty. Apparently this board was not set up, however, and the problem of discipline was left to the professors."[1] The first years of the university began with very little discipline. The faculty waited in vain for the students to inaugurate Jefferson's enlightened system and the students resolutely refused to inform on one another.

Without the restraints of family or of women, of religious observances or faculty control, the rough male code of fighting, sports, drinking and gambling, which dominated the wild sons of plantation gentry, took over. The rampant pranks and disrespect, the unrestrained wildness and violence, led to a high academic casualty rate. Of the total number of students who enrolled between 1825 and 1850, about one-third stayed longer than the first year, less than a quarter remained for two years and only ten percent completed three years.

Poe's English mother, his Scottish foster father, his English and Irish teachers in Stoke Newington and Richmond and his European professors at the university gave him an unusually cosmopolitan outlook. He registered for the Schools of Ancient and Modern Languages; and regularly attended classes in Greek and Latin, in French, Spanish and Italian.

Violence, in those days, was not confined to the students. Dr.

George Blaetterman, Poe's professor of modern languages, was an irascible German, with a strong foreign accent, who once horse-whipped his wife in the street. He was fired in 1838 at the request of the student body. George Long, the professor of ancient languages, was a more distinguished scholar and more pleasant man, and soon found an attractive young wife. Only nine years older than Poe, a Master of Arts and Fellow of Trinity College, Cambridge, Long collaborated on a book with Blaetterman. He later taught at the newly established University of London; translated and edited Herodotus, Epictetus, Plutarch, Cicero, Caesar and Marcus Aurelius; and wrote numerous books (many of them under the imprint of the Society for the Diffusion of Useful Knowledge) on biography, politics, history, geography, Egyptology, classical languages and education.[2]

Poe's classes in ancient languages met on Monday, Wednesday and Friday mornings from 7:30 to 9:30; in modern languages on Tuesday, Thursday and Saturday at the same time. Among the Latin authors, Poe read plays by Plautus and Terence, Cicero's *Epistles*, Virgil's *Georgics*, Horace's *Odes*, Tacitus' *Annals* and Juvenal's *Satires*. Professor Blaetterman once suggested that his class translate some lines of Torquato Tasso into English verse. At the next Italian lecture he announced that Poe was the only student who had responded to his request and complimented his polished performance. One classmate recalled that Poe rarely had to prepare his lessons in advance. His intellect and memory were so acute that he required only a few minutes of study before class in order to give the best recitation. At the beginning of December 1826 Poe, along with students who had completed their second year at the university, was examined for two to three hours in each subject by two former presidents of the United States: James Madison, who had succeeded Jefferson as rector, and James Monroe. Poe was awarded the highest honors in both ancient and modern languages.

II ⚌

At the university, as in later life, Poe had no intimate friends in whom he confided and who knew him well. Contemporary impressions of his appearance and character vary according to the individual informant. One student described him as "a pretty wild young man" who was interested in sports and could leap twenty feet in a running broad jump; another as a "sober, quiet and orderly young man . . . [whose]

deportment was uniformly that of an intelligent and polished gentleman." One classmate said Poe was "short of stature, thick and somewhat compactly set," while others maintained, more convincingly,
that "he was of rather a delicate and slender mold," his weight between 130 and 140 pounds. He had "finely marked features, and eyes
dark, liquid and expressive. He dressed well and neatly. He was a
very attractive companion, genial in his nature." Studious and careworn, Poe certainly wore "a sad, melancholy face always, and even
a smile, for I don't remember his ever having laughed heartily, seemed
to be forced."[3]

Several incidents reveal Poe's touchy, artistic, excitable, pugnacious
temperament—subject, as always, to violent swings of mood. One
evening he read a witty story to a group of friends in his room at 13
West Range and responded to their mild criticism by flinging his
manuscript into the fire: "thus was lost a story of more than ordinary
parts, and, unlike most of his stories, was intensely amusing, entirely
free from his usual sombre coloring and sad conclusions merged in a
mist of impenetrable gloom."

The most vivid account of Poe at Virginia comes from Miles
George, who later became a prominent Richmond doctor:

> [Poe] was fond of quoting poetic authors and reading poetic
> productions of his own, with which his friends were delighted
> and entertained; then suddenly a change would come over
> him; he would with a piece of charcoal evince his versatile
> genius by sketching upon the walls of his dormitory, whimsi-
> cal, fanciful and grotesque figures, with so much artistic skill,
> as to leave us in doubt whether Poe in future life would be
> Painter or Poet.—He was very excitable & restless, at times
> wayward, melancholic & morose, but again—in his better
> moods frolicksome, full of fun & a most attractive and agree-
> able companion. To calm and quiet the excessive nervous
> excitability under which he labored, he would too often put
> himself under the influence of that "Invisible Spirit of Wine."[4]

Poe once had a fistfight with Miles George, but shook hands with
him after a few rounds and remained on good terms. Other fights at
the university were much more serious. On one occasion, Poe wrote
to Allan, describing a fight he had witnessed: "Blow struck him with
a large stone on one side of his head—whereupon Smith drew a pistol
(which are all the fashion here) and had it not missed fire would have
put an end to the controversy." During another savage confrontation,

Poe recounted, a student with ferocious Berenice-like teeth, "after getting the other completely in his power, began to bite—I saw the arm afterward—and it was really a serious matter.—It was bitten from the shoulder to the elbow—and it is likely that pieces of flesh as large as my hand will be obliged to be cut out."[5] Discipline became entirely out of control by 1840, when a professor was murdered while trying to stop a student disturbance.

Poe had great talent and an appetite for work, but needed an external structure. At the university, where the pressure of his peers was too great, the impressionable youth sought to emulate the dissolute habits of the rich. Thomas Holley Chivers, who met Poe twenty years later, maintained that "his College-life in Virginia was the cause of all his after-inebriation." Though we cannot be quite so exact about the origins of Poe's alcoholism, all contemporary accounts agree that he drank and gambled in a joyless, maniacal fashion and tried to get intoxicated in the shortest possible time:

> Poe's passion for strong drink was as marked and as peculiar as that for cards. It was not the taste of the beverage that influenced him; without a sip or smack of the mouth he would seize a full glass, without water or sugar, and send it home with a single gulp. This frequently used him up. . . .
>
> Poe was particularly fond of playing cards—seven-up and loo being his favorite games. He played in such an impassioned manner as to amount to almost an actual frenzy. All of his card playing and drinking he did under a sudden impulse. . . . He would always seize the tempting glass . . . and without the least apparent pleasure swallow the contents, never pausing until the last drop had passed his lips. One glass at a time was about all that he could take.

Charles Baudelaire, who also indulged in mad binges, perceptively attributed Poe's drinking to his suicidal impulses: "he did not drink like an ordinary toper, but like a savage, with an altogether American energy and fear of wasting a minute, as though he was accomplishing an act of murder, as though there was *something* inside him that he had to kill."[6]

William Wertenbaker, the librarian of the university, recalled a conversation in Poe's room on a cold December night at the end of their academic year. Poe broke up a small table to rekindle the fire, expressed contrition about his gambling and promised to pay his debts—though he could not possibly do so:

He spoke with regret of the large amount of money he had wasted and of the debts he had contracted during the Session. . . . He estimated his indebtedness at $2000, and though they were gaming debts he was earnest and emphatic in the declaration, that he was bound by honor to pay at the earliest opportunity, every cent of them. He certainly was not habitually intemperate, but he may occasionally have entered into a frolick.

Poe's enormous losses not only suggest that he was particularly inept and unlucky at gambling, but also that he may have been victimized and cheated by his companions. One Virginia student, after losing $240 at a single session of cards, horsewhipped the adversary who, he felt, had cheated him.

The drinking and gambling that wrecked the life of Poe's William Wilson at Eton and Oxford were clearly based on his self-destructive experience at Virginia and on Allan's moral judgment of Poe's passionate dissipation. Poe narrates the story as if *he* were the ruthless, rich and sophisticated rake, rather than the victim of a gambling fraud. William Wilson describes how

I invited a small party of the most dissolute students to a secret carousal in my chambers. We met at a late hour of the night; for our debaucheries were to be faithfully protracted until morning. The wine flowed freely and there were not wanting other and perhaps more dangerous seductions. . . .

Having become an adept in this despicable science [of gambling, I] practiced it habitually as a means of increasing my already enormous income at the expense of the weak-minded among my fellow-collegians. . . . An ejaculation evincing utter despair on the part of Glendinning, gave me to understand that I had effected his total ruin.[7]

Though Poe was regarded as the heir of one of the richest men in Virginia, Allan sent him to the university with insufficient funds and virtually forced him to gamble in order to pay his essential expenses. His apparent, but not actual, riches at the university reflected the ambiguity of his relations with Allan at home. After Poe had lost an enormous amount of money, which he could not and Allan would not pay, Allan refused to support him any longer—despite his academic achievements—or allow him to continue his education. Thomas Ellis, the son of Allan's partner, attempting to exculpate Allan, explained how Poe was suddenly transformed from a student of classics to a slave of commerce:

> Mr. Allan went up to Charlottesville, inquired into his ways, paid every debt that he thought ought to be paid, and refusing to pay some gambling debts (which Mr. James Galt told me, in his lifetime, amounted to about $2,500) brought Edgar away in the month of December following, and for a time kept him in Ellis & Allan's countingroom (where they were engaged in winding up their old business)—thus attempting to give him some knowledge of book-keeping, accounts, and commercial correspondence.

In a bitter and most unwelcome letter to Allan, written four years after he had been forced to leave the university, Poe argued that his foster father was to blame for all his financial troubles, since he had placed him in an impossible situation. He complained (with characteristic self-pity) that Allan did not love him, and tried to excuse his astronomical gambling debts:

> I will boldly say that it was wholly and entirely your own mistaken parsimony that caused all the difficulties in which I was involved while at Charlottesville. The expenses of the institution at the lowest estimate were $350 per annum. [Most students needed at least $500.] You sent me there with $110. Of this $50 were to be paid immediately for board—$60 for attendance upon 2 professors—and you even then did not miss the opportunity for abusing me because I did not attend 3. Then $15 more were to be paid for room-rent—remember that all this was to be paid *in advance*, with $110.—$12 more for a bed—and $12 more for room furniture. I had, of course, the mortification of running in debt for public property— against the known rules of the institution, and was immediately regarded in the light of a beggar. You will remember that in a week after my arrival, I wrote to you for some more money, and for books.—You replied in terms of the utmost abuse—if I had been the vilest wretch on earth you could not have been more abusive than you were because I could not contrive to pay $150 with $110. . . .
>
> [Books were bought on credit.] In this manner debts were accumulated, and money borrowed from Jews in Charlottesville at extravagant interest—for I was obliged to hire a ser-

vant, to pay for wood, for washing, and a thousand other
necessaries. It was then that I became dissolute, for how could
it be otherwise? . . . I applied to James Galt [the adopted son
of Allan's benefactor, William Galt]—but he, I believe, from
the best of motives refused to lend me any—I then became
desperate, and gambled—until I finally involved myself irretrievably. . . . You would not let me return because bills were
presented you for payment which I never wished nor desired
you to pay. Had you let me return, my reformation had been
sure—as my conduct the last 3 months [at the university]
gave every reason to believe.[8]

But Allan did not, in fact, pay all of Poe's legitimate debts. The
bills sent in by Charlottesville merchants long after Poe had left the
university continued to exacerbate relations between father and son
by reminding Allan not only of Poe's "extravagance," but also of his
own disastrous negligence in this affair.

It seems that Allan deliberately sent the seventeen-year-old Poe to
the University of Virginia with insufficient funds, knowing full well
that this would place him in an impossible situation. It is curious that
Allan was willing to provide Poe with an expensive English education
when business was bad and he himself had little money, but unwilling
to spend less than this amount on Poe's education at Virginia when
he possessed a great fortune. Though there were no rational reasons
for Allan's behavior, it is possible to speculate on his tortuous motives.
He may have resented Poe's assumption that as the son of a wealthy
man he would always have plenty of money and wanted to disillusion
Poe about this. He may have wished to test Poe's self-sufficiency and
see how he would manage on his own (as Allan had to do when he
first began to make his way in the world). He may have thought it
better for Poe's character to keep him on short funds than spoil him
(as he had previously been accused of doing) by undue extravagance.
He may have resented (at the same time that he was proud of) Poe's
intellectual and artistic ability, and been jealous of his wife's devotion
to Poe. He may have unconsciously desired Poe to fail at the university, so that he would not become a professional man—superior to
the merchant Allan—but would instead be forced to enter Allan's
business and remain under his authority. Finally, he may have wanted
to punish Poe for some unspecified offence—quite possibly his criticism of Allan's adultery. In any case, Allan's attitude toward Poe's
higher education clearly reflects a radical change in feeling about his
errant foster child.

III ==

When Poe returned to Richmond in late December 1826, condemned to work without pay in his foster father's countinghouse, he suffered another blow. Elmira Royster's father—who had probably heard about Poe's dissipation and quarrel with Allan, and assumed that Poe would not become Allan's heir—had intercepted all Poe's letters to his daughter. Elmira, thinking that Poe had forgotten her, had become engaged to the more suitable Alexander Shelton. She later confessed (if her friend can be believed) that she had never loved her husband and more than once said: "I married another man, but the love of my life was Edgar Poe. I never loved anyone else."

Poe was bitterly disappointed by the termination of his university career, shocked and angered by Elmira's engagement, and miserably unhappy at the prospect of permanent confinement in the counting-house. On March 19, 1827, after less than three months of "book-keeping, accounts and commercial correspondence," Poe could no longer endure his intolerable situation. Like many young men, he decided to leave home and make his own way in the world. His letter to Allan, written from Richmond on that date, the progenitor of dozens of others written later in life, conveyed his decision in typically operatic style: with maudlin self-pity, defiant accusations, self-righteous indignation, wounded pride, abject demands for money, veiled warnings of self-destruction and threatened torments of guilt-ridden remorse. He berated Allan for his cruel treatment, lack of feeling, unjust accusations and insulting behavior (even the household slaves no longer respected and obeyed the young master), emphasized his own desperate poverty and blamed their quarrel on an obscure difference of opinion. This may have concerned the responsibility for Poe's disasters at the university (to which he still hoped to return), disagreements about his future career as a respectable merchant or criticism of Allan's sexual infidelities. Critical and rebellious by nature, Poe, by contradicting instead of cultivating Allan, hurt his chances of inheriting Allan's money. Poe wrote:

> My determination is at length taken—to leave your house and endeavor to find some place in this wide world, where I will be treated—not as *you* have treated me. . . .
>
> Since I have been able to think on any subject, my thoughts have aspired, and they have been taught by *you* to aspire, to eminence in public life—this cannot be attained without a good Education. . . .

But in a moment of caprice—you have blasted my hope because forsooth I disagreed with you in an opinion. . . . I have heard you say . . . that you had no affection for me.

You have moreover ordered me to quit your house, and are continually upbraiding me with eating the bread of idleness, when you yourself were the only person to remedy the evil by placing me to some business.—You take delight in exposing me before those whom you think likely to advance my interest in this world.

You suffer me to be subjected to the whims & caprice, not only of your white family, but the complete authority of the blacks. . . . [I hope] to place myself in some situation where I may not only obtain a livelihood, but lay by a sum which one day or another will support me at the University. . . . Send me I entreat you some money immediately—as I am in the greatest necessity.—If you fail to comply with my request—I tremble for the consequence.

The following day, unable to tolerate such severe criticism from his dependent, Allan hardened his heart, refused financial assistance and justified his own behavior: "I taught you to aspire, even to eminence in Public Life, but I never expected that Don Quixotte, Gil Blas [which Allan had sent to Poe], Jo: Miller['s Jests] & such works were calculated to promote the end. . . . The charge of eating the bread of idleness, was to urge you to perseverance & industry in receiving the classics, in perfecting yourself in the mathematics, mastering the French"—which was exactly what Poe had been doing at the university. Undaunted (as always) by this curt refusal, the starved and penurious Poe, unwilling or unable to seek refuge with his Richmond friends, and wandering madly about like the hero of "The Man of the Crowd," made on March 20 a last desperate, pitiful but futile plea: "I am in the greatest necessity, not having tasted food since Yesterday morning. I have no where to sleep at night, but roam about the Streets.—I am nearly exhausted."[9]

Poe survived, somehow, for four more days in Richmond. Then, on March 24, accompanied as far as Norfolk by his childhood friend Ebenezer Burling—with whom he had read *Robinson Crusoe* and sailed on the James River—he embarked (and may have worked his passage) on a coal vessel bound for his native Boston. Poe later described this episode when Arthur Gordon Pym leaves home, accompanied by Augustus Barnard, and ships aboard the *Grampus*. In that novella, two different characters named "Allen" suffer violent deaths.

The cruel termination of his career at Virginia, the stifling of his talent, the loss of Elmira, the bitter quarrel with Allan and expulsion from home, the lack of support from friends and relatives, and his rapid descent into poverty were terrible blows that split Poe's life in two. They seemed, all at once, to destroy his prospects, his hopes and his ambitions. As the critic Edward Davidson perceptively observed: "Part of Poe's personal tragedy was that he was carefully reared through the first eighteen years of his life to conform to the manners and code of the aristocratic, landed gentry [which were adopted] in the fashionable circles of sophisticated Richmond; then he was suddenly thrust into the business world where the only money he ever made came from that otherwise discredited instrument in the world of finance—a writer's pen."

Poe grew up and was educated in the Virginia of Thomas Jefferson and John Marshall. But his unhappy experience at the university led to a reaction against Jefferson's ideas, which seemed so natural to many nineteenth-century Americans who valued "the appeal to common sense rather than to subtlety, the assumption of the existence of a benevolent God and benevolent principles in human nature, and the support of religious faith through confidence in intuitive convictions.[10] Poe subscribed rather to the urbane, conservative thought of the statesman John Marshall, which reacted strongly against Jacksonian democracy and reform. He felt no need to change the Southern social order, and supported plantation life and slavery. In his stories, Poe replaced the "rational, disciplined and social" beliefs of his time with bizarre, wild and individualistic ideas that emphasized the supernatural, the human predisposition to evil and the materialistic view of the world.

Chapter 4

THE ARMY AND WEST POINT,
1827-1831

I ⸺

After arriving by ship in Boston in April 1827, Poe clerked for a month at a very small salary in a wholesale merchandise warehouse on the waterfront. He then secured work for a short time as clerk and reporter for P. P. F. De Grand's obscure commercial newspaper, the *Weekly Report*. Finally, on May 26, after he had exhausted all his resources and had no other prospects in view, he enlisted for five years, under the pseudonym "Edgar A. Perry," as a common soldier in the American army. Military records in the National Archives state that on Castle Island in Boston Harbor Poe gave his occupation as clerk and his age as twenty-two (though he was only eighteen years old); that he was five feet, eight inches tall, with gray eyes, brown hair and a fair complexion.

By leaving the university and joining the army, Poe sank into the lower class—as his father had done in 1803 by abandoning law for the stage. The army would alleviate his poverty, offer security and provide the basic necessities of life. Accustomed to living in boarding school and in college, and overwhelmed by the strain of surviving on his own for the last two months, the teenage Poe was attracted to the certainty, structure, order, discipline and paternal authority of regimental life. By enlisting in the ranks he could not only find a challenging new experience, but also escape his ambiguous social status, acquire a definite position and have the satisfaction of belonging to a group. He could also punish Allan ("look what you forced me to do") for his cruel treatment, and punish himself for gambling at the university and helping to ruin his own career. And he could expiate his guilt by burying his poetic talent and burning ambition in a sortie to the lower depths.

T. E. Lawrence's enlistment in the ranks of the RAF, his pleasurable relief in sinking to the bottom and knowing he could stand it, illuminates Poe's impulsive act. Lawrence wrote, with excruciating self-analysis: "I liked the things underneath me and took my pleasures and adventures downward. There seemed a certainty in degradation, a final safety. Man could rise to any height, but there was an animal level beneath which he could not fall. It was a satisfaction on which to rest."[1]

Poe's military service—along the Atlantic coast from Boston to Charleston—defined the geographical limits of his adult life. Once he had signed up, his officers recognized his superior education (not many soldiers had studied Greek at the university) and gave him more interesting work. He spent the first six months with Battery H of the First Artillery, stationed at Fort Independence in Boston Harbor, and as a private earned five dollars a month. At first, he rather liked the security and order of peacetime army life, and was reasonably content with his light duties as company clerk and assistant in the commissariat department. He prepared the routine papers of his battery, wrote letters dictated by the officers, prepared the payrolls and muster rolls, and served as messenger between his company and regimental headquarters.

II ===

Poe had been writing poems at the University of Virginia and at Ellis & Allan's countinghouse in Richmond, and continued to do so while serving in the army. He had accumulated a thin manuscript by now and may have gone to Boston because it was a literary and publishing center. His first work, *Tamerlane and Other Poems*, was paid for by Poe and published anonymously "By a Bostonian." Brought out by a young printer, Calvin Thomas of 70 Washington Street, in July 1827, when Poe was only eighteen years old, the forty-page pamphlet received no attention and fell stillborn from the press. Fifty copies were printed, of which only twelve have survived, making it the rarest and most valuable of American first editions. In the Preface, Poe apologized for the quality of his verse and magnified its merit by emphasizing his precocity. He claimed, with considerable exaggeration, that "the greater part of the Poems which compose this little volume, were written in the year 1821–2, when the author had not completed his fourteenth year." In the Advertisement to his second volume of poetry, he explained the indifferent reception of the first and suggested that malignant forces had stifled his talent. The title poem, Poe said, "was printed for publication in Boston, in the year 1827, but suppressed through circumstances of a private nature."

The epigraph to *Tamerlane* from William Cowper's "Tirocinium"—

> Young heads are giddy, and young hearts are warm,
> And make mistakes for manhood to reform—

excused himself and appealed to Allan for forgiveness. It also began the confessional mode of many of his later poems and stories, and employed his characteristic method of simultaneous concealment and revelation.

The historical Tamerlane was born near Samarkand, in remote and exotic central Asia, about forty years after Kubla Khan. This cruel Tartar warrior rose from humble origins—"A cottager, I mark'd a throne / Of half the world as all my own"—to become the conqueror of Persians, Russians, Indians, Arabs, Turks and Chinese, and to create an empire that extended from the Black Sea to the interior of Cathay. Though Tamerlane had been the subject of a play by Christopher Marlowe in 1590, Poe followed the "oriental" tradition of exotic settings and characters made famous in the eighteenth and early nineteenth centuries by Montesquieu's *Persian Letters*, Voltaire's *Zadig*, Johnson's *Rasselas*, Beckford's *Vathek*, Byron's *The Giaour* and Moore's *Lalla Rookh*. Poe, who knew virtually nothing about the real Tamerlane, but felt free to write about him, apologized for his ignorance and begged "the reader's pardon for making Tamerlane, a Tartar of the fourteenth century, speak in the same language as a Boston gentleman of the nineteenth: but of the Tartar mythology we have little information."[2]

Tamerlane is meant to be an allegory of Poe's poetic ambition and disappointed love for Elmira Royster. Poe's love for Elmira had, surprisingly, already been the subject of a prose sketch, "The Pirate"

(1827), by his older brother Henry and a play, *Merlin* (1827), by his friend Lambert Wilmer. In Poe's poem, the dying pagan conqueror absurdly confesses to a Christian friar that his overweening ambition and conquest of the world have deprived him of human love:

> How was it that Ambition crept,
>   Unseen, amid the revels there,
> Till growing bold, he laughed and leapt
>   In the tangles of Love's very hair?

III =====

The publication of Poe's first volume of poetry emphasized the fissure between his artistic and military lives, between his Romantic desire to be a writer and his quest for a socially acceptable career. After six months of undemanding duty in Boston, Poe's battery was ordered to Fort Moultrie on Sullivan's Island in Charleston Harbor. It embarked on the brig *Waltham* on November 8, 1827 and arrived ten days later. During his thirteen months in South Carolina, Poe was promoted to artificer—a soldier who prepared shells for artillery— and had his meager pay doubled to a still modest ten dollars a month, plus one ration of whiskey or rum per day.

A narrow channel separated Fort Moultrie from Fort Sumter, where the first engagement of the Civil War would take place in April 1861. Poe alludes to this area in three of his stories. The narrator in "The Oblong Box" embarks from Charleston on a voyage to New York; the English Flying Machine in "The Balloon-Hoax" arrives on Sullivan's Island; and most importantly, "The Gold-Bug" takes place on the narrow, miasmic, decrepit island, whose unusual flora Poe describes in some detail:

> This island is a very singular one. It consists of little else than the sea sand, and is about three miles long. Its breadth at no point exceeds a quarter of a mile. It is separated from the mainland by a scarcely perceptible creek, oozing its way through a wilderness of reeds and slime, a favorite resort of the marsh-hen. The vegetation, as might be supposed, is scant, or at least dwarfish. No trees of any magnitude are to be seen. Near the western extremity, where Fort Moultrie stands, and where are some miserable frame buildings, tenanted, during summer, by the fugitives from Charleston dust

and fever, may be found, indeed, the bristly palmetto; but
the whole island, with the exception of this western point,
and a line of hard, white beach on the sea-coast, is covered
with a dense undergrowth of the sweet myrtle so much prized
by the horticulturists of England.

After eighteen months in these dreary surroundings, with poor
pay, scant recreation, repetitive duties and no chance of advancement
to officer rank, Poe realized that he had come to a complete dead end.
He desperately wanted to escape from the remaining three and a half
years of his enlistment. He discussed the situation with his sympathetic superior, Lieutenant Howard, who agreed to discharge Poe
(still a minor) if he would effect a reconciliation with Allan and get
his permission to leave the army. In November 1828 Poe wrote to
Allan about this urgent matter, enclosing a report of his good character. But Allan, undoubtedly shocked by the unexpected news of Poe's
enlistment as a common soldier as well as relieved that he was safely
out of the way for the next few years, replied that Poe "had better
remain as he is until the termination of his enlistment."

Writing again from Fort Moultrie on December 1 and trying to
persuade Allan to change his mind, Poe tried a number of different
tactics. He said that he was concerned about Allan's recent illness, felt
wounded by Allan's belief that he was "degraded & disgraced, and
that any thing were preferable to my returning home & entailing on
yourself a portion of my infamy." Poe added that he had assured
Lieutenant Howard that Allan was "ready to forgive even the worst
offenses" and that the prime of his life would be wasted by five long
years in the army. He threatened (as usual) that he would "be driven
to more decided measures if you refuse to assist me" and claimed that
his character had dramatically improved: "I am altered from what
you knew me, & am no longer a boy tossing about on the world
without aim or consistency." Poe, knowing Allan would disapprove
of a literary career, failed to define exactly what his consistent aim
would be once he left the army. Allan, fearing Poe would again
become a financial burden and indifferent to his idle threats, thought
it prudent not to reply.

On December 11, 1828 the battery, having been transferred to
Fortress Monroe at Old Point Comfort near Hampton, Virginia,
sailed from South Carolina on the *Harriet* and arrived four days later
at Hampton Roads. On December 22 Poe, writing to Allan about
this matter for the third time, rather ineffectually repeated his plea

for permission to leave the army. Alternating between high-handed insults and groveling requests for assistance, he complained—though Allan's silence had made his answer quite obvious—that though his officers had taken a fatherly interest in his welfare, Allan, "who called me your son, should refuse me even the common civility of answering a letter." Thinking of his recently published volume of poetry, he begged his "father" not to "throw me aside as *degraded*. I will be an honor to your name." This time, instead of meaningless threats, he bade Allan a theatrical *adieu* and (like the hero of a melodrama) claimed that Allan's rejection would inspire his quest for success: "If you determine to abandon me—here take I my farewell.—Neglected—I will be doubly ambitious, & the world shall hear of the son whom you have thought unworthy of your notice."[3]

Ten days later, on January 1, 1829, Poe, having shot up in only nineteen months to the highest rank an enlisted man could attain, was promoted to regimental sergeant major. During his army service, the most practical and well-ordered years of his life, Poe had earned the respect of many officers who took a paternal interest in the talented soldier and told him about their life at West Point. A month after his promotion, Poe again changed his tack and came up with a new plan that would not only enable him to leave the army, but would utilize his experience and propel him toward a new career.

He now asked Allan to help him procure an appointment as cadet at the Military Academy. He argued—incorrectly, as it turned out—that his experience in the army would be a great advantage at West Point and, "having already passed thro' the practical part of the higher portion of the Artillery arm, my cadetship would only be considered as a necessary form which I am positive I could run thro' in 6 months." Attempting to escape Allan's censure, Poe tried to excuse his past behavior while, at the same time, falsely claiming that he had never meant to excuse it: "Whatever fault you may find with me [and Allan had found plenty] I have not been ungrateful for past services, but you blame me for the part which I have taken without considering the powerful impulses which actuated me.—You will remember how much I had to suffer upon my return from the University. I never meant to offer a shadow of excuse for the infamous conduct of myself & others at that place." Poe ends, as usual, with a threat: "I shall wait with impatience for an answer to this letter, for upon it depend a great many circumstances of my future life—the assurance of an honourable & highly successful course in my own country—or the prospect—no *certainty*, of an exile forever to another."[4] Clinging to the belief that

Allan was still attached to him, Poe could not face the fact that Allan was now indifferent to Poe's threats of exile and suicide, and would have been delighted to be finally rid of him.

Matters had reached an impasse when, on February 28, 1829, Frances Allan died in Richmond at the age of forty-three. Granted leave from the army, Poe did not reach home until the day after her funeral. Poe and Allan, both grieving for the woman they loved, achieved an emotional reconciliation that perhaps fulfilled her dying wish. Poe's next letter, written from Fortress Monroe on March 10, returned to his childhood form of address ("My dear Pa" instead of the formal "Dear Sir") and reflected their renewed intimacy. After Allan had finally allowed Poe to leave the army, Poe's colonel wrote to the commanding general saying that Allan had reinstated Poe "into his family and favor" and, since an experienced soldier had been found to take "Perry's" place, asked that he be discharged.

It was then customary for a soldier who wished to leave the army to pay for a substitute. Since his officers were absent on furlough when Poe's permission came through, he could not enlist the first recruit who offered himself at the standard rate of twelve dollars. Impatient and unwilling to await their return, and always incompetent with money, Poe agreed to pay an ex-soldier seventy-five dollars to take his place. Lacking the full amount, he paid twenty-five dollars in cash and gave the soldier a note for the remainder, a rash act that later on would cause serious trouble. On April 15, 1829 Poe was finally released from the United States Army.

In "The Business Man" Poe solemnly wrote: "In biography the truth is every thing, and in autobiography it is especially so." But the socially sensitive son of strolling players, ashamed of having lost caste by becoming a common soldier, later attempted to hide his years in the army. He concocted fantastic but circumstantial myths, inspired by the travels of his brother Henry, of joining a Byronic expedition to help the oppressed Greeks, then fighting for their liberty against the Turks, and of difficulties encountered on a trip to St. Petersburg, where he was supposedly rescued by Henry Middleton, the American minister. Poe's European fantasies were apparently confirmed in a bizarre undated manuscript by Alexandre Dumas. The famous French novelist maintained that Poe, armed with an introduction from Fenimore Cooper, met Dumas in Paris in 1832 (when Poe was actually living in Baltimore) and resided in Dumas' house for the duration of his stay in the city. Poe treated the house as his own, Dumas said, and like his fictional hero Auguste Dupin, went out only at night.[5]

IV ═══

During the next fourteen months, between leaving the army and entering West Point, Poe lived mainly in Baltimore, reading, writing and vainly looking for work while living in his cousin's house in Caroline Street. He concentrated on placating Allan and extracting some money from him, on gaining admission to the Military Academy and on publishing his second volume of poems. His "Dear Pa" letter of July 26, 1829, written three months after his discharge from the army, responded to Allan's wounding taunt that "men of genius ought not to apply to [his] aid." Poe lamely explained why he had had to pay seventy-five dollars instead of only twelve, said he had walked thirty-seven miles from Baltimore to Washington to see Major John Eaton, the secretary of war, and complained: "I am conscious of having offended you formerly—greatly—but I thought *that had been forgiven.* At least you told me so. I know that I have done nothing since to deserve your displeasure." To Allan, for whom the acquisition of money was the index of success, Poe's protestations were worthless. Since Poe could not survive without Allan's help, he was forced to reopen his financial wounds every time he begged for money. Since Allan never forgave or forgot, he continued to rake up Poe's past mistakes and abuse him for his pathetic inability to support himself.

The following month, dubiously claiming that he was "not so anxious of obtaining money from your good nature as preserving your good will," Poe sacrificed Allan's goodwill by requesting (as he did in almost every letter he ever wrote) more money. Toward the end of the year he reproached Allan for his angry tone and lack of forgiveness. And he pitifully told a literary friend, John Neal: "I have no father—nor mother."[6] In November the orphan, extremely pinched and almost without clothes, once again troubled his Pa for more money. And in December, driven to desperate expedients, he helped his aunt Maria Clemm assign the services of her slave to another master for a term of nine years. For this transaction, they received forty dollars.

While continuing to anger and alienate Allan, Poe also asked his help in securing an appointment to West Point. Poe first persuaded Colonel Worth—the commander of Fortress Monroe who had recently joined the regiment after a tour of duty as Commandant of Cadets at the Academy—to write a letter of recommendation. On April 20, 1829 Worth, impressed by Poe, rather rashly but obligingly stated that his military "deportment has been highly praise worthy &

deserving of confidence. His education is of a very high order and he appears to be free from bad habits. . . . I unhesitatingly recommend him as promising to acquit himself of the obligations of that [cadet] station studiously & faithfully."

Two weeks later, on May 6, Allan wrote an all too honest and potentially damaging letter to the secretary of war, which retailed some of the darker episodes in Poe's past, virtually disowned his foster son and reflected his generally hostile feelings.

> He left me in consequence of some Gambling at the university at Charlottesville, because (I presume) I refused to sanction a rule that the shopkeepers & others had adopted there, making Debts of Honour of all indiscretions.—I have much pleasure in asserting that He stood his examination at the close of the year with great credit to himself. His History is short. He is the Grandson of Quartermaster-General Poe of Maryland, whose widow as I understand still receives a pension for the Services or disabilities of Her Husband. Frankly, Sir, I declare that He is no relation to me whatever. . . . I do request your kindness to aid this youth in the promotion of his future prospects. . . . Pardon my frankness; but I address a soldier.

The letter from Colonel James Preston, the father of Poe's Richmond classmate, was much more sympathetic. It stressed only the positive aspects of Poe's university career and presented a strong contrast to Allan's equivocal recommendation: "I am acquainted with the fact of his having been born under circumstances of great adversity. I also know from his own [poetic] productions and other undoubted proofs that he is a young gentleman of genius and talents. I believe he is destined to be distinguished, since he has already gained a reputation for talents & attainments at the University of Virginia. I think him possessed of feelings & character peculiarly entitling him to public patronage."[7] The fourth letter of recommendation, written by Senator Powhaten Ellis of Mississippi and secured through his brother, Allan's former business partner, was decisive. This epistolary barrage finally secured Poe's appointment to West Point.

V ===

Poe pursued his poetic at the same time as his military ambitions. In May 1829, the month after his discharge from the army, the distinguished Philadelphia publishers, Carey, Lea & Carey, offered to bring out Poe's second volume of poetry if—following current practice with unknown authors—Poe would insure them against loss by paying one hundred dollars for the cost of publication. Poe, who of course did not have this money, appealed to Allan to underwrite the book and rather speciously argued that one hundred dollars "must be the limit of any loss, supposing not a single copy of the work to be sold.—It is more than probable that the work will be profitable [though Carey, Lea & Carey did not seem to think so] & that I may gain instead of lose, even in a pecuniary way." The pragmatic Allan, though once willing to publish Poe's schoolboy verses, knew a bad deal when he saw one. Predictably, he censured Poe's foolish request and refused any aid.

In December 1829, after further negotiations, Poe's seventy-two-page *Al Aaraaf, Tamerlane and Minor Poems* was finally published in Baltimore by a less prestigious firm, Hatch & Dunning, in an edition of 250 copies. The critic Floyd Stovall has noted that "the predominant moods of the 1827 volume as a whole are those of wounded pride and resentment for the wrongs, real or imagined, that he had suffered, and the dominant tone of the 1829 volume is one of disillusionment with the world and escape into some more congenial realm of dream or of the imagination."

The 264-line title poem was suffused with a fashionable Romantic melancholy and with a melodious incoherence—reminiscent of the fuzziest passages in Shelley's *Prometheus Unbound* (1820)—that made it extremely difficult, if not impossible, to understand. Poe's explanation did not clarify matters. He told his potential publisher Isaac Lea that the title of the poem came from a Limbo described in chapter seven of the *Koran*, "from the Al Aaraaf of the Arabians, a medium between Heaven & Hell where men suffer no punishment, but yet do not attain that tranquil & even happiness which they suppose to be the characteristic of heavenly enjoyment. . . . I have placed this 'Al Aaraaf' in the celebrated star discovered by [the Danish astronomer] Tycho Brahe which appeared & disappeared so suddenly. . . . Even after death, those who make choice of the star as their residence do not enjoy immortality—but, after a second life of high excitement, sink into forgetfulness & death. . . . The poem commences with a sonnet (illegitimate) a la mode de Byron in his 'Prisoner of Chillon.' But this is a digression."[8]

Poe's use of Tycho Brahe's discovery on November 11, 1572 of the star he called Al Aaraaf may have been influenced by Keats' use of the discovery in 1781 of the planet Uranus (which he compared to

the excitement he felt when first reading Homer in English) in his
sonnet "On First Looking into Chapman's Homer" (1816). Poe completed only two of the projected four parts of his longest poem (which
few readers have wished any longer) and seemed to suggest, in the
vaguest possible way, that one might avoid earthly sin through devotion to higher beauty. The best part of the poem is the lyrical apostro-
phe to the goddess of harmony, whose name he borrowed from one
of the Sirens and later used as the title of one of his best stories:

> Ligeia! Ligeia!
>   My beautiful one!
> Whose harshest idea
>   Will to melody run,
> O! is it thy will
>   On the breezes to toss?
> Or, capriciously still,
>   Like the lone Albatross,
> Incumbent on night
>   (As she on the air)
> To keep watch with delight
>   On the harmony there?

The failure of Poe's longest poem undoubtedly influenced his belief,
later expressed in "The Poetic Principle," that a poem, to be effective,
must be short.

The most accomplished poem in Poe's second volume was his
"Sonnet—To Science," a Romantic protest against scientific rational-
ism, which destroys the mythology that nourishes and sustains the
creative imagination:

> Why preyest thou thus upon the poet's heart,
>   Vulture, whose wings are dull realities? . . .
> Hast thou not dragged Diana from her car?
>   And driven the Hamadryad from the wood
> To seek a shelter in some happier star?

This theme had been similarly expressed in William Blake's antiration-
alist poem, "Mock on, Mock on, Voltaire, Rousseau" (1803):

> The Atoms of Democritus
> And Newton's Particles of Light

> Are sands upon the Red Sea shore,
> Where Israel's tents do shine so bright.

Poe's second volume, which received slightly more attention than his first one, provoked a satiric allusion in the anonymous *Musiad*, published in Baltimore in 1830:

> Next Poe who smil'd at reason, laugh'd at law,
> And played a tune who should have play'd at taw [marbles],
> Now strain'd a license, and now cracked a string,
> But sang as older children dare not sing.

In January 1830, however, Poe's second cousin Neilson Poe wrote to his future wife: "Edgar Poe has published a volume of Poems, one of which ["Tamerlane"] is dedicated to John Neal, the great autocrat of critics.—Neal has accordingly published Edgar as a Poet of great genius." Neal—a lawyer, novelist and editor—had prophetically written: "If the young author now before us should fulfil his destiny . . . he will be *foremost* in the rank of *real* poets."[9] But Poe's ardent desire to escape from the real into the dream world was sadly at variance with his long-nourished goal of becoming an army officer.

VI ═══

Poe was the only major American writer to attend West Point. He arrived there on about June 20, 1830 and easily passed the entrance examination, which consisted of little more than basic reading, writing and arithmetic. He then spent two months in the rigorous summer camp, where he lived in a tent, slept on the ground, practiced tactical movements and participated in the endless and exhausting drill, which began at 5:30 in the morning and lasted until 6:30 at night. During artillery drill, he wore leather harness in order to pull the heavy guns.

West Point, founded in 1802 to train and educate officers for the United States Army, was the first college in America to emphasize technical subjects. The superintendent, Colonel Sylvanus Thayer, closely followed the organization and curriculum of the French École Polytechnique. Robert E. Lee, who had graduated in 1829, the year before Poe entered the Academy, later succeeded Thayer and followed his traditions. In 1830 the library had 3,000 books on civil and military engineering, mathematics, chemistry and geology, strategy, tactics

and military history. It also subscribed to the *Edinburgh Review* and
the *London Quarterly Review*.

Poe was distinctly ill suited to the rigors of life at West Point. In
order to develop Spartan character and discipline in the cadets, the
Academy "required attendance at church, minute regulation of daily
life, cold rooms in winter and hot ones in summer, inferior food, and
no recreation." Thayer and his successors proscribed harmless as well
as pernicious pursuits, forbidding the cadets "to drink, play cards or
chess, gamble, use or possess tobacco, keep any cooking utensils in
their room, participate in any games, read novels, romances, or plays,
go off the post, bathe in the river, or play a musical instrument."
Unlike the University of Virginia, which encouraged Poe's tendency
to gamble and drink, the Academy imposed intolerable discipline and
severe punishments for any breach of the rules.

All the cadets wore the ill-fitting and uncomfortable uniform. The
high shoes were heavy and clumsy, the coat had three rows of eight
yellow buttons in front, and the high black leather hat, with polished
visor, had a decorative eight-inch plume. The cheap, stodgy and
unappetizing food, contracted out to the lowest bidder and served in
two Commons, consisted mainly of bread, coffee, boiled meat, boiled
potatoes and boiled pudding—sometimes supplemented by a stolen
chicken, roasted by the cadets over the logs of an open fireplace.
Water was carried in by the bucket and candles illuminated the
sparsely furnished and fanatically neat three-man rooms. While enjoying this life, the cadets were paid twenty-eight dollars a month,
plus subsistence and tuition.

One of the few outlets of escape at West Point was Benny Havens'
hospitable tavern, which served forbidden liquor to cadets. "As a
young man Benny had worked for a sutler but, having been discovered selling rum to a cadet, was fired. In 1824 he set up his own
tavern, which he continued to run until long after the Civil War. It
became the most famous establishment in all West Point history. . . .
Mrs. Havens did the cooking, specializing in buckwheat cakes and
roast turkey. Benny himself was a great talker who had deep sympathy for the plight of the cadets—he often extended credit or took
blankets or other stolen items for his excellent flip. Edgar Allan Poe,
who went often, thought Benny 'was the sole congenial soul in the
entire God-forsaken place.' "

The academic schedule, which began when Poe moved into No.
28 South Barracks and started classes on September 1, was as rigorous
and regimented as the summer camp. The cadets rose at sunrise,

attended classes until breakfast at 7:00 A.M., from 8:00 until 1:00, and again from 2:00 to 4:00 P.M. They practiced military exercises from after supper until 9:30, and put out the lights at 10:00 P.M. The only holidays were July 4 and Christmas day. After the freedom of release from his undemanding life in the army, and a fairly idle year in Baltimore, ex-Sergeant-Major Poe, three years older than the rest of his classmates, must have felt terribly constricted by the uniforms, the salutes, the roll calls, the drills, the crowded quarters, the uncomfortable conditions, the incessant study, the rigid discipline and the oppressive authority.

Like all first-year cadets, Poe took two courses: mathematics and French. The cold and dessicated Albert Church, who taught mathematics from 1828 to 1878, was a "short, stocky, brown-eyed, broad-faced man, with a complaining voice. There never was a colder eye or manner than Professor Church's. He seemed an old mathematical cinder, bereft of all natural feeling."[10] The Frenchman Claudius Berard, who taught the language for thirty-one years, had purchased a substitute to replace him in Napoleon's army, then fled France when that man was killed in the Peninsular campaign and he once again became liable to conscription. Berard had the cadets read Voltaire's *Histoire de Charles XII* (1731), which described the Swedish king's struggle with Peter the Great of Russia, and Lesage's picaresque satire, *Gil Blas* (completed 1735), which Allan had sent Poe at the university and then criticized as a worthless book. After his studies of classical and modern languages at Virginia, Poe had a great advantage in this course. Another notable faculty member was the round-faced, bold-eyed, disheveled Robert Weir. After studying in Italy, he came to West Point in 1833 and taught drawing there for forty-two years. A memorable line in Poe's "Ulalume," inspired by the Hudson River landscape, refers to "the ghoul-haunted woodland of Weir."

Thayer carefully ranked every student in every course. The cadets recited in class every day and took general examinations in each subject in January and in June. Poe, who was both scholarly and intelligent, repeated at West Point his distinguished academic performance at Virginia. At the end of the first half year he finished, in a class of eighty-seven, third in French and seventeenth in mathematics. Since standards were exacting and discipline rigid, the attrition rate was as high at West Point (where the students were more motivated) as it had been at Virginia. Only a quarter of the cadets in each class ever graduated; the rest were dismissed for bad conduct or scholastic deficiency.

The descriptions of Poe by his West Point contemporaries tend to ignore his academic accomplishments and seem retrospectively colored by the notoriety he achieved in later life. They reveal that he continued to read and write poetry, and to drink heavily, despite the strict rules. George Cullum remembered Poe as "a slovenly, heedless boy, very eccentric, inclined to dissipation, [who], of course, preferred making verses to solving equations"—though seventy classmates, who presumably preferred equations, ranked lower than he did. Poe's roommate Thomas Gibson, in the fullest account, also emphasized his poetic ability and unusual character: "His acquaintance with English literature was extensive and accurate, and his verbal memory [which he had exhibited as a child] wonderful. He would repeat both prose and poetry by the hour." When they first met, a forbidden volume of Thomas Campbell's poems was lying on Gibson's table. Mentioning an obsession that would later cause him a great deal of trouble, Poe contemptuously remarked that Campbell was a plagiarist. "He had a worn, weary, discontented look," Gibson continued, "not easily forgotten by those who were intimate with him. [The hypersensitive] Poe was easily fretted by any jest at his expense." Alluding to a problem that would plague Poe throughout his life, Gibson remarked: "I don't think he was ever intoxicated while at the Academy, but he had already acquired the more dangerous habit of constant drinking."

Allan Magruder, a classmate from Virginia who left the Academy in 1831, mentioned the intellectual ability that enabled Poe to excel without effort (as he had done at the university), but also stressed his lack of interest in routine military duties—which he had mastered during his two years in the army:

> [Poe] was very shy and reserved in his intercourse with his fellow-cadets—his associates being confined almost exclusively to Virginians. . . . He was an accomplished French scholar, and had a wonderful aptitude for mathematics, so that he had no difficulty in preparing his recitations in his class and obtaining the highest marks in these departments. He was a devourer of books, but his great fault was his neglect of and apparent contempt for military duties. His wayward and capricious temper made him at times utterly oblivious or indifferent to the ordinary routine of roll-call, drills, and guard duties. These habits subjected him often to arrest and punishment, and effectually prevented his learning or discharging the duties of a soldier.

And Timothy Jones noted, without offering an explanation, Poe's sudden change in attitude toward West Point: "He was certainly given to extreme dissipation within a very short time after he entered school. At first he studied hard and his ambition seemed to be to lead the class in all studies. . . . It was only a few weeks after the beginning of his career at West Point that he seemed to lose interest in his studies and to be disheartened and discouraged."[11]

One famous cadet who shared many of Poe's attitudes was James McNeill Whistler, who later became an eminent painter. He entered the Academy in 1851, spent three years of humiliating failure in everything except art (which he studied with Robert Weir) and was discharged in 1854 for gross deficiency after an examination in chemistry. "Had silicon been a gas," Whistler later observed, "I would have been a major general." Despite this failure, he constantly referred to himself as "a West Point man" and liked to deliver little sermons about "correct West Point principles"[12]—something Poe was never tempted to do.

Poe's classmates were probably unaware of the principal reasons for his neglect of drill and sudden lack of interest in his studies. Now, for the second time, he had cause to repent his long-term commitment to military life. He had originally told Allan that his previous experience as a soldier would undoubtedly allow him to "run thro' " the course at West Point in only six months. But once he had enrolled, he realized that he, like all his raw classmates, would have to spend four full years at the Academy before securing his commission as a lieutenant.

Moreover, changes in Allan's family life cast forbidding light on Poe's expectations. Allan's mistress gave birth to illegitimate twin sons in Richmond on about July 1, 1830 (sixteen months after his wife's death). And on October 5, 1830, during Poe's first term at West Point, Allan married another woman, Louisa Patterson of Elizabeth, New Jersey, with whom he was to have three children. The death of the first Mrs. Allan had led to a reconciliation with his foster father and entry into West Point; now, the marriage to the second Mrs. Allan dashed his hopes of an inheritance and made him decide to leave it. Allan had kept Poe as short of funds at the Academy as he had at the university. Realizing, at last, that the army was no place for a poor man and that without Allan's help he would not be able to live on a lieutenant's pay, Poe decided to abandon his military career.

But Poe could not leave West Point, any more than he could have left the army, without the consent of his foster father. And Allan, having helped Poe secure a position that made few financial demands on him, would lead to a profession and would make Poe independent, did not want him to abandon his career. He feared Poe was repeating at West Point his disastrous experience at Virginia.

On January 3, 1831 Poe wrote Allan a bitterly angry letter, rehearsing their unhappy history from the time of his adoption to his misery at West Point. Though he knew that "General" Poe had been reduced to poverty and could not adopt him, he now claimed that the wealthy "General," his "natural protector," had reluctantly surrendered his favorite grandchild after Allan had promised to give the boy a good education: "Did I, when an infant," Poe rhetorically asked, "solicit your charity and protection, or was it of your own free will, that you volunteered your services in my behalf? . . . Under such circumstances, can it be said that I have no *right* to expect any thing at your hands?" After blaming Allan for his disasters at the university and saying he had never valued Allan's love, he exclaimed: "You sent me to W. Point like a beggar. The same difficulties are threatening me as before at Charlottesville—and I must resign."

A month before entering West Point, on May 3, 1830, Poe had made one of the greatest mistakes of his mistake-filled life. Hounded for his debt of fifty dollars by his army substitute, Sergeant Samuel "Bully" Graves (who had reenlisted to get the bounty), Poe rashly remarked of his respectable, tightfisted foster father: "I have tried to get the money for you from Mr. A a dozen times—but he always shuffles me off. . . . Mr. A is not often very sober—which accounts for it." In December 1830 Graves, irritated that he had still not been paid, told Allan what Poe had said about him. Naturally furious at Poe's slanderous statement, Allan demanded an explanation. Now, in his emotional letter of January 3, 1831, Poe tactlessly suggested that his statement to Graves was *true* and blamed Allan for provoking it by his bitter taunts: "As regards Sergt. Graves—I *did* write him that letter. As to the truth of its contents, I leave it to God and your own conscience.—The time in which I wrote it was within a half hour after you had embittered every feeling of my heart against you by your abuse of my *family*, and myself, under your own roof—and at a time when you knew that my heart was almost breaking."

Allan did not reply to Poe's long letter of January 3, which marked a turning point in their unhappy relations. He clearly rejected Poe's version of the events described, regarding him as reckless, ungrateful and untrustworthy. And he wrote on this unfortunate letter: "I do not think the Boy has one good quality. He may do or act as he pleases, tho' I wd have saved him, but on his own terms & conditions.

I cannot believe a word he writes. His letter is the most barefaced one-sided statement."[13]

Since Allan would not allow him to resign from West Point, Poe decided to get himself court-martialed. Between January 7 and 27, 1831, he deliberately disobeyed orders from the officer of the day. He failed to report for parades, roll calls and guard duty thirteen times, and failed to attend church and class ten times. On January 28 Cadet Poe was tried on the charges of "Gross Neglect of Duty" and "Disobedience of Orders." He did not defend himself, and was found guilty of all charges. After confirmation of the verdict by the secretary of war on February 8, Poe was dismissed, as of March 6 (so he could collect his pay due on that date), from the service of the United States.

Undeterred by Allan's silence and wrath, Poe wrote again from New York on February 21, melodramatically blaming his self-induced court-martial on illness—and on Allan:

> I am obliged once more to recur to you for assistance.—It will however be the last time that I ever trouble any human being.—I feel that I am on a sick bed from *which* I shall never get up. . . . I, as I told you, neglected my duty when I found it impossible to attend to it, and the consequences were inevitable—dismissal. I have been dismissed—when a single line from you would have saved it.—The whole academy have interested themselves in my behalf because my only crime was being *sick*. . . . I shall never rise from my bed—besides a most violent cold on my lungs, my *ear* discharges blood and matter continually.

Allan's reaction to this letter was even more bitter and angry than his response to the previous one. After learning that Poe had actually carried out his threat and been dismissed from the Academy, he angrily annotated the letter, calling it a "precious relict of the Blackest Heart & deepest ingratitude, alike destitute of honour & principle. Every day of his life has only served to confirm his debased nature.— Suffice it to say my only regret is in Pity for his failings—his Talents are of an order that can never prove a comfort to their possessor." It is ironic that Allan, for all his lack of understanding, perceived that Poe could be destroyed by his own genius.

Considered a strange, melancholy loner who concentrated on his poetry, Poe nevertheless did well academically at both Virginia and West Point. His problems at Virginia were largely induced by Allan's meanness with money; though Poe wanted to continue his education, he was not allowed to do so. At West Point four years later, Poe realized that he did not want to be an army officer and, with a self-destructive compulsion that would recur throughout his life, deliberately ruined his second and last chance of a professional career. In doing so, he permanently alienated John Allan and destroyed all possibility of becoming his heir.

VII ═══

After the ignominy of a court-martial, we would expect Poe to have abandoned all thoughts of a military career. But almost immediately after being expelled from West Point, he had the nerve to ask the Superintendent for a letter of recommendation. In November 1830 the Poles had risen up against the Russian enemy who had occupied their country since 1772. They established a substantial army and had some initial success. On March 10, 1831—before the Poles were crushed and the Russians reentered Warsaw—Poe told Colonel Thayer of his plans and requested his assistance: "I intend by the first opportunity to proceed to Paris with the view of obtaining, thro' the interest of the Marquis de la Fayette [his family friend], an appointment (if possible) in the Polish Army. In the event of the interference of France [who had been Poland's ally during Napoleon's war against Russia] in behalf of Poland this may easily be effected."[14] Poe saw this war as a Byronic fantasy, with himself as the idealistic, sacrificial hero. But when France declined to save Poland from the Russian hordes, Poe concentrated all his efforts in publishing his third volume of poetry, a more likely arena for constructing a Romantic self-image.

Poe amused his classmates at West Point, as he had done at the university, with his own poetry. Timothy Jones, perceiving a new aspect of Poe's character after he had decided to leave the Academy, mentioned that "he would often write some of the most forcible and vicious doggerel. . . . I have never seen a man whose hatred was so intense." The only surviving example of Poe's West Point verse is a tame squib—rather than biting satire—on the martinet, Lieutenant Joseph Locke, who taught military tactics and, as Inspector, was responsible for reporting all infractions of the rules. Mentioning the eminent philosopher who shared the officer's surname, Poe wrote:

> John Locke was a notable name
>   Joe Locke is a greater; in short,

> The former was well known to fame,
>   But the latter's well known "to report."

Eager to see Poe's scandalous satires in print, most of the cadets subscribed seventy-five cents each to underwrite publication. This sum was deducted from their official accounts by the Treasurer of the Academy, who on April 23, 1831 sent Poe a check for $170. Poe's heavily revised and considerably augmented third volume, *Poems*, was brought out by Elam Bliss in New York the following month in an edition of about five hundred copies. In gratitude, it was dedicated to the "United States Corps of Cadets." But this volume was received by them "with a general expression of disgust." The puny, miserably produced booklet, bound in green boards and badly printed on coarse paper, "contained not one of the squibs and satires upon which his reputation at the Academy had been built up."[15]

Poe had published half his poems by 1831. But he had earned nothing from his verse, and the following year began writing stories out of financial necessity. Poe had made considerable poetic progress—not only in new, but also in revised poems—from 1827 to 1831, as he struggled to free himself from dependence on Allan and achieve artistic as well as personal maturity. His best poems from the early years are "Sonnet—To Science" (1829), the first "To Helen," "Israfel," "The Sleeper," "The Valley of Unrest" and "The City in the Sea" (all 1831).

Poe's major poetic themes include victimization, power and powerlessness, confrontations with mysterious presences, extreme states of being, dehumanization and its cure, the relation of body and soul, memory of and mourning for the dead, the need for spiritual transcendence and affirmation.[16] Israfel, according to the *Koran* and Poe's note to that poem, is an angel "whose heart-strings are a lute, and who has the sweetest voice of all God's creatures." In this mysteriously incantatory poem, Poe, aspiring to the heights of poetic inspiration, suggests that it would be much more difficult for the melodiously named Israfel, if burdened by mortal constraints, to sing joyously of earthly sorrows. Conversely, mortal poets would sing more beautifully if they enjoyed Israfel's celestial state:

> If I could dwell
> Where Israfel
>   Hath dwelt, and he where I,
> He might not sing so wildly well
>   A mortal melody,

> While a bolder note than this might swell
> From my lyre within the sky.

Poe found in Romantic poetry an artistic correlative for his own unhappy life. He believed the most beautiful poetry came from the deepest feelings (the "heart-strings"), but that it was difficult to write in a philistine world that constrained and ignored the poet's art.

"The Sleeper," "The Valley of Unrest" and "The City in the Sea" form a distinct thematic group and represent a self-conscious dramatization of doom. "The Sleeper" is Poe's first expression of his characteristic portrayal of the twilight state between life and death. The grieving lover wishes a peaceful sleep for the beautiful dead woman, and morbidly prays: "Soft may the worms about her creep!" But he also fears that her rest will be disturbed. In "The Valley of Unrest," the imaginary landscape reflects human sadness as nature weeps for man's loss of innocence. The restlessness of the sad valley is evoked by magnificently melancholy descriptions of its trees:

> Ah, by no wind are stirred those trees
> That palpitate like the chill seas
> Around the misty Hebrides!,

and of its flowers:

> They weep:—from off their delicate stems
> Perennial tears descend in gems.

"The City in the Sea"—inspired by accounts in Flavius Josephus' *History of the Jewish Wars* (written in the first century A.D.) of the wicked biblical city of Gomorrah that lay buried, decomposing and sinking beneath the hideously serene waters of the Dead Sea—portrays Poe's ghastly apocalyptic vision:

> But light from out the lurid sea
> Streams up the turrets silently—. . .
> Up many and many a marvellous shrine
> Whose wreathéd friezes intertwine
> The viol, the violet, and the vine. . . .
> While from a proud tower in the town
> Death looks gigantically down.

Poe had brought out accomplished volumes of verse when he was eighteen and twenty years old. But his *Poems* of 1831, an impressive achievement for a young man of twenty-two, was the best book written, thus far, by an American poet.

Though Thomas Gibson maintained that at West Point he had "never heard [Poe] speak in terms of praise of any English writer, living or dead," Poe's "Letter to B——," addressed to his publisher Elam Bliss and included as a preface to the *Poems* of 1831, contained very high praise for Samuel Taylor Coleridge. The older poet had a profound influence on Poe's poetic imagination, his critical principles and his speculative mind. In this "Letter," his first prose work, Poe praises Coleridge as a "giant in intellect and learning" who sometimes "goes wrong by reason of his very profundity," and then breathlessly extols his explosive imaginative force: "Of Coleridge I cannot speak but with reverence. His towering intellect! His gigantic power! . . . In reading his poetry, I tremble, like one who stands upon a volcano, conscious, from the very darkness bursting from the crater, of the fire and the light that are weltering below." In two reviews of 1836 Poe said Coleridge had composed "the purest of all poems" and, identifying with the neglected Coleridge, called him a " 'myriad-minded man,' and ah, how little understood, and how pitifully vilified!"[17]

In the "Letter to B——" Poe lifted a sentence, without acknowledgment, from chapter XIV of Coleridge's *Biographia Literaria* (1817). Coleridge wrote:

> A poem is that species of composition, which is opposed to works of science, by proposing for its *immediate* object pleasure, not truth,

and Poe repeated:

> A poem, in my opinion, is opposed to a work of science by having, for its *immediate* object, pleasure, not truth.

Floyd Stovall, who called Coleridge "the guiding spirit of Poe's entire intellectual life," has effectively summarized his extensive debt to the English poet. Like Coleridge, Poe believed that poetry gives pleasure by being indefinite, music is an essential element in poetry, beauty is the sole province of the poem, poetic beauty has the quality of strangeness, the poem must have unity of effect, the true poem must be brief, passion and poetry are discordant, and the tone of the poem should be melancholy.[18]

VIII ====

Poe's love for Frances Allan had bound his foster father to him. But he now sealed his doom by alienating both John Allan and his second wife, Louisa. She had not only supplanted his beloved foster mother, but also effectively cut him off from his inheritance. A portrait of the unattractive Louisa depicts her round, jowly face, large nose, full lips and heavy creases that run from her nostrils to the edges of her mouth. Though John Hewitt, a Baltimore journalist, declared that the cause of Poe's rupture with Allan "originated from Poe's too close attention to his benefactor's wife when the old gentleman was on a visit to Europe," his assertion was nothing more than a libelous rumor. But there were other, more realistic grounds for the quarrel between the "masculine" Louisa and the hypersensitive Poe. He falsely told one young lady that Louisa Patterson had been Allan's housekeeper. And Susan Archer Talley, a Richmond friend, reported that after Louisa had emphasized Poe's dependent position and reminded him that he was "an object of 'charity' in her house," he retaliated by accusing her of having married for money.[19] Louisa's niece claimed that her aunt (who lived until 1881) "always felt it bitterly that the public so often blamed her for the estrangement when she had nothing to do with it." But Poe's wife showed a friend an important letter from Louisa, written after Allan's death, which "expressed a desire to see [Poe], and acknowledged that she alone had been the cause of his adopted father's neglect."

Poe's undated "Autobiography" throws some light on this crucial but murky quarrel. Poe states that before Allan's second marriage he was "regarded always as [Allan's] son and heir—he having no other children." Poe admits that he had led a very dissipated life and, after Allan had refused to pay his debts of honor, had run away from home "without a dollar." Though he does not specify the cause of their argument—which may have been sparked by Louisa's insult about their "charity"—he clearly states that "Mrs. A. and myself quarrelled, and he, siding with her, wrote me an angry letter."[20]

Poe had quarrelled with Allan during his adolescent rebellion in Richmond and again after his gambling debts at the university, but he had always managed—perhaps with the help of Frances Allan— to achieve a reconciliation. But his much more serious quarrels with both Allan and Louisa after his expulsion from West Point led—despite one more hopeless attempt to appease the sickly old man—to a final rupture that condemned Poe to a life of degrading poverty. Poe's quarrels with Allan reenacted the tragedy of his earliest years and caused great psychological as well as material damage. The death of Frances Allan reflected the death of his mother; the rejection by John Allan mirrored the desertion of his father; and the adopted orphan, having lost his foster parents, was orphaned once again.

Chapter 5

BALTIMORE: MARIA CLEMM AND EARLY STORIES, 1831–1834

I ═══

After Allan's second marriage and their recent quarrels, Poe knew that the house in Richmond was now closed to him. In May 1831 he returned to Baltimore, which then had 80,000 inhabitants and was the third-largest city in America. In that red-brick town his ancestors had resided, "General" Poe had achieved patriotic eminence and the remnant of his original family now lived. But there was a powerful contrast between Allan's imposing mansion and Poe's humble quarters, first in Mechanics Row, Wilks Street, then at 3 Amity Street, a narrow, shabby, two-story house, with shuttered windows and a mean front door. Both places had the austerity of his military barracks.

Born in poverty, the child of a broken home, and orphaned at the age of two; unable to complete his university education, expelled from West Point and rejected by his foster father; traumatized by the deaths of the women who had loved him—Eliza Poe, Jane Stanard and Frances Allan—Poe was well prepared for a perfectly wretched life. Despite all efforts to improve his fortunes, his descent into the lower class was to prove permanent. This celebrated delinquent became the saddest and strangest figure in American literature, "socially dislocated, emotionally starved, and torn in spirit."[1] He kept no diaries, had no intimate friends and confided in no one.

Poe's strange, melancholy loneliness, his obsession with plagiarism, his sensitivity to criticism, his frequent requests for money, his threats of rash behavior, his overweening pride, his humiliating self-abasement and his compulsive self-destruction all contributed to his caustic and corrosive character. Yet his sense of social grievance, his brooding temperament, his fecklessness, his excitable, imperious nature were balanced by his Castilian courtesy, "polished manners, enormous erudition, formidable conversational abilities, and indescribable personal magnetism."

The life of the "wild, eccentric, audacious, tortured, horror-haunted, sorrowing, beauty-loving"[2] Poe was defined by the unbearable tensions in his paradoxical character. He was a Virginia gentleman and the son of itinerant actors, the heir to a great fortune and a disinherited outcast, a university man who had failed to graduate, a soldier bought out of the army, a court-martialed cadet. Later in life he would become a husband with an unapproachable child-bride, a brilliant editor and low-salaried hack, a world-renowned but impoverished author, the fiancé of two women who would not marry him, a normally temperate man and an uncontrollable alcoholic, a rationalist with a mystical cast of mind, a materialist who yearned for a final unity with God.

The sharp inward division between the impressive force of Poe's rational mind and the overpowering strength of his irrational apprehension was reflected not only in his poems and stories but also in his conflict with authority, his anxious welcome of personal disaster and his sad compulsion to destroy his own life. Poe portrays his divided personality in his autobiographical tale, "William Wilson." The narrator, like Poe himself in certain moods, has an "imaginative and easily excitable temperament" and is "self-willed, addicted to the wildest caprices, and a prey to the most ungovernable passions." He is tormented and pursued by his double—an inseparable companion in Dr. Bransby's school, at Eton and Oxford, and on the Continent—who mimics all his actions. Finally, unable to escape his tiresome other self, he stabs him to death. Only then does he realize that he has destroyed his conscience, or finer part of himself. He has become dead to the moral world and no longer has a meaningful existence. The story expresses Poe's dual impulses: to act destructively and to censure his own irrational behavior.

Poe quarreled with nearly everyone he ever met and alienated nearly

everyone who was capable of helping him. Though sadly dependent
upon patronage, his touchy pride and deep hostility to paternal authority led to consistently uneasy relations with his superiors: with
John Allan (who intensified Poe's instability by refusing to define his
status and expectations), with the officials at the university and the
officers at West Point, and with the magazine owners who exploited
his talent and paid subsistence wages—with anyone, in fact, who
impugned his dignity, status or genius. Prompted by memories of
his early oppression, he once shocked a listener by exclaiming, with
satanic pride: "My whole nature utterly *revolts* at the idea that there
is any Being in the Universe superior to *myself*!" But, till the very
end of his life, he was forced to apologize to figures of authority and
to explain the reasons for his irresponsibility, his poverty and his
drunkenness.

Poe's quarrels were provoked by his merits as well as by his faults.
As one friend shrewdly perceived, "others disliked him, naturally
enough, because he was a man of superior intellect." In *Marginalia*,
Poe considered the ambivalent "fate of an individual gifted, or rather
accursed, with an intellect *very* far superior, to that of his race. . . .
Since his opinions and speculations would differ wildly from those of
all mankind—that he would be considered a madman, is evident."[3]
His consciousness of intellectual superiority, especially when he was
confined to a humble position, inspired the enmity or mockery of
ordinary men. There was a limited tolerance in journalistic circles for
Poe's odd character, intellectual arrogance and pretentious learning.

In "Eleonora" Poe discussed a related idea—which had begun with
Plato and evolved through the centuries to the Romantic poets—that
genius was connected to madness, that the diseased imagination could
transcend intellect and create the deepest artistic visions: "the question
is not yet settled, whether madness is or is not the loftiest intelligence—whether much that is glorious—whether all that is profound—does not spring from disease of thought—from *moods* of
mind exalted at the expense of the general intellect."

The unusually intelligent and extremely neurotic Poe was driven
by what he called "the human thirst for self-torment." Defining the
reasons for his own irrational behavior in "The Imp of the Perverse,"
he wrote that some men were motivated by self-destructive impulses,
that "the assurance of the wrong or error of any action is often the
one unconquerable *force* which impels us, and alone impels us to its
prosecution." His own unhappy life—as well as that of his fictional
characters—seemed dominated by this fatal principle. The guilt-
obsessed narrator of "The Black Cat," for example, is also possessed

by this profound and apparently inexplicable impulse: "The spirit of perverseness, I say, came to my final overthrow . . . this unfathomable longing of the soul *to vex itself*—to offer violence to its own nature—to do wrong for wrong's sake only."

The unbearable tensions in Poe's divided personality led him to perversely self-destructive behavior, to conflict with authority and sometimes to morbid despair. He would communicate this dark mood to his correspondents in an attempt to elicit their pity and sympathy; and kindly friends would offer encouragement and try to coax him out of his melancholy. One of them advised Poe to "subdue this brooding and boding inclination of your mind." Another insisted that "life is too short & there is too much to be done in it, to give one time to *despair*," and urged him to "exorcise that devil, I beg of you, as speedily as possible." But Poe's deep-rooted gloom went far beyond the characteristic melancholy of Byron and Coleridge, and could not, despite encouragement from friends, be readily dismissed. After searching his soul, he recorded one of his most personal and profound beliefs: "to be *thoroughly* conversant with Man's heart, is to take our final lesson in the iron-clasped volume of Despair."[4] There is no escape to the dream world in "To One in Paradise," where—as in "Alone"—ineradicable grief overshadows the present and blights the future:

> Ah, dream tòo bright to last!
>   Ah, starry Hope! that didst arise
> But to be overcast!
>   A voice from out the Future cries,
> "On! on!"—but o'er the Past
>   (Dim gulf!) my spirit hovering lies
> Mute, motionless, aghast!

II ══

During his years in Baltimore, the least documented and most obscure period of his life, Poe lived in humble and sometimes desperate circumstances. He rediscovered his family and shared quarters with his father's widowed sister, Aunt Maria Clemm, and her child, his nine-year-old cousin Virginia, who would later become his wife. Born in 1790, Maria had in 1817 married William Clemm, a socially prominent Baltimore widower whose late wife was Maria's first cousin. Maria had three children, one of whom died in infancy. At the time of Clemm's death in 1826, his property had disappeared, and his widow (like Poe) was left desolate and unprotected. When Poe joined the household in May 1831—four months after his court-martial and the same month he published his third volume of poems in New York—Maria was barely managing to support herself by sewing, by keeping occasional boarders in her tiny house and by a $240 annual pension, paid to her paralyzed, bedridden mother, Elizabeth, the widow of "General" Poe.

The large, forty-one-year-old Maria Clemm had the face and figure of a man. A daguerreotype portrays her in a white widow's bonnet with long streamers, trim white collar and pleated black dress. She had a large forehead, deep-set, widely spaced eyes with overhanging brows, a broad nose, lined cheeks, long narrow mouth, firm chin and puffy jowls. The kindly, energetic and tactless Maria was absolutely devoted to Poe. She believed in his genius, cared for him with a maternal solicitude and willingly made great sacrifices on his behalf. The Irish novelist Mayne Reid has provided the best account of the numerous services Maria performed for the ever-impractical Poe (who published his first stories while living with her in Baltimore) and of her constant attempts to protect him from the harsh realities of the world:

> She was the ever-vigilant guardian of the house, watching it against the silent but continuous sap of necessity, that appeared every day to be approaching closer and nearer. She was the sole servant, keeping everything clean; the sole messenger, doing the errands, making pilgrimages between the poet and his publishers, frequently bringing back such chilling responses as "The article is not accepted," or "The cheque not to be given until such and such a day,"—often too late for his necessities. And she was also the messenger to the market; from it bringing back, not "the delicacies of the season," but only such commodities as were called for by the dire exigencies of hunger.

Poe was closer to Maria than to anyone else he ever knew. His intense emotional attachment to both Maria and Virginia Clemm was forged when, rejected by his foster father, he had returned to his own blood relations, to the aunt and cousin who comprised his third family. Maria too had suffered bereavement, having lost her husband and child. Poe's deeply felt though somewhat morbid and sentimental sonnet, "To My Mother," is dedicated not to Eliza Poe or Frances

Allan, who were never entirely satisfactory mothers, but to Maria Clemm. She was also bound to him as the mother of his future wife and he addresses her with the passion of a lover:

> Because I felt that, in the Heavens above,
>   The angels, whispering to one another,
> Can find, among the burning terms of love,
>   None so devotional as that of "Mother,"
> Therefore by that dear name I long have called you—
>   You who are more than mother unto me. . . .
> My mother—my own mother, who died early,
>   Was but the mother of myself; but you
> Are mother to the one I love so dearly,
>   And thus are dearer than the mother I knew.

Poe's residence with the Clemms in Baltimore renewed his sporadic contact with his older brother, Henry, who had been brought up by "General" Poe. Henry had corresponded with Edgar in the 1820s, visited him in Richmond and accompanied him to the house of Elmira Royster, the subject of his prose sketch, "The Pirate." In the late 1820s Henry had made several sea voyages to the Mediterranean, the Near East and possibly Russia, as well as to the West Indies and Montevideo, aboard the American frigate *Macedonian*. Edgar incorporated Henry's actual journeys into his own fantastic biography. Upon returning to Baltimore in 1827, Henry had published an account of his journey and, along with his invalid widowed grandmother, had taken up residence with the perennial standby, Maria Clemm.

A thin, dark-eyed young man who resembled his brother, Henry shared Edgar's dreamy Romanticism, morbid melancholy, wild streak and weakness for liquor. In August 1829, four months after his discharge from the army, Poe had described their hopelessly miserable household in a letter to Allan: "My grandmother is extremely poor & ill (paralytic). My aunt Maria if possible still worse & Henry entirely given up to drink & unable to help himself, much less me." Henry, who had been in poor health for some time and continued to drink heavily, died of tuberculosis on August 1, 1831, at the age of twenty-four. Edgar replaced Henry in the household and in the affections of his aunt.

During his years in Richmond (both before and after his Baltimore years) Poe occasionally saw his younger sister, Rosalie, who continued to live with the prosperous Mackenzies, her adopted family. A dull, tedious, pathetic figure, Rosalie had failed to develop mentally after the age of twelve. Though Edgar was repelled by her and would tease her about her strange dress and peculiar behavior, she adored him and clung to him. "She was a very plain person," a Richmond friend recalled, "and he with his fastidious ideas could not tolerate her want of feminine tact and taste."[5]

III

The wretched conditions recounted in Poe's letter of August 1829 prevailed throughout the Baltimore years. During the autumn of 1831 this misery once again forced Poe to grovel before Allan in the hope of extracting a pittance that would enable them all to survive. Both Allan and Poe had grown up in anticipation of inherited wealth. Though William Galt had left Allan a great fortune, Allan hoped to establish his foster son in a business or profession that would make him independent, and left none of Galt's money to the starving Poe. Later on, remembering Allan's harsh, erratic treatment, Poe described him as "a man of a gross & brutal temperament, though *indulgent to him* & at *times* profusely lavish in the matter of money—at others, penurious and parsimonious." An acute passage in "Three Sundays in a Week" reveals that Poe saw Allan's potential bequest as a *repayment* for the gift of a beautiful infant, that Allan had loved him after a fashion but treated him very badly, and that he had used his wealth to control Poe by alternately promising to give him a fortune or leave him nothing at all: "My parents, in dying, had bequeathed me to him as a rich legacy. I believe the old villain loved me as his own child . . . but it was a dog's existence that he led me, after all. . . . From fifteen to twenty, not a day passed in which he did not promise to cut me off with a shilling."

On October 16, 1831—eight months after Allan had condemned his black heart and deep ingratitude and two months after Allan's first legitimate son was born—Poe wrote a regretful, conciliatory letter that asked no favors, flattered the old man, berated himself and echoed Job's "let the day perish wherein I was born": "When I look back upon the past and think of every thing—of how much you tried to do for me—of your forbearance and your generosity, in spite of the most flagrant ingratitude on my part, I can not help thinking myself the greatest fool in existence.—I am ready to curse the day when I was born."

Having softened Allan up with this letter, Poe applied in earnest to

"Dear Pa" the following month after (he claimed) he had been arrested for an unspecified debt, "which I never expected to have to pay, and which was incurred as much on [his dead brother] Henry's account as on my own." Though no evidence for his actual arrest has been found, Poe, if in debt, was clearly in real danger. In 1832 half the prisoners in the Baltimore City Jail were insolvent debtors. Poe ended with his by now familiar pleas and threats: "If you will only send me this one time $80, by Wednesday next, I will never forget your kindness & generosity.—If you refuse God only knows what I shall do, & all my hopes & prospects are ruined forever." But it took more than theatrical declarations of doom to move Allan, who ignored this letter as he had ignored the previous one.

On December 15 and again on the 29th, the increasingly miserable Poe tried to touch Allan's heart with two last, sad pleas for help:

> When I beg and entreat you in the name of God to send me succour you will still refuse to aid me. I know that I have offended you past all forgiveness, and I know that I have no longer any hopes of being again received into your favour, but, for the sake of Christ, do not let me perish for a sum of money which you would never miss, and which would relieve me from the greatest earthly misery. . . .
>
> No person in the world I am sure, could have undergone more wretchedness than I have done for some time past— and I have indeed no friend to look to but yourself—no chance of extricating myself without your assistance.

Finally moved by Poe's misery and self-abasement as well (perhaps) by charitable feelings appropriate to the Christmas season, on December 7 Allan asked a business friend in Baltimore "to procure his liberation [from debt or jail] & to give him $20 besides to keep him out of further difficulties."[6] Unfortunately, through oversight or design, Allan failed to send the money until January 12, 1832—thus prolonging Poe's agony for another five weeks.

IV ===

In May 1831, the month Poe moved to Baltimore, the Philadelphia *Saturday Courier* offered a prize of one hundred dollars for the best original story. Poe submitted several of his works, but the prize was awarded to Delia Bacon's "Love's Martyr." The judges must have been favorably impressed, however, for throughout 1832 the paper published five of his stories, beginning with "Metzengerstein" on January 14.

This story, originally subtitled "A Tale in Imitation of the German," capitalized on the current vogue, made popular by Ludwig Tieck and E. T. A. Hoffmann, of depicting pathological emotional states, subconscious criminal impulses and a poetic atmosphere that combined realistic and supernatural worlds. The hero's parents, like Poe's, left him an orphan at an early age. Baron Metzengerstein's father "died young. His mother, the Lady Mary, followed him quickly." After quarreling with his Hungarian neighbor Count Berlifitzing, the depraved baron sets fire to his enemy's stable and the count dies while trying to rescue his favorite horse. The spirit of the dead count then takes possession of the horse that had fled from his fire, and the baron, unaware of this, uses it as his own mount. During another fire that now breaks out in Metzengerstein's residence, this wild horse becomes uncontrollable. It "bounded far up the tottering staircases of the palace, and, with its rider, disappeared amid the whirlwind of chaotic fire."

In this vengeful tale about the overwhelming power of evil, which recoils back upon itself and destroys the destroyer, Poe first dramatized his own violent emotions and employed many of the Gothic properties that characterize his classic stories: an ancient, decayed, remote, secluded, vast and gloomy building, with strangely shaped rooms, armorial trophies, artificial lighting, vivid colors, underground vaults and somber tapestries—one of which portrays a gigantic steed that, after the death of the count, supernaturally alters its position in the work of art. The "dense and livid mass of ungovernable fire" that finally destroys the baron may have been based on Poe's childhood memories of the terrible fire in the Richmond Theater which, three weeks after the death of his mother in December 1811, had killed seventy-two people.

The other four stories published in 1832 included "The Duc de l'Omelette," "A Tale of Jerusalem" and "Bon-Bon." "*Intended* for half banter, half satire," they are, like most of his comic tales, tedious elaborations of witless jokes. "Loss of Breath," whose title hints at the high incidence of lung disease in Poe's immediate family, is equally absurd but more interesting. This comic story describes the sensations felt by a man who is tortured and hanged for the benefit of an enthusiastic audience—"I did my best to give the crowd the worth of their trouble. My convulsions were said to be extraordinary. My spasms it would have been difficult to beat. The populace *encored*"—and foreshadows the theme of the artist sacrificed to the public in Kafka's "A Hunger Artist."

Poe's literary career brought him into close contact with his first writer-friend, Lambert Wilmer. A Baltimore journalist, satirist and poet, and close friend of Henry Poe, Wilmer had written a verse drama on Edgar's romance with Elmira Royster. Poe told Wilmer that he had traveled to St. Petersburg, and appeared to be "delicate and effeminate, but never sickly or ghastly." (Though University classmates had described Poe as athletic, with luminous eyes, another Baltimore acquaintance, noting the effects of urban poverty, portrayed him as "a slim, feeble young man, with dark inexpressive eyes.") Wilmer also described Poe as an attentive listener and perceptive speaker: "He did not monopolize the discourse, but seemed to be quite as willing to listen as to talk. Though he seldom said anything very startling, his remarks were generally shrewd. . . . I never knew him to speak in warm terms of admiration of any poetical writer, except Alfred Tennyson. Among prose authors, Ben. D'Israeli [whose *Vivian Grey* influenced "King Pest"] was his model."[7]

In June 1833 the Baltimore *Saturday Visiter*, which had recently been edited by Wilmer, offered two prizes in order to encourage literature and procure the finest works for their readers: fifty dollars for the best tale in prose and twenty-five dollars for the best short poem. Poe submitted a poem, "The Coliseum," and six tales: "Four Beasts in One," "Lionizing," "Silence," "The Assignation," "A Descent into the Maelström" and "MS. Found in a Bottle." The last story won the prize. In announcing the winner, the judges defined the characteristic qualities of Poe's works and justly stated that "these tales are eminently distinguished by a wild, vigorous and poetical imagination, a rich style, a fertile invention, and varied and curious learning." Poe's claim that he had won *both* prizes and that the poetry award was given to the second-best poem after he had obtained the prize for the story, was later substantiated by one of the judges, John Latrobe.

Poe's aggressive behavior on the streets of Baltimore when he encountered John Hewitt, the editor of the *Saturday Visiter*, who had submitted his own poem under a pseudonym and won the prize, showed his deep resentment about this matter and provoked a physical assault. According to Hewitt, Poe approached him with an ominous scowl and sternly said:

"You have used underhanded means, sir, to obtain that prize over me."

"I deny it, sir," was my reply.

"Then why did you keep back your real name?"

"I had my reasons, and you have no right to question me."

"But you tampered with the committee, sir."

"The committee are gentlemen above being tampered with, sir." . . .

"I agree that the committee are gentlemen," replied he, his dark eyes flashing with anger, "but I cannot place *you* in that category."

My blood mounted up to fever heat in a moment, and with my usual impulsiveness, I dealt him a blow which staggered him, for I was physically his superior."

The prize-winning "MS. Found in a Bottle" is a shipwreck story—like "A Descent into the Maelström" and *The Narrative of Arthur Gordon Pym*—that was partly inspired by his childhood favorite *Robinson Crusoe* and by Coleridge's "The Rime of the Ancient Mariner." The narrator of this story also has some traits in common with Poe. He is five feet, eight inches tall and has been estranged from his family by ill usage. Having survived one terrifying shipwreck, he lands on a second ship—ten times as large—that is manned by an ancient crew who fail to notice his ghost-like appearance. This ship is sucked down by a whirlpool into a vast hole at the center of Antarctica. The narrator writes his bizarre account at the very edge of the abyss and until the very last moment of his life; the manuscript survives in the bottle and the fatal story is posthumously told. In this tale Poe gives verisimilitude to an incredible adventure in which the hero is carried by simoon, tempest, hurricane and tornado into unknown and mysterious regions. He conveys with uncanny suggestiveness the presentiment of evil in the ghastly crew, which resembles the sailors of the *Flying Dutchman*. He describes the overwhelming force and destructive power of nature. And he convincingly portrays the desire to pass, psychologically as well as physically, from known to unknown worlds.

The sailor-novelist Joseph Conrad, whose "Secret Sharer" may have been influenced by the theme of the double and the divided personality in "William Wilson," awarded high praise to both the realism and the art of Poe's story: "The indifference of [Coleridge's] animated corpses to the living people resembles the indifference of the secular ghosts in the overgrown ship in E. A. Poe's impressive version of the Flying Dutchman ('MS. Found in a Bottle'). A very fine piece of work—about as fine as anything of that kind can be—and so authentic in detail that it must have been told by a sailor of a sombre and poetical genius in the invention of the phantastic."[8]

Poe used the five stories he had published in the Philadelphia *Saturday Courier*, along with the six stories submitted for the Baltimore *Saturday Visiter* prize, to make up a volume called *Tales of the Folio Club*. According to Poe's plan, the tales were supposed to be the work of the eleven "Dunderheads" in this club, who each read a story at their monthly meetings. Waiving all remuneration, Poe tried for several years to publish this collection, but was never able to do so.

Though Poe was always quick to accuse others of plagiarism, his early stories reveal that he too cannibalized his literary ancestors. He adopted four major conventions from the influential Scottish monthly, *Blackwood's Magazine*: "the creation of a literary personality, the 'self-consciously learned pose,' the exploitation of the hoax, and the burlesque and horror tale as major fictional modes." In addition to borrowings from *Blackwood's*, Tieck, Hoffmann, Coleridge and D'Israeli, Poe—early and late in his career—also appropriated material from Milton, Thomas Moore, Byron, Shelley, Keats, Thomas Hood, Elizabeth Barrett and Alfred Tennyson. As he told his fellow poet James Russell Lowell: "I am profoundly excited by music, and by some poems—those by Tennyson especially—whom, with Keats, Shelley, Coleridge (occasionally) and a few others of like thought and expression, I regard as the *sole* poets."[9] Yet Poe, at once derivative and original, both absorbed and transformed the work of his predecessors. He recognized sympathetic temperaments in past writers and discovered in them forms of expression that could be reaffirmed and recreated.

V ═══

One of the judges who awarded the story prize to Poe was the handsome John Pendleton Kennedy, a successful lawyer and prominent citizen of Baltimore. He had published his first novel, *Swallow Barn*, in 1832, and became Poe's first literary patron. He found Poe (who had not exaggerated his misery in the letters to Allan) in a state of starvation; gave him clothing, generous hospitality and a horse to ride whenever he wished; and advised him about the publication of *Tales of the Folio Club*. In fact, Kennedy "brought him up from the very

verge of despair." Kennedy, who appreciated Poe's talent and sympathized with his destitution, emphasized the almost schizoid quality of
his noble and debased personality: "I have never known, nor heard
of any one, whose life so curiously illustrated that twofold existence
of the *spiritual* and the *carnal* disputing the control of the man, which
has often been made the theme of fiction. He was debauched by the
most grovelling appetites and exalted by the richest conceptions of
genius."

Another judge of the contest, John Latrobe, a Baltimore lawyer
and inventor, recalled Poe's military bearing, his somber dress, his
neat but threadbare clothing (carefully maintained by Maria Clemm)
and his ill-concealed destitution:

> He was, if anything, below the middle size, and yet could not
> be described as a small man. His figure was remarkably good,
> and he carried himself erect and well, as one who had been
> trained to it. He was dressed in black, and his frock-coat was
> buttoned to the throat, where it met the black stock, then
> almost universally worn. Not a particle of white was visible.
> Coat, hat, boots, and gloves had very evidently seen their
> best days, but so far as mending and brushing go, everything
> had been done, apparently, to make them presentable. On
> most men his clothes would have looked shabby and seedy,
> but there was something about this man that prevented one
> from criticising his garments. . . . The impression made,
> however, was that the award in Mr. Poe's favor was not
> inopportune.[10]

Poe's pressing need for money, sense of responsibility to Maria and
Virginia Clemm, and all-too-human concern for his own uncertain
future inspired a final attempt at reconciliation with John Allan. In
April 1833, after a fifteen-month silence, the outcast wrote a last,
futile letter. He did not mention his recent literary success, but hoped
to arouse Allan's sense of pity and charity: "I am perishing—absolutely perishing for want of aid. And yet I am not idle—nor addicted
to any vice—nor have I committed any offense against society which
would render me deserving of so hard a fate. For God's sake pity me,
and save me from destruction."

When this letter failed to elicit a response from his coldhearted Pa,
Poe tried a direct confrontation. On February 14, 1834, when Allan
was seriously ill with dropsy, Poe returned to Richmond for a final

visit. According to his childhood friend Thomas Ellis, Louisa Allan opened the door herself:

> A man of remarkable appearance stood there, & without giving his name asked if he could see Mr. Allan. She replied that Mr. Allan's condition was such that his physicians had prohibited any person from seeing him except his nurses. The man was Edgar A. Poe, who was, of course, perfectly familiar with the house. Thrusting her aside & without noticing her reply, he passed rapidly upstairs to Mr. Allan's chamber, followed by Mrs. Allan. As soon as he entered the chamber, Mr. Allan raised his cane, & threatening to strike him if he came within his reach, ordered him out.[11]

Cursed instead of blessed by his father, and driven from the family home by the enraged old man, Poe passed out of Allan's life forever.

Allan once said that he rarely suffered unavailing regrets. Influenced by his kindly first wife, he had been affectionate, generous, even extravagant during Poe's childhood. But after their bitter quarrels and Allan's second marriage, he wrote Poe off, with few pangs of conscience, as a bad lot. When he died six weeks after Poe's rash visit, on March 27, 1834, Allan made good his threat to "turn him adrift" and left Poe absolutely nothing. Poe had been taught the habits and tastes of a gentleman, but denied the means to support them.

Poe portrayed the methodical materialism of men like Allan in "The Business Man," in which the satiric victim expresses intense hostility to the artist: "If there is any thing on earth I hate, it is a genius. You geniuses are all arrant asses—the greater the genius, the greater the ass. . . . Especially, you cannot make a man of business out of a genius." The bitter lines from Yeats' "September 1913" express Poe's response to the philistine business mentality that ignored or despised his genius:

> What need you, being come to sense,
> But fumble in a greasy till
> And add the halfpence to the pence
> And prayer to shivering prayer, until
> You have dried the marrow from the bone?

Unfortunately, Allan's tragic lack of forgiveness dried the marrow from Poe's bone as well as from his own.

Chapter 6

RICHMOND: THE *SOUTHERN LITERARY MESSENGER* AND MARRIAGE, 1835-1836

I

Soon after his return to Baltimore, on March 15, 1835, Poe asked John Pendleton Kennedy's help in applying for a teaching job. Kennedy invited him to Sunday dinner and Poe, replying with self-abasing pride about the disgraceful state of his wardrobe, refused for reasons that would normally be kept hidden from the host: "Your kind invitation to dinner to day has wounded me to the quick. I cannot come—and for reasons of the most humiliating nature in my personal appearance. You may conceive my deep mortification in making this disclosure to you—but it was necessary. If you will be my friend so far as to loan me $20 I will call on you to morrow—otherwise it will be impossible, and I must submit to my fate." It is not clear whether Kennedy, unexpectedly hit for a loan, thought it worth twenty dollars to have shabby Edgar as a dinner guest. But this incident led to a major turning point in Poe's literary career.

Kennedy had helped choose Poe for the story prize in 1833. Realizing his desperate need, he now recommended Poe to Thomas Willis White, the publisher of the *Southern Literary Messenger* in Richmond: "He is very clever with his pen—classical and scholar-like. He wants experience and direction, but I have no doubt he can be made very useful to you. And, poor fellow! he is *very* poor. . . . [He is] highly imaginative, and a little given to the terrific." Kennedy later recalled the erratic career of that "bright but unsteady light": "I then got him employment with Mr. White, in one department of the editorship of the *Southern Literary* newspaper at Richmond. His talents made that periodical quite brilliant while he was connected with it. But he was irregular, eccentric, and querulous, and soon gave up his place for other employments of the same character in Philadelphia and New York. His destiny in these places was as sad and fickle as in Richmond. He always remembered my kindness with gratitude, as his many letters to me testify."[1]

Thomas Willis White, twenty years older than Poe, was small, florid faced, soft featured, curly haired, pleasant and conciliatory. An uneducated and unsophisticated man, the son of a tailor, he became a printer and began to publish the *Southern Literary Messenger*, a monthly of sixty-four double-column pages, in August 1834. "Devoted to Every Department of Literature and the Fine Arts," the magazine contained tedious essays, sentimental stories and mediocre verse. It emphasized middle-class morality and was the spokesman of Southern culture. As White wrote in the first issue, the journal intended "to stimulate the pride and genius of the South, and awaken from its long slumber the literary exertion of this portion of our country."

White published Poe's first contribution in the March issue, solicited his advice during the spring and in June asked if Poe would be willing to join the magazine. He would handle the correspondence, do the proofreading and write all the critical notices—which eventually became the greatest attraction of the journal. His modest salary of about fifteen dollars a week seemed like a windfall, for the death of his seventy-nine-year-old grandmother in July 1835, and the consequent loss of her annual pension, had been a serious blow to the family.

At the height of the summer Poe returned to Richmond with mixed feelings. He had forfeited his place in that small society and was embittered by the loss of his inheritance. Brought up with the expectations of a fortune and with no profession of his own, he had few job possibilities and no resources. Now part of a different and less prestigious world, he was reluctant to approach his old friends and acquaintances. Nothing was sadder than remembering past happiness in his present misery.

Soon after arriving Poe applied for a job teaching English at the Richmond Academy. When he failed to secure this position, he began his editorial connection with the first of his five magazines. But it was inevitable that Poe's personality and values, his stories and criticism,

would clash with the controlling ethic of the *Messenger* and its proprietor. White admired Poe's intelligence, talent and editorial skill, which
would bring him considerable profits, but was shocked by his emotional instability, his savage book reviews and his alcoholic binges.

The first crisis occurred only two weeks later, at the end of August.
Separated from the Clemms and extremely lonely, Poe became terrified of losing his vital connection with his surrogate mother and the
adolescent girl he intended to marry. While in Richmond, he learned
that his cousin Neilson Poe, the owner of a Baltimore newspaper,
had invited Virginia to live with his family. Neilson, whom Poe called
his "bitterest enemy," knew of his attachment to Virginia and disliked
the prospect of their marriage. He offered to become Virginia's guardian, to educate her, to provide a comfortable life and to introduce her
to polite society. On August 29 Poe responded to this threat by sending Maria Clemm the most personal and agonizing letter he ever
wrote. He declared his passionate love for Virginia, expressed his fears
that she would leave him, admitted that the prosperous Neilson could
provide more security and material comfort, yet begged Virginia to
refuse Neilson's offer and remain loyal to him. He asked if Virginia
and Maria still loved him; and said that his whole life was at stake,
that losing them would kill him, that he would have nothing to live
for. Wounded to the soul by their cruelty, he dreamed of their cosy
life together in Richmond and begged Virginia not to break his heart.

> I am blinded with tears while writing this letter.—I have no
> wish to live another hour. Amid sorrow, and the deepest
> anxiety your letter reached [me]—and you know how little I
> am able to bear up under the pressure of grief. My bitterest
> enemy would pity me could he now read my heart. . . . I
> love, *you know* I love Virginia passionately, devotedly. I can-
> not express in words the fervent devotion I feel towards my
> dear little cousin—my own darling. . . . [I would take pride]
> in making you both comfortable & in calling her my wife.—
> But the dream is over. O God have mercy on me. What have
> I *to live for*? Among strangers with *not one soul to love me*. . . .
> The tone of your letter wounds me to the soul.—O Aunty,
> Aunty you loved me once—how can you be so cruel
> now? . . . Are you sure she would be more happy [with
> Neilson]. Do you think any one could love her more dearly
> than I? . . . Virginia, My love, my own sweetest Sissy, my
> darling little wifey, think well before you break the heart of
> your cousin. Eddy.

In mid-September, with this emotional crisis still unresolved, Poe sent Kennedy, his latest father figure, a pitiful plea for help: "I am suffering under a depression of spirits such as I have never felt before. I have struggled in vain against the influence of this melancholy. . . . I am still miserable in spite of the great improvement in my circumstances. . . . My heart is open before you. . . . I am wretched, and know not why. Console me—for you can. . . . [This] depression of spirits will ruin me should it be long continued."[2] In September, White recorded the dramatic, negative changes in Poe, to whom he had assigned the most menial tasks. White told Lucian Minor—a temperance advocate and frequent contributor to the *Messenger*—that drink and depression had driven the unstable young man to the verge of suicide: "Poe is now in my employ—not as Editor. He is unfortunately rather dissipated,—and therefore I can place very little reliance upon him. His disposition is quite amiable. He will be some assistance to me in proof-reading. . . . Poe has flew the track already. His habits were not good.—He is in addition the victim of melancholy. I should not be at all astonished to hear that he has been guilty of suicide." White's letters may have started the rumor in the literary world that Poe was not quite sane.

In late September, despite an encouraging reply from Kennedy, Poe remained tormented by the fear of losing Virginia. Under considerable emotional strain, he sought oblivion in heavy drinking and was fired by White. Then, without any employment, he went to Baltimore to convince the Clemms to remain with him. While Poe was away, White wrote a frank, fatherly letter, expressing concern for his welfare. He doubted Poe's promises to reform, warned him about the dangers of drink, offered to protect him from this vice in his own household and agreed to reinstate him if he promised to separate himself "from the bottle and bottle companions, for ever!":

> That you are sincere in all your promises, I firmly believe. But, Edgar, when you once again tread these streets, I have my fears that your resolve would fall through,—and that you would again sip the juice, even till it stole away your senses. . . .
>
> How much I regretted parting with you, is unknown to any one on this earth, except myself. I was attached to you— and am still,—and willingly would I say return, if I did not dread the hour of separation very shortly again.
>
> If you could make yourself contented to take up your quarters in my family, or in any other private family where liquor

is not used, I should think there was hope of you.—But, if
you go to a tavern, or to any other place where it is used at
table, you are not safe. . . .

Tell me if you can and will do so—and let me hear that it
is your fixed purpose never to yield to temptation.

If you should come to Richmond again, and again should
be an assistant in my office, it must be especially understood
by us that all engagements on my part would be dissolved,
the moment you get drunk.

No man is safe who drinks before breakfast! No man can
do so, and attend to business properly.

By October, the emotional crisis had passed. White had rehired
him, Poe had persuaded the Clemms to reject Neilson's offer and had
assumed financial responsibility for them. Moved by the almost insane
expression of Poe's tormented feelings, by love for and loyalty to
him, and by fears for his life, the Clemms sacrificed material prospects
and put their fate in Poe's hands. As soon as he had settled into his
new job, he brought them to Richmond, where they all lived in Mrs.
Yarrington's boarding house at Twelfth and Bank streets, on Capitol
Square. In December, White officially announced that Poe had become editor of the *Southern Literary Messenger*. In January 1836 Poe
told Kennedy that he wanted to be appointed guardian of both Virginia and her brother Henry, and wrote one of his rare positive letters:
"My health is better than for years past, my mind is fully occupied,
my pecuniary difficulties have vanished, I have a fair prospect of
future success—in a word, all is right."[3]

II ═══

The need to produce a massive amount of copy now intensified Poe's
reading and writing. His poems, stories and criticism were filled with
references to classic authors and to recondite books. But some of his
erudition was clearly bogus. He liked making up quotations and
attributing them to famous authors, and inventing the titles of obscure
volumes in order to give his work a scholarly tone. When not familiar
with the original books, he gathered numerous tags and epigraphs
from secondary sources. Poe had read widely at school, at the university and at West Point. He received a great many review copies, which
he read or skimmed through, and then sold. He borrowed books
from friends like Kennedy, who owned extensive collections. But he

must have done most of his reading, to make up for deficiencies in his formal education as well as to gather material for the magazine, in public libraries.

In Baltimore he used the library at the City Assembly Rooms, the circulating library of Joseph Robinson and the subscription library of ten thousand volumes at the Baltimore Library Company. Richmond, with a population of only 20,000, had less extensive holdings. But even there Poe had access to the circulating libraries, the Richmond Library (founded in 1806) and the State Library. During these years Poe also began to build up his own cherished collection of books, though in difficult times he would often have to sell them. His own library, he proudly said, was "no very large one, certainly, but sufficiently miscellaneous; and, I flatter myself, not a little *recherché.*" But, he maintained, true erudition, based on extensive and diversified reading, "is certainly discoverable—is positively indicated—only in its ultimate and total *results.*" He made effective use of his unusually wide knowledge of classical and English poetry, of European and English literature, of philosophy and science, in all his writing.

Lambert Wilmer thought Poe was one of the most hardworking men he had ever known. He visited Poe at all hours and—driven as Poe was by the need to earn money—always found him at work. A fluent writer, Poe usually composed in the morning and, if the occasion demanded, continued till late afternoon. He would then relax by reading and reciting poetry, taking long walks in the countryside and (when he had one) working in his flower garden. Though Poe turned out an enormous quantity of critical hack work and trashy stories during his short career, his best work—as his "Philosophy of Composition" suggests—was always analytical, elaborately forged and finely polished. One friend remarked that "the form of his manuscript was peculiar: he wrote on half sheets of note paper, which he pasted together at the ends, making one continuous piece, which he rolled up tightly. As he read he dropped it upon the floor. [His fair copy] was very neatly written, and without corrections, apparently."[4]

Emphasizing his free spirit, Poe described his tendency to put off creative (as opposed to critical) work when he did not feel inspired. But he also said that his thoughts during these apparently aimless wanderings would suddenly strike a spark and lead to a frenzy of writing: "I know too well the unconquerable procrastination which besets the poet. . . . Were I to be seized by a rambling fit—one of my customary *passions* (nothing less) for vagabondizing through the woods for a week or a month together—I would not—in fact I *could* not be put out of my mood. . . . I can feel for the 'constitutional

indolence' of which you complain—for it is one of my own besetting
sins. I am excessively slothful, and wonderfully industrious—by
fits. . . . I have thus rambled and dreamed away whole months, and
awake, at last, to a sort of mania for composition."[5]

III

In December 1835 Poe celebrated his appointment as editor by publishing in the *Southern Literary Messenger* scenes from his unfinished
closet drama *Politian*. Though it was named after an Italian poet, and
imitated the hackneyed apparatus and tedious conventions of Jacobean
tragedy, the play was actually based on the notorious incident that
had taken place in Frankfort, Kentucky, in 1825. Colonel Solomon
Sharp, a politician, had seduced Ann Cook, who bore him a child.
When the child died, he broke his promise and refused to marry her.
Jereboam Beauchamp, an attorney, though much younger than Ann,
sought her hand. She finally agreed to marry him if he promised to
kill Sharp before the wedding. Beauchamp challenged him to a duel,
but Sharp, being in the wrong, refused to fight. At 2:00 A.M. on
November 7, Beauchamp called Sharp to the door of his house and
stabbed him in the heart. After a trial, Beauchamp was condemned
to death and Ann acquitted of complicity in the crime. Both attempted
suicide. Ann died, Beauchamp survived and was hanged on July 7,
1826. This story of revenge also inspired Thomas Holley Chivers'
Conrad and Eudora (1834) and William Gilmore Simms' *Beauchampe*
(1842) as well as Robert Penn Warren's *World Enough and Time* (1950).
When reviewing Simms' novel, Poe wrote: "No more thrilling, no
more romantic tragedy did ever the brain of a poet conceive than was
the tragedy of Sharp and Beauchamp."

Unfortunately, Poe knew no more about Renaissance Italy than he
did about Central Asia at the time of Tamerlane. The wooden hero,
archaic style and melodramatic plot of *Politian* did not do justice to
this tragic story. There was a vast, fatal chasm between his theory
and practice; and this play did precisely what he would warn against
in his own dramatic criticism. "The first thing necessary," Poe later
wrote, "is to burn and bury the 'old models,' and to forget, as quickly
as possible, that ever a play had been penned. . . . A closet-drama
[not meant to be performed on stage] is an anomaly—a paradox—a
mere figure of speech. . . . The proof of the *dramatism* is the capacity
for representation."

In the play, Poe names the characters after historical figures. But

he conflates the Italian poet Angelo Poliziano with the English Earl of
Leicester (a contemporary of Shakespeare). Leicester, who is visiting
Rome, represents Beauchamp. Baldassare Castiglione (the real author
of *The Book of the Courtier*) is Sharp. Both men are rivals for the love
of Lalage. The pointless repetition of banalities in one brief excerpt
suggests the astonishing awfulness of this play:

> *Di Broglio*: I've news for you both. Politian is expected
> Hourly in Rome—Politian, Earl of Leicester!
> We'll have him at the wedding. 'Tis his first visit
> To the imperial city.
> *Alessandra*: What! Politian
> Of Britain, Earl of Leicester?
> *Di Broglio*: The same, my love.
> We'll have him at the wedding.[6]

It is not surprising that Kennedy, after reading this play, advised
Poe to abandon tragedy and write farces after the manner of French
vaudevilles.

IV

Oppressed by hack work, Poe wrote no original tales in 1836. But
during 1835 and 1836 he reprinted in the *Southern Literary Messenger*
seven *Tales of the Folio Club*, published three others (written in 1833)
from this collection and brought out three significant new stories:
"Berenice," "Morella" and "The Unparalleled Adventure of One
Hans Pfaall" (all 1835). In "Berenice"—the first story with an obsessed, monomaniacal, rivetting narrator—Poe found his authentic
voice. He made Gothic horrors more realistic and sophisticated, and
dramatized terrors in concrete images that commanded belief. In the
Greek poem by Callimachus, Berenice (whose four-syllable name
means "bringer of victory"), wife of King Ptolemy of Egypt, promised her hair to Aphrodite if her husband returned safely from the
wars. Instead of voluntarily sacrificing her hair for her husband, Poe's
Berenice loses her teeth and her life to her mad fiancé. The narrator
of Poe's story, Egaeus, is named after Aegeus, father of Theseus and
King of Athens, who killed himself when he mistakenly thought that
his son had lost his life on a mission to kill the Minotaur. But Poe's
Egaeus, after inadvertently killing Berenice, his cousin and lover,
survives to be tormented by remorse.

Egaeus lives in his gloomy, hereditary halls, surrounded by towers and filled with tapestries. There he dissipates his youth in intense, abnormal meditations about the nature of good and evil. His own mental disease, a kind of morbid irritability during which he loses all sense of motion and physical existence, is matched in the beautiful Berenice by epilepsy—a physical disease that frequently terminates in a trance that resembles death.

Though Egaeus has never loved Berenice, who is more of a dream than a reality to him, they are (like so many of Poe's characters) locked in a pathological symbiosis. As the day of their wedding approaches, she shrinks into a corpse-like emaciation. He suddenly becomes obsessed by the perfection of her dazzling white teeth and seriously believes that her teeth represent *ideas*: "*Therefore* it was that I coveted them so madly! I felt that their possession could alone ever restore me to peace, in giving me back my reason." Teeth, which (unlike bone) are visible and seem perfect, can restore Egaeus because they endure, survive and transcend death. But his monomania is temporarily interrupted when Berenice dies in an epileptic seizure and is promptly buried.

Egaeus then falls into one of his own trances. He hears the piercing shriek of a female voice and tries to remember what had caused it. A menial disturbs his reveries to announce that Berenice's grave has been violated and that she had been buried while still alive. The servant then tactlessly points out Egaeus' spade, muddy garments clotted with gore and hand "in*dent*ed" with the mark of human nails. This leads to the horrifying discovery of some instruments of dental surgery and a box that spills out Berenice's thirty-two small white teeth.

Egaeus' mad desire to preserve something permanent from Berenice, which would last beyond the grave, led him to extract her teeth when she was still alive. He murdered her during this grisly operation (for she could not possibly survive, in her debilitated state, the loss of a tremendous quantity of blood), and retained the teeth as telling evidence of his own sickness, madness and crime. Always fascinated by abnormality, Poe composed in "Berenice" the first of many stories in which the living are nearly dead and the dead still living. This irrational tale of the possessor possessed is made believable not only because of the cunning way Poe draws us into the demented mind of the narrator, but also—as he suggests in the Latin quotation from the Church Father, Tertullian—because of the element of logic in its absurdity.[7]

Though White published the ghastly story, he did not like it. In the issue in which it appeared, he commented: "Whilst we confess that we think there is too much horror in his subject, there can be but one opinion as to the force and elegance of his style." Responding to the harsh criticism that White had expressed in a letter, Poe—who had *not* described the dental extractions—conceded that he had gone too far. He had offended contemporary taste (though not the morbid taste of our own time): "Your opinion of it is very just. The subject is by far too horrible. . . . In respect to Berenice individually I allow that it approaches the very verge of bad taste—but I will not sin quite so egregiously again." He then explained that he had achieved his horrible effects by exposing the most bizarre subconscious impulses and by forcing human emotions to morbid excess and pathological extremes: "the ludicrous [is] heightened into the grotesque: the fearful coloured into the horrible: the witty exaggerated into the burlesque: the singular wrought out into the strange and mystical."

"Morella" explores the essential oneness of mother and daughter (which is suggested by the epigraph from Plato's *Symposium*: "*one,* everlastingly, and single") and portrays the theme of malign reincarnation. The narrator cannot love his erudite, mystical wife, Morella, whose name in Italian means "blackish" and suggests the dark mystery of her identity. The essential question in the story, derived from her philosophical reading, is whether or not personal identity is lost at death. The narrator, whose dislike of his wife intensifies, wishes for her death as she pines away. But she seems to have discovered the secret of survival and predicts: "I am dying, yet shall I live." Though she dies in childbirth, her daughter (also called Morella) survives and grows up to resemble her dead mother. The narrator suggests the satanic evil of the serpent and the torments of those who have transgressed against the Lord by alluding to Isaiah 66:24 and comparing the young Morella to "a worm that *would* not die." When she also dies, he bears her to the tomb "and laughed with a long and bitter laugh as I found no traces of the first, in the charnal where I laid the second, Morella." The philosophical mother has fulfilled her prophecy by preserving her identity and prolonging her own life through the life of her daughter.

"Hans Pfaall," a very different kind of story, shows Poe's inexhaustible invention and tendency to experiment. His first science fiction tale and the first of his imaginary voyages capitalizes on contemporary interest in the development of the hot-air balloon, which was invented by the Montgolfiers in 1783. The first balloon ascent by man took place that year and the first balloon voyage across the English Channel occurred in 1785. John Latrobe, a judge in the

Baltimore story contest, left a vivid account of Poe's animated description of this long tale, which took two weeks of hard work to complete:

> I asked him whether he was then occupied with any literary labor. He replied that he was engaged on a voyage to the moon, and at once went into a somewhat learned disquisition upon the laws of gravity, the height of the earth's atmosphere and the capacities of balloons, warming in his speech as he proceeded. Presently, speaking in the first person, he began the voyage, after describing the preliminary arrangements . . . and leaving the earth, and becoming more and more animated, he described his sensation, as he ascended higher and higher, until, at last, he reached the point in space where the moon's attraction overcame that of the earth, when there was a sudden *bouleversement* of the car and a great confusion among its tenants. By this time the speaker [Poe] had become so excited, spoke so rapidly, gesticulating much, that when the turn-up-side-down [of the balloon] took place, and he clapped his hands and stamped with his foot by way of emphasis, I was carried along with him, and . . . may have fancied myself the companion of his aerial journey.

"Hans Pfaall" describes a voyage to the moon by a bankrupt Dutch bellows-mender who is fleeing from his creditors. It combines the factual reality of Defoe with the weird fantasies of Hoffmann, and introduces a knowledge of scientific methods into the sphere of art. The tale opens like a news report—"By late accounts from Rotterdam, that city seems to be in a high state of philosophical excitement"—and then descends into several pages of burlesque and buffoonery. The pseudo-scientific tone begins after Hans examines his equipment, like a child with a new chemistry set, and, on April Fool's Day, finally leaves the earth. The best parts of the story are the descriptions of his difficulty in breathing amidst the intense atmospheric pressure, and the striking accounts of the aerial views that seem to diminish the works of man and increase the power of nature:

> At a vast distance to the eastward, although perfectly discernible, extended the islands of Great Britain, the entire Atlantic coasts of France and Spain, with a small portion of the northern part of the continent of Africa. Of individual edifices, not a trace could be discovered, and the proudest cities of mankind

had utterly faded away from the face of the earth. . . . The
convexity of the ocean had become so evident, that the entire
mass of the distant water seemed to be tumbling headlong
over the abyss of the horizon.

After Hans' cursory description of the lunar scenery and weird
inhabitants, he promptly returns to earth. Poe then reverts to the
comic mode, undermines the reality of the story and suggests that the
whole business has been nothing but a hoax. He later admitted that
the tale was faulty and wanted to revise it. Though he "saw at once
that the chief interest of such a narrative must depend upon the
reader's yielding his credence in some measure as to details of actual
fact . . . [he mistakenly] fell back upon a style half plausible, half
bantering."[8]

The successful publication in the *Southern Literary Messenger* of his
latest stories, which had surpassed his earlier ones in both seriousness
and sophistication, encouraged him to try once again to publish the
Tales of the Folio Club. But in June 1836 Harper's rejected the book
for the same reasons that inhibit today's publishers from bringing out
collections of short stories: most of them had already been printed,
they were separate tales rather than a continuous narrative, and they
were too learned and mystical to appeal to the average reader.

V ═══

After joining the *Messenger* Poe continued to write stories in his spare
time but devoted most of his energy to earning his meager salary as
editor and critic. Poe had the journalist's interest in whatever was
current and fashionable. He wrote about balloon flights, daguerreotypes, phrenology, mesmerism, galvanism, exploration, shipwrecks,
hidden treasure, epidemics, detection, murder, premature burial and
apocalyptic prophecies. He even introduced a series of articles on
"Autography," which discussed how handwriting revealed character,
included physical descriptions of the authors who sent in their signatures and indulged in a bit of literary gossip.

W. H. Auden expressed a commonly held view of Poe's literary
journalism by stating that "much of his best criticism will never be
read widely because it lies buried in reviews of totally uninteresting
authors." Yet the ninety-four pieces he wrote from December 1835
to August 1836 on philosophy, science, romance, poetry, travel, navi-
gation, physiology and law include many works by the leading au-

thors of his time: Irving, Cooper and Bryant among the older
generation of American writers; Godwin, Coleridge, Southey, Hazlitt, Frances Trollope and Bulwer-Lytton among his English contemporaries.

It was not primarily the subject matter that made many of Poe's
reviews "repetitious, prejudiced, sentimental, or simply dull." They
were also limited by the overwhelming number of books that had to
be noticed; by lack of time, shortage of money, poor working conditions and ill health. As George Orwell, who also served time as a
Grub Street hack, remarked in "Confessions of a Book Reviewer":
"the prolonged, indiscriminate reviewing of books is a quite exceptionally thankless, irritating and exhausting job. . . . In much more
than nine cases out of ten the only objectively truthful criticism would
be 'This book is worthless.' "[9]

Though Poe eagerly sought out the smallest newspaper notice
about himself and his work, and was extremely sensitive to criticism,
his unusually cutting attacks on his fellow authors created many enemies and provoked severe retaliation. His models of harshness were
the savage critics of the great British quarterly reviews: John Wilson
in *Blackwood's*, William Gifford in the *London Quarterly*, Francis Jeffrey
in the *Edinburgh* (whose attack on Byron's "Hours of Idleness" Byron
had answered in his "English Bards and Scotch Reviewers") and John
Croker in the *Quarterly*, whose attack on "Endymion" had supposedly
killed Keats, as Byron remarked in Canto XI of *Don Juan*: "'Tis
strange the mind, that very fiery particle, / Should let itself be snuff'd
out by an article."

Poe adopted this harsh critical approach because he had few literary
friends and was free to speak frankly. He was envious about the
undeserved success of mediocre writers and embittered about his own
poverty and lack of recognition. He also wanted to establish his critical
reputation and, through notoriety, to increase the circulation of his
journal. Most importantly, he wished to banish parochialism, curb
the literary monopoly of New England writers and create serious
standards in contemporary letters. As he insisted in *Marginalia*: "As
for American Letters, plain-speaking about *them* is, simply, the one
thing needed. They are in a condition of absolute quagmire."

Though most of Poe's reviews were actually favorable, the negative
ones were the most witty and memorable:

> *The Swiss Heiress* should be read by all who have nothing
> better to do. . . .

[*Ups and Downs*] is a public imposition. . . . [It] should have
been printed among the quack advertisements. . . .

[*Paul Ulric*] is too purely imbecile to merit an extended critique. . . . As one of the class of absurdities with an inunda-
tion of which our country is grievously threatened—we shall
have no hesitation, and shall spare no pains, in exposing fully
before the public eye its four hundred and forty-three pages
of utter folly, bombast, and inanity. . . . Such are the works
which bring daily discredit upon our national literature.[10]

Though readers must have enjoyed the critical fireworks, the press
disapproved. The *Richmond Courier* sententiously remarked: "The
criticisms are pithy and often highly judicious, but the editors must
remember that it is almost as injurious to obtain a character for regular
cutting and slashing as for indiscriminate laudation." The New York
Knickerbocker, accusing him of both prejudice and favoritism, frankly
maintained: "His criticisms, so called, are generally a tissue of coarse
personal abuse or personal adulation." Even the mild-mannered
White, who had profited from Poe's criticism but did not pay him
enough to do a thorough job, later conceded that Poe "read through
few [books]—unless it were some trashy novels,—and his only object
in reading even these, was to ridicule their authors."

More reckless, honest and outspoken than any other critic dared to
be, Poe made many bitter and dangerous enemies. Theodore Fay, the
editor of the *New York Mirror*, published a two-volume novel, *Norman
Leslie*, which his newspaper repeatedly puffed. By attacking its plot
as "a monstrous piece of absurdity" and calling it "the most inestima-
ble piece of balderdash with which the common sense of the good
people of America was ever so openly or so villainously insulted,"[11]
Poe created a sensation, antagonized many of Fay's influential friends
and provoked a powerful group of writers. They would soon fight
back and try to destroy his growing reputation.

The great exception to Poe's severe strictures was Alfred Tennyson,
whom, like Coleridge, he consistently praised. Poe admired his
mournful lyricism, his "poetical excitement," his pure idealism and
his ethereal beauty. He later read from "The Princess" during his
public lectures, and was pleased when his own work was compared
to Tennyson's. Poe spoke of his "magnificent genius," said "for
Tennyson, as for a man imbued with the richest and rarest poetic
impulses, we have an admiration—a reverence unbounded," and ec-

statically concluded, "I consider Tennyson not only the greatest Poet in England, at present, but the greatest one, in many senses, that England, or any other Country, ever produced." Tennyson reciprocated Poe's feelings. After Poe's death, Tennyson said he had long admired his works, spoke of him as "so strange & fine a genius [with] so sad a life," and generously called Poe "the most original genius that America has produced," one "not unworthy to stand beside Catullus, the most melodious of the Latins, and Heine, the most tuneful of the Germans."[12]

VI ═══

In Richmond Poe's small but steady salary allowed him to provide the Clemms with minimal comforts; and the stability of their reassembled family enabled him to write his stories and churn out his criticism. Though they had all once been used to a more luxurious existence, before Poe left home and Maria became widowed, life in Richmond was much better than the extreme poverty they had experienced in Baltimore and would suffer again later on.

During their four years together Poe had exerted a considerable influence on Virginia's character, molding her into the kind of woman he wanted to marry. Though she clearly lacked the intellectual ability and spiritual understanding of a mature woman (later, as a widower, he would seek these qualities in a series of bluestocking poets), she was an attractive girl with a sweet and gentle disposition. Lambert Wilmer noted Poe's serious efforts to develop the mind and talents of his future wife: "While he was editor of the *Southern Literary Messenger* he devoted a large part of his salary to Virginia's education, and she was instructed in every elegant accomplishment at his expense. He himself became her tutor at another time, when his income was not sufficient to provide for a more regular course of instruction. I remember once finding him engaged, on a certain Sunday, in giving Virginia lessons in Algebra."

Virginia became an accomplished singer and musician. As an adult, she was a good enough poet to write an idyllic Valentine poem, which alluded to their secluded life and to her menacing illness, and whose initial letters spelled his name:

> Ever with thee I wish to roam—
> Dearest my life is thine.
> Give me a cottage for my home

> And a rich old cypress vine,
> Removed from the world with its sin and care
> And the tattling of many tongues.
> Love alone shall guide when we are there—
> Love shall heal my weakened lungs;
> And Oh, the tranquil hours we'll spend,
> Never wishing that others may see!
> Perfect ease we'll enjoy, without thinking to lend
> Ourselves to the world and its glee—
> Ever peaceful and blissful we'll be.

The plump little Virginia retained her girlish looks throughout her life. She had a round face, dark brown hair, violet eyes, pale complexion and a slight lisp. Modest and shy, easily amused and utterly devoted to Poe, she remained a silent and admiring listener when visitors came to their house. Two lady friends later commented on her charming good nature, Poe's tender consideration and the domestic tranquility that seemed to shut out the cares of the world. Even as an adult, she was

> fair, soft, and graceful and girlish. Every one who saw her was won by her. Poe was very proud and very fond of her, and used to delight in the round, child-like face and plump little figure, which he contrasted with himself, so thin and half-melancholy looking, and she in turn idolized him. She had a voice of wonderful sweetness, and was an exquisite singer, and in some of their more prosperous days, when they were living in a pretty little rose-covered cottage . . . she had her harp and piano. . . .
>
> [At home] the character of Edgar Poe appeared in its most beautiful light. Playful, affectionate, witty, alternately docile and wayward as a petted child—for his young, gentle and idolized wife, and for all who came, he had even in the midst of his most harassing literary duties, a kind word, a pleasant smile, a graceful and courteous attention.[13]

On May 16, 1836, after they had been living together in Richmond for seven months, the twenty-seven-year-old Poe married the nearly fourteen-year-old Virginia. A witness swore that she was twenty-one and the Reverend Amasa Converse, the Presbyterian minister who performed the modest ceremony in their boarding house, raised no objections. Despite her childlike qualities, Virginia must have had a well-developed figure and behaved in a mature manner in order to appear more than seven years older than she actually was. The couple spent their honeymoon in Petersburg, Virginia, about twenty miles south of Richmond.

Though Virginia began by seeing Edgar as a cousin and friend, she ended by accepting him as a husband and lover. One reliable witness testified that "although he loved her with an undivided heart he could not think of her [at first] as his wife, as any other than his sister, and indeed he did not for two years assume the position of husband, still occupying his own chamber by himself." Several biographers, most notably Joseph Wood Krutch, have insisted (without convincing evidence) that Poe and Virginia did not have a normal married life and that "prolonged illness made sexual relations with her impossible after she reached maturity."[14] Krutch and his followers assume that her illness would have prevented sexual relations, but ignore the four healthy years (1838–42) between the time she reached sixteen and the onset of her first tubercular hemorrhage.

Autobiographical elements in Poe's works suggest that their sexual life was *normal*. Annabel Lee ("my life and my bride"), who is partially based on Virginia, "lived with no other thought / Than to love and be loved by me." The hero of "Three Sundays in a Week" overcomes serious obstacles to marry his adored fifteen-year-old cousin. And in a crucial passage in "Eleonora," the narrator, his cousin and her mother lived innocently for fifteen years "before Love entered within our hearts" and became physical passion: "It was one evening at the close of the third lustrum [five-year period] of her life, and of the fourth of my own, that we sat, locked in each other's embrace. . . . We had drawn the god Eros from that wave, and now we felt that he had enkindled within us the fiery souls of our forefathers. The passions which had for centuries distinguished our race, came thronging with the fancies for which they had been equally noted, and together breathed a delicious bliss over the Valley."

VII

Despite his domestic happiness, Poe was still under considerable strain, heightened perhaps by his sexual frustration during the first years of marriage. His menial work, his heavy financial responsibilities and his intellectual incompatibility with White weighed heavily upon him. Ignoring White's well-intentioned warnings, he began to drink again, put his job at risk and threatened the welfare of his family.

When asked what actual, concrete things harm a writer, Hemingway fatalistically replied: "Politics, women, drink, money, ambition. And the lack of politics, women, drink, money and ambition." Except for politics, Poe was deeply troubled by all these things—and especially by drink. The vicious "bottle companions" who led Poe into temptation were never named by White or by anyone else, probably because Poe did not need much encouragement. Temperance was for him more difficult than abstinence; drunkenness followed sobriety as the night the day. Once he started to drink, he was unable to stop until he ran out of money or fell into a stupor. Poe was the kind of alcoholic who could abstain for months at a time and then suddenly lose control, start to drink excessively and continue to do so for days at a time. As he tried to explain to a potential patron, with more optimism than truth: "Intemperance with me, has never amounted to a habit; and had it been ten times a habit it would have required scarcely an effort on my part to shake it from me at once and forever. I have been fully awakened to the impolicy and degradation of the course hitherto pursued, and have abandoned the vice altogether, and without a struggle."

Alcoholism in Poe's time—when churches and temperance unions exerted a powerful influence on society—was considered as morally reprehensible as drug addiction is today. It was thought of as a moral defect rather than a psychological affliction; and few people were as sympathetic and tolerant as White. Drink brought out the split in Poe's personality. It reversed his normal nature and transformed the courtly gentleman into a frenzied beast. All his friends agreed that a *single* glass of wine, to most men a moderate stimulus, turned him into a madman. He drank to excess, became coarse and vulgar, fell into fits of the deepest gloom and finally became so sick that he could not drink any more. These drinking bouts were always followed by several days of sickness. John Daniel, a Richmond editor, described Poe's drinking as a joyless and compulsive self-destruction: "His taste for drink was a simple disease—no source of pleasure or excitement. When the poison had passed his lips, he would go at once to a bar and drink off glass after glass as fast as its tutelar genius could mix them, until his faculties were utterly swallowed up."[15]

There is a considerable amount of drinking in Poe's stories. He usually describes its negative effects, with a moral disapproval that suggests he shared contemporary attitudes and was passing judgment on his own disreputable behavior. In one story a victim is lured by the offer of fine Sherry and then permanently sealed up in a catacomb filled with Amontillado. In "The Angel of the Odd" he describes the

physical symptoms, "a rumbling in my ears—such as a man sometimes experiences when getting very drunk." In "The Man of the
Crowd" he autobiographically reveals the telltale signs of alcoholism
in those degenerates with a shabby-genteel appearance and a mad
glint in their eyes: "Others [were] clothed in materials which had
once been good, and which even now were scrupulously well-
brushed—men who walked with a more than naturally firm and
springy step, but whose countenances were fearfully pale, whose eyes
were hideously wild and red." In the opening chapter of *The Narrative
of Arthur Gordon Pym*, the hero's friend Augustus Bernard is degraded
to the level of an animal: "He was drunk—beastly drunk—he could
no longer either stand, speak, or see. His eyes were perfectly glazed;
and as I let him go in the extremity of my despair, he rolled like a
mere log into the bilge-water." Most significantly, in "Hop-Frog"
the dwarf jester cannot tolerate alcohol: "it excited the poor cripple
almost to madness. . . . His eyes *gleamed*, rather than shone; for the
effect of wine on his excitable brain was not more powerful than
instantaneous." After he is forced to drink, the dwarf takes a fiery
and fatal revenge on the sadistic king and his ministers.

The origins of Poe's alcoholism go back to his infancy, when his
nurse tranquilized him with bread soaked in gin, and to his childhood,
when he toasted the dinner guests with glasses of sweetened wine.
At the university he compulsively gulped down alcohol during his
drinking bouts and at West Point frequently drank at Benny Havens'
tavern. Though Poe needed no excuse to start drinking, he sought
relief in alcoholic binges during times of emotional stress. He drank
when he was in danger of losing Virginia, after her first hemorrhage
and after her death. He drank when overwhelmed by work and by
poverty at the *Southern Literary Messenger* and at all the other magazines he edited. He drank to calm his nerves (though drinking actually
excited them) before crucial meetings with President Tyler and with
the poet James Russell Lowell. He drank before and after his public
lectures in New York and Boston, incapacitating himself for the
former and disgracing himself after the latter. And he drank heavily
during the frenetic courtships of women at the end of his life.

Poe's alcoholism was partly hereditary. We now know that "alcoholism runs in families. Children of alcoholics become alcoholics
about four times more often than children of nonalcoholics," and
that most alcoholics have suffered childhood trauma and emotional
deprivation. Poe's father and brother were both alcoholics, and drinking certainly contributed to their early deaths. Poe frequently stressed
that he was an orphan and lamented the loss of parental love and

support. His susceptibility to drink was also physiological. The chemical composition of his body gave Poe a low tolerance for alcohol. He got drunk after only one glass, but continued to drink, rapidly passing from intoxication to stupor. Drinking in Poe's time was a common and potentially dangerous form of social activity for men (as the temperance movement attested), both at home, where the host dispensed lavish liquors, or in the many taverns where men gathered to exchange gossip and do business. But what for others was a harmless pastime, for Poe was a dangerous and potentially fatal addiction.

The long series, beginning with Poe, of alcoholic American writers suggests a strong connection between that intense, lonely profession and the compulsive need to drink.[16] Like De Quincey, Coleridge and Novalis with opium, Baudelaire with hashish, Verlaine and Rimbaud with absinthe, Poe found in liquor an instant relief from the oppressive strain of writing as well as an anodyne for the even greater torments of creative sterility. It was always easier to drink than to work. As Hemingway wrote toward the end of his life, when his alcoholism became dangerous and he was forced to revert to ancestral teetotalism: "Trouble was all my life when things were really bad I could always take a drink and right away they were much better. When you can't take a drink is different. Wine I never thought anybody could take away from you. But they can." Poe explained that his desperate need for stimulants was a compensatory attempt to recover essential things that had been lost—love, wealth, social status and literary reputation: "The earnest longing for artificial excitement, which, unhappily, has characterized too many eminent men, may thus be regarded as a psychal want, or necessity,—an effort to regain the lost,—a struggle of the soul to assume the position which, under other circumstances, would have been its due." It is significant, and ironic, that Poe's worldly prospects were ruined in part by his false accusation that John Allan was "not very often sober."

Poe drank to escape the misery of poverty and his wife's serious illness, to blunt his hypersensitivity to criticism and to find social approbation in the tavern. As he grew older he became increasingly bitter and began to lose faith in mankind. He had considerable insight about this disease—though not the ability to use this insight to cure himself—and came close to the heart of the matter when he observed: "I have absolutely *no* pleasure in the stimulants in which I sometimes so madly indulge. It has not been in the pursuit of pleasure that I have perilled life and reputation and reason. It has been the desperate attempt to escape from torturing memories, from a sense of insupportable loneliness, and a dread of some strange impending doom."[17]

The torturing memories concerned his dead mother and later his dead wife, his unbearable loneliness without them and his fear that a similar fate would destroy every woman that he loved. Poe's drinking—which Baudelaire compared to killing something inside himself—was a form of suicide that expressed his wish to escape from "The sickness—the nausea— / The pitiless pain—/ . . . the fever called 'Living' / That burned in my brain."[18]

VIII ===

Drinking, especially before breakfast, was the principal cause of all Poe's difficulties with his employers. It not only made him incapable of doing his editorial work, but also brought out the negative side of his personality, decreased his inhibitions and prompted him to express contempt for the less talented men who paid his wages. As White's messenger boy observed: "Mr. Poe was a fine gentleman when he was sober. He was ever kind and courtly, and at such times every one liked him. But when he was drinking he was about one of the most disagreeable men I have ever met."

Though Poe was one of the best editors of his time, he was never given complete editorial control, and never received sufficient compensation. While he struggled to maintain a bare existence, he saw the huge profits—earned by his ideas and his labor—go entirely to the owner. Poe gave a partial, though not entirely truthful account of why he left the *Messenger* in an elegantly phrased letter to his great-uncle William Poe: "The situation was disagreeable to me in every respect. The drudgery was excessive; the salary was contemptible. . . . I stood no chance of bettering my pecuniary condition, while my best energies were wasted in the service of an illiterate and vulgar, although well-meaning man, who had neither the capacity to appreciate my labors, nor the will to reward them."

Poe remained hard-pressed for money during 1836, and continued to write begging letters to relatives and friends. Like Samuel Johnson's touchy companion Richard Savage, Poe had experienced trauma in childhood, lived as a writer in wretched poverty, quarreled with most of his friends and died in his forties in degrading circumstances. Like Savage, Poe was "without any other support than accidental favours and uncertain patronage afforded him; sources by which he was sometimes very liberally supplied, and which at other times were suddenly stopped."[19]

Despite the impressive fact that Poe had made the *Southern Literary*

Messenger nationally known, had increased the circulation from 500 to 3,500 and had earned a handsome annual profit of ten thousand dollars, White complained that Poe was "continually after me for money. I am as sick of his writings as I am of him." White's wife was dying of cancer and he was extremely depressed. Their disputes inevitably flared into a crisis in late December 1836. White—who had condemned Poe's drinking, questioned his sanity and feared for his life—told Beverley Tucker, a professor of law and frequent contributor to the *Messenger*, that he had dismissed Poe for drinking in September. Though he had reinstated him, after Poe had begged for one more chance, he was about to relieve him of his duties for the third and final time:

> Highly as I really think of Mr. Poe's talents, I shall be forced to give him notice, in a week or so at farthest, that I can no longer recognize him as editor of my *Messenger*. Three months ago I felt it my duty to give him a similar notice,—and was afterwards overpersuaded to restore him to his situation on certain conditions—which conditions he has again forfeited. Added to all this, I am cramped by him in the exercise of my own judgment, as to what articles I shall or shall not admit into my work. . . . I mean to dispense with Mr. Poe as my editor. . . . If he chooses to write as a contributor, I will pay him well.

In January 1837 the *Messenger* published Poe's valediction—"With the best wishes to the Magazine, and to its few foes as well as to its many friends, he is now desirous of bidding all parties a peaceable farewell"[20]—and relapsed into its former role as an innocuous family magazine. Poe's experiences at the *Southern Literary Messenger* established a recurrent pattern in his life. He would strive intensely for a desperately desired goal and, when it was nearly in reach, destroy his own chance of achieving it. Poe's self-destructive drinking seemed to be a way of punishing himself for some deep-rooted guilt, which may have been related to his irrational but powerful feeling of responsibility for the premature deaths of his beloved women.

Chapter 7

PHILADELPHIA: *BURTON'S MAGAZINE,* 1837-1840

I ===

Following his custom, Poe moved to a new city to begin again after his disastrous experiences in the previous one. In February 1837 he took his family to New York, where they lived first on Sixth Avenue and Waverley Place, then at 113½ Carmine Street, near Washington Square. But in May the New York City banks suspended specie payments, starting the great Panic of 1837 that led to one of the worst depressions in American history. Poe thus found it difficult to obtain work; and the family survived somehow on his occasional publications and on the meager profits from the boardinghouse run by the ever-resourceful Maria Clemm. In New York, as in Philadelphia the following year, the family was often quite destitute. They suffered from lack of food and were forced to live solely on bread and molasses for weeks at a time. Yet William Gowans, a Scotsman who was their lodger and later became a well-known bookseller, recorded that Poe (on his best behavior after his dismissal in Richmond) was strictly sober, that his young wife mothered him and that the family—as long as they were together—seemed remarkably happy:

> For eight months, or more, "one house contained us, us one table fed." During that time I saw much of him, and had an

opportunity of conversing with him often, and I must say I never saw him the least affected with liquor, nor even descend to any known vice, while he was one of the most courteous, gentlemanly, and intelligent companions. . . . He had a wife of matchless beauty and loveliness, her eye could match that of any houri, and her face defy the genius of a Canova to imitate; a temper and disposition of surpassing sweetness; besides, she seemed as much devoted to him and his every interest as a young mother is to her first born. . . . Poe had a remarkably pleasing and prepossessing countenance, what the ladies would call decidedly handsome.

When conditions became impossible in New York, the transients moved south to Philadelphia in the summer of 1838, living first at 127 Arch Street, near the Delaware River, and then in the western part of the city, in a small house on Sixteenth Street near Locust. In that city Poe met the engraver John Sartain and the young doctor Thomas Dunn English, who was struck by his "undoubted genius." Scrutinizing Poe with an artist's eye, Sartain confirmed Gowans' opinion that Poe was handsome and (like many others) emphasized his dramatic forehead: "Although his forehead when seen in profile showed a receding line from the brow up, viewed from the front it presented a broad and noble expanse, very large at and above the temples. His lips were very thin and very delicately modelled." English, who frequently visited Poe's family, remembered (as John Latrobe did) his shabby-genteel appearance, his charming demeanor and his domestic tranquility: "I was impressed favorably with the appearance and manner of the author. He was clad in a plain and rather worn suit of black which was carefully brushed, and his linen was especially notable for its cleanliness. His eyes at that time were large, bright and piercing, his manner easy and refined, and his tone and conversation winning. . . . Mrs. [Virginia] Poe was a delicate gentlewoman, with an air of refinement and good breeding, and Mrs. Clemm had more of the mother than the mother-in-law about her."[1]

The most vivid and incisive descriptions of Poe's physical appearance in his late twenties were the idealized self-portraits in his fiction. Making the most of his capacious frontal bone, he equated this feature, in a review of a book on phrenology, with superior intellect: "a skull which is large, which is elevated or high above the ears, and in which the head is well developed and thrown forward . . . may be presumed to lodge a brain of greater power." His autobiographical description of the reluctant duelist John Hermann, deleted from later printings of

"Mystification" (1837), depicts the attractive, intellectual Romantic hero in suggestive phrenological terms:

> His head was of colossal dimensions, and overshadowed by a dense mass of straight raven hair, two huge locks of which, stiffly plastered with pomatum, extended with a lachrymose air down the temples, and partially over the cheek bones. . . . The forehead was massive and broad, the organs of ideality over the temples, as well as those of causality, comparison, and eventuality, which betray themselves above the *os frontis*, being so astonishingly developed as to attract the instant notice of every person who saw him. The eyes were full, brilliant, beaming with what might be mistaken for intelligence, and well relieved by the short, straight, picturesque-looking eyebrow. . . . The aquiline nose, too, was superb; certainly nothing more magnificent was ever beheld, nothing more delicate nor more exquisitely modelled.

Poe's delineation of Roderick Usher's brilliant eyes, sensual lips, aquiline nose, lustrous black hair and forehead of unusual breadth complements the earlier self-portrait and suggests the sickly, dissipated, decadent side of his own character:

> A cadaverousness of complexion; an eye large, liquid, and luminous beyond comparison; lips somewhat thin and very pallid but of a surpassingly beautiful curve; a nose of a delicate Hebrew model, but with a breadth of nostril unusual in similar formations; a finely molded chin, speaking, in its want of prominence, of a want of moral energy; hair of a more than web-like softness and tenuity;—these features, with an inordinate expansion above the regions of the temple, made up altogether a countenance not easily to be forgotten.

While living in Philadelphia Poe had a large enough garden to be offered, by a friend in Richmond, a pet fawn to amuse the young Virginia. Though he could not find a way to transport the animal, he was pleased to imagine the little fellow already nibbling the grass before his window. During these years, however, he did acquire a remarkably agile and intelligent cat called Catterina, who had learned how to unlock a latched door with her cunning springs: "The writer of this article is the owner of one of the most remarkable black cats in the world—and this is saying much; for it will be remembered that black cats are all of them witches. The one in question has not a white hair about her, and is of a demure and sanctified demeanor. That portion of the kitchen which she most frequents is accessible only by a door, which closes with what is termed a thumb-latch; these latches are rude in construction, and some force and dexterity are always requisite to force them down. But puss is in the daily habit of opening the door." The portrayal of the clever cat in this unusually lighthearted essay reveals the gentle and witty side of Poe. It may have influenced his description of the ourang-outang who opens the spring-fastened windows in "The Murders in the Rue Morgue" and the favorite pet in "The Black Cat."

In mid-1838, desperate as always for money, Poe tried for a short time to learn the art of lithography. And in July he asked James Kirke Paulding—a New York author who thought Poe was the best American writer, had taken a friendly interest in his literary career and had just been appointed secretary of the navy—if Paulding could rescue him from the endless tedium of Grub Street, even if it meant separation from his family: "Could I obtain the most unimportant Clerkship in your gift—*any thing, by sea or land*—to relieve me from the miserable life of literary drudgery to which I, now, with a breaking heart, submit, and for which neither my temper nor my abilities have fitted me."[2] But this attempt, like all other efforts to secure a non-literary position, failed. Poe was permanently condemned to live by his pen.

II ═══

When rejecting the *Tales of the Folio Club* in June 1836, Harper's had told Poe that American readers have a strong preference for works of fiction in which a single and connected story occupies the whole book. They also informed him, through James Kirke Paulding—who had approached the publishers on his behalf—that if he would cut out the arcane references and eliminate the mystification, if he would "lower himself a little to the ordinary comprehension of the generality of readers, and prepare . . . a single work, and send [it] to the Publishers, previous to [its] appearance in the *Messenger,* they will make such arrangements with him as will be liberal and satisfactory."

Poe's only novel, published on satisfactory if not liberal terms in July 1838, attempted—but failed—to meet these requirements and reach a popular audience. Poe followed his publishers' injunction to write a single work. But it was scarcely more unified than a series of stories, and contained a good deal of arcane material and mystification. Its monstrous subtitle gives some idea of its contents, which include entrapment, mutiny, murder, starvation, cannibalism, landslides, exploding ships, miraculous escapes, strange landscapes and weird people: *The Narrative of Arthur Gordon Pym of Nantucket. Comprising the Details of a Mutiny and Atrocious Butchery on Board the American Brig Grampus, on Her Way to the South Seas, in the Month of June, 1827. With an Account of the Recapture of the Vessel by the Survivers; Their Shipwreck and Subsequent Horrible Sufferings from Famine; Their Deliverance by Means of the British Schooner Jane Guy; the Brief Cruise of this Latter Vessel in the Antarctic Ocean; Her Capture, and the Massacre of Her Crew Among a Group of Islands in the Eighty-Fourth Parallel of Southern Latitude; Together with the Incredible Adventures and Discoveries Still Farther South to Which That Distressing Calamity Gave Rise.*

Poe had made two transatlantic voyages as a child. But, like Melville and Conrad after him, he also made extensive use of factual sources to fill in the huge gaps in his knowledge: Benjamin Morrell's *Narrative of Four Voyages to the South Seas and Pacific, 1822–1831* (1832) and Jeremiah Reynolds' *Address on the Subject of a Surveying and Exploring Expedition to the Pacific Ocean and South Seas* (1836), which Poe had favorably reviewed in the *Messenger* in January 1837. Moreover, Poe freely adapted details of geography and natural history in chapters XIV to XVI to pad out the story when invention failed him.

Though *Pym* belongs with the imaginary journeys described in "Hans Pfaall" and *Julius Rodman*, and with the shipwrecks portrayed in "MS. Found in a Bottle" and "A Descent into the Maelström," its deceptive title suggests the story is a realistic first-person account of Pym's actual experiences at sea and the South Pole, a region about which almost nothing was known at that time. (Antarctica had not even been discovered until 1820.) Poe had published two installments, under his own name, in the *Messenger* of January and February 1837. After being fired from the magazine, he abandoned the novel. He resumed work on it while living in New York that year, but reached an imaginative dead end with his hero adrift in Antarctic waters. Unable to find a way to bring Pym back to Nantucket after his descent into the chasm, to get him out of the fantastic realm and back into the real world, Poe left the book unfinished.

The published novel appeared without Poe's name on the title page and with a Preface by "A. G. Pym," claiming that some gentlemen in Richmond had urged him to write an account of his marvelous adventures, and that Poe had merely ghostwritten the earlier sections and published them as fiction because of their strange content. We are asked to believe that the whole narrative is a true story. To substantiate this, the novel contains extracts of diaries and references to logbook entries. And chapter XXIII includes drawings of hiero-glyphic inscriptions that Pym and his half-breed Indian companion, Dirk Peters, discover on the island of Tsalal.

Pym concludes with a Note regretting that two or three chapters of Pym's manuscript have been lost "through the accident by which he perished himself." Poe, the gentleman mentioned in the Preface, declines to finish the novel because he does not believe the final chapters are truthful. And Peters, though still alive in Illinois, cannot be found to tell the rest of the story. The Note concludes with a solemn discussion of the rock inscriptions.

Even readers as sophisticated as the American publisher George Putnam were at first taken in by Poe's artful documentary effects, and believed the narrative was a genuine travel book and a serious contribution to geographical science. As Putnam told his English copublisher, alluding to the hieroglyphics that Poe had lifted from a traveler's book on Petra, in the Jordanian desert: "This man has reached a higher latitude than any European navigator. Let us reprint this for the benefit of Mr. Bull [the typical Englishman]." Putnam later realized that "the grave particularity of the title and of the narra-tive misled many of the critics as well as [himself]." He was amused to note that "whole columns of these new 'discoveries,' including the hieroglyphics (!) found on the rocks, were copied by many of the English country papers as sober historical truth."[3]

One of the greatest difficulties Poe had with the novel was deciding on a tone that would sustain the narrative. The novel begins in the realistic manner invented by Defoe and perfected by Swift in *Gulliver's Travels* to frame their imaginary voyages: "My name is Arthur Gor-don Pym. My father was a respectable trader in sea-stores at Nan-tucket, where I was born." Pym's biography and middle-class background is sketched in some detail, so we expect the narrator's world-view to play a role, as it does in Defoe and Swift, in illuminat-ing the nature of the adventures he undergoes.

The series of exciting episodes that follows Pym's first brush with death arouses and sustains the reader's interest, but departs radically from the initial mode of narration. Poe soon lapses into the conven-tions of melodrama, giving physiological descriptions of fear ("My hair stood erect on my head—I felt the blood congealing in my veins—my heart ceased utterly to beat") instead of conveying this fear to the reader. Pym's journey carries him from the respectable world of Nantucket, where his grandfather has laid by "a tolerable

sum of money" that he expects to inherit, to fantastic southern lati-
tudes where he endures extreme hardship and becomes implicated in
killing. Pym breaks out of the eighteenth-century conventions as soon
as he changes from an ironic observer to an active participant.

Poe's elaborate attempt to frame Pym's fantastic journey in a sober
scholarly format allows him to convey two contradictory messages
to his audience. The Preface suggests that the novel is a factual record
of real travels; the final Note casts doubt on its authenticity and slyly
indicates that Poe, the putative "editor," thinks the whole thing is a
lot of nonsense. The incomplete journal form also allows Poe to
disguise and excuse his own inability to control the plot and complete
the novel. He had criticized Captain Marryat's episodic novel *Joseph
Rushbrook* for its lack of artistic unity: "One incident begets another,
and so on, *ad infinitum*. . . . There is none of that *binding* power
perceptible, which often gives a species of unity (the unity of a writer's
individual thought) to the most random narrations." And, well aware
of *Pym*'s obvious defects, Poe "did not appear in his conversation to
pride himself much upon it." He realized it was carelessly composed,
could not take it seriously and called it "a very silly book."

Contemporary reviewers tended to agree with Poe's estimate of his
work and were quick to point out its radical defects. The harshest
notice came from his future employer William Burton, who, in his
own magazine, waxed indignant at what he took to be Poe's attempt
to deceive his gullible readers with a "rapid succession of improbabili-
ties": "A more impudent attempt at humbugging the public has never
been exercised. . . . Arthur Gordon Pym puts forth a series of travels
outraging possibility, and coolly requires his insulted readers to believe his [account]. . . . We regret to find Mr. Poe's name in connexion with such a mass of ignorance and effrontery."

Lewis Gaylord Clark, a New York writer who had been enraged
by Poe's attack on Theodore Fay's novel *Norman Leslie*, compared
Pym's faults to those in Defoe's famous novel, and complained about
its careless style and disgusting details: "There are a great many tough
stories in this book, told in a loose and slip-shod style, seldom cheq-
uered by any of the more common graces of composition, beyond a
Robinson Crusoe-ish sort of simplicity of narration. The work is one
of much interest, with all its defects, not the least of which is, that it
is too liberally stuffed with 'horrid circumstance of blood and battle.' " A third critic agreed about the horrors and justly complained
that the story remained unfinished: "There are too many atrocities,
too many strange horrors, and finally, there is no conclusion to it; it
breaks off suddenly in a mysterious way, which is not only destitute

of all *vraisemblance*, but is purely perplexing and vexatious. We cannot, therefore, but consider the author unfortunate in his plan."[4]

In our time, *The Narrative of Arthur Gordon Pym* and *The Journal of Julius Rodman*, a similar adventure tale that takes place on land instead of at sea, have struck Leslie Fiedler "as improbable books for Poe to have attempted, concerned as they are with the American scene and the great outdoors." Though these masculine adventures seem to contradict the hermetic, cadaverous image of Poe portrayed in the character of Roderick Usher, Pym's energy and resourcefulness actually reflect Poe's own athletic prowess, his keen interest in physical activity and his passion for wandering through the natural landscape.

Other modern critics, Patrick Quinn and Richard Wilbur, have written brilliant, if ingenious, interpretations of *Pym*. The former has noted the themes of recurrent revolt, reality and appearance, deception and the double in this "strictly organized and skillfully developed" story; while the latter has read it as an allegory of cosmic unity. Though it is difficult to see *Pym* as a masterpiece, it does have some striking passages amidst the manic succession of misadventures. In chapter X, a spectral Dutch ship with a dead crew (another example of the influence of Coleridge's "Ancient Mariner") passes by; and an ominous seagull, who has been gnawing on the corpses, drops a ghastly gobbet of human flesh at the feet of the sailor Parker. Later on, when the shipwrecked sailors are all starving, Parker suggests they resort to cannibalism; but he draws the short straw, and is appropriately killed and eaten. The seagull foreshadows Parker's fate in the same way that the *Ariel*, the name of Pym's Nantucket sailboat and of the boat in which Shelley drowned in 1822, prefigures his shipwreck.

On January 19 (Poe's birthday) Pym and Dirk Peters reach Tsalal, on the coast of Antarctica, which is inhabited by treacherous black savages with long woolly hair. As the voyagers pass from the real into the dream world, the tone of the novel—which starts like Defoe and ends like Coleridge—changes from the factual to the fantastic. While they are exploring the interior, Pym becomes trapped in a chasm and descends by rope the side of a precipitous cliff. As his imagination becomes wildly excited by the depths below him, he vainly tries to suppress his dangerous thoughts: "The more earnestly I struggled *not to think*, the more intensely vivid became my conceptions, and the more horribly distinct. At length arrived that crisis of fancy, so fearful in all similar cases, the crisis in which we begin to anticipate the feelings with which we *shall* fall—to picture to ourselves the sickness, and dizziness, and the last struggle, and the half swoon, and the final bitterness of the rushing and headlong descent. . . . My whole soul was pervaded with a *longing to fall*; a desire, a yearning, a passion utterly uncontrollable." In this psychologically perceptive passage, Poe anticipates Hemingway's insight about the *danger* of the imagination in moments of extreme crisis: "Cowardice . . . is almost always simply a lack of ability to suspend the functioning of the imagination. Learning to suspend your imagination and live completely in the very second of the present minute with no before and no after is the greatest gift a soldier [or a sailor] can acquire."[5]

The end of *Pym*, though inconclusive, is extremely effective. In 1818 Captain John Symmes had set forth the unusual theory that the earth is "hollow, habitable, and widely open about the poles"; and the idea of "holes at the poles" was taken seriously until the late nineteenth century. Like the unfortunate narrator of "MS. Found in a Bottle," Pym and Peters fall into one of those "holes"—and Pym somehow survives to tell the story. As they paddle south through the sullen darkness and through the warm, milky waters, "we rushed into the embraces of the cataract, where a chasm threw itself open to receive us. But there arose in our pathway a shrouded human figure, very far larger in its proportions than any dweller among men. And the húe of the skín of the fígure / was of the pérfect whíteness of the snów." The hypnotic cadence of the final sentence is achieved through four anapestic, prepositional phrases, divided into two ten-syllable lines, each with three strong accents. The majesty of this poetic sentence brilliantly recalls the menacing white beasts and the destructive prophecies of the end of the world in Revelation 1:14: "His head and his hairs were white like wool, as white as snow; and his eyes were as a flame of fire."

III ===

All of Poe's more ambitious long works—"Al Aaraaf," *Politian, Pym* and *The Journal of Julius Rodman*—remained unfinished. After these relative failures, he abandoned long poems, verse drama and episodic travel books, and devoted himself to lyric poetry and the short story, making "unity of effect" the keystone of his aesthetic theory. During his early years in Philadelphia Poe perfected his characteristic themes, published his first great works of short fiction—"Ligeia," "The Fall of the House of Usher" and "The Man of the Crowd"—and brought out his first book of stories. Their concentrated form helped him to focus his imagination and achieve an intense but coherent tone.

In a review of 1840, he illuminated his fictional technique and showed how he transformed reality when creating his imaginative works: "All novel conceptions are merely unusual combinations. The mind of man can *imagine* nothing which has not really existed. . . . Thus with all which seems to be *new*—which appears to be a *creation* of the intellect. It is resoluble into the old." Even Poe's most bizarre stories, as George Orwell shrewdly remarked, are governed by convincing logic: "though Poe is fantastic he is never arbitrary. Even his least naturalistic stories . . . are psychologically correct, in the sense that they deal with perfectly intelligible motives."

In contrast to the noble idealism and exalted sentiments of the poetry, Poe's early stories plunge into sadism and violence. His best works, as Daniel Hoffman has noted, derive from four traditions of popular fiction: the science fiction story, the tale of exploration, the detective story and the Gothic horror tale. These genres enabled Poe to portray unnatural and irrational states of consciousness—dreams, visions, swoons, stupors, fevers, fainting, epilepsy, melancholia, intoxication, claustrophobia and hallucination—that freed the mind from the bonds of reason and allowed it to enter the realm of the imagination. His morbid mentality externalized these inner states of consciousness and portrayed deranged heroes who were at or over the edge of madness. With astonishing intensity, the orphan and outcast described the effects of the deprivation of love, and the ambiguous conjunctions of affection and hatred. He frequently depicted an isolated individual in a horrible situation and then—while hinting at the existence of other things too awful to be described—analyzed with agonizing precision the growing terror that overwhelmed him. Joris-Karl Huysmans, the French novelist who was drawn to Poe's aestheticism and mysticism, observed that his characters, "convulsed by hereditary neuroses, maddened by moral choreas . . . lived on their nerves."[6]

The striking openings of Poe's best works suck the reader, like a vertiginous whirlpool, into the depths of the story. The antagonistic narrator of "The Tell-Tale Heart" insists on his sanity while revealing his madness: "True!—nervous—very, very dreadfully nervous I had been and am; but why *will* you say that I am mad?" The demented hero of "The Pit and the Pendulum" is nearly driven mad by physical torture: "I was sick—sick unto death with that long agony; and when they at length unbound me, and I was permitted to sit, I felt that my senses were leaving me." The hyperbolic hero of "The Cask of Amontillado" attempts to justify his exquisitely conceived retaliation: "The thousand injuries of Fortunato I had borne as best I could; but when he ventured upon insult, I vowed revenge."

Though Poe's works are unique in the literature of his time, they have striking affinities with two painters who were his contemporaries. Poe and Francisco Goya (1746–1828) both helped define the origins of the modern temper in literature and in art. Sadism, cruelty, horror, executions and tortures in underground vaults appear in *The Disasters of War* and "The Pit and the Pendulum," which takes place during the Spanish Inquisition. The grotesque dental extractions in Goya's "Out Hunting for Teeth" (*Caprichos*, no. 12) suggests "Berenice"; the decayed but deceptively dressed old crone in "Until Death" (*Caprichos*, no. 55) prefigures the decrepit great-great-grandmother whom the nearsighted hero nearly marries in "The Spectacles"; and the nightmares of flying demons in "The Sleep of Reason Produces Monsters" (*Caprichos*, no. 43) foreshadow the morbid opium dreams in "Ligeia" and the monstrous nightmares in "Dream-Land":

> By the dismal tarns and pools
>   Where dwell the Ghouls,—
> By each spot the most unholy—
> In each nook most melancholy,—
> There the traveller meets aghast
> Sheeted Memories of the Past.

Poe's connection with the English visionary painter John Martin (1789–1854) is even more remarkable. In June 1841 Poe wrote a charming fantasy, "The Island of the Fay," to accompany an engraving, by his Philadelphia friend John Sartain, after a painting by John Martin. But his closest affinities are with Martin's gigantic, apocalyptic paintings (as Poe wrote in "Dream-Land") of

> Mountains toppling evermore
> Into seas without a shore;
> Seas that restlessly aspire,
> Surging, unto skies of fire.

Like John Martin, Poe portrays—in works like "The City in the Sea" and *The Narrative of Arthur Gordon Pym*—ancient cities overwhelmed and devastated by cataclysmic floods; fantastic, menacing, fire-swept, blood-soaked landscapes; demonic figures, claustrophobic caverns, eerie turreted castles hanging on the edge of jagged mountains; and monstrous boulders thundering down to the depths of desolate valleys.[7]

Both moralistic Victorian writers and modern psychoanalytical critics have equated Poe's mad characters with their creator and, on the basis of his fiction, variously diagnosed him as epileptic, manic-depressive, necrophiliac, impotent and syphilitic. Though there are autobiographical elements in the stories, it is wrong—as a Philadelphia friend pointed out in 1852—to attribute "that perfection of horror which abounds in his writings . . . to some moral defect in the man." Though well aware of his own volatile moods and mental instability, Poe believed in the rational basis of art and rejected the Romantic equation of genius and madness: "What the world [wrongly] calls 'genius' is the state of mental disease arising from the undue predominence of some one of the faculties. The works of such genius are never sound in themselves and, in especial, always betray the general mental insanity."

Poe's belief that the dead are not entirely dead to consciousness, his hope that love could transcend death and his "prescient ecstasy of the beauty beyond the grave" were inspired by the early deaths of his mother, of Jane Stanard and of Frances Allan. These three losses—in infancy, adolescence and young manhood—were the most profound emotional experiences of Poe's youth. In "The Philosophy of Composition" he expressed a crucial aesthetic principle by categorically stating: "the death of a beautiful woman is, unquestionably, the most poetical topic in the world." (Ugly women, dead or alive, were presumably not worth a story.) But the slow, prolonged death of a beautiful woman was to Poe even more moving. His attractive heroines have an extremely high mortality rate; and stories like "Berenice," "Morella," "Ligeia" and "Eleonora" are filled with sickly women who often die, like the victims of tuberculosis, of suffocation. In a perceptive observation, Dylan Thomas noted the limitations of the egoistic, necrophiliac attachments in Poe's fiction: "the most beautiful thing in the world to Poe was a woman dead; Poe is not to be challenged on the grounds of taste but on those of accuracy, for a woman dead is not a woman at all, the spirit that made her a woman being fled and already metamorphosed. To love a dead woman does not appear to me to be unnecessarily unhealthy, but it is a love too onesided to be pure."[8]

Poe believed that "Ligeia," a tale of a powerful and beautiful woman who returns from the dead, was the best story he had ever written. It was suggested, Poe wrote, by a dream in which the eyes of the heroine produced an intense effect upon him; and the oneiric quality of Ligeia pervades the story. As Poe wrote of Tennyson, when defining the disembodied nature of the women in his poems, "he excels most in his female portraitures; but while delicate and graceful they are indefinite; while airy and spiritual, are intangible." Edward Davidson elaborated his idea of ethereal heroines by stating that "Poe's poems and tales are ritual incantations to the erotically desirable young woman who is forever white, aloof, reserved, virginal, bridal, whether she lies in the wedding bed or the funeral bier." The crucial point in Poe's stories, where the woman is *more* attractive on the funeral bier, is to preserve her *after* death.

In "Ligeia" (1838) Poe recreates, with significant variations, the themes of metempsychosis and psychic survival that he had first essayed in "Morella." The idea of the story, expressed in the epigraph attributed to (but not to be found in) the seventeenth-century English clergyman and philosopher Joseph Glanvill, is repeated no less than three times in the text. This epigraph suggests that powerful human volition can, in certain extraordinary conditions, actually circumvent death: "Man doth not yield himself to the angels, nor unto death utterly, save only through the weakness of his feeble will."

The first name of the heroine (the narrator-husband never knew her surname) means "clear-toned." She first appeared as the goddess of harmony in "Al Aaraaf" and speaks, in this story, with a musical language. Shrouded in mystery and exceptionally beautiful, she has raven hair and (like Virginia Poe) fabulous *houri* eyes. She is prey to tumultuous passion and has mastered "*all* the wide areas of moral, physical, and mathematical science." And she is, of course, stricken with a fatal illness. Before being overwhelmed by the conqueror worm of death, she reaffirms her idolatrous love for the narrator.

After Ligeia's inevitable death, the narrator moves from his decaying city on the Rhine to a gloomy abbey in a remote region of England. Suddenly, the fair-haired and blue-eyed Lady Rowena Trevanion, of Tremaine—who is given her full and quite elaborate title, name and birthplace, derived from the heroine of Scott's *Ivanhoe* and a village in north Cornwall—materializes out of nowhere and instantly marries the grieving widower. He then describes not the bride but the phantasmagoric bridal chamber. Compounded of Venetian, Gothic, Druid, Saracen, Indian, Egyptian and Norman styles, it bears a strong resemblance to a Hollywood set.

Preferring, as always, the dead to the living wife, the narrator develops a preternatural hatred for Rowena. She, in turn, falls ill, becomes emaciated and eventually dies. While Rowena is dying, the narrator, who is addicted to opium and lives in a drug-induced dreamworld, seems to hear slight sounds amidst the heavy tapestries and gentle footfalls on the carpet. He seems to feel invisible objects passing near his body, seems to perceive faint shadows thrown from a lighted censer, seems to see drops fall into a goblet as from some invisible spring.

The death of the loathsome Rowena revives his memories of the beloved Ligeia. At midnight, a sob from Rowena's deathbed startles him from his reverie and makes him aware that she is still alive. Throughout the night Rowena repeatedly comes back to life and shrivels up again into a corpse. Each vacillation between her recovery and relapse is marked by a low sob from the region of her ebony bed. Finally, Rowena rises from her bier, walks toward the narrator, unwinds the ghastly cerements that have covered her face, loosens her long disheveled hair and slowly opens her eyes. At this startling moment, she reveals the raven tresses and dark luminous orbs of the lady Ligeia, who has possessed the body of her rival in love. Poe describes this transformation with unusual subtlety and, by combining the suggestive details of a spectral presence with the unreality of an opium dream, persuades the reader to suspend disbelief.

Poe responded to a literary friend's criticism of "Ligeia" in a fascinating letter of September 1839. He admitted that Ligeia's possession of Rowena was too sudden and surprising, and that a gradual realization of her reincarnation would have been much more effective. But since he had already embodied this idea in "Morella," he was forced to use a less persuasive variant in the second story. In retrospect, Poe believed that the theme of the will expressed in the epigraph should not have been realized in the story, that it would have been better if Ligeia had permanently died:

> Touching "Ligeia" you are right—all right—throughout. The *gradual* perception of the fact that Ligeia lives again in the person of Rowena is a far loftier and more thrilling idea than the one I have embodied. It offers, in my opinion, the widest possible scope to the imagination—it might be rendered even sublime. And this idea was mine—had I never written before I should have adopted it—but then there is "Morella." . . . I was forced to be content with a sudden half-consciousness, on the part of the narrator, that Ligeia stood before him. One point I have not fully carried out—I should have intimated that the *will* did not perfect its intention—there should have been a relapse—a final one—and Ligeia (who had only succeeded in so much as to convey an idea of the truth to the narrator) should be at length entombed as Rowena—the bodily alterations having gradually faded away.[9]

Poe's attraction to the dying and attachment to the dead have always appealed to the morbid but universal feelings of his readers.

IV ═

Poe's failure to achieve popular success with *The Narrative of Arthur Gordon Pym* and his lack of an editorial salary forced him to accept a commission for his grossest piece of hack work: *The Conchologist's First Book: or, A System of Testaceous Malacology [Shell-Covered Mollusks], Arranged expressly for the use of Schools*, published in April 1839. In 1838 Thomas Wyatt had published his expensive *Manual of Conchology*, which contained many illustrations of shells and cost eight dollars. Since the price of this book was too high for both beginners and advanced students, Wyatt wished to bring out a concise yet comprehensive edition that would cost only $1.50 and could be used as a school book. But Harper's, not wanting to spoil the sale of their expensive book, rejected the idea of a cheap edition so soon after the original publication. Thus, the only way to bring out an abridgment was to publish it "with the name of some irresponsible person whom it would be idle to sue for damages, and [the perfectly irresponsible] Poe was selected for the scape goat."

Poe had provided an overelaborate description of the *biche-de-mer* mollusk in chapter XX of *Pym*. And in 1839 (an instant expert on the subject) he said that Wyatt, the author of *A Synopsis of Natural History*, was "favourably known to the public as the author of an exceedingly well arranged, accurate, and beautifully illustrated *Conchology*." For a fee of fifty dollars Poe now agreed to allow his somewhat tarnished name to appear on the title page of the abridged edition. He also translated Georges Cuvier's accounts of the little animals, and wrote the brief Preface and Introduction. The book aimed to give a simple and accurate anatomical account of each animal and the shell it inhabits. But Poe's boring, pedantic and hair-splitting Preface was absolutely guaranteed to torment and discourage even the most passionately interested schoolboy: "A treatise concerning the shells, exclusively, of this greater portion, is termed, in accordance with general usage, a Treatise upon Conchology or Conchyliology; although the word is somewhat improperly applied, as the Greek *conchylion*, from which it is derived, embraces in its signification both the animal and the shell. Ostracology would have been more definite."

This slightly shady undertaking landed Poe in hot water. He had acknowledged his debt to Cuvier and to Wyatt's *Manual of Conchology*, which in turn had been based on Captain Thomas Brown's recently published *Conchologist's Text-Book* (3d edition, Glasgow, 1835). Though he *had* infringed copyright, Poe was accused by a Philadelphia newspaper of plagiarism—a charge he hotly denied. Furthermore, when he tried to publish his stories with Harper's (who had brought out *Pym*) five years later, in 1844, he was informed that the firm was still angry with him for undercutting the sale of their expensive edition. "They have *complaints* against you," a friend told Poe, "grounded on certain movements of yours, when they acted as your publishers some years ago; and appear very little inclined at present to enter upon the matter which you have so much at heart."[10] It is therefore extremely ironic that though the large first edition of Poe's abridgment was well received, adopted as a textbook in many schools and sold out within two months, he earned no royalties. *The Conchologist's First Book*, Poe's most obscure work, was the only one of his books to go into a second edition in his lifetime.

V ==

Poe had not had a regular salary since his dismissal from the *Messenger* in December 1836. He had earned only $143, or sixteen cents a day, during the last two and a half years, and the fifty-dollar fee from the conchology book (the equivalent of a month's wages) could not sustain him for very long. In May 1839, a month after this book appeared, he approached William Burton, the proprietor of *Burton's Gentleman's Magazine*, about securing an editorial position. The hearty, rotund Burton, the son of a scholar and printer, had been born in London in 1802 and attended St. Paul's School. After failing to establish a monthly magazine, he had had a successful theatrical career in England. He emigrated to Philadelphia in 1834, became a popular comic actor on the American stage, and was particularly admired for his portrayal of Shakespeare's Falstaff and Sir Toby Belch. He also wrote two successful plays. The sharp-tongued Lewis Gaylord Clark, who had reviewed *Pym*, condemned Burton's morals as well as his style, calling him "a vagrant from England, who has left a wife and offspring behind him there, and plays the bigamist . . . with another wife, and his whore besides; one who cannot write a paragraph in English to save his life."

Burton had issued the first number of his magazine, to which he frequently contributed, in July 1837. He then bought out his partner and became sole owner in December 1838. *Burton's* had a large, beautifully printed format, and published light, entertaining articles. Since acting tours often took him away from Philadelphia for long periods of time, he needed an assistant editor. After his success on the *Messenger*, Poe seemed well suited to the job. On May 11, 1839 Burton, responding to Poe's letter, complained about high expenses and offered a lower salary than Poe had suggested:

> I wish to form some such engagement as that which you have proposed, and know of no one more likely to suit my views than yourself. The expenses of the Magazine are already woefully heavy; more so than my circulation warrants. . . . Competition is high—new claimants are daily rising. . . . My contributors cost me something handsome, and the losses upon credit, exchange, etc., are becoming frequent and serious. I mention this list of difficulties as some slight reason why I do not close with your offer, which is indubitably liberal, without any delay.
>
> Shall we say ten dollars per week for the remaining portion of this year? Should we remain together, which I see no reason to negative, your proposition shall be in force for 1840. A month's notice to be given on either side previous to a separation.
>
> Two hours a day, except occasionally, will, I believe, be sufficient for all required.
>
> I shall dine at home today at 3. If you will cut your mutton with me, good. If not, write or see me at your leisure.

At *Burton's* Poe moved from unpaid to salaried literary drudgery. His routine and frequently trivial work included proofreading, compiling short fillers, revising and preparing manuscripts for the press, and supervising the printing of the magazine. All this often took much more than two hours a day. Unlike White, who recognized Poe's intellectual superiority and treated him with paternal solicitude, the imperious Burton—an eminent man with a considerable reputation as actor, playwright and editor—considered Poe a mere employee and never gave him any editorial opportunities. Burton also objected to his caustic reviews and to the savage disrespect with which he treated the revered James Fenimore Cooper. Cooper's recent works, Poe wrote, are "a flashy succession of ill-conceived and miserably executed literary productions, each more silly than its predecessor . . . [which] had taught the public to suspect a radical taint in the intellect, an absolute and irreparable mental leprosy."

Burton's absences from Philadelphia, financial worries, condescending attitude and criticism of Poe's reviews, combined with Poe's low salary, disgust at the frivolity of the magazine, hypersensitivity about his menial position and embittered moods, led to a serious argument before the end of Poe's first month. Poe sent Burton an angry letter defending his literary criticism. On May 30 Burton frankly censured Poe and replied: "I am sorry you have thought it necessary to send me such a letter. Your troubles have given a morbid tone to your feelings, which it is your duty to discourage. I myself have been as severely handled by the world as you can possibly have been, but my sufferings have not tinged my mind with melancholy, nor jaundiced my views of society. . . . I cannot permit the magazine to be made a vehicle for that sort of severity which you think 'so successful with the mob.' . . . You must, my dear sir, get rid of your avowed ill-feelings towards your brother-authors. You see I speak plainly; I cannot do otherwise upon such a subject."[11]

Burton's strictures were not shared by influential members of the press, who recognized Poe's achievements as editor and author. The *St. Louis Bulletin*, for example, in an extract that Poe wanted his cousin Neilson to reprint in his newspaper, commented on Poe's tenure at the *Messenger*: "The first impetus to the favor of *literary men* . . . was given by the glowing pen of Edgar A. Poe, now assistant editor of *Burton's Gentleman's Magazine*; and, although he has left it, [it] has well maintained its claims to respectability. There are few writers in this country . . . who can compete successfully, in many respects, with Poe. With an acuteness of observation, a vigorous and effective style, and an independence that defies control, he unites a fervid fancy and a most beautiful enthusiasm. His is a high destiny."

When Neilson failed to respond to his suggestion, Poe recalled his cousin's opposition to his marriage and attempt to lure Virginia away from him. And he condemned the wealthy but selfish Neilson in an unusually angry letter to the Baltimore physician and editor Joseph Snodgrass: "I believe him to be the bitterest enemy I have in the world. He is the more despicable in this, since he makes loud professions of friendship. . . . I cannot account for his hostility except in being vain enough to imagine him jealous of the little literary reputation I have, of late years, obtained. But enough of the little dog."[12] Despite his connection with *Burton's*, Poe's financial problems continued. At the end of 1839 he sent a letter to his former Philadelphia landlord apologizing for his inability to repay a debt of fifty dollars.

Poe's editorial job at *Burton's* gave him a new outlet for his stories. He published "The Man That Was Used Up" in the August 1839 issue and his masterpiece, "The Fall of the House of Usher," in September. Like "Loss of Breath," "The Man That Was Used Up: A Tale of the Late Bugaboo and Kickapoo Campaign" is a "comic" story with one interesting idea. The satire on war heroes and military glory in the Kickapoo campaign against the Illinois Indians may have been based on the Virginian, General Winfield Scott, who was a close relative of John Allan's second wife and had met Poe. Scott—who had fought in the Seminole and Creek campaigns, had been severely wounded and been breveted major general—was later defeated as Whig candidate for president. Martial heroes like Admiral Horatio Nelson, who had lost an eye in combat in Corsica and an arm in battle in Tenerife, were traditionally honored for their sacrificial valor. But Poe reveals how his grievously wounded American hero has been "used up" and reduced by his war wounds to nothing but naked aggression.

Every day this hero has to be built up again to regain his identity— lost in the slaughter of war—and resemble a human being. With the assistance of his servant Pompey, the grotesque old soldier screws his cork leg and arm on to his amputated stumps, slips his shoulder and bosom on to the concavities of his torso, covers his scalped head with a wig, replaces his bashed-in teeth with dentures, fits a glass eye into his gouged-out socket and restores his slashed tongue with a palate. Only at this point does the observant narrator begin "very clearly to perceive that the object before me was nothing more nor less than my new acquaintance, Brevet Brigadier-General John A. B. C. Smith. The manipulations of Pompey had made, I must confess, a very striking difference in the personal appearance of the man."

Poe's story bears a striking resemblance to Jonathan Swift's savagely satiric poem "A Beautiful Young Nymph Going to Bed," and both works have a common source in Juvenal's satires. The nauseating nymph and the repulsive general are both observed at their *toilette*: but she deconstructs while he reconstructs himself. In both works the author brutally portrays the deliberate, disgusting dismantling or reassembling of an artificial body. Swift satirizes woman's vanity, Poe man's barbarity.[13]

"The Fall of the House of Usher" synthesizes in an extraordinarily effective way Poe's quintessential elements: gloomy landscape, crumbling mansion, somber interior, sorrowful atmosphere, terrified narrator, neurasthenic hero, tubercular heroine, opium dreams, arcane books, premature burial, oppressive secrets, tempestuous weather, supernatural elements, return from the grave and apocalyptic conclusion. The mournful cadence of the opening sentence—which mentions the dying year, the heavy sky, the isolated narrator and the deathly darkness that surrounds the mansion—sets the mood of the story and foreshadows the doom of the family: "During the whole of a dull, dark, and soundless day in the autumn of the year, when the clouds hung oppressively low in the heavens, I had been passing alone, on horseback, through a singularly dreary tract of country, and at length found myself, as the shades of evening drew on, within view of the melancholy House of Usher." Though unnerved by the desolate setting, the narrator notices the eye-like windows that personify the house, as well as the barely perceptible fissure in the wall and the lurid tarn that reappear significantly at the end of the story.

The narrator arrives for a visit at the urgent request of his boyhood friend Roderick Usher, and is "ushered" into a strange chamber to greet his host. The weirdly eccentric Usher is an irreclaimable eater of opium, which intensifies experience at the same time that it allows him to escape from reality. He suffers excruciatingly "from a morbid acuteness of the senses; the most insipid food was alone endurable; he could wear only garments of a certain texture; the odors of all flowers were oppressive; his eyes were tortured by even a faint light; and there were but peculiar sounds, and these from stringed instruments, which did not inspire him with horror." After Usher's twin sister Madeline passes through the chamber like an apparition, the narrator learns that she is gradually wasting away with chronic Poe's disease.

A decadent but singularly talented hermit, Usher improvises musical dirges, paints phantasmagoric conceptions of long sealed tunnels bathed with ghastly and inappropriate rays, and writes an allegorical poem, "The Haunted Palace," in which a "hideous throng" of "evil things" prophesy his doom. Poe explained that "by the Haunted Palace I mean to imply a mind haunted by phantoms—a disordered brain." The poet-critic A. E. Housman admired the sensual music of this poem, but felt the allegory in the first four stanzas—before the mood changes to suggest desolation and destruction—was too insistently schematic:

> *The Haunted Palace* is one of Poe's best poems so long as we are content to swim in the sensations it evokes and only vaguely to apprehend the allegory. We are roused to discomfort, at least I am, when we begin to perceive how exact in detail the allegory is; when it dawns upon us that the fair palace door is Roderick Usher's mouth, the pearl and ruby his teeth and lips, the yellow banners his hair, the ramparts plumed and pallid his forehead, and when we are reduced to

hoping, for it is no more than a hope, that the wingéd odours
have no connexion with hair-oil.

Usher identifies with his rotting house, is passionately absorbed in
it and believes its very stones have human feelings: "The conditions
of the sentience had been here, he imagined, fulfilled in the method
of collocation of these stones—in the order of their arrangement, as
well as in that of the many *fungi* which overspread them, and of the
decayed trees which stood around—above all, in the long undisturbed
endurance of this arrangement, and in its reduplication in the still
waters of the tarn." The lake emphasizes the twin motif and the
unreality of the house by reflecting the reflection of the eye-like windows.

Madeline, finding in the narrator no hope of rescue from her hermetic existence, dies during his visit and is promptly entombed in the
family vault that lies in the depths of the dungeon. The reading by
Usher and the narrator of the medieval tale of the "Mad Trist" is
interrupted by a screaming sound and signals the second dramatic
appearance of Madeline. As Usher regretfully exclaims: "*We have put
her living in the tomb!*" Her bloody robes reveal her desperate struggle
to escape from the vault. As she clasps her brother in a vengeful
death-embrace, he finally succumbs to the terrors he had anticipated
throughout the story. When the narrator flees the house during a
violent storm, its fissure widens and he hears the final death cry of
Madeline: "my brain reeled as I saw the mighty walls rushing asunder—there was a long tumultuous shouting sound like the voice of a
thousand waters—and the deep and dark tarn at my feet closed sul-
lenly and silently over the fragments of the '*House of Usher.*' "

The House of Usher is brought down by psychological as well as
architectural stress; and the deeper significance of the story is hidden
below the dazzling surface. The word "mystic," Poe wrote, is applied
by German critics "to that class of composition in which there lies
beneath the transparent upper current of meaning an under or *suggestive* one. What we vaguely term the *moral* of any sentiment is its
mystic or secondary expression." D. H. Lawrence was the first to
perceive that the story portrayed the unconscious impulses of the
characters; that Poe "was an adventurer into the vaults and cellars and
horrible underground passages of the human soul." The decay and
disintegration of the aristocratic family is inextricably related to the
"oppressive secret" that Usher is unable to divulge and to his complex
motives for burying his sister while she is still alive. As Lawrence
saw, the story powerfully suggests the incestuous relations of the twin

brother and sister. Though Usher tries to repress that terrible secret by premature burial, Madeline manages to escape from the tomb and to punish him for his crime.[14]

VI =====

The publication of "The Fall of the House of Usher" in September 1839 helped establish Poe's reputation as a serious writer and enabled him to publish his first collection of stories. The Philadelphia firm Lea & Blanchard agreed to bring out in December of that year a two-volume edition of his *Tales of the Grotesque and Arabesque*. These volumes included the twenty-five varied and extremely uneven stories he had written thus far and had extensively revised for this edition. But the publishers would not pay royalties, and allowed him only twenty free copies for distribution to friends.

The "grotesque" tales were comic or satiric; the "arabesque," which recalled the Middle Eastern influence on "Tamerlane" and "Al Aaraaf," were serious, imaginative and poetic. The book was dedicated to the eminent congressman and judge Colonel William Drayton, who had befriended Poe in Philadelphia and may have subsidized the publication of the book. In the brief Preface, Poe defended himself against the charges of Germanism and gloom, and justly insisted: "If in many of my productions terror has been the thesis, I maintain that terror is not of Germany, but of the soul,— that I have deduced this terror only from its legitimate sources, and urged it only to its legitimate results."

The anonymous reviews of the book were mixed, even contradictory. The harsh, bewildered reaction of the *Boston Notion*, which was looking for moral uplift, suggested that Poe's bizarre imagination was more suited to the taste of future readers than to that of his own time: "[The tales] fall below the average of newspaper trash. . . . They consist of a wild, unmeaning, pointless, aimless set of stories, outraging all manner of probability, and without anything of elevated fancy or fine humor to redeem them. . . . The congregation of nonsense is merely caricature run mad." *Alexander's Weekly Messenger*, by contrast, called the tales a "playful effusion of a remarkable and powerful intellect." The *New York Mirror*, responsive to Poe's style and themes, agreed that the stories revealed "the development of great intellectual capacity, with a power for vivid description, an opulence of imagination, a fecundity of invention, and a command over the elegances of diction which have seldom been displayed, even by writers who

have acquired the greatest distinction in the republic of letters." The
Philadelphia Saturday Courier also recognized the originality of Poe's
work and ended with an apt comparison: "They are generally wildly
imaginative in plot; fanciful in description, oftentimes to the full
boundaries of the grotesque; but throughout indicating the polished
writer, possessed of rare and varied learning. Some of them will bear
good comparison with the productions of Coleridge."

Despite its extraordinary originality and the generally favorable
reviews, the book was too far ahead of its time and did not sell well.
In August 1841, a year and a half after publication, Poe proposed a
second edition with eight new stories, including "The Murders in
the Rue Morgue" and "A Descent into the Maelström," and again
volunteered to forfeit all royalties. But the publishers promptly declined his offer: "We very much regret to say that the state of affairs
is such as to give little encouragement to new undertakings. As yet
we have not got through the edition of the other work and up to this
time it has not returned to us the expense of its publication."[15]

In January 1840 Poe published in *Burton's Magazine* the first of six
installments of *The Journal of Julius Rodman: Being an Account of the
First Passage across the Rocky Mountains of North America ever Achieved
by Civilized Man*. Like *Politian* and *Pym*, this work was left unfinished.
When he left *Burton's*, Poe abandoned Rodman in Montana, a long
way from the promised end of his journey. Like *Pym*, it is heavily
reliant on sources, several of which are mentioned in the text: Sir
Alexander Mackenzie's *Voyages in 1789 and 1793* (1801), *History of
the Expedition under the Command of Captains Lewis and Clark* (1814),
Washington Irving's *Astoria*, an account of the Northwest fur trade,
which Poe had reviewed in 1836, and Captain Benjamin Bonneville's
The Rocky Mountains (1837).

Julius Rodman, an adventurous account of exploration by land in
1792, complements *Pym*'s account of exploration by sea in 1827. Both
Pym and *Julius Rodman* are shamelessly padded with factual details of
the scenery, weather, geology and geography of the then unknown
country; and both contain a breathless series of episodic incidents.
Julius Rodman describes dangerous illnesses, capsized boats, stamped-
ing antelopes, attacks by bears and ferocious fights with treacherous
Sioux Indians, whom Rodman considers "an ugly ill-made race."
Rodman undertakes the journey as a health cure and his Usher-like
hereditary hypochondria drives him "to seek, in the bosom of the
wilderness, that peace which his peculiar disposition would not suffer
him to enjoy among men." Though delicate and sensitive, he seizes
every opportunity to blast the Indians with his superior weapons:

"The effect of the discharge was very severe, and answered all our purposes to the full. Six of the Indians were killed, and perhaps three times as many badly wounded."[16]

Despite its fictional absurdities, *Julius Rodman* (like *Pym*) was accepted in some quarters as an actual historical document. Poe must have been pleased to discover that a paragraph from his skillful pastiche of fact and fantasy was incorporated into an official report on the Oregon Territory, prepared for the United States Senate in 1840. Poe's desperate need for money forced him to waste his talents on such potboilers, which failed to achieve popular success. But during the same year, he also produced a work that was as profound and original as *Julius Rodman* was puerile and conventional.

"The Man of the Crowd" (November 1840), Poe's most underrated story, conveys an astonishingly prescient sense of modernity. It blends realistic and surrealistic elements, and employs sophisticated techniques to show the transit of time and the alternation of daylight and darkness. It also expresses several subtle themes: the alienation of man in the modern city, the isolation of the artist, who observes his own double, and the distrust of democracy—exemplified by the chaotic mob.

In the opening paragraph the narrator mentions vague secrets, mysteries and crimes that burden the conscience, and hints that they will illuminate the bizarre behavior of the man of the crowd. The story proper begins in a Dickensian London coffee-house at the close of evening in autumn. The narrator, convalescing from ill health and still feverish, is in a happy mood (quite unusual in Poe), and experiences enjoyment, pleasure and calm from his newspaper and cigar, from observing the company in the room and the people in the street. As darkness closes in, he emphasizes the press of the crowded thoroughfare, the tides of population, the sea of human heads, the aggregate relations of the masses. (In 1840 London had a population of about 750,000 and was the largest city in the world.) And he acutely notes the paradox that urban people feel "solitude on account of the very denseness of the company around."

Glassed off from the swarming mob, the narrator observes the different types of people in the street and (like Poe's detective hero, Auguste Dupin) deduces their social class and occupation from their physical characteristics. Clerks, who place their pens on their lobes, have bent right ears; gamblers have unusually extended thumbs. He also describes, amidst the throng, peddlers, beggars, invalids, working girls, lepers, prostitutes and drunkards. As the story progresses, the narrator notes the precise passage of time during the next twenty-four hours as well as the change of light from late evening, the advent of darkness, the deepening of night and the garish luster of gas lamps struggling with the dying day, to full nightfall, near daybreak, sunrise, daylight and the shades of the second evening. When the more respectable daylight folk have gone home, the shining gas lamps reveal the harsher types of nocturnal people.

Exactly halfway through the story, the narrator notices a decrepit old man with an idiosyncratic expression of supreme despair. Infected by the intense emotions he perceives in the man and determined to discover his dreadful secret, the narrator follows him into the crowd. The old man—dressed in ragged clothes and fine but filthy linen—is short, thin and very feeble. A rent in his cloak reveals a dagger and a diamond—the weapon and the spoils, it would seem, of his criminal practice.

For Poe, as for modern writers, the city does not represent industry, pleasure and civilization, but rootlessness, isolation and despair—a population massed together with no sense of community. Instead of describing the external horrors of the city, as Friedrich Engels did in his *Condition of the Working Classes in England* (1845), Poe portrays the psychic scars caused by these horrors. In Romantic literature, the isolated hero is opposed to the ravenous mob. In Poe's story, the *isolado* joins the mob and actually likes "the madding crowd's ignoble strife." Forever wandering the streets—outcast, aimless and distressed—the old man joins his inner chaos to that of the deracinated and atomized crowd. As Blake wrote in "Mad Song," at the beginning of the Industrial Revolution:

> Like a fiend in a cloud
>   With howling woe,
> After night I do crowd,
>   And with night will go.

Poe ingeniously describes the manic-depressive divagations, the direction and vacillation, as the narrator, pursuing his prey, follows him (for precise periods of time) through the humid fog and heavy rain, on the main thoroughfare, through a narrow street, in and out of shops, and into the East End of London, the noisome quarter of dreadful poverty and crime. During this circuitous route, the old man's mood and gait suffer violent alterations. He first walks hesitatingly, his eyes rolling wildly, then regains his persevering stride. He next rushes actively about, with a vacant stare, then runs with incredible swiftness (for a "feeble" septuagenarian), gasping for breath and with a look of intense agony.

The narrator, "at a loss to comprehend the waywardness of his actions," cannot possibly understand them because there is *no point* in the old man's wanderings. Like Hemingway's sense of *nada* or Camus' existential despair, the very inability to define the cause and nature of the depressing obsession is precisely what makes it so terrible.

The festering atmosphere of the London slums reflects the old man's desolation and his spirits flicker like a lamp near its death hour. He reaches a gin palace (a place inspired, perhaps, by Fielding and Hogarth), enters the throng with a shriek of joy, but feels intense despair when the host closes for the night and he is once again cast into the darkness of the street. As the sun rises the old man retraces his steps to the center of the city and walks all day through the turmoil of the streets, until the shades of the second evening appear. Though the old man has not stopped for food, drink or rest during these twenty-four hours, his manic energy is undiminished. But the much younger narrator—who has come a long way from the cosiness of the coffeehouse and whose behavior has become as irrational as that of his prey—is weary unto death and can go on no longer. He confronts the wanderer, stares into his face to divine his mystery and concludes that he "is the type and the genius of deep crime"—though he has never actually seen him *commit* a crime. "He refuses to be alone. *He is the man of the crowd.* It will be in vain to follow; for I shall learn no more of him, nor of his deeds." Later writers would have hinted at rather than mentioned the "deep crime" that propelled and perpetuated the man of the crowd.

John Henry Ingram, the leading nineteenth-century authority on Poe, described the story as "this weird record of a solitude-dreading mortal—this impersonation of La Bruyère's *'grand malheur, de ne pouvoir être seul.'* "[17] But the story actually gives an ironic twist to Poe's epigraph. The old man's inability to endure solitude springs from the crimes he has committed, rather than from the troubles he suffers, in the modern metropolis. His obscure guilt, frenetic desperation and terrible loneliness not only arouse our interest but also evoke our sympathy.

"The Man of the Crowd" is also an allegory of the artist who follows and observes his alter ego in order to explore, understand and write about the dark side of his own personality. The old man, the narrator's double, resembles the pictorial incarnations of the fiend, shudders when he comes into momentary contact with a shopkeeper, has tireless superhuman strength and represents aged yet ageless evil: a demonic criminal found and flourishing in a crowd. In this reading, the old man's psychological anguish and "supreme despair" are not primarily caused by committing a crime or rejecting a moral code, but by a deep division within himself which forces him to take refuge in a crowd that provides a semblance and parody of the human community.

VII ══

In May 1840 the smoldering antagonism between Burton and Poe ignited. Burton, who had frequently remained on tour while retaining control of the magazine, was now focusing his attention on building his own National Theater in Philadelphia. On May 21, realizing that he had more work than he could handle, he announced that *Burton's Gentleman's Magazine* was for sale. It had produced an income of three to four thousand dollars a year while Poe, who did most of the work, earned only five hundred. Concluding that he would soon lose his job, Poe drew up the announcement of the *Penn Magazine*, which he hoped would fulfill his long-cherished dream of a journal of his own. Burton, knowing that Poe's forthcoming announcement would decrease the sale price of his own magazine, rebuked him for planning the *Penn* and fired him on the spot.

According to Thomas Dunn English, Poe became abusive and stomped out of the office in uncontrollable disgust at Burton's "chicanery, arrogance, ignorance and brutality." He then sent Burton a furious letter that expressed all the resentment and contempt—both pecuniary and personal—that had accumulated during his year of servitude:

> You first "enforced," as you say, a deduction of salary [to pay off Poe's debts]; giving me to understand thereby that you thought of parting company.—You next spoke disrespectfully of me behind my back—this as an habitual thing— to those whom you supposed your friends, and who punctually retailed me, as a matter of course, every ill-natured word which you uttered. Lastly you advertised your magazine for sale without saying a word to me about it. . . .
>
> Your attempts to bully me excite in my mind scarcely any other sentiment than mirth. . . . If by accident you have taken

it into your head that I am to be insulted with impunity, I can
only assume that you are an ass.

During their dispute, Poe had called Burton a blackguard and
scoundrel for initiating a fraudulent premium scheme. In November
1839 Burton had advertised prizes totaling one thousand dollars for
the best stories, poems and essays that were written for his magazine.
In April 1840, alleging that the submissions had been inadequate, he
suddenly announced the cancellation of the contest. In June Poe exposed Burton's infamous conduct in a letter to Joseph Snodgrass.
Disguising the fact that he had been fired, he declared that Burton
had no intention of paying the premiums. For this reason, Poe said,
he had abruptly severed his connection with the magazine.

Meanwhile, Poe went ahead with plans for his *Penn Magazine*,
which he had conceived as early as 1834, and told prospective patrons
that he had left *Burton's* in order to establish a superior magazine of his
own. *Penn* would have fine paper, clear type and superior woodcuts; it
would feature boldness in criticism and originality in fiction. His
prospectus of June 1840 mentioned his earlier disagreement with the
Messenger's editorial policy and announced that *Penn*, with a subscription of five dollars a year, would be more serious and more severe,
as well as more expensive, than most of its rivals.

> Having in [the *Messenger*] no proprietary right, my objects
> too, in many respects being at variance with those of its
> worthy owner, I found difficulty in stamping upon its pages
> that *individuality* which I believe essential to the perfect success
> of all similar publications. . . . The *Penn Magazine* will retain
> this trait of severity in so much only as the calmest and sternest
> sense of literary justice will permit. . . . [It will offer] upon
> all subjects, an honest and fearless opinion. . . .
>
> Its aim, chiefly, shall be *to please*; and this through means
> of versatility, originality and pungency. It must not be sup-
> posed, however, that the intention is never to be serious.
> There *is* a species of grave writing, of which the spirit is
> novelty and vigor, and the immediate object the enkindling
> of the imagination.[18]

In October Burton sold his magazine, which had 3,500 subscribers,
to George Graham, a Philadelphia editor, for $3,500. In December
Poe, confined to bed by illness and unable to find financial supporters,

announced that he was forced to postpone publication of the *Penn Magazine* until the following March. Though he would try again with the *Stylus* in 1843 and the *Broadway Journal* in 1845, his dream of owning a successful journal was never to be realized.

Apart from his many disagreements with Burton, Poe was also dismissed for heavy drinking. Burton alluded to this problem in his issue of September 1840 by writing that Poe's " 'infirmities' have caused us much annoyance." He also spread word of Poe's alcoholism when retailing his version of their quarrel. Poe denied these damaging charges in a furious but unconvincing letter to Joseph Snodgrass. He admitted his past aberrations, but maintained that he was now completely sober:

> I could prove their falsity and their malicious intent by witnesses who, seeing me at all hours of every day, would have the best right to speak. . . . In fact, I could prove the scandal almost by acclamation. . . . I have always told [Burton] to his face, and everybody else, that I looked upon him as a blackguard and a villain. . . . I pledge you, before God, the solemn word of a gentleman, that I am temperate even to rigor. . . .
>
> At no period of my life was I ever what men call intemperate. I never was in the *habit* of intoxication. . . . But, for a brief period . . . I certainly did give way, at long intervals, to the temptation held out on all sides by the spirit of Southern conviviality. My sensitive temperament could not stand an excitement which was an everyday matter to my companions. In short, it sometimes happened that I was completely intoxicated.

But his claim to sobriety is contradicted by Thomas Dunn English's report that Poe was often found drunk in the streets of Philadelphia. He sometimes felt an irresistible urge to escape from literary drudgery and indulge in a drinking spree with male friends. English himself had once found Poe stupefied in the gutter and helped him stumble back to Mrs. Clemm. When English knocked on their front door, she opened it and scolded him by crying: "You make Eddie drunk, and then you bring him home." His tongue loosened by alcohol, Poe, in a rare flash of humor, expressed resentment of her moral censure and oppressive domesticity. As English was hastily turning to leave, Poe grasped him by the shoulder and exclaimed: "Never mind the old———; come in."[19]

Chapter 8

PHILADELPHIA: *GRAHAM'S MAGAZINE,* 1841-1843

I ==

The severe illness that had forced Poe to postpone the publication of the *Penn Magazine* confined him to bed until the beginning of January 1841. A month later, a financial crisis disrupted the operations of the Philadelphia banks, which—like the New York banks in 1837—suspended specie payments. Money was again difficult to obtain, and Poe was forced to abandon all hope of bringing out his new magazine in the foreseeable future.

The Philadelphia lawyer and publisher George Graham, the owner of the *Casket,* had bought *Burton's.* In December 1840 he combined the two magazines into *Graham's* and had a total of 5,000 subscribers—five times more than Poe thought was the minimum necessary to start the *Penn.* In February 1841 Graham hired Poe as editor at a salary of eight hundred dollars a year. Four years younger than Poe, Graham had worked as a cabinet maker while studying for the bar. Expansive, genial, social and liberal with his most popular writers (though not with Poe), he became—with Poe's help—an extremely rich man.

Graham's paid three hundred dollars a year more than *Burton's* and Poe, relieved of the routine drudgery that was now handled by an assistant editor, had a good deal less work to do. He did not have to deal with incoming manuscripts, but wrote the book reviews, contributed a story each month and read the final proofs. A typical issue of *Graham's* contained several short stories, a number of lyric, narrative and didactic poems, essays on nature, art, biography and manners, articles on literature and travel, book reviews, colored fashion plates and several well-executed engravings.

Poe's innovative tales, rigorous reviews, original ideas, good taste and literary contacts soon made *Graham's* the most important and astonishingly successful magazine in America. Beginning with a circulation of 5,000, *Graham's* printed 20,000 in September, 25,000 in December, and 40,000 in February 1842. But Poe's salary remained exactly the same. He had cordial relations with Graham, who (unlike Burton) was usually civil and kind. But after working on the middlebrow magazine for only a few months, he felt increasingly disgusted with his situation.

At *Graham's*, Poe aroused the interest of subscribers by continuing the series on "Autography" (reading character from signatures) that he had started at the *Messenger* in 1836. He also encouraged readers to send in ciphers—with the key phrase in English, Greek, Latin, French, Italian, Spanish or German, or in any dialects of these languages— and boasted that he would solve every one of these coded messages. "This challenge excited, most unexpectedly," Poe noted in an essay on "Secret Writing," "a very lively interest among the numerous readers of the journal. Letters were poured in upon the editor from all parts of the country; and many of the writers of these epistles were so convinced of the impenetrability of their mysteries, as to be at great pains to draw him into wagers on the subject. . . . Foreign languages were employed. Words and sentences were run together without interval. Several alphabets were used in the same cipher. . . . Out of, perhaps, one hundred ciphers altogether received, there was only one which we did not immediately succeed in resolving. This one we *demonstrated* to be an imposition—that is to say, we fully proved it a jargon of random characters, having no meaning whatever."

When Poe's own difficult cipher could not be solved, he offered a year's subscription to the magazine to anyone who could solve it *with the key*. Finally, overwhelmed by the torrent of ingenious ciphers and wearied by the enormous amount of time he had spent on this popular enterprise, he reluctantly closed the contest. He had proved to his readers what he would later repeat and demonstrate in "The Gold-Bug": "human ingenuity cannot concoct a cipher which human ingenuity cannot resolve." Though Poe felt a truly difficult cipher required a great deal of patient thought, he did not pride himself on his solutions. In fact, he wrote despondently in 1843, "I feel little pride about anything."[1]

After assuming control of *Graham's Magazine*, Poe began to publish his stories for an ever-widening circle of readers. "The Murders in the Rue Morgue" (April 1841), the first detective story, had an immense impact and changed the history of world literature. The brilliant title logically links "murders" with "morgue," connects the dramatic action to the exotic place where it occurs and immediately arouses interest in the *identity* of the murderer. (Though there was no Rue Morgue in Paris, the word "morgue," which suggests "morbid," was the name of the building in that city that housed dead bodies.) The criminal did not, as the title implies, commit a sequence of killings, but was responsible for two hideous deaths at the same time. The murderer was undoubtedly inspired by the huge, hairy, red ourang-outang that was exhibited before astonished crowds at the Masonic Hall in Philadelphia in July 1839.

This story introduces the detective, Auguste Dupin, who is—with Roderick Usher—Poe's most interesting fictional character. But while Usher is gradually losing his mind, Dupin, the logical Frenchman, is in full control of his rational faculties and exercises great ingenuity in detecting the murderer. Like Poe—who had studied mathematics at West Point, had an analytical mind and could decipher cryptographs—Dupin "is fond of enigmas, of conundrums, hieroglyphics; exhibiting in his solutions of each a degree of *acumen* which appears to the ordinary apprehension praeternatural." Dupin solves problems by means of a pure disembodied intellect that combines scientific logic with artistic imagination.

The aristocratic and highly eccentric Dupin has other characteristics in common with his creator. Both come from wealthy families but have been reduced, by a variety of untoward circumstances, to dire poverty. Both "managed, by means of a rigorous economy, to procure the necessities of life, without troubling [themselves] about its superfluities." Books were the sole luxuries of both men, who astonished friends by the vast extent of their reading.

The narrator lives in a fourth-floor flat with the detective, adjusts to his gloomy way of life and fancies himself Dupin's double. Like Roderick Usher, they inhabit a time-eaten and grotesque mansion, "tottering to its fall" in a lonely and desolate quarter of the city. Stimulated by silence and darkness, which turns their thoughts inward and sharpens their wits, they live in perfect seclusion; they shut out the rays of the day and leave the house only at night. Dupin demonstrates his analytic powers by reading the mind of the bewildered narrator and then showing—through a series of logical associations—precisely how he was able to do it. Though Dupin's mind is a mystery to the narrator, his thoughts are transparent to Dupin.

Immediately after this prelude, the narrator quotes a newspaper account that gives several dramatic details of the brutal murders. These crimes have taken place in a fourth-story flat, a fact that links the victims with the detective. Madame L'Espanaye's throat was so thoroughly cut that when the police tried to raise her, her head suddenly fell off. Her daughter was rammed feet-forward up the chimney, so that her dress and underwear presumably fell downward over her head and exposed her sexual parts. Like Dupin and the narrator, the women lived an extremely retired life and saw almost no one. Since the four thousand francs in gold, which had been delivered by a bank clerk three days before the murder, were not stolen, there seems to be no motive for the atrocities. Though there is no evidence against him, the bank clerk Adolphe Le Bon, despite his propitious name, has been arrested and imprisoned.

All the evidence that Dupin eventually uses to solve the crime is available in the apartment, but the newspapers (obtuse as the police) report that there is not the slightest clue to this perplexing mystery. They also say that the police have interviewed a surprisingly cosmopolitan array of witnesses—including an Italian, an Englishman, a Spaniard, a Dutchman and a Frenchman—who had heard screams and rushed to the scene of the crime. All of them heard a man speaking French, but none could correctly identify the shrill language of the murderer (whom they did not see). All were certain, however, that the shrill voice was babbling in a tongue they did not know.

The narrator, as puzzled as the police and the reporters, states, when probed by Dupin, that there was nothing *peculiar* at the scene of the crime. But Dupin, already on the scent, remarks that the murderer could not have escaped through the door and down the stairs without being seen by the witnesses. And he warns against the common error of confounding the unusual with the abstruse. He then reasons that the unusually agile assassin escaped through the sash window. This dropped of its own accord and became fastened by a concealed spring, but *seemed* to be closed shut by a nail.

The astounding agility, the superhuman strength, the brutal ferocity, the motiveless butchery and the grotesque horror all suggest that the murderer is a madman—till Dupin perceives that the reddish hair clutched in Madame L'Espanaye's fingers is *not human*. Nor, it transpires, are the prehensile marks around her severed neck those of a human hand. From this Dupin deduces that an ourang-outang has committed the crime. He advertises in the newspaper for the owner of the ape; and when a sailor turns up to claim the beast, the detective—knowing he is innocent—convinces him to reveal everything.

When the pet ourang-outang, brought back from a voyage to Borneo, escaped with his razor, the sailor followed him through the deserted streets, climbed onto the roof of the L'Espanayes' flat and watched helplessly as the wild brute, armed with a frightening weapon, committed the ghastly crimes. Dupin is delighted that he has outwitted the prefect of police. By ignoring the evidence and blaming Le Bon (who is immediately released from prison), the prefect—"too cunning to be profound"—failed to solve the murders.

"A Descent into the Maelström," a very different kind of story, which Poe published in *Graham's* the following month, is closely related to "MS. Found in a Bottle" and *The Narrative of Arthur Gordon Pym.* In this minor work, set in Norway, the first-person survivor gives a retrospective account of how he was shipwrecked and sucked into a whirlpool, but escaped by clinging to a cask. The fisherman emphasizes the destructive power of nature and objectively describes his own imminent death.

Rushed to complete the story in time for the May issue and knowing he could not possibly equal the brilliant achievement of the "Rue Morgue," Poe confessed that the conclusion of "Maelström," so often the weakest part of his work, was imperfect. It was extremely ironic that the author of the article on "Whirlpool" in the ninth edition of the *Encyclopedia Britannica* gave Poe credit for information that Poe had lifted from an earlier edition of the same *Encyclopedia,* and then quoted as facts the parts of the story that Poe himself had invented. In this case, as when *Pym* was assumed to be an account of a scientific journey in the English newspapers and *Julius Rodman* was absorbed into a Senate Report, Poe's fantastic fictions were accepted as factual truth.

II ═══

In April 1841, the month he published "Rue Morgue," Poe met Rufus Griswold, an influential literary journalist who later became a dangerous enemy. The coarse-featured, blunt-nosed, thick-lipped, bearded and balding Griswold was six years younger than Poe. Born in Rutland, Vermont, the son of a small farmer, he was a rigid Calvinist in religion. After meager schooling and superficial training as a Baptist clergyman, he was licensed to preach in 1837 but never had a permanent congregation. After working as a printer and journalist in New England and New York, he joined the Philadelphia *Daily Standard* in November 1840.

Griswold combined immense energy with a notable lack of talent, and was clearly on the make in the world of letters. A successful literary parasite and indefatigable compiler, he gained considerable reputation, influence and power during the 1840s and 1850s through a series of immensely popular literary anthologies. James Russell Lowell, alluding to the shepherd in Virgil's First Eclogue, neatly speared him with a couplet in *A Fable for Critics* (1848): "But stay, here comes Tityrus Griswold, and leads on / The flocks whom he first plucks alive, and then feeds on." Griswold was, like Poe, both caustic and hypersensitive. Known for his savagery when attacked and for his "constitutional infirmity which prevents his speaking the simple truth," Griswold was also "careless, erratic, dogmatic, pretentious, and vindictive."[2] The death of his wife and son, just after the infant's birth, and an unhappy second marriage made him increasingly bitter and despondent.

Poe and Griswold suppressed their mutual dislike and presented a facade of mutual cordiality. Poe wanted to be included in Griswold's anthologies; Griswold wanted Poe's critical praise. *The Poets and Poetry of America* appeared in 1842 and revealed the limitations of Griswold's taste. It included only three poems by Poe—"The Coliseum," "The Sleeper" and "The Haunted Palace" (from "Usher")—as compared to seventeen poems by Lydia Sigourney and forty-five by Charles Fenno Hoffman, both of whom are now forgotten.

Griswold was blatantly hypocritical in his attitude to Poe. In January 1845, smarting from Poe's harsh criticism, he tried to disarm his rival by pompously claiming: "Although I have some cause of quarrel with you, as you seem to remember, I do not under any circumstances permit, as you have repeatedly charged, my personal relations to influence the expression of my opinions as a critic." In a review of Poe's *Tales* that year he conceded that Poe "has a great deal of imagination and fancy, and his mind is in the highest degree *analytical*. . . . [His stories are] the results of consummate art." But in December 1843 he had attempted to ingratiate himself, in a private letter to Longfellow, by condemning Poe's "personal and malignant" criticism of Longfellow and warning him of Poe's base character: "It would be very like Poe, since he cannot find a publisher for his 'criticism,' to attempt again to win your friendship with his praise."[3]

Poe was equally insincere with Griswold. During their mutual exploitation, he trimmed his critical views to match the winds that fanned their fiery relations. In 1841, while still courting Griswold's favor, Poe characterized him as "a gentleman of fine taste and sound judgment." The following year he called Griswold's anthology "the best collection of the American Poets that has yet been made, whether we consider its completeness, its size, or the judgment displayed in its selection." But that same month he wrote to Joseph Snodgrass, who was not a poet and had no personal stake in the anthology, condemning it as "outrageous humbug" and urging his friend to "use it up." And in a long review of a later edition of this work, written after several personal and literary quarrels, Poe followed the advice he had given to Snodgrass. After savaging Griswold's character, intellect and taste, and alluding to the wicked servant in Matthew 25:26, he concluded with an amazingly accurate prophecy:

> [Is] the Reverend Mr. Griswold the man of varied talents, of genius, of known skill, of overweening intellect, he was somewhere pictured, or is he the arrant literary quack he is now entitled by the American press? . . .
>
> That he has *some* talents we allow, but they are only those of a *mediocre* character. . . . As a critic, his judgment is worthless. . . .
>
> The [prefatory] biographies are miserably written . . . simply because reason and thinking are entirely out of Mr. G.'s sphere. . . .
>
> Forgotten, save only by those whom he has injured and insulted, he will sink into oblivion, without leaving a landmark to tell that he once existed; or, if he is spoken of hereafter, he will be quoted as *the unfaithful servant who abused his trust.*[4]

Deeply wounded by this blistering attack, Griswold bided his time and took vengeance after Poe's death.

III ═══

In 1841 the Poe family moved from Sixteenth Street to a small row house at 2502 Coates Street, near Fairmount Park, on the northwest outskirts of the city. The rooms, as always, were neat and orderly, but everything about the place revealed its shabby poverty, its hunger, cold and despair.

On the evening of January 20, 1842 (the day after Poe's thirty-third birthday), while the undernourished and debilitated Virginia was singing and playing the piano, she suddenly broke a blood vessel and began to hemorrhage in a terrifying way. The blood gushed from her mouth and her life was in danger. She partially recovered, only to sink, like a drowning survivor, again and again.

One attentive visitor noticed that the confined quarters impeded her recovery and that her illness had a devastating effect on Poe:

> She could not bear the slightest exposure, and needed the utmost care; and all those inconveniences as to apartment and surroundings which are important in the care of an invalid were almost a matter of life and death to her. And yet the room where she lay for weeks, hardly able to breathe except as she was fanned, was a little place with the ceiling so low over the narrow bed that her head almost touched it. But no one dared to speak—Mr. Poe was so sensitive and irritable. . . . And he would not allow a word about the danger of her dying—the mention of it drove him wild.

George Graham recalled Poe's anxious solicitude (which now reversed the mother-son relations that their lodger William Gowans had noted) and attributed to her illness Poe's tragic sense of life:

> His love for his wife was a sort of rapturous worship of the spirit of beauty which he felt was fading before his eyes. I have seen him hovering around her when she was ill, with all the fond fear and tender anxiety of a mother for her first-born, her slightest cough causing in him a shudder, a heart-chill that was visible. I rode out, one summer evening, with them, and the remembrance of his watchful eyes eagerly bent upon the slightest change of hue in that loved face, haunts me yet as the memory of a sad strain. It was the hourly *anticipation* of her loss that made him a sad and thoughtful man, and lent a mournful melody to his undying song.

Frederick Thomas—the Charleston writer and lawyer who became Poe's closest confidant—thought Virginia was charming but doomed: "Her manners were agreeable and graceful. She had well formed, regular features, with the most expressive and intelligent [Ligeia-like] eyes I ever beheld. Her pale complexion, the deep lines in her face and a consumptive cough made me regard her as the victim for an early grave." And Thomas Holley Chivers, the wealthy Georgia doctor and poet, saw Virginia nearly choke to death during one of her coughing fits: "She addressed him with the endearing appellation of *My Dear*! But she was not a healthy woman. . . . At irregular intervals—even while we were talking—she was attacked with a terrible paroxysm of coughing whose spasmodic convulsions seemed to me almost to rend asunder her very body. This was so severe at times as to threaten her with strangulation."[5]

Poe's emotions were finely tuned to the fluctuating state of Virginia's health and his fading hopes for her recovery were, in Andrew Marvell's words, "begotten by Despair / Upon Impossibility." Two weeks after the hemorrhage, Poe told Frederick Thomas that Virginia was out of immediate danger and mentioned the agony he had suffered. In late May he rejoiced that his adored wife was much better and had strong hopes that she would ultimately regain her health. But in early June she had another dangerous hemorrhage "from the lungs," and Poe thought it was now folly to hope for improvement. She was still seriously ill in late August, when Poe had faint hope of her recovery. In March 1843 she was the same (if no worse), but suffered great mental stress from her chronic condition and her fear of death. From then on, she seemed to flutter on the very edge of existence.

"Eleonora" (published in September 1842) offers a positive complement to the wife-hating (or second-wife-hating) narrators of "Berenice," "Morella" and "Ligeia." More importantly, it illuminates Poe's feelings about the moribund Virginia. As in "The Black Cat" and "The Tell-Tale Heart," the narrator immediately mentions his own madness. The demented narrators in the first two stories confess the horrible crimes provoked by their condition, while the narrator of "Eleonora" finds an unusual peace, inspired by the spirit of love.

At the beginning of the story the narrator, his young cousin and her mother live a coolly serene existence in an idyllic setting—the Valley of Many-Colored Grass—whose name was inspired by a line in Shelley's "Adonais": "Life, like a dome of many-coloured glass." When Eleonora is fifteen, their suppressed passions surge to the surface and they become locked in carnal embrace. But it is all too perfect to last. Soon afterward she sees "the finger of Death [pointing to tuberculosis] upon her bosom" and realizes "she had been made perfect in loveliness only to die." Since the childlike Eleonora is saddened to think the narrator might love another woman after her death, he vows never to remarry. This immediately relieves her jealous anxiety, "as if a deadly burthen had been taken from her breast."

Eleonora dies in tranquility. Driven out by the anguished memories of his dead wife, the narrator leaves the happy valley for the temptations and turbulence of the real world. Inevitably, he falls in love with the princess Ermengarde. Despite her ethereal quality, the fever of his ecstasy surpasses his passion for Eleonora. Ignoring his vow and Eleonora's dreaded curse, he marries the royal maiden. But he also escapes Eleonora's bitterness. She comes to him in the silence of the night (which recalls the River of Silence in their happy valley) to absolve him from his vows and direct him to "Sleep in Peace" with Ermengarde.

The story reveals Poe's guilt-ridden desire to rebuild his emotional life and Virginia's generous willingness to grant him freedom. By killing off the beloved Eleonora while the doomed Virginia was still alive, Poe expressed his unconscious desire for Virginia's death, which would free him from intolerable guilt and emotional anguish. It would also allow him to marry a wealthy woman ("the king's daughter"), who would not only provide emotional support but also pay for his long-cherished magazine.

IV ═══

Poe contributed several monthly reviews and an occasional minor poem, as well as frequent stories, while serving as editor of *Graham's*. Though he wrote about many inferior works during 1841 and 1842, he also reviewed books by several important authors: Bolingbroke, Goldsmith, Thomas Campbell, Cooper, Marryat, Macaulay, Bulwer-Lytton, Longfellow, Tennyson and Lowell. Poe continued to delight readers with his lethal criticism of both established and unknown authors. *Mercedes of Castile*, he said, was "the worst *novel* ever penned by Mr. Cooper." And he wittily remarked that if James McHenry (author of *The Antediluvians*) "should be arraigned for writing poetry, no sane jury would ever convict him."

In the spring of 1842, however, a few months after Virginia's hemorrhage, Poe came into contact with two of the greatest writers of his time—Charles Dickens and Nathaniel Hawthorne. At the beginning of their careers, he shrewdly recognized their extraordinary talent and promise. By May 1842 Poe had already reviewed Dickens' *Sketches by Boz, Nicholas Nickleby, The Old Curiosity Shop, Master Humphrey's Clock, The Pic-Nic Papers* and the serial version of *Barnaby Rudge*, in which he correctly predicted, from the opening chapters, "that Barnaby, the idiot, is the murderer's own son." Poe later boasted to friends that he had been completely right in his predictions about the plot and that Dickens had sent him a letter of flattering acknowledgment, asking if his prophecies had been inspired by dealings with the devil. In fact, only the first of his five predictions about the novel was correct, and there is no evidence that Dickens ever sent an admiring letter. When reviewing the completed novel, Poe dismissed his own errors as insignificant and disingenuously attributed them to Dickens' inconsistency: "if we did not rightly prophesy, yet, at least, our prophecy *should have been* right."[6]

Poe corresponded with Irving, Cooper, Bryant, Elizabeth Barrett, Longfellow and Hawthorne, but the only major writers he actually met were Dickens, James Russell Lowell and Walt Whitman. On March 6, 1842, when Dickens was lecturing in Philadelphia during his popular American tour, Poe sent copies of his *Tales of the Grotesque and Arabesque* along with two reviews of *Barnaby Rudge*. He requested an interview and received a cordial response: "I shall be very glad to see you, whenever you will do me the favor to call. I think I am more likely to be in the way between half past eleven and twelve, than at any other time. I have glanced over the books you have been so kind as to send me; and more particularly at the papers to which you called my attention. I have the greater pleasure in expressing my desire to see you, on their account."

The following day Poe had two long interviews with Dickens at the United States Hotel on Chestnut Street. They discussed the state of American poetry, Poe read a poem by Emerson and Dickens promised to help Poe place his work in England. He later described Poe as a man with "shiny straight hair and turned down shirt-collar, who taketh all of us English men of letters to task in print, roundly and uncompromisingly." Dickens kept his promise to help Poe, though he was unsuccessful, as he wrote in late November, in finding an English publisher: "I should have forwarded you the accompanying letter from Mr. Moxon before now, but that I have delayed doing so in the hope that some other channel for the publication of your book on this side of the water would present itself to me. I am, however, unable to report any success. I have mentioned it to publishers with whom I have influence, but they have, one and all, declined the venture."[7] Despite this disappointment, the two authors retained fond memories and mutual respect. When Dickens returned to America after Poe's death, he made a special effort to find Maria Clemm and contribute to her support.

Poe was even more enthusiastic about Hawthorne than he was about Dickens. Though Hawthorne (eight years before he published

The Scarlet Letter) had not yet established his reputation, he promised to enhance the greatness of American literature. In April and May 1842, just after he met Dickens, Poe published an important two-part review of *Twice-Told Tales*. He clearly identified with the mind and character of the slightly older writer when he observed: "these effusions of Mr. Hawthorne are the product of a truly imaginative intellect, restrained, and in some measure repressed, by fastidiousness of taste, by constitutional melancholy, and by indolence." He quirkily accused Hawthorne of plagiarizing "Howe's Masquerade" from "William Wilson," though the earliest version of Hawthorne's story had appeared *before* Poe's. But he also awarded him the highest praise: "Of Mr. Hawthorne's tales we would say, emphatically, that they belong to the highest region of Art. . . . We look upon him as one of the few men of indisputable genius to whom our country has as yet given birth."

Poe used the occasion of this review to set forth his ideas on brevity, point and structure, in both poems and tales, which have had a powerful influence on all subsequent theories of the short story. "A rhymed poem [should] not," Poe wrote, "exceed in length what might be perused in an hour. Within this limit alone can the highest order of true poetry exist. . . . In almost all classes of composition, the unity of effect or impression is a point of the greatest importance. . . . Unity cannot be thoroughly preserved in productions whose perusal cannot be completed at one sitting. . . . Thus a long poem is a paradox." This theory applied to tales as well as to poems: "Having conceived, with deliberate care, a certain unique or single *effect* to be wrought out, [the author] then invents such incidents—he then combines such events as may best aid him in establishing this preconceived effect. . . . In the whole composition there should be no word written, of which the tendency, direct or indirect, is not to the one pre-established design."[8] Though he failed to apply these principles in his long, unfinished works, Poe did realize his aesthetic ideas and achieve dramatic intensity in his finest short works.

Poe's review of *Mosses from an Old Manse* in November 1847 also began with an autobiographical reflection. Noting the difference between his achievement and reputation, he called Hawthorne "*the* example, *par excellence*, in this country, of the privately-admired and publicly-unappreciated man of genius." He praised Hawthorne's true originality, condemned his allegory, which interfered with unity of effect (though this condemnation has not prevented many allegorical interpretations of Poe's own works) and showed how, despite his use of allegory, Hawthorne had achieved unity of effect in his most skillful tales. Poe concluded with a generous, even ecstatic appreciation that must have given great pleasure to his neglected contemporary: "He has the purest style, the finest taste, the most available scholarship, the most delicate humor, the most touching pathos, the most radiant imagination, the most consummate ingenuity." Before this review appeared, Hawthorne had written Poe an amiable letter, which praised his honest criticism but urged him to concentrate on his own imaginative work:

> I have read your occasional notices of my productions with great interest—not so much because your judgment was, upon the whole, favorable, as because it seemed to be given in earnest. I care for nothing but the truth; and shall always much more readily accept a harsh truth, in regard to my writings, than a sugared falsehood.
>
> I confess, however, that I admire you rather as a writer of tales than as a critic upon them. I might often—and often do—dissent from your opinions in the latter capacity, but could never fail to recognize your force and originality, in the former.[9]

V

Poe continued to publish some of his best stories—"The Masque of the Red Death," "The Mystery of Marie Rogêt," "The Gold-Bug," "The Black Cat" and "The Tell-Tale Heart"—during the early 1840s. "The Masque of the Red Death" appeared in the same May 1842 issue of *Graham's* as his Hawthorne review. It effectively combines elements from Boccaccio's *Decameron,* in which aristocrats flee to a secluded retreat while attempting to avoid the plague; from Defoe's *Journal of the Plague Year,* which provided many grim pathological details; and from the cholera epidemic he had witnessed in Baltimore in 1831.

The opening paragraph roots this supernatural story in reality by vividly describing the ravaging plague, the morbid symptoms and the rapid death of the victims. The emphasis on "profuse bleeding" and on "the horror of blood" only four months after Virginia's terrifying hemorrhage is personal and poignant:

> The "Red Death" had long devastated the country. No pestilence had ever been so fatal, or so hideous. Blood was its Avatar and its seal—the redness and the horror of blood.

There were sharp pains, and sudden dizziness, and then profuse bleeding at the pores, with dissolution. The scarlet stains
upon the body and especially about the face of the victim,
were the pest ban which shut him out from the aid and from
the sympathy of his fellow-men. And the whole seizure,
progress, and termination of the disease, were the incidents
of half an hour.

The lavish, operatic masked ball that Prince Prospero organizes
to divert his courtiers during the sixth month of their escape from
contagion takes place in seven differently colored rooms. The eastern
chamber is blue, the others are purple, green, orange, white and
violet, and the western room, where the sun sets, leading to night
and suggesting death, is black. The seventh room also alludes to the
opening of the seventh seal in chapter 8 of Revelation, which brings
"hail and fire mingled with blood" and a minatory voice crying:
"Woe, woe, woe, to the inhabiters of the earth." The zigzag construction of the rooms (which recalls the fissure on the House of Usher)
represents the twists and turns of life that lead to the inevitable end.

Suddenly, amidst the "grotesque" and "arabesque" costumes of
the revelers, a tall, gaunt, masked figure appears. He is shrouded from
head to foot in the blood-smeared "habiliments of the grave" and his
visage resembles that of a stiffened corpse. Prince Prospero orders the
mocking figure to be seized, unmasked and executed. But all the
courtiers shrink back in terror as he walks with solemn step through
the seven rooms. Prospero himself, with drawn dagger, follows this
morbid figure. But as the masked man turns to confront his pursuer,
Prospero drops his dagger and falls prostrate in death. The revelers
seize this figure in the black apartment and gasp in horror at finding
the grave cerements and corpselike mask "untenanted by any tangible
form." The Red Death has come "like a thief in the night." The
thematic allusion to Job 24:14: "The murderer rising with the light
killeth the poor and needy, and in the night is as a thief" suggests the
transience of life and the futility of trying to escape from death.

"The Mystery of Marie Rogêt" (November 1842) is subtitled "A
Sequel to 'The Murders in the Rue Morgue.'" But the sequel is
distinctly inferior to the original story, and there is no connection
between the two except for the Parisian setting and the character of
Auguste Dupin, who, in a fine moment, dozes behind green spectacles
while the prefect of police sets forth his boring explanation of the
case. In "Rue Morgue," Dupin analyzes the evidence, makes sense of
it and uses it to solve the crime. In "Marie Rogêt," which also relies

heavily on newspaper accounts of the murder, Dupin endlessly disputes the mistaken theories of the journalists. Though he suggests how the crime *could* be solved, he never actually names the murderer. The story concludes weakly with vague speculations about the Calculus of Probabilities and—like *Pym*—remains vexatiously unfinished. Unwilling to commit himself to a solution that might prove wrong, Poe changed a murder story into a tale of ratiocination and frustrated readers by refusing to solve the mystery.

Like *Politian*, "Marie Rogêt" is based on an actual murder but translated to a different setting.[10] In July 1841, the year before the story was written, the body of Miss Mary Rogers, a pretty salesgirl in a Manhattan cigar store, was found floating in the Hudson River. Poe had successfully demonstrated the fallacy of the theory, accepted by the newspapers, that the girl was the victim of a *gang* of ruffians and argued that her lover, probably a sailor, had strangled her. But he was not—any more than in his review of *Barnaby Rudge*—correct in his prophecies. In fact, a naval officer later confessed his share of responsibility for the death of Mary Rogers, which took place during an abortion in a New Jersey inn run by a Mrs. Loss. After Mary had died on the operating table, she was tied up and thrown into the river.

When Poe reprinted the story in his *Tales* of 1845, he said, in an important note, that though her "death occasioned an intense and long-enduring excitement, the mystery attending it remained unsolved at the period when the present paper was written and published." He then boasted in the note that *he* had solved the crime in this tale: "The confessions of two persons . . . made, at different periods, long subsequent to the publication, confirmed, in full, not only the general conclusion, but absolutely *all* the chief hypothetical details by which that conclusion was attained."

The subsequent confessions *seemed* to confirm "absolutely *all* the chief hypothetical details" only because, as John Walsh discovered, Poe made, in the 1845 reprint, "fifteen small, almost undetectable changes in the story, all of which definitely accommodate the possibility of an abortion death at the inn of Madame Deluc (the fictional name for Mrs. Loss)." Only these surreptitious additions—for example: "There might have been a wrong *here*, or, more possibly, an accident at Madame Deluc's"—allowed the story to "enjoy a long and totally absurd existence as one of the supreme examples of Poe's analytical powers."[11] In "Marie Rogêt," Poe seemed more concerned with suggesting a solution to the crime than with writing a good story.

"The Gold-Bug," another tale of analytic ratiocination and "sober mystification," won the hundred-dollar story prize of the Philadelphia

Dollar Newspaper in June 1843 just as, ten years earlier, "MS. Found in a Bottle" had won the fifty-dollar prize in the *Baltimore Saturday Visiter*. Like the heroes in "Rue Morgue" and "Eleonora," William Legrand has some autobiographical connection with Poe. When he sends an urgent letter begging the narrator to come immediately to Sullivan's Island, the narrator wonders: "What new crochet possessed his excitable brain? . . . I dreaded lest the continued pressure of misfortune had, at length, fairly unsettled the reason of my friend." When he arrives on the island, the astonished narrator, a Dr. Watson-like foil to the shrewd Legrand, exclaims: "I am as much in the dark as ever. With all the jewels of Golconda awaiting me upon the solution of this enigma, I am quite sure that I should be unable to earn them."

The story utilizes Poe's knowledge of cryptography, which he had demonstrated by solving all the ciphers sent to *Graham's* and had explained in his essay "Secret Writing." The reclusive Legrand has found on the island a real gold bug and an old piece of parchment which, when accidentally heated, reveals a mysterious cipher. After Legrand finds the fabulous gold and jewels that had been buried, with his murdered colleagues, by the notorious pirate Captain Kidd (who wanted to keep the entire treasure himself), Legrand explains how he cracked the cipher that led him to the treasure. The narrator and Legrand's black servant Jupiter, who witnessed the discovery, are now, ironically, in the same dangerous position as Captain Kidd's late associates.

The unusual setting, the contrasting characters, the comic relief provided by Jupiter's Negro dialect, the adventurous quest for hidden wealth, the puzzle-solving ingenuity and the gradual revelation of the mystery made "The Gold-Bug" Poe's most popular story. In May 1844 he boasted to Lowell that 300,000 copies had been circulated, though it is unlikely he had been paid anything beyond the original prize money.

The story also inspired some absurd controversies that reveal the debased state of contemporary journalism. In June 1843, the month of publication, the Philadelphia *Daily Forum* falsely accused Poe (as Poe had accused John Hewitt in 1833) of collusion with the prize committee; and Poe initiated a libel suit against the editor, Francis Duffee. The following month, in the Philadelphia *Spirit of the Times*, John Du Solle (knowing of Poe's obsession with this matter) jokingly accused him of plagiarizing "The Gold-Bug" from "Imogine," a story by a thirteen-year-old schoolgirl. By the end of the month the fires had died down. Duffee publicly retracted the charge of collusion and Poe withdrew the libel suit. In August the story was hastily dramatized in Philadelphia to cash in on its popularity. But, John Du Solle reported, though the acting was good, the play "dragged, and was rather tedious. The frame work was well enough, but wanted filling up."[12]

"The Black Cat" (August 1843) continued Poe's perverse portrayals of alcoholics, criminals, murderers and madmen. It also has some fascinating parallels with Poe's life. The narrator is especially fond of sagacious black cats and mentions, as Poe had in "Instinct vs. Reason," that black cats are popularly regarded as witches in disguise. The narrator is dominated by the "Fiend of Intemperance" and cursed by the disease of alcohol, which causes him to experience "a radical alteration for the worse." Returning one evening completely intoxicated, he grabs the frightened cat, who bites him. In a fit of fiendish malevolence, he gouges out one of its eyes with a penknife and drowns out the memory with more drink.

The Poe-like narrator is driven by the "spirit of *Perverseness*." Just as Poe was disinherited, so the narrator's worldly wealth had been destroyed in a sudden fire, and he too is forced to live in poverty. The narrator too has an uncomplaining wife who is "the most patient of sufferers." Like Poe, he unconsciously resents her humble devotion. Provoked by the reproachful one-eyed cat, he swings at it with an axe but is arrested by the moderating hand of his wife. Then, giving way to his murderous impulses, he buries the axe in her brain. To escape detection, he walls up her corpse in the cellar. But distracted and tormented by guilt, he also walls up the cat, who represents his conscience, within her tomb. The wailing shrieks of the wounded animal, who sits on the head of the decayed corpse, give away his crime and consign him to the hangman. Though Poe expressed his love for Virginia in words, letters and domestic devotion, this story provided an essential outlet for his remorse, resentment and rage.

"The Tell-Tale Heart," written for the first issue of Lowell's short-lived *Pioneer* in January 1843, is the complement and mirror image of "The Black Cat." In both stories a mad narrator confesses the repulsive unmotivated murder of an innocent victim: the devoted wife and the harmless old man. In both the crime is provoked by an evil eye. In both he takes great pains to conceal the body and stands right next to the corpse as the suspicious but imperceptive police search the premises. In both, driven by remorse of conscience, he gives himself away when he hears—or thinks he hears—the cat's shrieks or the beating of the dead man's tell-tale heart. Driven to produce a story each month, Poe repeated in "The Tell-Tale Heart" the extremely effective formula of "The Black Cat" just as in "Ligeia" he repeated (but surpassed) the theme of "Morella."

VI ==

Graham's editorial salary of eight hundred dollars a year was not sufficient to support Poe's family, especially after the dramatic increase in Virginia's medical expenses, and they continued to live in soul-destroying poverty. The hardship and illness explain Poe's irrational behavior, wild drinking sprees and expressions of murderous rage in his stories. As Samuel Johnson wrote of the poet William Collins: "in a long continuance of poverty, and long habits of dissipation, it cannot be expected that any character should be exactly uniform. There is a degree of want by which the freedom of agency is almost destroyed."

Poe was the first American writer, as Alexander Pope had been the first in England, to support himself entirely by his writing. Emerson was a clergyman, Longfellow and Lowell were professors, Cooper was consul in Lyons, Irving attaché in Spain and Hawthorne consul in Liverpool. The main problem, as Poe repeatedly pointed out, was the lack of an international copyright law—which was not adopted until 1891. American publishers were reluctant to pay writers like Poe if they could publish Dickens for nothing. As Poe wrote in the aptly named essay "Some Secrets from the Magazine Prison-House": "The want of an International Copy-Right Law, by rendering it nearly impossible to attain anything from the booksellers in the way of remuneration for literary labor, has had the effect of forcing many of our best writers [like himself] into the service of the Magazines and Reviews." But many of the magazines paid nothing at all or, when they did offer fees, tormented the writers by paying late. "A young author," Poe wrote with personal anguish, "struggling with Despair itself in the shape of a ghastly poverty, has no alleviation—no sympathy from an every-day world, that cannot understand his necessities." Maria Clemm, who resorted to desperate expedients in order to get money, would retrieve rejected manuscripts from Poe's wastebasket and sell them—as well as books he had borrowed—without his knowledge. After Poe's death she contrasted the coddled child with the indigent adult and told Neilson Poe: "I attended to his literary business, for he, poor fellow, knew nothing about money transactions. How should he, brought up in luxury and extravagance?"[13]

Like most serious modern writers—Lewis, Joyce, Lawrence, Pound and Eliot—Poe's work was, as Harper's had told him, too difficult to reach a popular audience. And like these writers, he had difficulty in selling his work—even when he waived royalties—and was always poorly paid. Cooper usually received two thousand dollars for the American edition of his novels, the once-popular Nathaniel Willis earned fourteen hundred dollars a year from four magazines and James Kirke Paulding agreed to write a monthly five-page article for *Graham's* for fifty dollars. This fee was three weeks' salary for Poe, who (by contrast) earned only four dollars a page.

Since he was paid the same rates for his best work and his worst, he was forced to fend off starvation by churning out a great quantity of trash. He warmly agreed with Hawthorne that writing for magazines was "the most unprofitable business in the world." During the three years following his resignation from *Graham's*, he earned only $121 from his writing. His total income from all his books, written over a period of more than twenty years, came to less than $300. A single copy of *Tamerlane* has been recently sold for much more money than Poe ever earned in his entire life.

Most of Poe's letters, early and late, contained humiliating pleas for money or some other form of assistance. In March 1843, for example, he offered one acquaintance a real bargain: "If you cannot spare $30 I would be exceedingly glad of $20." His correspondents, hardening their hearts against his constant demands, always dreaded and usually ignored them. In a personal aside about payment to authors, Poe bitterly noted that compensation amounted to "little more than any common scavenger might have earned in the same period, upon our highways." And in an early review, he passionately condemned the materialistic mentality—exemplified by John Allan as well as by the editors who employed him—that despised and demeaned the idealistic artist: "When *shall* the artist assume his proper situation in society—in a society of thinking beings? How long shall he be enslaved? How long shall mind succumb to the grossest materiality? How long shall the veriest vermin of the Earth, who crawl around the altar of Mammon, be more esteemed of men than they, the gifted ministers to those exalted emotions which link us with the mysteries of Heaven?"[14]

In the spring of 1842, prompted by feelings that his talents were being debased, Poe fell into a familiar pattern of behavior. When he had no editorial position and was on the verge of starvation, he was very glad to accept a regular salary for doing literary drudgery. But after he had been toiling at it for a while, his resentment built up

again. He got fed up with working hard for little pay, desperately
wanted a magazine of his own, and was either fired or quit the job.
Poe's frustration and anger were fueled by his loyal friends. Thomas
Holley Chivers, for example, felt Poe, who was responsible for Graham's extraordinary success, was shamefully underpaid:

> He ought to give you ten thousand dollars a year for supervis-
> ing it. It is richly worth it. I believe it was through your
> editorial ability that it was *first* established. If so, he is greatly
> indebted to you. It is not my opinion that you ever have been,
> or ever will be, paid for your intellectual labours. You need
> never expect it, until you establish a Magazine of your
> own. . . .
>   There is, in the perspicuous flow of your pure English, a
> subtle delicacy of expression which always pleases me—*except
> when you tomahawk people.*

Referring to his experience on the *Messenger* and on *Burton's*, Poe
told a friend, just before joining *Graham's*, that he had made serious
intellectual as well as financial sacrifices: "I have not only labored
solely for the benefit of others (receiving for myself a miserable pittance) but have been forced to model my thoughts at the will of men
whose imbecility was evident to all but themselves." This bitterness
also appeared in his review of an early book by Dickens. Poe observed
that the need to crank out mechanical work for money stifled the
imagination and turned the genius into the hack: "To write well, the
man of genius must write in obedience to his impulses. When forced
to disobey them; when constrained, by fetters of a methodical duty,
to compose at *all* hours, it is but a portion of his nature—it is but
a condition of his intellect—that he should occasionally grovel in
platitudes of the most pitiable description."[15] Shortly after leaving
Graham, who had made a $25,000 profit while paying him $800 a
year, Poe told a friend that if Graham had given him a tenth-interest
in the magazine instead of a paltry salary, he would have been a rich
man.

In April 1842 Poe returned to the office after a brief illness to find
that Charles Peterson, the other editor, had taken over his duties.
Unduly upset by this trivial incident, which triggered the memory of
numerous grievances, he impulsively resigned from *Graham's*. Rufus
Griswold became his successor at the higher salary of one thousand
dollars a year. Torn between his desire to edit a successful magazine
and his scorn for the middlebrow contents that made it popular, Poe

explained that "my reason for resigning was disgust with the namby-pamby character of the Magazine—a character which it was impossible to eradicate. I allude to the contemptible pictures, fashion-plates, music and love tales. The salary, moreover, did not pay me for the labor I was forced to bestow. With Graham who is really a very gentlemanly, although exceedingly weak man, I had no misunderstanding." Despite Poe's disclaimer, their relations had not been entirely harmonious. On the morning after Virginia's hemorrhage, when Poe was not indebted to Graham, he had asked for an advance of two months' salary to help him over the crisis, and was abruptly and discourteously refused.

Moreover, when Poe had temporarily abandoned the *Penn Magazine* to join *Graham's*, Graham had promised to subsidize *Penn* within a year. Since Graham had money and Poe did not, he agreed to this plan. But the more work Poe did for *Graham's*, the more profitable he made the magazine, the less willing Graham was to support a rival journal and lose his brilliant editor. In the end, he did not keep his promise. In September 1842, when Graham became unhappy with Griswold, Poe refused a good offer to return. And in an anonymous review of Griswold's anthology, Poe fired a parting shot by mentioning "the brilliant career of *Graham's Magazine* under Mr. Poe's care, and its subsequent trashy literary character [under Griswold] since his retirement." Though Graham did little to alleviate Poe's poverty, he was certainly aware of its disastrous effects. Graham later wrote two essays explaining the reasons for Poe's alcoholism and defending his character against the vicious attacks made by Griswold after Poe's death:

> The sufferings caused by poverty to the sensitive, proud, educated gentleman are agonies indescribable, temptations irresistible; and Poe's poverty was at times excessive, extending to the want of the mere necessaries of life. . . .
> [Despite his struggle with adverse fate,] he was always the same polished gentleman, the quiet, unobtrusive, thoughtful scholar, the devoted husband, frugal in his personal expenses, punctual and unwearied in his industry, *and the soul of honor* in all his transactions.[16]

Cautioned by his great-uncle William Poe that a "free use of the Bottle" was the great enemy of their family, Poe had generally abstained from alcohol since his dismissal from *Burton's Magazine*. But after leaving *Graham's*, the strain of intense work, debilitating poverty and anxiety about Virginia's illness drove him back to drink. In Philadelphia Poe met the lively Northern Irishman Mayne Reid, who became his faithful drinking companion. A schoolmaster, corn-factor in New Orleans, tutor, trapper and traveler in the American West, Reid later became a captain during the Mexican War, a successful author of adventure novels and, for a time, the inmate of an insane asylum. Poe, who had rarely moved inland from the East Coast, was fascinated by this fluent, inexhaustible and exuberantly inventive raconteur. He called Reid "a colossal but most picturesque liar" and then added: "he fibs on a surprising scale, but with the finish of an artist, and that is why I listen to him attentively."

The loyal Mayne Reid, acknowledging that Poe sometimes joined him on binges, playfully tried to diminish and excuse their force and their frequency:

> I feel satisfied that Edgar Allan Poe was not, what his slanderers have represented him, a rake. I know he was not; but in truth the very opposite. I have been his companion in one or two of his wildest frolics, and can certify that they never went beyond the innocent mirth in which we all indulge when Bacchus gets the better of us. With him the jolly god sometimes played fantastic tricks—to stealing away his brain, and, sometimes, too, his hat—leaving him to walk bareheaded through the streets at an hour when the sun shone too clearly on his crown, then prematurely bald.
>
> While acknowledging this as one of Poe's failings, I can speak truly of its not being habitual; only occasional, and drawn out by some accidental circumstance—now disappointment; now the concurrence of a social crowd, whose flattering friendship might lead to champagne, a single glass of which used to affect him so much that he was hardly any longer responsible for his actions.[17]

Lambert Wilmer, his old Baltimore friend, took a darker and more realistic view of Poe's alcoholism. "It gives me inexpressible pain," he told a mutual friend, "to notice the vagaries to which he has lately become subject. Poor fellow!—he is not a teetotaller by any means and I fear he is going headlong to destruction, moral, physical, and intellectual."

Two incidents that occurred a few months after Virginia's hemorrhage and Poe's resignation from *Graham's* confirm Wilmer's prophetic remarks. In June 1842 Poe took a ferry across the Hudson River

Poe's slightly tilted head, asymmetrical face and contorted expression, curling into a contemptuous sneer, reveal his ravaged condition four days after his suicide attempt in November 1848. Library of Congress

The petite actress Eliza Poe was praised for her interesting figure, her correct performance, and her sweetly melodious voice.
Valentine Museum, Richmond

John Allan "was sharp and exacting, and with his long, hooked nose, and small keen eyes looking from under his shaggy eyebrows, he always reminded me of a hawk."
Poe Museum, Richmond

Frances Allan, an unusually attractive woman, suffered from poor health and a nervous disposition. Valentine Museum, Richmond

The rather masculine Maria Clemm had a large forehead, deep-set, widely spaced eyes with overhanging brows, broad nose, lined cheeks, long narrow mouth, firm chin, and puffy jowls. From a daguerreotype formerly owned by Annie Richmond

"Poe was proud and very fond of Virginia, and used to delight in the round, child-like face, and plump little figure." Humanities Research Center, University of Texas, Austin

The caustic and hypersensitive Rufus Griswold was known for his savagery when attacked and for his "constitutional infirmity which [prevented] his speaking the simple truth."
New York Public Library

James Russell Lowell: "A young poet, to whom others than ourselves have assigned a genius of the highest rank."
From an 1844 daguerreotype

Fanny Osgood was "about medium height and slender, complexion unusually pale; hair black and glossy; eyes a clear, luminous grey, large, and with a great capacity for expression." John Sartain's engraving of a portrait by Samuel Osgood

Helen Whitman clothed her fragile beauty in silken draperies and floating veils, and sniffed strong-smelling ether as a stimulant for her weak heart. The Providence Athenaeum

Annie Richmond: "*This peculiar expression of the eye, wreathing itself occasionally into the lips, is most powerful.*" University of Massachusetts, Lowell

Elmira Shelton's "*voice was very low, soft and sweet, her manners exquisitely refined, and she was a woman of education and force of character.*" From a daguerreotype owned by her daughter, Ann Elizabeth

to New Jersey, where Mary Rogers had died, been trussed up and thrown into the water. Maria Clemm did not know where he was and Virginia was frantic with anxiety. After a search was made, he was finally discovered in the woods outside Jersey City, wandering around like a crazy man. The following month, he got uncontrollably and obliviously drunk on another short business trip to New York, and was forced to send a feeble apology to his friends when he returned to Philadelphia: "Would you be kind enough to put the best possible interpretation upon my behavior while in N–York? You must have conceived a *queer* idea of me—but the simple truth is that Wallace [a Kentucky-born poet] would insist upon *the juleps*, and I knew not what I was either doing or saying."[18]

VII ==

The release from *Graham's* and the increasingly urgent need for money shot Poe in many different directions. He tried to find a job in the Philadelphia Custom House through the Tyler administration in Washington. He resurrected plans for his own magazine and arranged for the publication of an important biographical sketch of himself. He brought out a pamphlet with two stories and began his career as a public lecturer. As usual, he had terrible luck and failed in most of these enterprises.

The idea of a government sinecure that would pay a comfortable salary while providing sufficient leisure for writing had always appealed to Poe. But a letter of May 1841 from Frederick Thomas, who had just landed a cushy job in Washington, describing the attractive security and idleness, inspired him to pursue this will-'o-the-wisp for the next two years. Thomas wrote:

> How would you like to be an office holder here at $1,500 per year payable monthly by Uncle Sam who, however slack he may be to his general creditors, pays his officials with due punctuality. How would you like it? You stroll to your office a little after nine in the morning leisurely, and you stroll from it a little after two in the afternoon homeward to dinner, and return no more that day. If during office hours you have anything to do it is an agreeable relaxation from the monstrous laziness of the day. You have on your desk everything in the writing line in apple-pie order, and if you choose to lucubrate in a literary way, why you can lucubrate.

Thomas, a close friend of President Tyler's son Robert, tried to use his influence to get Poe a position in the Philadelphia Custom House. But the old Collector of Customs refused, for political reasons, to make the appointment and Poe had to wait until a new man took over. In October 1842 the new collector arrived, but there were over 1,200 applications for a few dozen jobs, and Poe did not have the necessary influence or prestige to get one. When the list of successful candidates was posted, he saw the name "Pogue" and optimistically thought it was a mistake for his own. After four futile interviews with the collector, in which he held out false hopes and Poe became increasingly short-tempered, Poe was rudely told that all the positions had been filled. As Poe complained to Thomas in November:

> He has treated me most shamefully. . . . He told me, upon my first interview after the election, that if I would call on the fourth day he would swear me in. I called & he was not at home. On the next day I called again & saw him, when he told me that he would send a Messenger for me when ready:—this without even inquiring my place of residence— showing [though Poe did not see it at the time] that he had, from the first, no design of appointing me. Well, I waited nearly a month, when, finding nearly all the appts made, I again called. He did not even ask me to be seated—scarcely spoke—muttered the words "I will *send* for you Mr. Poe"— and that was all.

Undaunted by this humiliating rejection, Poe bounced back the following March, when he went to Washington to present his case to the president. Nervous and excited, overeager and excessively convivial, he got horribly drunk on port wine, washed down with rum coffee. He went around with his coat turned inside out, became petulant and vexatious, publicly mocked Thomas Dunn English (who was also visiting the capital) and was sick for several days. He was in no condition to meet President Tyler and, by showing the worst side of his character at the worst possible time, completely destroyed his chance of getting a job.

John Hewitt—who in 1833 had brawled with Poe in the streets of Baltimore over the poetry prize awarded to Hewitt by the *Baltimore Saturday Visiter*—now met him on Pennsylvania Avenue. Drunk and destitute, Poe needed help and was unusually conciliatory. Hewitt described him as

> *Un homme blasé*—seedy in his appearance and woe-begone.
> He came boldly up to me, and, offering me his hand, which
> I willingly took, asked me if I would forget the past. He said
> he had not had a mouthful of food since the day previous,
> and begged me to lend him fifty cents to obtain a meal.
> Though he looked the used-up man all over—still he showed
> the gentleman. I gave him the money—and I never saw him
> afterwards.[19]

The ever vigilant Maria Clemm, taking no more chances, was waiting at the Philadelphia train station to cart him home.

Reports of Poe's self-destructive behavior soon reached Philadelphia. One friend who had tried to help him in Washington told the publisher Thomas Clarke, a potential backer for Poe's new magazine, that Poe could handle politicians no better than he could handle drink or money: "He exposes himself here to those who may injure him very much with the President, and thus prevents us from doing for him what we wish to do and what we can do if he is himself again in Philadelphia. He does not understand the way of politicians, nor the manner of dealing with them to advantage. How should he?" And Frederick Thomas, who had unfortunately been confined to bed by sickness during Poe's visit, tactfully revealed (in a note on Poe's letter) that port wine did in Washington what mint juleps had done in New York: "he presented himself in Washington certainly not in a way to advance his interests. I have seen a great deal of Poe, and it was his excessive, and at times marked sensibility which forced him into his 'frolics,' rather than any mere marked appetite for drink, but if he took but one glass of weak wine or beer or cider the Rubicon of the cup was passed with him, and it almost always ended in excess and sickness."

The day after returning from the drunken debacle in Washington, Poe sent a cheeky letter to his patrons urging them to press his hopeless case and to tell Robert Tyler that "if he *can* look over matters & get me the Inspectorship I will join the Washingtonians [a temperance society] forthwith." This letter, which recalls the earlier one asking Colonel Thayer for a recommendation after his court-martial from West Point, reveals that Poe had the alcoholic's tendency to deny reality. Poe pretended that his disasters had never occurred and naively wanted everyone else to do so as well.

Despite the failure of Lowell's *Pioneer*, Poe never swerved from the grand purpose of his life. While pursuing political sinecures, he also revived the idea of a new magazine—this time to be called the *Stylus*. "How dreadful is the present condition of our Literature!" he lamented to Lowell. He then set forth his two lifetime obsessions: "We want two things, certainly:—an International Copy-Right Law, and a well-founded Monthly Journal, of sufficient ability, circulation, and character, to control and so give tone to, our Letters."

To this end, early in 1843, he formed a partnership with Thomas Clarke, the publisher of the Philadelphia *Saturday Museum*, to publish the *Stylus*. In February he issued a prospectus. As with the *Penn* announcement, Poe emphasized its high standards, contrasted it to the tripe published in rival journals and promised, beginning with the opening number in May, a series of critical and biographical sketches of American writers that would surpass Griswold's work:

> It will endeavor to be, at the same time, more varied and more unique [*sic*];—more vigorous, more pungent, more original, more individual, and more independent. It will discuss not only the Belles-Lettres, but, very thoroughly the Fine Arts, with the Drama; and, more in brief, will give each month, a Retrospect of our Political History. . . .
>
> It shall, in fact, be the chief purpose of the *Stylus*, to become known as a journal wherein may be found, at all times, upon all subjects within its legitimate reach, a sincere and a fearless opinion.[20]

By May, when the first issue was due, Poe's idealistic plans had collapsed. Disturbed by Poe's drinking and in serious difficulties with his own magazine, Clarke withdrew his support for the *Stylus* and let him down as badly as Graham had done. Though the magazine never appeared, Poe gathered subscriptions for it till the end of his life.

In February 1843, while this project was still alive, Henry Hirst—an eccentric Philadelphia poet who later became addicted to absinthe and spent his final years in a lunatic asylum—published an important biographical essay on Poe. It appeared in the same issue of Clarke's *Saturday Museum* that contained the *Penn* prospectus. This essay, intended to puff the editor of the new magazine, was based on material supplied by Poe. It did not mention his army service, but described his fictional journeys to Greece and St. Petersburg, and his return from Europe on the night of Frances Allan's funeral. These biographical myths were not exploded for a hundred years. Accompanied by his portrait, lengthy extracts from his poetry and thirty-two laudatory comments on his stories, the essay concluded with a physical description that suggested the decisive character of the thirty-four-year-old Poe: "He is now but little more than thirty years of age; in person, he is somewhat slender, about five feet, eight inches in height, and well proportioned; his complexion is rather fair; his eyes are grey and restless, exhibiting a marked nervousness; while the mouth indicates great decision of character; his forehead is extremely broad. . . . His hair is nearly black and partially curling." Poe approved of (and may even have written) this description. But he disliked the portrait, which was neither a good likeness nor even a vague resemblance. The crude woodcut portrays Poe sitting stiffly in a wooden armchair and looking much older than his actual age. Dressed in a waistcoat, frock coat and high collar, he has sideburns down to his bare chin and thick, thundercloud eyebrows. "I am ugly enough God knows," he exclaimed, "but not quite so bad as that."

In July 1843, after the *Stylus* had collapsed, Poe made his last, half-hearted attempt to find a career outside literature. He registered in the district court of Philadelphia to study law in Hirst's office, but did not get very far with Blackstone's *Commentaries*. In 1845, attempting to repay his friend, he generously wrote that Hirst "has not only given indication of poetical genius, but has composed some *very* commendable poems. His imagination is vigorous, bold, and at the same time delicate." But he also reverted to his old obsession with plagiarism that year and wounded Hirst with a caustic comment: "provided you purloin my poetry *in a reputable manner*, you are welcome to just as much of it as you (who are a *very* weak little man) can conveniently carry away."[21]

In the spring of 1843 poverty, debts, restlessness, desire for change or search for healthier quarters propelled the Poes to their fourth house in Philadelphia. The narrow, five-story brick cottage, with a garden on one side and a porch in the rear, was at 234 North Seventh Street, in the Spring Garden District, on the northern edge of town. A schoolgirl neighbor later recalled that Maria Clemm focused her considerable energy on cleaning up the place and on looking after the essential lodger who was crammed into the small house: "Mrs. Clemm was always busy. I have seen her of mornings clearing the front yard, washing the windows and the stoop, and even white-washing the palings. You would notice how clean and orderly everything looked. She rented out her front room to lodgers, and used the middle room, next to the kitchen, for their own living room or parlor. They must have slept under the roof." Poe was frequently unable to pay the modest rent. But the landlord, a wealthy plumber, was unusually tolerant and not disposed to cause him distress.

In July, a few months after moving to Spring Garden, William Graham of 98 Chestnut Street in Philadelphia published a little pamphlet, *The Prose Romances of Edgar A. Poe*, containing two unrelated stories: "The Murders in the Rue Morgue" and "The Man That Was Used Up." Though it was announced as the first in a "Uniform Serial Edition" and cost only twelve and one-half cents, sales were insufficient to warrant the publication of further stories in this series.

Poe's last bid for money and fame in Philadelphia were more successful than all the others. In an 1841 review of Dickens' *The Old Curiosity Shop*, he had mocked "the present absurd rage for lecturing," which Dickens would do so successfully on his American tour the following year. But, utilizing material he had planned to publish in the *Stylus*, Poe began his own career as a lecturer on November 21, 1843 with a talk in Philadelphia on "Poetry of America." The popularity of "The Gold-Bug" and his tomahawk reputation excited public interest and drew an overflow audience. Hundreds of other people, unable to gain admission, missed his witheringly severe attack on Griswold's anthology, *The Poets and Poetry of America*. Poe repeated the lecture in Wilmington a week later and in New York the following February.

Poe was an extremely effective speaker and an eloquent reciter of poetry. His voice was soft, mellow and melodious. Paying particular attention to rhythm, he "almost sang the more musical versifications." The expert delivery and controversial content of his maiden speech led to a rapturous reception. One newspaper said, "the Lecture was received with the most enthusiastic demonstrations of applause, and it was agreed by all, that it was second to none, if not superior to all lectures ever delivered before the Wirt Institute." And in the *Saturday Museum*, Thomas Clarke awkwardly remarked: "Quite a large, and certainly highly intelligent audience, attended the Lecture on American Poetry. . . . The fact of the Lecturer himself possessing talents, as a poet, of a high order, and therefore capable of more truly appreciating his subject, with great analytical power, and that command of language and strength of voice which enables a speaker to give full expression to whatever he may desire to say, it will be readily perceived that the Lecturer combined qualities which are rarely associated in a public speaker."[22] The good crowd earned Poe the substantial sum of about one hundred dollars.

Despite considerable hardship and Virginia's tragic illness, Poe had accomplished a great deal during his six years in Philadelphia. He had successfully edited two important national magazines, had published thirty-one stories, including most of his masterpieces, and had collected them in a two-volume book. He had consolidated his reputation as a critic and author, reached the height of his achievement as a literary man and, in his stories, revitalized the portrayal of the fantastic and the unreal.

Chapter 9

A LION IN NEW YORK,
1844-1845

I ===

In April 1844 Poe left Philadelphia, as he had left Baltimore and Richmond after his previous failures. In New York he resumed the rootless and impoverished life that his actor-parents had led, and continued to pursue the dream of obtaining his own literary magazine. After being sacked from the *Southern Literary Messenger*, he had lived a wretched life, during 1837 and 1838, in a wooden shanty on Carmine Street in Manhattan. But New York, with a population four times greater than Philadelphia, was the newspaper and book publishing center of America. Poe felt that the cosmopolitan city, where he would spend the remaining years of his life, offered better opportunities than Philadelphia for the man of letters.

Poe and Virginia took a train from Philadelphia to Perth Amboy, New Jersey, and then traveled by steamer across the Hudson River to New York. While Virginia waited aboard ship, chatting to the other lady passengers, Poe quickly rented a room in a boarding house at 130 Greenwich Street, near the southern tip of Manhattan. His unusually domestic letter to his mother-in-law—familiarly addressed to "My dear Muddy," oddly referring to his young wife as "Sis," and signed "Eddie,"—mentioned a number of details that would interest Maria Clemm and portrayed himself as a model husband and son. He recounted the journey, the weather, Virginia's health, his small purchases and the money that remained; and described the dinner and breakfast with a relish that suggests he had not eaten a substantial meal for a very long time:

> Last night, for supper, we had the nicest tea you ever drank, strong & hot—wheat bread & rye bread—cheese—tea-cakes (elegant) a great dish (2 dishes) of elegant ham, and 2 of cold veal, piled up like a mountain and large slices—3 dishes of cakes, and every thing in the greatest profusion. No fear of starving here. The landlady seemed as if she couldn't press us enough, and we were at home directly. . . . [This morning] I ate the first hearty breakfast I have eaten since I left our little home. Sis is delighted, and we are both in excellent spirits. She has coughed hardly any and had no night sweat. She is now busy mending my pants which I tore against a nail.[1]

After mentioning his strict temperance, he sent greetings to their clever pet, Catterina, and assured Maria that they hoped to send for her *very* soon. In a postscript, Poe urged Maria to return the copy of the *Southern Literary Messenger* to Henry Hirst, who had borrowed it, at Poe's request, from William Duane. Instead of following his instructions, Maria, always resourceful and desperate to raise the cash for the trip to New York, sold it to Leary's bookstore in Philadelphia. Duane, who had to buy back his own signed copy from a Richmond bookseller, sent angry and insulting letters to Poe.

After Maria had joined them in New York, the family continued to move around the city, searching for a quiet place for Poe to work and a healthy locale for Virginia. When they could not pay the rent, the landlords became impatient and they were forced to find cheaper rooms. In the summer of 1844 they lodged in Patrick Brennan's isolated two-story house, at 84th Street and Broadway, which was surrounded by a two-hundred-acre farm that extended west from Central Park to the Hudson River. In September Poe told Frederick Thomas that he had been living like a hermit in rural Manhattan and had not seen anyone but his family. In January 1845 the gypsies moved downtown to 154 Greenwich Street; in May they took rooms on the second floor of 195 East Broadway; and in September 1845 they shifted to a three-story house at 85 Amity Street, near Washington Square. Poe's imaginative genius and caustic criticism had made him a popular lecturer, and he supported his family during this time by public speaking, by copious journalism and (as usual) by pressing all his friends and acquaintances for urgently needed loans.

In May 1844 Poe told Nathaniel Willis—graduate of Yale, poet, European correspondent and editor of the New York *Evening Mirror*—that he was in poor health and miserably depressed. In October, after Poe had been writing trivial pieces for the *Mirror* for a year and a half, Willis offered him a salary of $750 a year as assistant editor and "mechanical paragraphist" on his daily newspaper. "It was his business," Willis apologetically wrote, "to sit at a desk, in a corner of the editorial room, ready to be called upon for any of the miscellaneous work of the moment—announcing news, condensing statements, answering correspondents, noticing amusements—everything but the writing of a 'leader,' or constructing any article upon which his peculiar idiosyncrasy of mind could be impressed." Though this was a humble, if not actually degrading, position for the former editor of several prominent national monthlies, Poe was forced to accept the job. In November he began to publish in the *Mirror* the learned and gossipy paragraphs of "Marginalia," which were based on his extensive reading, and continued to bring them out in various journals until 1849.

Poe had generously called Willis' *Tortesa, the Usurer* "by far the best play from the pen of an American author." In his account of the New York "Literati," he identified himself with Willis' tempestuous character: "Mr. Willis' career has naturally made him enemies among the envious host of dunces whom he has outstripped in the race for fame; and these his personal manner (a little tinctured with reserve, *brusquerie*, or even haughtiness) is by no means adapted to conciliate. . . . He is impulsive, generous, bold, impetuous, vacillating, irregularly energetic." Willis reciprocated by encouraging Poe's work and, after his death, by writing sympathetic accounts of his refined and sad-mannered friend. But Willis' recollections, intended to counteract the slanders of Griswold, sound more like a condescending letter of recommendation than a memoir about a genius: "We had seen but one presentment of the man,—a quiet, patient, industrious, and most gentlemanly person, commanding the utmost respect and good feeling by his unvarying deportment and ability."[2]

II ===

While dutifully completing his tedious tasks on the *Mirror* in 1844, Poe published "Dream-Land," a major poem of considerable technical skill, in *Graham's*; and placed four significant stories in several popular journals: "A Tale of the Ragged Mountains" in *Godey's*, "The Balloon-Hoax" in the *Sun*, "The Purloined Letter" in the *Gift* and "The Premature Burial" in the *Dollar Newspaper*. All these stories show Poe's extraordinary originality, his unique combination of realistic detail and fantastic subjects, and his capacity to convince and disturb.

"Dream-Land"—a land of death, of the unconscious and of nightmare—explores unknown areas of the human mind as the dreamer awakens and describes his vision:

> By a route obscure and lonely,
> Haunted by ill angels only,
> Where an Eidolon [phantom], named Night,
> On a black throne reigns upright,
> I have reached these lands but newly
> From an ultimate dim Thule—
> From a wild weird clime that lieth, sublime,
> Out of Space—out of Time.

In this hypnotic poem the traveler-narrator has escaped from the agonizing time and space of the real world into the disintegrating phantasmagoric landscapes of the painter John Martin, where he encounters spectral "Memories of the Past." But this mysterious though strangely soothing land hides its mournful meaning from him. His sad soul can behold it, like St. Paul in I Corinthians 13:12, only through a darkened glass that obscures his perception but diminishes his pain.

"A Tale of the Ragged Mountains" takes place on the southern outskirts of Charlottesville and describes another kind of dreamland. In this supernatural tale of narcotic visions, reincarnation and tragically foreshadowed death, the invalid hero, Augustus Bedloe, is physically peculiar and—like Roderick Usher and the narrator of "Ligeia"—addicted to opium. Baudelaire, in his essay "Eugène Delacroix," alluded to this story and said Poe believed "the effect of opium upon the senses is to invest the whole of nature with a supernatural intensity of interest, which gives to every object a deeper, a more wilful, a more despotic meaning." Bedloe's large dose of morphine (a drug based on opium) certainly heightens his sensory perceptions: "In the quivering of a leaf—in the hue of a blade of grass— in the shape of a trefoil—in the humming of a bee—in the gleaming of a dew-drop—in the breathing of the wind—in the faint odors that came from the forest—there came a whole universe of suggestion—a gay and motley train of rhapsodical and immethodical thought."

While under the influence of the drug, Bedloe has a vision of an exotic Indian city. He enters the town, is killed in battle and describes his own death—which he has seen in this vision. When he wakes up and returns to Charlottesville, he discovers from his doctor that this was exactly how Oldeb, Bedloe's physical double, had died while fighting the rebellious natives in Benares in 1780. A week later, Bedloe himself dies after the doctor has accidentally applied a poisonous leech to his right temple—at exactly the place where an arrow had fatally wounded Oldeb in the vision. Inspired by narcotics, Bedloe foresees but cannot avoid his own doom.

In a minor tale, "The Angel of the Odd," Poe described his method of inventing subjects for his science-fiction stories. "Knowing the extravagant gullibility of the age," he wrote, he tried to imagine "improbable possibilities." In "The Balloon-Hoax" he returned to the locale of his army service and of "The Gold-Bug," and deceived even more people than he had gulled with "Hans Pfaall."

Despite the title's clear signal that "The Balloon-Hoax" is a fantasy, Poe's densely factual narration and the circumstantial inclusion of the English novelist Harrison Ainsworth among the passengers gave the editors of the New York *Sun* sufficient scope to boost circulation and convince fifty thousand avid readers that this voyage had actually taken place. The morning headline in the *Sun* of April 13, 1844, printed above an illustration of the balloon, dramatically announced: ASTOUNDING INTELLIGENCE BY PRIVATE EXPRESS FROM CHARLESTON VIA NORFOLK!—THE ATLANTIC OCEAN CROSSED IN THREE DAYS!!—ARRIVAL AT SULLIVAN'S ISLAND OF A STEERING BALLOON INVENTED BY MR. MONCK MASON!! Poe's story was issued, following this fanfare, as a one-page broadside that same afternoon.

The following month, Poe described the wild enthusiasm his story had aroused: "On the morning (Saturday) of its announcement, the whole square surrounding the *Sun* building was literally besieged, blocked up—ingress and egress being alike impossible, for a period soon after sunrise until about two o'clock P.M. . . . I never witnessed more intense excitement to get possession of a newspaper. As soon as the first few copies made their way into the streets, they were bought up, at almost any price, from the news-boys, who made a profitable speculation." Poe received his regular fee for this story but, as usual, did not share the profits of this enormous success.

In the story itself, Poe put his "readers in possession of the minutest particulars respecting this extraordinary voyage." Anticipating the hyperbolic rhetoric of modern space programs, he concluded ironically by calling this farfetched account "unquestionably the most stupendous, the most interesting, and the most important undertaking ever accomplished or even attempted by man. What magnificent events may ensue, it would be useless now to think of determining." Though Poe enjoyed perpetrating a hoax in order to show how easy it was to deceive the public, this story also had a more serious purpose. "The Balloon-Hoax" is a telling satire not only on human gullibility, but also on the contemporary infatuation with the idea of progress. As Poe shrewdly told Thomas Chivers: "I disagree with you in what you say of man's advance towards perfection. Man is now only more active, not wiser, nor more happy, than he was 6,000 years ago."[3]

"The Purloined Letter" has many subtle connections to "The Murders in the Rue Morgue." In both stories Dupin easily and amiably triumphs over the rather obtuse prefect of police. The Latin epigraph of the later story—translated as "Nothing is more distasteful to good sense than too much cunning"—echoes Dupin's earlier judgment that the "Prefect is somewhat too cunning to be profound." Dupin's narrator-friend is characteristically "astonished" in one story and "astounded" in the other by the detective's brilliant revelations. In the first tale Dupin repays the good service of the bank clerk Le Bon by proving him innocent and releasing him from prison; in the second, his solution of the mystery enables him to extract revenge for the evil the minister had once done to him in Vienna. Both stories end with aphoristic quotes from classical authors in French.

In the opening paragraph of "The Purloined Letter" the two friends—one naive, the other analytical—are silently smoking pipes in Dupin's study at 33 Rue Dunôt, reflecting on "the affair of the Rue Morgue, and the mystery surrounding the murder of Marie Rogêt," when the door is suddenly thrown open by the baffled prefect of police, who arrives to seek the detective's help. Like the narrator, the prefect is a foil for Dupin. He informs Dupin that the minister has stolen a private letter from a royal personage, by substituting a similar one, and used it to blackmail her. And he explains that an exhaustively thorough search of the apartment of Minister D——has failed to produce the missing item. When the prefect asks for advice, Dupin emphasizes his colleague's ineptitude by telling him "to make a thorough re*search* of the premises."

Dupin's innovative method is to identify his own intellect with that of his criminal opponent. In fact, the detective and the minister, whose names both begin with the letter "D," have several traits in common. When Dupin, wearing characteristic green spectacles to cover his eye movements, visits the minister at home, he finds him "yawning, lounging, and dawdling, as usual, and pretending to be in the last extremity of *ennui*, [though] he is, perhaps, the most really energetic human being now alive." This deceptive lethargy recalls the portrayal of Dupin in the opening paragraph of the story, meditating in the smoke-filled library in the Faubourg St. Germain. And when Dupin realizes that the minister—despising ordinary concealment and driven to simplicity—has prevented discovery by leaving the stolen letter in full view, he recovers it by duplicating the minister's crime, substituting a facsimile for the real one and stealing it back from the thief. By doing this, he gives the royal lady power over the minister, condemns him to destruction and neatly repays his evil deed.

Poe's creative imagination ranged from the detective story that was meant to entertain by appealing to the intellect to "The Premature Burial" that was designed to terrify by appealing to the emotions. The latter achieved its effect by describing a fear that was deeply rooted in Western culture during the nineteenth century. The source of this morbid preoccupation came from the earlier age of great plagues and epidemics when, during the frenzied disposal of the mass of corpses, amidst the dead-carts and the grave pits, the living were sometimes mistaken for the dead. In this period, sophisticated coffins, using the latest technology, were invented to allay the possibility of premature burial, a topic frequently discussed in contemporary books and journals.

Works like Joseph Taylor's *The Danger of Premature Interment, Proved From Many Remarkable Instances of People Who Have Recovered After Being Laid Out* (1816), published in Poe's lifetime, and Franz Hartmann's *Buried Alive* (1895), recounted numerous case histories and expressed the fears of the age. In 1834 Jean-Sébastien Fontenelle had listed a great number of conditions—"Asphyxia, Hysterics, Lethargy, Hypochondria, Convulsions, Syncope, Catalepsis, excessive loss of blood, Tetanus, Apoplexy, Epilepsy and Ecstasy [sexual orgasm]"—which caused a partial and momentary suspension of life. And the *Quarterly Review* of 1844 convincingly asserted that hungry cadavers and cries from the tomb were frequent occurrences: "There exists among the poor of the metropolitan districts an inordinate dread of premature burial; and very terrible stories are told of bodies being found in coffins in positions that seemed to indicate that a struggle had taken place after the lid had been closed."

Philippe Ariès observes that "the living corpse became a constant theme, from baroque theater to the Gothic novel." It did not remain confined to the world of the imagination, however, but invaded everyday life. A doctor was not exaggerating when he wrote in 1876 that " 'a universal panic' had taken hold of people's minds at the idea of being buried alive, of waking up in the bottom of a grave." And Joseph Taylor exclaimed: "Amongst the many dreadful calamities incident to human nature, none surely is more horrid, nor can the thought be more appalling, than even *in idea* to be buried alive;—the very soul sickens at the thought."[4]

It was therefore inevitable that people took precautions while still alive. They instructed heirs to test their corpses with fire and knife, with burns and slashes on the soles of their feet, and to delay burial for several days. In the late eighteenth century, before the advent of technological advances in the manufacture of coffins, small bells were sometimes attached to the bodies of the dead, to ring at any unexpected movement. In 1845 a medical correspondent told the alcoholic Poe: "I did actually restore to active animation a person who died from excessive drinking of ardent spirits. He was placed in his coffin ready for interment." The debate over apparent death raised the possibility that death could be, at least for a time, an ambiguous condition, and this aroused Poe's serious interest.

In "How to Write a Blackwood Article" (1838) and again in "The Premature Burial," Poe—always obsessed with the ghoulish aspects of contemporary subjects—refers to an anonymous tale, "The Buried Alive," in *Blackwood's Magazine* of October 1821. In the former, Poe satirizes the macabre story at the same time that he imitates it: "There was 'The Dead Alive,' a capital thing!—the record of a gentleman's sensations when entombed before the breath was out of his body— full of taste, terror, sentiment, metaphysics, and erudition. You would have sworn that the writer had been born and brought up in a coffin."

In the horrific "Buried Alive," whose realistic details preyed on the fears of its readers, the first-person narrator suffers not only premature burial but also the depredations of grave robbers and the torments of medical dissection. But, after a knife pierces his breast, he experiences a miraculous return to life:

> I exerted my utmost power of volition to stir myself, but I could not move even an eyelid. . . . The world was then darkened, but I still could hear, and feel, and suffer. . . . I soon after found the undertakers were preparing to habit me in the garments of the grave. . . . The day of interment ar-

rived. . . . The hearse began to move. . . . Dreadful was the
effort I then made to exert the power of action. . . . This is
death, thought I. . . .

I heard a low and undersound in the earth over me, and I
fancied that the worms and reptiles of death were coming. . . . Presently I felt the hands of some dreadful being
working about my throat. They dragged me out of the coffin. . . .

Previous to beginning the dissection, he proposed to try
on me some galvanic experiment—and an apparatus was arranged for that purpose. The first shock vibrated through all
my nerves: they rang and jangled like the strings of a harp.
The students expressed their admiration at the convulsive
effect. The second shock threw my eyes open. . . . But still
I was as dead.[5]

Poe's preoccupation with unnatural states of consciousness inevitably attracted him to this theme. The silence and darkness of the
grave, the enclosure, isolation and helplessness, the fear of imminent
suffocation, of which the still-alive corpse is dimly or acutely aware,
approximates, defines and illuminates an understanding of the physical state of death. As Claudio tells Isabella in *Measure for Measure*,
imagining a corpse still aware of the results of death: "Ay, but to die,
and go we know not where, / To lie in cold obstruction and to rot."

The posthumous heroines of Poe's earlier stories—"Morella," "Ligeia" and "The Fall of the House of Usher"—suffer the early though
temporary entombment of the "dead alive." Arthur Gordon Pym
experiences two symbolic burials—first in a provisioned box to which
a long cord is attached, then by a convulsion of nature that entombs
him alive under caved-in rocks—and he laments the supreme "mental
and bodily distress . . . of living inhumation. The blackness of darkness which envelops the victim, the terrific oppression of lungs, the
stifling fumes from the damp earth . . . [are] not to be tolerated."
Variations of this theme obsessively recur—like the theme of the
double or the death of beautiful women—in "Loss of Breath," "The
Colloquy of Monos and Una," "Berenice," "The Black Cat" and
"The Cask of Amontillado," and find their fullest expression in "The
Premature Burial."

This psychologically acute story begins with an irrefutable premise—"To be buried while alive is, beyond question, the most terrific
of these extremes which has ever fallen to the lot of mere mortality"—

and is prefaced by four case histories that describe body-snatchers and galvanic restoration as well as struggles within the coffin, morbid lethargy and hopeless states of stupor. These lead to living death and to "the clinging to the death garments—the rigid embrace of the narrow house—the blackness of the absolute Night—the silence like a sea that overwhelms—the unseen but palpable presence of the Conqueror Worm."

The narrator, who suffers from cataleptic trances and provides a pathological description of his symptoms, then recounts his own personal experience with these terrors. Obsessed with the case histories and with his fears of premature interment, he takes elaborate precautions to prevent his fears from being realized:

> I had the family vault so remodeled as to admit of being readily opened from within. The slightest pressure upon a long lever that extended far into the tomb would cause the iron portals to fly back. There were arrangements also for the free admission of air and light, and convenient receptacles for food and water, within immediate reach of the coffin intended for my reception. The coffin was warmly and softly padded, and was provided with a lid, fashioned upon the principle of the vault-door, with the addition of springs so contrived that the feeblest movement of the body would be sufficient to set it at liberty. Besides all this, there was suspended from the roof of the tomb, a large bell, the rope of which, it was designed, should extend through a hole in the coffin, and so be fastened to one of the hands of the corpse.

Despite all these well-contrived securities, the narrator seems to fall into a trance while away from home and is buried alive in a distant grave. Finally, he reveals that he merely dreamed of burial while sleeping in the narrow berth of a ship. The tortures endured in his imagination, however, were quite equal to those of a real sepulcher. After the terrifying hallucination, he gives an analytical account of his psychological obsession, which matches the description of his physical symptoms at the beginning of the story. By confronting his fears, by suffering and surviving this cathartic experience, he frees himself from his charnal apprehensions and from his cataleptic disorder, and is able, for the first time, to lead a normal life.

In a Poe-like story, "The Body-Snatcher" (1884), Robert Louis Stevenson satirized grave robbing and the murderers who supplied the corpses. Fettes' pathological duty in the Edinburgh school of medicine is to "receive and divide the various subjects" who (in a nicely ambiguous phrase) "supplied the table" in the anatomy class. This unnatural occupation runs counter to all funerary conventions and leads to the fictional equivalent of Rembrandt's *Anatomy Lesson*. In this grimly ironic story Stevenson suggests the dangers of premature *dis*interment, the thin partition between life and death, the gruesome contrast between the physical and spiritual aspects of man: "To bodies that had been laid in earth, in joyful expectation of a far different awakening, there came that hasty, lamplit, terror-haunted resurrection of the spade and mattock" and the exposure of the body "to uttermost indignities before a class of gaping boys."[6]

Although in his horror stories Poe exploited the gruesome fears of grave robbing, his attitude toward dissection itself was admirably progressive. In "Disinterment," an obscure article of 1840 (not included in Poe's *Complete Works*), he opposed a law that would have made it illegal to dig up the dead for scientific purposes and defended human dissection as "the surest and truest basis, indeed the only sure basis, of all medical knowledge.—A blow struck legally at it, is a vital blow to the best and most important interests of the human family."[7]

III ═══

Poe continued to write criticism at the same time as he was publishing his fiction. In the *Broadway Journal* of January 1845 he reviewed *The Drama of Exile and Other Poems* by Elizabeth Barrett (who had not yet married Robert Browning). Poe admired Barrett almost as much as he did Coleridge and Tennyson, and exclaimed that "her poetic inspiration is the highest—we can conceive nothing more august. Her sense of Art is pure in itself." He later wrote that "with the exception of Tennyson's 'Locksley Hall,' I have never read a poem combining so much of the fiercest passion with so much of the most delicate imagination, as the 'Lady Geraldine's Courtship' of Miss Barrett."

Barrett took the name of her heroine from Coleridge's "Christabel" ("My sire is of a noble line, / And my name is Geraldine"); Poe indicated his high opinion of Barrett's work by imitating its complicated rhyme and rhythm in "The Raven." In "Lady Geraldine's Courtship" Barrett wrote:

With a murmurous stir uncertain, in the air the purple curtain, and Poe echoed this with:

And the silken, sad, uncertain rustling of each purple curtain.

Barrett, when writing to their mutual friend, the English poet Richard Henry Horne, found "The Raven" unaccountably weird and caught a careless error in Poe's erudite review: "There is certainly a power—but ["the Raven"] does not appear to me the natural expression of a sane intellect in whatever mood. . . . Mr. Poe, who attributes the *Oedipus Coloneus* to Aeschylus [instead of to Sophocles] (*vide* review on me), sits somewhat loosely, probably, on his classics." A month later, in May 1845, she had second thoughts, felt she had not been sufficiently grateful and asked Horne to thank Poe for his perceptive notice: "Will you tell him—what is quite the truth—that in my own opinion he has dealt with me most generously, and that I thank him for his candour as for a part of his kindness. Will you tell him also that he has given my father pleasure; which is giving it to *me* more than twice. Also, the review is very ably written, and the reviewer had so obviously and thoroughly *read* my poems as to be a wonder among critics."[8]

When "The Raven" appeared as the title poem of Poe's book in November 1845, he prefaced the volume with a gracious tribute:

> To the Noblest of her Sex—
>   To the author of
> *The Drama of Exile*—
>   To Miss Elizabeth Barrett Barrett,
>   Of England,
> I Dedicate This Volume
> With the most Enthusiastic Admiration
> And with the most Sincere Esteem.

Acknowledging his tribute the following April, Barrett described the unnerving effect "The Raven" had had in England and cunningly praised the rhythm that Poe had stolen from her own poem:

> Receiving a book from you seems to authorize or at least encourage me to try to express what I have long felt before— my sense of the high honour you have done to me in your country and mine, of the dedication of your poems. . . .
>   Your "Raven" has produced a sensation, a "fit horror," here in England. Some of my friends are taken by the fear of

it and some by the music. I hear of persons haunted by the "Nevermore," and one acquaintance of mine who has the misfortune of possessing a "bust of Pallas" never can bear to look at it in the twilight. I think you would like to be told our great poet, Mr. Browning . . . was struck much by the rhythm of that poem.

Barrett expressed her most serious and sincere response to Poe's character and criticism, and to morbid stories like "The Facts in the Case of M. Valdemar," in her letters of 1845 and 1846 to Robert Browning. She was puzzled and amused by what she took to be the strange mixture of praise and hostility in Poe's review of her book: "He wrote a review of me in just that spirit—the two extremes of laudation and reprehension, folded in one another.—You would have thought it had been written by a friend & foe, each stark mad with love & hate, & writing the alternate paragraphs—a most curious production indeed."

Barrett also perceived the element of madness in both Poe's personality and his fiction. Despite the manifest flaws of the stories, she could not quite explain their powerful impact and the conflicting emotions they had inspired:

You shall have his poems with his mesmeric experience & decide whether the outrageous compliment to me or the experiment on M. Valdemar goes furthest to prove him mad. There is poetry in the man, though, now & then, seen between the great gaps of bathos. *Politian* will make you laugh— as the "Raven" made *me* laugh, though with something in it which accounts for the hold it took upon people. . . .

[Mrs. Osgood] tells me that I ought to go to New York only "to see Mr. Poe's wild eyes flash through tears" when he reads my verses.[9]

Poe's symbolic raven—which follows the Romantic tradition of Coleridge's albatross, Shelley's skylark and Keats' nightingale—was influenced not only by Barrett's "Lady Geraldine's Courtship" but also by Grip, the raven, "the embodied spirit of evil," in Dickens' *Barnaby Rudge* (1841). In one scene of that early novel, which describes the destructive events that took place in London in 1780, "Barnaby has been arrested and imprisoned for his part in the Gordon Riots. Grip, the raven, remains faithful to his master. They sit and brood in the semidarkness of the cell, and the sunlight filters through the narrow window, casting the shadow of the bars upon the floor, and Grip's shadow, too, when he chooses to sit upon the window ledge. The whole atmosphere of the prison is somber and chilled. The flames of the fiercely burning city sometimes reflect in Grip's eyes."

Poe had pondered for several years the mournful sound of the long "o" in the key word, "Nevermore," as well as the foreboding central symbol in the poem. He wrote "Lenore" in 1831; he named one kind of benign quiet "no more" in "Silence" (1840); he used the word "evermore" in "The Conqueror Worm" (1843); and "nothing more," "evermore" and "word Lenore" finally evolve into "Nevermore" in "The Raven" (1845). Poe explained the dramatic action of the poem in "The Philosophy of Composition": "A raven, having learned by rote the single word 'Nevermore,' and having escaped from the custody of its owner, is driven at midnight, through the violence of a storm, to seek admission at a window from which a light still gleams—the chamber-window of a student, occupied half in poring over a volume, half in dreaming of a beloved mistress deceased."

An incantatory first-person narrative, with cunning internal rhyme, "The Raven" portrays (like so many of Poe's stories) the monomaniacal obsession of a melancholy man who is hovering on the edge of madness. The marble bust of Pallas represents intellectual wisdom, the plumed, ill-omened raven stands for intuitive truth. As grief dominates hope, the deranged speaker demands a comforting answer that the monodic bird—"emblematical [Poe said] of *Mournful and Never-ending Remembrance*"—cannot provide. All his questions are answered negatively, all consolation refused. As his self-torturing anguish intensifies, the hopeless, suffering narrator is forced to realize that there will be no reunion, after death, with his lost Lenore:

> "Prophet!" said I, "thing of evil!—prophet still, if bird or devil!
> By that heaven that bends above us—by that God we both
>   adore—
> Tell this soul with sorrow laden if, within the distant Aidenn,
> It shall clasp a sainted maiden whom the angels name Lenore—
> Clasp a rare and radiant maiden whom the angels name
>   Lenore."
>   Quoth the Raven "Nevermore."

In his fascinating, highly original but not strictly accurate essay, "The Philosophy of Composition" (1846), Poe gave an idealized and rationalized account of how he conceived, composed and completed his most famous poem. After considering the length, effect to be conveyed, tone, refrain and character of the crucial, oft-repeated word, he chose "Nevermore" and a nonreasoning creature that was capable of speech, combining "a lover lamenting his deceased mistress and a Raven continuously repeating the word 'Nevermore.' " Ignoring his debt to Elizabeth Barrett, Poe claimed that "nothing ever remotely approaching this [stanzaic] combination has ever been attempted." He then explained the masochistic impulse of the narrator, who questions the raven "half in superstition and half in that species of despair which delights in self-torture. . . . He experiences a phrenzied pleasure in so modeling his questions as to receive from the *expected* 'Nevermore' the most delicious because the most intolerable of sorrow."[10]

Poe was delighted with his poem. When he met the Kentucky poet William Ross Wallace on the streets of New York, he expressed his naive and egoistical enthusiasm:

> "Wallace," said Poe, "I have just written the greatest poem that ever was written."
> "Have you?" said Wallace. "That is a fine achievement."
> "Would you like to hear it?" said Poe.
> "Most certainly," said Wallace.
> Thereupon Poe began to read the soon-to-be-famous verses in his best way—which . . . was always an impressive and captivating way. When he had finished it he turned to Wallace for his approval of them—when Wallace said:
> "Poe—they are fine; uncommonly fine."
> "Fine?" said Poe, contemptuously. "Is that all you can say for this poem? I tell you it's the greatest poem that was ever written."

"The Raven," which told a concrete, dramatic story, was an immediate sensation, and Poe awoke—like Byron after the publication of *Childe Harold's Pilgrimage*—to find himself famous. Surpassing the popularity of any previous American poem, "The Raven" was reprinted throughout the country and inspired a great number of imitations and parodies. In contrast to the hermit's existence he had led during his first nine months in New York, Poe frequently appeared, throughout 1845, as a literary lion in fashionable salons.

An extremely effective orator of his own and others' works, Poe—dressed, as always, in mournful raven black—would often be asked to read his poem. Adjusting the atmosphere to suit the mood of his work, "he would turn down the lamps till the room was almost dark," one listener recalled, "then standing in the center of the apartment he would recite those wonderful lines in the most melodious of voices. . . . So marvelous was his power as a reader that the auditors would be afraid to draw breath lest the enchanted spell be broken." Elmira Royster Shelton, the Richmond sweetheart who met Poe again at the end of his life, remembered that his recitals could terrify as well as bewitch his audience: "When Edgar read 'The Raven,' he became so wildly excited that he frightened me, and when I remonstrated with him he replied he could not help it—that it set his brain on fire."[11]

One of his hostesses, the strict and proper schoolteacher and poetess Anne Lynch, emphasized the modest, refined demeanor that complemented the self-destructive side of his personality. Though his life had been impoverished and chaotic, he was perfectly at ease in genteel society: "Poe always had the bearing and manners of a gentleman—interesting in conversation, but not monopolising; polite and engaging, and never, when I saw him, abstracted or dreamy. He was always elegant in his toilet, quiet and unaffected, unpretentious in his manner." Poe had written this celebrated poem, he frankly told Frederick Thomas, to achieve popularity, and had surpassed his wildest expectations: " 'The Raven' has had a great 'run'—but I wrote it for the express purpose of running—just as I did the 'Gold-Bug,' you know. The bird beat the bug, though, all hollow."[12]

IV ═══

Poe's fame was enhanced in February 1845 by the publication of a laudatory biographical essay by James Russell Lowell in *Graham's Magazine*—which had rejected "The Raven." The charming and gentlemanly Lowell, the descendant of a distinguished colonial family, was born in Cambridge and graduated from Harvard. He later became a prominent poet, Longfellow's successor at Harvard, the editor of the *Atlantic Monthly*, and minister to Spain and to England. Though they held very different political views, the Southerner and New Englander had great respect for each other's work. Poe generously called Lowell "a young poet, to whom others than ourselves have assigned a genius of the highest rank. . . . He has given evidence of at least as high a poetical genius as any man in America—if not a loftier genius than any." Lowell, ten years younger than Poe, reciprocated with a flattering comparison: "Your early poems display a maturity which astonished me & I recollect no individual (and I believe I have all the poetry that was ever written) whose early poems were anything like as good. Shelley is nearest, perhaps."

The original idea had been for Poe to write a biographical essay on Lowell. But after the sudden success of "The Raven," Lowell—adopting some of the romantic fantasies that had appeared in Hirst's biographical sketch of 1843—wrote one on Poe. The most serious and substantial essay published on Poe during his lifetime was favorable but not fawning. Lowell censured Poe for the severity of his criticism and said he ignored the moral element in poetry. But he shrewdly concluded that Poe had made a significant contribution to American literature—which was by no means clear at the time—and that his reputation would survive:

> Mr. Poe is at once the most discriminating, philosophical, and fearless critic upon imaginative works who has written in America . . . [but he] seems sometimes to mistake his phial of prussic-acid for his inkstand. . . .
>
> Mr. Poe has two of the prime qualities of genius, a faculty of rigorous yet minute analysis, and a wonderful fecundity of imagination. . . .
>
> As a critic, Mr. Poe was aesthetically deficient. Unerring in his analysis of dictions, meters, and plots, he seemed wanting in the faculty of perceiving the profounder ethics of art. His criticisms are, however, distinguished for scientific precision and coherence of logic. They have the exactness and, at the same time, the coldness of mathematical demonstrations. Yet they stand in strikingly refreshing contrast with the vague generalisms and sharp personalities of the day. If deficient in warmth, they are also without the heat of partisanship. They are especially valuable as illustrating the great truth, too generally overlooked, that analytic power is a subordinate quality of the critic.
>
> On the whole, it may be considered certain that Mr. Poe has attained an individual eminence in our literature, which he will keep. He has given proof of power and originality.[13]

Lowell's essay in *Graham's* was accompanied by a steel engraving of Poe executed by Welch & Walter after a watercolor by A. C. Smith. This portrait depicts Poe with a back-sloping forehead, long nose, thin lips and whiskers running along the jawline to a clean-shaven, pointed chin. His narrow shoulders fall at a grotesque angle and there is an uncharacteristically benign expression on his triangular face. A contemporary justly observed that this peculiar portrait bore no more resemblance to Poe than it did to any other of *Graham's* contributors.

Their first and only meeting, as Lowell passed through New York in late May 1845, failed to match their mutual expectations. "I was very much disappointed," Poe told Chivers, "in his appearance as an intellectual man. He was not half the noble-looking person that I expected to see." The Southern, déclassé, conservative Poe, eager to win Lowell's approbation, may perhaps have been nervous at the prospect of encountering a New England, upper-class, ardent Abolitionist. Maria Clemm, attempting "to remove your wrong impression of my darling Eddie," euphemistically told Lowell that on the day they met "he *was not himself.*" Lowell found Poe's oddly triangular head rather reptilian, and perceptively described, in letters to Poe's early biographers, his strange appearance and behavior:

> He was small; his complexion of what I should call a clammy-white; fine, dark eyes, and fine head, very broad at the temples, but receding sharply from the brows backwards. His manner was rather formal, even pompous. . . .
>
> [I] found him a little tipsy, as if he were recovering from a fit of drunkenness, & with that over-solemnity with which men in such cases try to convince you of their sobriety. I well remember (for it pained me) the anxious expression of his wife.[14]

Poe (like Wyndham Lewis and Ernest Hemingway later on) tended to assert his independence by attacking people who had helped him and kicking down the ladder by which he rose. He was always torn by the desire to cultivate the friendship of influential people and the need to cut them down to size. Lowell's visit left Poe embarrassed and hostile. In the August *Broadway Journal*, he accused Lowell of plagiarizing from Wordsworth. Feeling that he had been stabbed in the back, Lowell made the kind of moral judgment which (Poe felt) was typical of New England writers, and told a mutual friend: "I have made Poe my enemy by doing him a service. . . . Poe, I am afraid, is wholly lacking in that element of manhood which, for want of a better name, we call character." After Poe's death, he added: "Had he possessed conscience in any proportion to his brain, our literature could hardly have had a greater loss."[15]

Lowell took another jab at Poe in his rough satiric poem, *A Fable for Critics* (1848). He commented on the source of "The Raven," on Poe's overelaborate prosody, on the element of fraud and bombast in his works, on his exaggerated emphasis on analysis and reason, and on his unjust accusations against Lowell's friend Longfellow:

> There comes Poe, with his raven, like Barnaby Rudge,
> Three-fifths of him genius and two-fifths sheer fudge;
> Who talks like a book of iambs and pentameters
> In a way to make people of common sense damn meters;
> Who has written some things quite the best of their kind,
> But the heart somehow seems all squeezed out by the mind;
> Who—But hey-day! What's this? Messieurs Matthews and Poe,
> You mustn't fling mud-balls at Longfellow so!

Ignoring the generous fraction of genius, Poe angrily attacked Lowell's poem in the *Southern Literary Messenger* of March 1849. He justified his learned discourse on metrics and, appealing to Southern resentment of Yankee interference in their traditional way of life, gave a final kick by condemning Lowell's politics:

> The *Fable* is essentially "loose"—ill-conceived and feebly executed, as well in detail as in general. . . . [It is] a book at once so ambitious and so feeble—so malevolent in design and so harmless in execution—a work so roughly and clumsily yet so weakly constructed. . . .
>
> So far from Mr. P.'s talking "like a book" on the topic at issue, his chief purpose has been to demonstrate that there exists *no* book on the subject worth talking *about*; and "common sense," after all, has been the basis on which *he* relied, in contradistinction from the *un*common nonsense of Mr. L. and the small pedants. . . .
>
> Mr. Lowell is one of the most rabid Abolition fanatics; and no Southerner who does not wish to be insulted, and at the same time revolted by a bigotry the most obstinately blind and deaf, should ever touch a volume by this author.[16]

Chapter 10

NEW YORK:
THE *BROADWAY JOURNAL,*
1845

I ====

In December 1844, when he was still on good terms with Poe, Lowell wrote to the Nantucket-born Charles Briggs—who had served as a sailor and written the satiric novel *The Adventures of Harry Franco* (1839)—recommending Poe for his new magazine, the *Broadway Journal*. With Lowell's help, Poe's prospects suddenly improved. He became Briggs' assistant editor in January; and on February 21 contracted with the publisher, John Bisco, to become coeditor, to supervise the general conduct of the magazine and to write one page of original work each week. For these duties Poe would be given a third of the profits and paid at the end of each month.

The *Broadway Journal* was more serious and intellectual, and therefore less financially successful, than the *Southern Literary Messenger, Burton's, Graham's* and the *Mirror.* Though it emphasized literary reviews, the magazine also published art, theater and music criticism as well as poetry and political articles. The *Journal's* young clerk, Alexander Crane, remembered Poe as a model of decorum and industry, who had offered sympathetic assistance when the boy fainted from the heat: "Poe was a quiet man about the office, but was uniformly kind and courteous to everyone, and, with congenial company, he would grow cheerful and even playful. I saw him every day, for . . .

office boy and editor were pretty close together. He came to the office
every day about 9 o'clock and worked until 3 or 4 in the afternoon, and
he worked steadily and methodically, too. . . . His act of kindness,
coupled with his uniform gentle greetings, when he entered the office
of a morning, together with frequent personal inquiries and words of
encouragement, made me love and trust my editor."

But another young man's account of Poe's irrational behavior at
the *Broadway Journal* that summer revealed how he could just as often
make enemies by tactless and hostile conduct. In July Richard Henry
Stoddard, a nineteen-year-old would-be poet, submitted his "Ode on
a Grecian Flute" to Poe's magazine. After a few weeks of silence, he
boldly went to the offices of the *Broadway Journal* and then to Poe's
nearby house. Poe received him kindly and promised to print the
poem the following week. "I was struck with his polite manner
toward me, and with the elegance of his appearance," Stoddard later
wrote. "He was slight and pale, I saw, with large, luminous eyes,
and was dressed in black. When I quitted the room I could not but
see Mrs. Poe, who was lying on a bed, apparently asleep. She too
was dressed in black, and was pale and wasted. 'Poor lady,' I thought;
'she is dying of consumption.' "

Eagerly seeking his poem in the pages of the *Broadway Journal* the
following week, Stoddard found instead a printed notice saying that
it had been mislaid. He returned to the office and this time found Poe,
under pressure of work and no doubt weary of being badgered, in a
surly and irascible mood. Poe expressed doubts about the poem's
authenticity, and Stoddard assured him that it was genuine. But when
Poe refused to believe him and, using strong language, threatened to
throw him out of the office, Stoddard "could not understand why
[he] had been subjected to such an indignity."[1] Stoddard later published several versions of this quarrel and dined out on this continuously elaborated anecdote for the rest of his life. He also wrote a
nasty memoir for his edition of Poe's works; and composed a poem,
"Miserrimus" (most miserable), in which he agreed with Griswold
that Poe's "faults were many, his virtues few." This episode shows
how Poe provided his enemies with ample ammunition and how his
minor lapses were used to condemn him after his death.

While working for the *Mirror* and the *Broadway Journal* during 1844
and 1845 Poe wrote many appreciative reviews of works by Milton,
Burns, Lamb, Hazlitt, Hunt, Shelley, Hood, Barrett, Tennyson, Pres-
cott and Lowell. But he continued to use his "tomahawk" to counteract the wholesale and indiscriminate inflation of mediocre works
which then prevailed in American criticism as well as to retaliate for

his own lack of worldly success. One of his favorite expressions was "I have scalped him!" Justifying his savage severity, he would add: "feeble puffing is not my forte. It will do these fellows good to hear the truth, and stimulate them to worthier efforts."

Reviewing William Lord's *Poems* in the *Broadway Journal* of May 1845, Poe used harsh language to vilify the unfortunate hack and concluded with a heavy-handed pun on the author's name: "We are heartily tired of the book, and thoroughly disgusted with the impudence of the parties who have been aiding and abetting in thrusting it before the public. To the poet himself we have only to say—from any further specimens of your stupidity, good Lord deliver us!" Poe also denigrated the stage performance of Sophocles' *Antigone* and called the whole affair "an unintentional burlesque." Rubbing salt in the wounds, he then quoted an absurd letter from the outraged theater manager, who had provided free tickets and expected the play to be praised: "I do not feel *myself* called upon to offer *facilities* to any one, to do me *injury* by *animadversions* evidently marked by ill *feeling*."[2]

The most unsavory episode in Poe's critical career—the "Longfellow War"—took place in March 1845. Poe's relations with Henry Wadsworth Longfellow resembled the destructive pattern of his friendship with Lowell. It began with mutual praise and with Poe's requests for contributions to his magazines. But as his bilious resentment built up, he unjustly accused Longfellow of gross plagiarism, became embroiled in undignified controversy, severed their friendly connection and made yet another powerful enemy.

Writing to Longfellow in May 1841, Poe spoke of "the fervent admiration which [your] genius has inspired in me." When reviewing Griswold's anthology the following year, he called Longfellow "unquestionably the best poet in America." Longfellow responded to Poe's praise with reciprocal admiration. "You are mistaken in supposing that you are not 'favorably known to me,' " he wrote. "On the contrary, all that I have read from your pen has inspired me with a high idea of your power; and I think you are destined to stand among the first romance writers of the country, if such be your aim."[3]

But Poe, eternally overworked and underpaid, resented Longfellow's chair at Harvard and his marriage to a wealthy woman. He also disliked the simplistic and moralistic aspects of his poetry, which was so different from his own, and his secure but inflated reputation. So he began to temper appreciation of Longfellow's verse with charges that his rival was not only "a determined imitator and a dexterous adapter of the ideas of other people," but also an outright literary thief.

In a review of February 1840 Poe had accused Longfellow of plagiarizing "Midnight Mass for the Dying Year" from Tennyson's "Death
of the Old Year." After quoting both poems in full, Poe exclaimed:
"We have no idea of commenting, at any length, upon this plagiarism,
which is too palpable to be mistaken, and which belongs to the most
barbarous class of literary robbery: that class in which, while the
words of the wronged author are avoided, his most intangible, and
therefore his least defensible and least reclaimable property is purloined." But Poe failed to prove his case. Though the poems are
vaguely similar in theme, there is certainly no palpable plagiarism.
The following year, in a letter to the unsympathetic Griswold, Poe
returned to his old obsession by maintaining that Longfellow had
taken "The Beleaguered City" from his own "Haunted Palace"
(which had appeared in "The Fall of the House of Usher"): "the
whole tournure [shape] of the poem is based upon mine, as you will
see at once. Its allegorical conduct, the style of its versification &
expression—all are mine."

Poe also found fault with Longfellow's pervasive and obtrusive
didacticism, which violated his own fundamental aesthetic principles.
In an 1841 review of Longfellow's *Ballads*, Poe defined pure poetry
as "the *Rhythmical Creation of Beauty*" and (echoing Shelley) compared
the ideal quest for Beauty to "the desire of the moth for the star."
And he added, while condemning Longfellow's poetic practice: "If
truth is the highest aim of either Painting or Poesy, then [the realistic
Dutch painter] Jan Steen was a greater artist than [Michel] Angelo,
and Crabbe is a more noble poet than Milton."[4]

The rather tepid "Longfellow War" finally broke out, after this
complicated prelude, when an unknown writer, employing the pseudonym "Outis" (Greek for "No-man," the name Odysseus used when
mocking the blinded Cyclops), objected to Poe's recent attack on
Longfellow's *The Waif*. Imitating Poe's manner, "Outis" farcically
claimed that "The Raven" was based on a sentimental poem "The
Bird of the Dream" in order to show the absurdity of Poe's charges.
Poe responded to this provocation with five successive and fairly
feeble articles, which attempted to stir up controversy and attract
readers to the *Broadway Journal*. Poe claimed (among other things)
that Longfellow's "The Spanish Student" was stolen from his own
Politian. Poe's monomaniacal obsession with plagiarism was undoubtedly connected to his own propensity to steal ideas, plots and phrases
from other authors. His vicious attacks on contemporary writers were
actually an attempt to exonerate himself.

During all this time Longfellow, who disliked all controversy and violent discussion, maintained a dignified silence. Just after Poe died, Longfellow (in contrast to Lowell) magnanimously praised his work and acutely attributed his unbalanced criticism to a deep-rooted grievance and bitter sense of injustice:

> What a melancholy death is that of Mr. Poe—a man so richly endowed with genius! I never knew him personally, but have always entertained a high appreciation of his powers as a prose-writer and a poet. His prose is remarkably vigorous, direct and yet affluent; and his verse has a particular charm of melody, an atmosphere of true poetry about it, which is very winning. The harshness of his criticisms, I have never attributed to anything but the irritation of a sensitive nature, chafed by some indefinite sense of wrong.[5]

In 1850, he bought five copies of Griswold's edition of Poe's works in order to help the destitute Maria Clemm.

II ═══

While editing the *Broadway Journal*, Poe's sudden fame and popularity in New York literary society led to the first of many passionate but platonic encounters with poetic women. They were attracted to his creative genius, his prestige and power in the world of letters, his notorious character and his tragic demeanor. As Lady Caroline Lamb said of the reckless Byron, "he was mad, bad, and dangerous to know." These ladies wanted to domesticate the literary lion, protect Poe from himself, nourish his genius and inspire his art. Margaret Fuller—the dynamic New England author and bluestocking, friend of Hawthorne and editor of the *Dial*—perceptively told Elizabeth Barrett Browning that Poe's love affairs were based on illusion, that he always remained terribly isolated and that he liked to assume a tragic Byronic pose: "several women loved him, but it seemed more with a passionate illusion, which he amused himself by inducing, than with sympathy; I think he really had no friend. I did not know him, though I saw and talked with him often, but he always seemed to me shrouded in an assumed character."

Poe met the first of these ladies, Frances Sargent Osgood, while battling with Longfellow in March 1845. A sentimental Massachusetts poetess of slight talent but great charm, two years younger than Poe and in delicate health, Fanny was a lively, kindly and attractive woman with two children. "In character she is ardent and sensitive," Poe wrote, with considerable warmth, "a worshipper of beauty; universally admired, respected, and beloved. In person she is about the medium height and slender; complexion usually pale; hair black and glossy; eyes a clear, luminous grey, large, and with great capacity for expression." They soon established a sympathetic rapport, and Poe felt she was the only friend who really understood him.

The Osgoods were already separated when Fanny met Poe, and neither her husband nor Poe's wife objected to their intensely emotional friendship. Samuel Osgood painted Poe's portrait in 1845; Virginia Poe, who believed Fanny could save Poe from drink and destruction, sanctioned—like the heroine of "Eleonora"—her affectionate interest. "I maintained a correspondence with Mr. Poe," Fanny later told Griswold, who became Poe's rival for her love, "in accordance with the earnest entreaties of his wife, who imagined that my influence over him had a restraining and beneficial effect."[6]

In that small literary society, several of Poe's lady friends knew each other. On March 16 Fanny aroused the interest, and ambition, of Sarah Helen Whitman—another New England poetess with whom Poe would become passionately involved in 1848—by breathlessly describing how Poe had earned her esteem: "Did you see how beautifully Mr. Edgar Poe spoke of me in his lecture on the Poets—the other night?—He recited a long poem of mine exquisitely, they said—& praised me very highly.—He is called the severest critic of the day—so it was a real compliment—& he did not know me then—I was introduced to him afterwards—& like him very much."

When they were finally introduced by Nathaniel Willis at the Astor House, Fanny was deeply moved by Poe's grave courtesy, appealing character, poetic appearance ("And all should cry, Beware! Beware! / His flashing eyes, his floating hair!"). Her enthusiastic description of their first meeting, written on her deathbed, was included, as a gesture of fairness, in Griswold's hostile memoir of 1850:

There was a peculiar and irresistible charm in the chivalric, graceful, and almost tender reverence with which he invariably approached all women who won his respect. . . .

With his proud and beautiful head erect, his dark eyes flashing with the elective light of feeling and of thought, a peculiar, an inimitable blending of sweetness and hauteur in his expression and manner, he greeted me, calmly, gravely, almost coldly; yet with so marked an earnestness that I could not help being deeply impressed by it.

Thomas Dunn English, observing them together in a literary salon, described them from a cynical and envious point of view. "In the center stands Poe," he wrote, "giving his opinions in a judicial tone and occasionally reciting passages with telling effect. . . . At my feet little Mrs. Osgood, doing the infantile act, is seated on a foot-stool, her face upturned to Poe."[7]

Flattered by Fanny's adoration and influenced, as always, by his personal relations with the author he was reviewing, Poe continued, in later comments, to puff her mediocre verse in precisely the manner he had always condemned. In December 1845 he echoed her epistolary style and rapturously exclaimed: "A happy refinement—an exquisite instinct of the pure—the delicate—the graceful—gives a charm inexpressible to everything which flows from her pen." The following March, he placed her above Elizabeth Barrett Browning: "In fancy . . . in delicacy of taste, in refinement generally, in *naiveté*, in . . . *grace* she is absolutely without a rival, we think, either in our own country or in England." And in April 1849, six months before his own death and a year before Fanny died (like so many of Poe's women) of tuberculosis, he exalted her work and emphasized her future promise: "Mrs. O. has lately evinced a *true* imagination, with a '*movement*' . . . or energy. . . . *Beyond all question the first of American poetesses*:—and yet we must judge her less by what she has done than by what she shows ability to do. A happy refinement—an instinctive sense of the pure and delicate—is one of her most noticeable merits. She *could* accomplish much—*very* much."

An incident that took place during one of Fanny's visits to Poe's home reveals the playful side of his character and Virginia's involvement in his flirtatious performance. It also shows that he sometimes used his influence as a literary critic to win a woman's heart:

> I found him just completing his series of papers entitled "The Literati of New-York." "See," said he, displaying, in laughing triumph, several little rolls of narrow paper (he always wrote thus for the press), "I am going to show you, by the difference of length in these, the different degrees of estimation in which I hold all you literary people. In each of these, one of you is rolled up and fully discussed. Come, Virginia, help me!" And one by one they unfolded them. At last they came to one which seemed interminable. Virginia laughingly ran to one corner of the room with one end and her husband to the opposite with the other. "And whose lengthened sweetness long drawn out is that?" said I. "Hear

her!" he cried, "just as if that little vain heart didn't tell her
it's herself!"[8]

Poe and Fanny also enhanced and etherealized their courtship by
writing self-consciously literary poems to each other. Like many other
writers, Poe extracted the maximum benefit from each of his poems.
The utterly conventional, all-purpose and continuously recycled "To
F——S O——D" was originally written in 1834 for his cousin Elizabeth Herring, addressed the following year to Eliza White (the daughter of the publisher of the *Southern Literary Messenger*) and finally
touched up to praise Fanny's virtues: fidelity, gentleness, grace and
beauty. In a similar fashion, the cost-efficient "To F——" was originally addressed in 1835 "To Mary" and retitled ten years later. In this
poem—whose lines, "And thus thy memory is to me / Like some
enchanted far-off isle," echo the famous opening lines of "To
Helen"—the dreams and memory (rather than the reality) of Fanny
grant him peace and solace, and allow him to escape from a troubled,
stormy world. The third poem, "A Valentine," written on February
14, 1846, was the only one composed expressly for Fanny. In these
verses Poe says that her name (revealed by reading the first letter of
the first line, the second letter of the second line, and so on), often
uttered by poets, is a "synonym for Truth."

While first courting Fanny in the summer of 1845, Poe also met
the sentimental, mystical and highly eccentric Georgia poet, Thomas
Holley Chivers. The author of *Conrad and Eudora* (based, like *Politian*,
on the Kentucky tragedy) was a great admirer of Poe. Persistently
but unsuccessfully, Poe tried to persuade the wealthy Chivers to back
the *Stylus* and the *Broadway Journal*. Chivers sent subscriptions and
small sums, promising much more while protesting his appreciation
of Poe's genius, but evaded all requests for more substantial loans that
might have founded—or saved—Poe's magazines.

Poe's comments on Chivers' work were naturally more temperate
and qualified than his exaltation of Fanny Osgood. In December 1841
he offered a backhanded compliment by stating that even Chivers'
"worst nonsense (and some of it is horrible) has an indefinite charm
of sentiment and melody." Reviewing *The Lost Pleiad* four years later,
he echoed his praise of Lowell and considered " many of the pieces
in the volume before us as possessing merit of a very lofty—if not
the very loftiest order."

In his extensive memoir, Chivers described Poe's attractive appearance and odd way of walking, his lively and reckless character, and
his hunger for praise:

His face was rather oval—tapering in the contour rather suddenly to the chin, which was very classical—and, especially
when he smiled, really handsome. . . .

His form was slender, and by no means prepossessing—
and appeared to me, in walking, to lean a little forward with
a kind of meditative or Grecian bend. . . .

One of the most striking peculiarities of Mr. Poe was, his
perfect *abandon* —boyish indifference—not only in regard to
the opinions of others, but an uncompromising independence
of spirit, which seemed to say that he was obnoxious to the
prejudices of every body. . . . Yet no man living loved the
praises of others better than he did.

Chivers also recalled Poe's not-so-gentle art of making enemies.
Encountering Lewis Gaylord Clark, the influential editor of the *Knickerbocker Magazine*, in the streets of New York, the hostile and confron-
tational Poe demanded to know "what business you had to abuse me
in the last number of your Magazine?" Clark angrily replied: "Why,
by God! Poe! . . . how did I know the Article referred to, was yours?
You had always attached your name to all your articles before, and
how, in Hell, did I know it was yours?" After they parted, Poe spat
out: "A damned coward! by God!"[9]

In February 1847, Chivers echoed John Pendleton Kennedy's earlier
offer of clothes, board and horse, and hospitably invited Poe to reside
permanently on his plantation: "If you will come to the South to live,
I will take care of you as long as you live—although, if ever there
was a perfect mystery on earth, you are one—and one of the most
mysterious." Reluctant to abandon literary life in New York for rural
Georgia, fearful of being bored by Chivers' constant company,
sceptical about his promises and unwilling to become a dependent,
Poe refused the well-intentioned offer. But he also expressed warm
feelings for the would-be patron who had so often disappointed him:
"Except yourself I have never met the man for whom I felt that
intimate *sympathy* (of intellect as well as soul) which is the sole basis
of friendship."[10]

III ===

In June 1845, capitalizing on the tremendous success of "The Raven,"
Wiley & Putnam brought out Poe's *Tales*, his first substantial book
in five years. The twelve reprinted stories (out of the seventy that

Poe had written) were chosen by Wiley & Putnam's editor, Evert Duyckinck. In an enthusiastic account of his generous character, Poe wrote that Duyckinck was "distinguished for the *bonhomie* of his manner, his simplicity, and single-mindedness, his active beneficence, his hatred of wrong done even to any enemy, and especially for an almost Quixotic fidelity to his friends." Duyckinck later justified this tribute by his staunch support of Herman Melville. But Duyckinck's selection was rather strange, for he omitted three stories that Poe had called his best—"Ligeia," "William Wilson" and "The Tell-Tale Heart"—as well as "Eleonora" and "The Masque of the Red Death." These significant omissions, and the inclusion of distinctly minor works like "Lionizing," disrupted the unity of effect that Poe had hoped to achieve in this book.

The reviews, both in America and in England, were generally favorable. Charles Dana, writing in the *Harbinger*, the journal of the Brook Farm Transcendentalists, disliked the stories but (like Elizabeth Barrett) recognized their pathological force: the "tales are clumsily contrived, unnatural, and every way in bad taste. There is still a kind of power in them; it is the power of disease." The London *Spectator* praised the three tales of ratiocination and detection: "To unfold the wonderful, to show that what seems miraculous is amenable to almost mathematical reasoning, is a real delight of Mr. Poe. . . . He exhibits great analytical skill in seizing upon the points of circumstantial evidence and connecting them together. He also has the faculty essential to the story-teller by 'the winter's fire,' who would send the hearers trembling to their beds." And in the New York *Daily Tribune*, the always perceptive Margaret Fuller recognized Poe's great originality and imagination: "The writings of Mr. Poe are a refreshment, for they are the fruit of a genuine observation and experience, combined with an invention . . . a penetration into the causes of things which leads to original but credible results. His narrative proceeds with vigor, his colours are applied with discrimination, and where the effects are fantastic, they are not unmeaningly so."[11] One of Poe's French translators, Émile Forgues, also published a favorable review of the *Tales* in the *Revue des deux mondes*.

When reviewing a book on diseases of the abdomen, Poe wrote that "the pathology of fever in general has been at all times a fruitful subject of discussion." "The Facts in the Case of M. Valdemar," published in December 1845, six months after the *Tales* appeared, is the most extreme—and most effective—example of Poe's use of pathological details to portray what Charles Dana called "the power of disease." In this story, a man dying of "confirmed phthisis" agrees to be hypnotized just as he is about to die in order to determine if death might be arrested by this mesmeric process:

> His face wore a leaden hue; the eyes were utterly lustreless; and the emaciation was so extreme, that the skin had been broken through by the cheek-bones. . . .
> The left lung had been for eighteen months in a semiosseous or cartilaginous state, and was, of course, entirely useless for all purposes of vitality. . . . The lower region [of the right lung] was merely a mass of purulent tubercules, running one into another. Several extensive perforations existed; and, at one point, permanent adhesion to the ribs had taken place.

The morbid details, the uneasy mixture of fascination and repulsion, the hopeless desire for a last-minute reprieve, were not only based on a textbook of tuberculosis, but also on Poe's close, anxious and horrified observation of Virginia, who was inexorably declining toward death.

In the story, after M. Valdemar's life has been artificially prolonged for nearly seven months, his doctors question him about his wishes. In a "gelatinous and glutinous" voice that both expresses and anticipates his final state, and suggests that he has been sentient and suffering, Valdemar puns on the archaic word for "alive" and begs: "For God's sake!—quick!—quick!—put me to sleep—or, quick!—waken me!—quick!—*I say to you that I am dead!*" But when they attempt to defy death and wake him from his long trance, he suddenly disintegrates into a viscous pulp: "his whole frame at once—within the space of a single minute, or less, shrunk—crumbled—absolutely *rotted* away beneath my hands. Upon the bed, before that whole company, there lay a nearly liquid mass of loathsome—of detestable putrescence." It is quite possible that Valdemar's name—which in Spanish means "valley of the sea"—suggests the solid and liquid states of his putrid body.

Poe was surprised to find that the vividly morbid details made this clinical case history, despite his disclaimer, widely reprinted and received as truth. A gullible Boston enthusiast told Poe: "Your account of M. Valdemar's case has been universally copied in this city, and has created a very great sensation. . . . I have not the least doubt of the *possibility* of such a phenomenon." The Virginia poet Philip Pendleton Cooke, whose opinions Poe respected, wrote him an insightful letter, praising his unnerving but convincing details:

["Valdemar" is] the most damnable, vraisemblable, horrible, hair-lifting, shocking, ingenious chapter of fiction that any brain ever conceived, or hand traced. That gelatinous, viscous sound of man's voice! there never was such an idea before. . . .

I have always found some remarkable thing in your stories to haunt me long after reading them. The *teeth* in Berenice— the changing eyes of Morella—that red & glaring crack in the House of Usher—the pores of the deck in the MS. Found in a Bottle—the visible drops falling into the goblet in Ligeia.[12]

IV ═══

In October 1845—while still enjoying the popularity of "The Raven," his *Tales* and his numerous public lectures—Poe was invited to read an original poem before the Boston Lyceum for a fee of fifty dollars. James Russell Lowell had secured this invitation, despite Poe's recent attack on him. Poe had mixed feelings about Boston, which had played a significant role in his life. He had been born in poverty in Boston while his parents had been on tour; had fled there from Richmond after quarreling with John Allan; had enlisted and served his first months in the army there; had published his first volume, "By a Bostonian," there; he had criticized the integrity of one of their most prominent authors in the "Longfellow War"; and had for many years conducted a running battle in the literary reviews with the puritanical and provincial New England Transcendentalists. Boston, for Poe, was enemy territory. But he entered it with reckless audacity.

Poe, the perennial outsider, despised Boston's literary coteries and its mutual admiration (analogous to the complacent superiority of the Bloomsbury Group in the modern era), and considered it "the chief habitation, in this country, of literary hucksters and phrase mongers." More significantly, he disliked what he called the pretenders and sophists among the Transcendentalists; and condemned—as a rationalist—their fuzzy thought and lack of intellectual rigor. And he deplored the pernicious Germanic, especially Kantian influence that had filtered through their prophet, Thomas Carlyle. "Emerson belongs to a class of gentlemen," Poe wrote of their leading thinker, "with whom we have no patience whatever—the mystics for mysticism's sake. . . . His present *rôle* seems to be the out-Carlyling of Carlyle." Despite favorable reviews of his works by Margaret Fuller (a Boston bluestocking who later married an Italian marquis), he attacked her as a grossly dishonest and detestable old maid. Poe called the Transcendentalists "Frogpondians," after the actual Frog Pond on the Boston Common, and urged Frederick Thomas to puncture their inflated egos: "They are getting worse and worse, and pretend not to be aware that there *are* any literary people out of Boston."[13] In his own savage fashion, Poe was determined to attack their complacency and teach them a salutary lesson, to express his enmity and remind them of his own existence.

The program at the Odeon Theater on the evening of October 16 began with an oration by the Massachusetts politician and statesman Caleb Cushing, who had recently returned from a diplomatic mission to China and had opened their ports to American trade. Cushing droned on for two and a half hours, completely exhausting the interest and attention of the audience. Poe then began his reading with some prefatory remarks condemning didacticism in poetry (a specialty of Longfellow). But instead of delivering the original work he had promised for this occasion, he read his most turgid and opaque poem, "Al Aaraaf." The weary, baffled audience inevitably began to file out of the auditorium, and only a few remained to hear Poe conclude the program by reciting "The Raven."

Two firsthand accounts of the evening—one hostile, one sympathetic—have survived. Cornelia Walter, the vitriolic editor of the *Boston Evening Transcript,* resented Poe's criticism of the Boston literati and wrote a series of articles ridiculing the obfuscation of his public performance:

> The poet immediately arose; but, if he uttered poesy in the first instance, it was certainly of a most prosaic order. The audience listened in amazement to a singularly didactic exordium, and finally commenced the noisy expedient of removing from the hall, and this long before they had discovered the style of the measure, or whether it was rhythm or blank verse. . . . The audience had now thinned so rapidly and made so much commotion in their departure that we lost the beauties of the composition. . . . Another small poem succeeded. This was "The Raven"—a composition probably better appreciated by its author than by his auditory.

By contrast, Thomas Wentworth Higginson—who was then a Harvard student and later became a Unitarian minister, a Civil War colonel and the editor of Emily Dickinson's poems—was impressed and enchanted by Poe's somewhat menacing appearance and by his unusual way of reading the long, early poem:

> I distinctly recall his face, with its ample forehead, brilliant eyes, and narrowness of nose and chin; an essentially ideal face, not noble, yet anything but coarse; with the look of oversensitiveness which when uncontrolled may prove more debasing than coarseness. It was a face to rivet one's attention in any crowd; yet a face that no one would feel safe in loving. . . .
>
> When introduced he stood with a sort of shrinking before the audience and then began in a thin, tremulous, hardly musical voice, an apology for his poem. . . . The audience looked thoroughly mystified. . . . In walking back to Cambridge my comrades and I felt that we had been under the spell of some wizard.

Poe not only insulted his Boston audience by reading an unintelligible poem, but also bragged about it to his hosts. Though his sponsors were confused and disappointed, they treated Poe with great courtesy and gave him a good supper. But, excited by the occasion and the free-flowing champagne, he boasted that he had deliberately hoaxed them with a poem he had written when he was only ten years old!

Provoked by Cornelia Walter's merciless attacks, Poe replied in the *Broadway Journal* of November 1 and 22, 1845. In editorials on "Boston and the Bostonians," Poe gave his own arrogant but witty account of this bizarre episode. He described the opening comments that advocated pure poetry, boasted about his use of a wretched old poem, mocked the ignorant audience (or what was left of it) for swallowing his ruse and finally expressed his delight in perpetrating an insult:

> On arising, we were most cordially received. We occupied some fifteen minutes with an apology for not "delivering," as is usual in such cases, a didactic poem: a didactic poem, in our opinion, being precisely no poem at all. After some farther words—still of apology—for the "indefiniteness" and "general imbecility" of what we had to offer—all so unworthy of a *Bostonian* audience—we commenced, and, with many interruptions of applause, concluded. . . .
>
> It could scarcely be supposed that we would put ourselves to the trouble of composing for the Bostonians anything in the shape of an *original* poem. We did not. We had a poem

(of about 500 lines) lying by us—one quite as good as new. . . . *That* we gave them—it was the best we had—for the price—and it *did* answer remarkably well. . . .

We do not, ourselves, think the poem a remarkably good one:—it is not sufficiently transcendental. Still it did well enough for the Boston audience—who evinced characteristic discrimination in understanding, and especially applauding, all those knotty passages which we ourselves have not yet been able to understand. . . .

Were the question demanded of us—"What is the most exquisite of sublunary pleasures?" we should reply . . . "kicking up a bobbery." . . .

If we cared a fig for their wrath we should not first have insulted them to their teeth, and then subjected to their tender mercies a volume of our Poems.[14]

This undignified episode revealed Poe's difficult relationship with his popular audience. Ambivalent about Boston and about literary readings that put him on exhibition like a showman, he was characteristically hypersensitive and nervous in that hostile atmosphere. Instead of making the best of the situation by reading a poem that would have impressed his listeners, he chose to expose their pretentiousness and to retaliate with rudeness for their low fee and lack of appreciation.

V ═══

The success of Poe's *Tales* in June encouraged Wiley & Putnam to bring out *The Raven and Other Poems*, in a similar format, in November. This edition, dedicated to Elizabeth Barrett, contained twelve (out of the thirty) poems—including "The Haunted Palace," "The Conqueror Worm," "Silence," "Dream-Land" and "The Raven"— that had been written since the youthful volume of 1831, and several others that had been extensively revised.

Poe's brief Preface was curiously confessional and defensive. He deprecated his own work (as if to forestall hostile critics) and expressed regret that he had had to give up writing poetry for financial reasons: "I think nothing in this volume of much value to the public, or very creditable to myself. Events not to be controlled have prevented me from making, at any time, any serious effort in what, under happier circumstances, would have been the field of my choice." As he told Chivers, serious poetry would always be unsalable in America. Poe also justified reprinting his eleven youthful poems—including "Tamerlane" and "Al Aaraaf"—in order to prove the originality of his poetry: "Private reasons—some of which have reference to the sin of plagiarism, and others to the date of Tennyson's first poems—have induced me, after some hesitation, to re-publish these, the crude companions of my earliest boyhood. They are printed verbatim—without alteration from the original edition—the date of which is too remote to be judiciously acknowledged."[15]

A heavily ironic review in the Brook Farm Phalanx noted Poe's extreme provocation of influential authors and critics as well as his tendency toward megalomania: "Edgar Poe, acting the constabulary part of a spy in detecting plagiarisms in favorite authors [i.e., Longfellow], insulting a Boston audience, inditing coarse editorials against respectable editresses [Cornelia Walter], and getting singed himself in the meanwhile, is nothing less [in poems like "Al Aaraaf"] than the hero of a grand mystic conflict of the elements." Despite his self-deprecating Preface and the hostility he had aroused, The Raven received many favorable reviews. His old employer and friend, Nathaniel Willis, called Poe "unquestionably, a man of genius" and urged him to abandon destructive criticism and to concentrate on his poetry. Thomas Dunn English agreed that Poe's "power to conceive and execute the [poetic] effect, betokens the highest genius" and pronounced him "the first poet of his school." The South Carolina novelist William Gilmore Simms, despite having suffered rough handling in Poe's reviews, expressed his high opinion of Poe's imaginative powers and characterized him as "a fantastic and a mystic—a man of dreamy mood and wandering fancies." Noting the difficulty of Poe's work, Simms said "his scheme of poem requires that his reader shall surrender himself to influences of pure imagination." And Margaret Fuller, in an unusually fair-minded review, wrote that Poe's poems "breathe a passionate sadness, relieved sometimes by touches very lovely and tender."[16]

While involved in the fiasco with the Boston Lyceum and in the publication of The Raven, Poe had serious trouble at the Broadway Journal. At this magazine, he compulsively repeated—rather than avoided—the personal conflicts, financial problems and alcoholic disasters that had destroyed his career at the Southern Literary Messenger, at Burton's and at Graham's. His coeditor Charles Briggs was at first extremely enthusiastic about Poe, despite his notorious reputation, and in January 1845 wrote his friend James Russell Lowell: "I like Poe exceedingly well; Mr. Griswold has told me shocking bad stories about him, which his whole demeanor contradicts." In March Briggs mentioned Poe's manic obsession with plagiarism, but still thought him a very decent fellow. By late June, however, disillusioned by Poe's all-too-frequent drinking bouts, he threatened "to haul down Poe's name" from the *Broadway Journal* and told Lowell that "he has latterly got into his old habits and I fear will injure himself irretrievably." On June 26, aware of the imminent danger, Poe alluded to his intense depression and to Virginia's chronic illness, and asked the faithful Evert Duyckinck if he would buy him out before he was fired: "I am still dreadfully unwell and fear that I shall be very seriously ill. Some matters of domestic affliction have also happened which deprive me of what little energy I have left—and I have resolved to give up the *B. Journal* and retire to the country for six months, or perhaps a year, as the sole means of recruiting my health and spirits. Is it not possible that yourself or [your friend and colleague, Cornelius] Matthews might give me a trifle for my interest in the paper?"[17]

In July Briggs, thoroughly fed up with Poe, attempted to buy out the publisher, John Bisco, and obtain complete control of the magazine. When Bisco unexpectedly demanded more than the agreed price, Briggs withdrew. Poe and Bisco missed an issue, and then limped on without Briggs. As a colleague told Griswold, mentioning Poe's young assistant: "The *Broadway Journal* stopped for a week to let Briggs step ashore with his luggage, & they are now getting up steam to drive ahead under Captains Poe & [Henry] Watson." In August Briggs, outmaneuvered by the man he had intended to sack, fired a parting shot at Poe. Criticizing his selfishness and mean-mindedness in an angry and morally superior letter to Lowell, Briggs wrote: "I have never met a person so utterly deficient of high motive. He cannot conceive of anybody's doing anything, except for his own personal advantage. . . . It is too absurd for belief, but he really thinks that Longfellow owes his fame mainly to the ideas which he borrowed from Poe's writings in the *Southern Literary Messenger*. . . . The Bible, he says, is all rigmarole. . . . He knows that I am possessed of the secret of his real character and he no doubt hates me for it."

By October Bisco, who had tried to make a go of it, abandoned all hope of earning any money from the barely solvent *Broadway Journal*, and sold it to Poe for only fifty dollars. But Poe, who did not even have this trivial amount, gave Bisco a note, endorsed by the famous editor of the New York *Daily Tribune*, Horace Greeley, which Poe never repaid and which Greeley still had in 1868. In this circuitous fashion, Poe finally achieved his lifelong ambition. On October 24, 1845 he became sole editor and proprietor of the *Broadway Journal*.

In late November a young poet, Walt Whitman, stopped by the

office and found the new owner, who had recently published his poem, somewhat dissipated but still personable and appealing: "Poe was very cordial, in a quiet way, appeared well in person, dress, etc. I have a distinct and pleasing remembrance of his looks, voice, manner and matter; very kindly and human, but subdued, perhaps a little jaded."[18]

Unfortunately, Poe had no business ability and could not do for his own magazine what he had previously done for the *Messenger*, for *Burton's* and for *Graham's*. The death of the *Broadway Journal*, only two months later, was one of the saddest events of his sad life. His two main problems, as always, concerned money and drink. As Poe's fame increased, his income declined. He had received twenty free copies for *Tales of the Grotesque and Arabesque* in 1840, and his publishers had refused to bring out a second collection on the same terms. Though "The Gold-Bug" sold over 300,000 copies, he earned no more than the hundred-dollar prize money. He was paid only nine dollars for the endlessly reprinted "Raven." He never found another job after 1845 and, without a regular place to publish, wrote—and earned—less. His total—and thoroughly inadequate—income would be $288 in 1847, $166 in 1848 and $275 in 1849. One scholar has reliably calculated that Poe's "lifetime earnings as a professional author, editor and lecturer" amounted to only $6,200.

Since Poe had absolutely no money of his own, and had borrowed money to buy the *Broadway Journal*, he tried desperately to extract cash from his friends in order to keep the magazine alive. He first turned to Chivers, who considered Poe one of the greatest men who ever lived. Despite protestations of his sincere interest in Poe's welfare and happiness, Chivers did *not* send the fifty dollars that was needed to pay for paper, printing and postage. Poe's pleas were also refused by George Poe, John Pendleton Kennedy and Evert Duyckinck, but he managed to get money (which was not repaid) from Neilson Poe, Griswold and the poet Fitz-Greene Halleck, to whom he wrote, with a touch of paranoia: "There is a deliberate attempt now being made to involve me in ruin, by destroying The Broadway Journal. I could easily frustrate them, but for my total want of money. . . . I venture to appeal to you. The sum I need is $100."

In November Poe persuaded Thomas Lane, a customs official and friend of Thomas Dunn English, to buy half interest in the magazine and to pay all recent debts up to forty dollars. But this was merely a temporary solution. It was not surprising, as Poe told Duyckinck in mid-November, that the intense strain made him feel (like so many of his fictional characters) on the verge of a mental breakdown: "[I am] dreadfully sick and depressed, but still myself. I seem to have just awakened from some horrible dream, in which all was confusion, and suffering. . . . I really believe that I have been mad—but indeed I have had abundant reason to be so. . . . My object in writing you this note [and how his friends must have dreaded such notes] is (once again) to beg your aid. Of course I need not say to you that my most urgent trouble is the want of ready money."[19]

In order to escape from this intolerable agony, Poe began to drink heavily. He had abstained from alcohol for more than eighteen months, but as early as May 1845 became frequently incapacitated. In June, unable to write a new poem for a literary celebration at New York University, he became intoxicated, was carried home in wretched condition and stayed in bed for an entire week. The following month, after borrowing money from Briggs and complaining of ill-treatment, he indulged in yet another drunken spree.

In September Chivers, a strict Prohibitionist, gave him a fiery sermon on the evils of drink. He had seen both the noble and bestial sides of Poe's character—reflected in so many of his fictional doubles—and exclaimed: "Why should a Man whom God, by nature, has endowed with such transcendent abilities, so degrade himself into the veriest automaton as to be moved only by the poisonous steam of Hell-fire?" When Chivers carried the stupefied Poe back home one summer evening (as Thomas Dunn English had done in 1839), Maria Clemm became hysterical. She believed that Poe had been driven nearly insane by Virginia's illness, which she euphemistically called "bronchitis," and that his drinking was hastening Virginia's death:

> Oh! Dr. C! how I have prayed that my poor Eddy might not get in this way while you were here! But I knew, when he went away from here this morning, that he would not return in his right senses! Oh! I do believe that the poor boy is deranged! His wife is now at the point of death with Bronchitis, and cannot bear to see him! Oh! my poor Virginia! She cannot live long! She is wasting away, day by day—for the Doctors can do her no good. But if they could, seeing this continually in poor Eddy, would kill her—for she dotes upon him! Oh! She is devoted to him! She fairly adores him! But would to God that she had died before she had ever seen him! My poor child! He has been in bed here for a whole week with nothing in the world the matter with him—only lying

here pretending to be sick, in order to avoid delivering the
Poem promised, before one of the Literary Societies of the
City: now he is in this deranged state again.

In late December Poe, with no one to cover for him, went off on
another alcoholic binge, leaving one and a half empty columns just
as the *Broadway Journal* was about to go to press. His partner, Thomas
Lane, tried for several days to restrain Poe and make him sober. But
since the magazine continued to lose readers and money, and Poe
remained out of control, Lane decided to end publication. On January
3, 1846 Poe published his jaunty but transparently tragic valediction:
"Unexpected engagements demanding my whole attention, and the
objects being fulfilled, so far as regards myself personally, for which
the *Broadway Journal* was established, I now, as its Editor, bid farewell—as cordially to foes as to friends."[20]

Eighteen forty-five was Poe's *annus mirabilis*. He achieved instant
fame after publishing "The Raven"; his portrait and laudatory biography by Lowell appeared in *Graham's*; after long months as a recluse, he
entered fashionable New York literary society; he met Fanny Osgood,
Thomas Holley Chivers, James Russell Lowell and Walt Whitman;
he brought out his *Tales* and *The Raven and Other Poems*, and was
called in print "a genius"; the first French review of his work appeared
in Paris; and he seemed to achieve his lifelong dream by becoming
editor and eventually sole proprietor of the *Broadway Journal*. All this,
for anyone but Poe, would have led to wealth, security and permanent
fame.

But Poe's "tomahawk" reviews, the attacks on Longfellow and his
Lyceum reading brought a great deal of adverse publicity. His poverty
and alcoholism (each exacerbating the other) led to the loss of the
magazine that might eventually have made him rich. After losing the
Broadway Journal, his last editorial position, Poe wrote less and less,
and wandered, as George Graham remarked, "from publisher to publisher, with his fine, print-like manuscript, scrupulously clean and
neatly rolled, [finding] no market for his brain."

During the final years of his life, as his physical and mental health
began to break down, the rootless outcast drifted, like a ship cut loose
from its moorings, through a series of personal disasters. Though
tormented, as Graham wrote, by "those morbid feelings which a life
of poverty and disappointment is so apt to engender in the heart of
man—the sense of having been ill-used, misunderstood, and put aside
by men of far less ability," Poe's idealistic pride in the glory of
literature remained as steadfast as ever. In 1809 Poe's impoverished

father, David, had written to his cousin George Poe, Jr., insisting that he had "joined a [theatrical] profession which I then thought and now think an honorable one." And in November 1845, when his world was collapsing all around him, David's impoverished son, Edgar, wrote to George's son, courageously insisting that he too had achieved an honorable place in the literary profession: "I have perseveringly struggled, against a thousand difficulties, and have succeeded, although not in making money, still in attaining a position in the world of Letters, of which, under the circumstances, I have no reason to be ashamed."[21]

Chapter 11

FORDHAM AND
LITERARY QUARRELS,
1846-1847

I ═══

Embittered by the failure of the *Broadway Journal*, by his persistent poverty and poor health, and by the serious illness of his wife, Poe became involved in 1846 in the two most damaging quarrels of his career: first with the minor Southern poet Mrs. Elizabeth Ellet; then with his former friend, the Philadelphia doctor and writer Thomas Dunn English. These scandalous episodes, following soon after his outrageous provocation at the Boston Lyceum, had a disastrous effect on Poe's personal and literary reputation. The retaliatory attacks by his enemies publicized his drunkenness and stigmatized his behavior as insane.

Encouraged by Poe's faint praise of her work—"Some of [the poems] have merit. Some we think unworthy of the talents which their author has undoubtedly displayed"—Ellet fell in love with, pursued and wrote emotional letters to the charismatic author of "The Raven." Pleased and perhaps amused by her devotion, Poe dutifully showed her letters to his invalid wife. Ellet was intensely jealous of his friendship with her rival, Fanny Osgood, a more attractive woman and more talented poet, whose relations with Poe had been encouraged by Virginia. According to one account, Ellet was enraged to find Osgood and Virginia Poe (who was excited by the attention her husband had aroused) reading one of her letters aloud and laughing hysterically.

While visiting Poe's house at 85 Amity Street in late January 1846, Ellet discovered a letter from Osgood to Poe which she considered extremely indiscreet. This officious guardian of morality then persuaded Osgood (who, fearful of her reputation, allowed herself to be manipulated) to ask Poe to return all her letters. Ellet sent two of her friends—Margaret Fuller and the prominent New York hostess Anne Lynch—to convey this request. Intensely irritated by their meddling in his personal affairs, Poe brusquely handed over Osgood's correspondence and sharply remarked that Ellet should have been more concerned about her *own* letters to him. As soon as Fuller and Lynch departed with their bounty, Poe gathered Ellet's compromising letters and left them at her house.

Indignant at Poe's remark, unhappy about losing his friendship and anxious to redeem her reputation, Ellet retaliated by sending her pugnacious brother, Colonel William Lummis, to confront Poe and demand her letters. Since he had already returned them, Poe could not hand them over. But the implacable Lummis, doubting Poe's word and bent on revenge, threatened to kill him if he did not immediately produce the letters. Unnerved by Lummis, Poe went to the house of Thomas Dunn English and asked to borrow a pistol to defend himself. English not only refused to help, but also provoked Poe by doubting that he had ever possessed any letters from Ellet. He urged Poe to save his skin by retracting his base charges against her.

Outraged at being called a liar, Poe punched English and started a fistfight. (He had also fought with John Hewitt in Baltimore in 1833.) Thomas Lane, his short-lived partner on the sinking *Broadway Journal*, happened to be present. He reported that Poe, though badly beaten, had kept up a brave front: "Poe was drunk and getting the worst of it, and was finally forced partly under the sofa, only his face being out. English was punching Poe's face, and at every blow a seal ring on his finger cut Poe. [He] hastened to separate them, when Poe cried out, 'Let him alone. I've got him just where I want him.' " Poe's version of this incident, retailed to Henry Hirst a few months later, contradicted Lane's account and portrayed himself as the triumphant fighter: "I gave E. a flogging which he will remember to the day of his death—and, luckily, in the presence of witnesses. He thinks to avenge himself by lies—but I shall be a match for him by means of simple truth."[1]

After the fight Poe took to his bed and made things even worse by instructing his doctor to deliver an inept apology to Ellet. In this letter Poe denied having commented that her correspondence was improper and claimed that if he had ever made such a wild accusation, he must have been suffering from temporary insanity. This absurd alibi was taken up by his enemies, who publicized this remark and reinforced his reputation as a madman. As early as April 1846, the St. Louis *Reveille* reported: "A rumor is in circulation in New York, to the effect that Mr. Edgar A. Poe, the poet and author, has been deranged, and his friends are about to place him under the charge of Dr. Brigham, of the Insane Retreat at Utica."

This self-destructive episode ruined Poe's reputation as a chivalrous Southern gentleman and his social standing with the New York blue-stockings (Anne Lynch struck his name from her guest list). It aroused the eternal enmity of Elizabeth Ellet and alienated the affection of Fanny Osgood. Poe later took a parting shot by depicting Ellet as a mercenary *Hausfrau*, insisting that her articles "have the disadvantage of *looking* as if hashed up for just so much money as they will bring" and describing her as "short and much inclined to *embonpoint*." But she continued to torment him for rejecting her love until the end of his life.

In the fall of 1848 Poe bitterly characterized Ellet to Sarah Helen Whitman (whom he was then courting) as "the most malignant and pertinacious of all fiends—a woman whose loathsome love I could do nothing but repel with scorn—[who] slanders me, in private society, without my knowledge and thus with impunity." He warned Whitman to beware of Ellet's maneuvers, diabolically designed to sabotage his relations with other women, and claimed that she had hastened the death of his hypersensitive wife: "Her whole study, throughout life, has been the gratification of her malignity by such means as any other human being would rather die than adopt. You will be sure to receive anonymous letters so skillfully contrived as to deceive the most sagacious. You will be called on, possibly, by persons whom you never heard of, but whom she has instigated to call & vilify me. . . . My poor Virginia was continually tortured (although not deceived) by her anonymous letters, and on her death-bed declared that Mrs. E. had been her murderer."[2]

In July 1846 Samuel Osgood, provoked by Ellet's malicious gossip, told her she would have to apologize formally to his wife or be hauled into court for libel. Frightened by this threat, she sent Fanny a letter, retracting her defamations, placing all the blame on Poe and Virginia, and—even now—obdurately attempting to justify her own behavior. Referring to Fanny's letter, which she had seen in Poe's house, Ellet maintained: "Had you seen the fearful paragraphs which Mrs. Poe first repeated and afterwards pointed out—which haunted me night and day like a terrifying spectre—you would not wonder I regarded you as I did."

After Poe's death, Fanny also attempted to exonerate herself from blame in this bizarre and rather sordid incident. She told Griswold how Poe had been relentlessly pursued by a group of poetical ladies, both before and after Virginia's death: "It is too cruel that I, the only one of these literary women who did not seek his acquaintance—for Mrs. Ellet asked an introduction to him and followed him every-where, Miss Lynch begged me to bring him there and called upon him at his lodgings, Mrs. Whitman besieged him with valentines and letters long before he wrote or took any notice of her, and all others wrote poetry and letters to him,—it is too cruel that I should be singled out after his death as the only victim to suffer from the slanders of his mother."[3] (Griswold's intense hostility to Maria Clemm was provoked by her attacks on Fanny Osgood.) Fanny later realized that Ellet—not Poe—had been at fault, and warmly praised Poe, in a long letter to Griswold, written at the end of her life.

II ===

In February 1846, distancing himself from the fashionable literary salons, Poe moved uptown from 85 Amity Street to Turtle Bay, where 47th Street meets the East River. He still retained some of the athletic ability of his youth, and liked to borrow a rowboat from his landlord and pull himself out to Blackwell's (now Welfare) Island for "a voyage of discovery and exploration" and an afternoon swim.

In May—when Poe was suffering from an unspecified feverish illness—he moved once again and took a year's lease on a snug little workman's cottage in the rural village of Fordham. It was fourteen miles north of the city and was served by a train on the Harlem Railroad that ran every four hours. The modest two-story frame building (which still exists as a Poe museum) stood at the top of Fordham hill at 192nd Street and Kingsbridge Road. There was a sitting room, a small bedroom and a kitchen on the first floor, Poe's study and Maria's bedroom in the unheated attic. The parlor floor was covered with matting, and had a round table, light chairs and, hanging on the wall, a French print of a young girl. The cottage had a small front porch where Poe kept caged songbirds and was surrounded by lilacs and cherry trees. The extreme simplicity of the cottage provided a strong contrast to the elaborate and opulent decor described in Poe's essay "The Philosophy of Furniture."

Poe was a moderate eater, preferred simple foods and was fond of fruit, buttermilk and curds. A typical breakfast consisted of a pretzel, a crust of bread with salt herring and two cups of strong coffee. His favorite walk, during his Fordham years, was to High Bridge, where granite arches, one hundred and fifty feet high, supported the aqueduct that carried water across the Harlem River.

The cottage was adjacent to the Jesuit priests of St. John's College (later Fordham University). Poe soon met the sympathetic Father Edward Doucet, who allowed him to use their excellent library. Father Doucet, like so many others, was struck by Poe's aristocratic demeanor and acute intelligence: "In bearing and countenance, he was extremely refined. His features were somewhat sharp and very thoughtful. He was well informed on all matters. I always thought he was a gentleman by nature and instinct." Poe returned the compliment by observing that the Jesuits "smoked, drank, and played cards like gentlemen, and never said a word about religion."

The peaceful setting, the charming countryside, the simple life and the stimulation of the Catholic priests seemed to inspire Poe's writing. One visitor to Fordham recalled that Poe composed his works with his favorite tortoiseshell cat (who had replaced the black Catterina) wrapped around his shoulders. And Fanny Osgood was impressed by the way he captured, "in an exquisitely clear chirography and with almost superhuman swiftness, the lightning thoughts . . . as they flashed through his wonderful and ever wakeful brain."[4]

From May, the month he moved to Fordham, until October 1846 Poe published in *Godey's Lady's Book* his controversial essays on "The Literati of New York City." Many of these literary figures had welcomed Poe as a celebrity after the publication of "The Raven," and then excluded him after his scandalous behavior with Elizabeth Ellet. These articles contained gossipy personal descriptions as well as Poe's all-too-frank opinions of their literary merit.

Louis Godey—a plump, kindly, simplehearted man—was neither an able writer nor a good literary critic. But he paid competitive fees. His popular journal, directed to a vast female audience, published many elegant fashion plates and thousands of extremely moral and sentimental tales. Poe disparaged it as "a milliner's magazine." Alluding to its editorial harem, he wittily remarked that "Godey keeps almost as many ladies in his pay as the Grand Turk."

Poe naturally knew many of the people he anatomized in the New York Literati—Nathaniel Willis, Charles Briggs, Evert Duyckinck,

Thomas Dunn English, Margaret Fuller, Fanny Osgood and Lewis Gaylord Clark—and his criticism of that compact society was, as always, intensely personal. Godey, therefore, was confidently able to announce: "We are much mistaken if these papers of Mr. Poe do not raise some commotion in the literary emporium." Though most of the essays were unexpectedly mild and gentle, Poe's fierce and implacable side erupted often enough to create a tremendous sensation. All copies of the high-circulation magazine were quickly sold out, and Poe did for *Godey's* what he had been unable to do for the faltering *Broadway Journal*.

In a gratuitous aside about the popular *Knickerbocker* magazine, Poe took a typically savage cut at an old adversary and described it as "tottering, month after month, through even that dense region of unmitigated and unmitigable fog—that dreary realm of outer darkness, of utter and inconceivable dunderheadism . . . in the august person of one Lewis Gaylord Clark." The ironic mode and the clear allusion to Alexander Pope's *Dunciad* revealed Poe's desire to scourge modern folly. Many readers bought the magazine, as they had bought *The Dunciad*, to see their contemporaries cut up and abused. And like Pope's enemies, Poe's potential victims, fearful that they might be subject to his satire, made vigorous attempts to placate him. In 1846 Poe could justly claim, as Pope had claimed a century earlier: "Yes, I am proud; I must be proud to see / Men not afraid of God, afraid of me."[5]

Poe's attacks on Clark and other influential figures inevitably provoked retaliation, and several writers seized this opportunity to settle old scores. Charles Briggs, Poe's coeditor at the *Broadway Journal*, had been intensely irritated by Poe's drinking bouts, had threatened to fire him, had unsuccessfully attempted to take control of the magazine and had condemned his character in a series of letters to Lowell. Briggs also exposed a radical flaw in Poe's character and agreed with Lowell that "One of the strange parts of his strange nature was to entertain a spirit of revenge towards all who did him a service. . . . He rarely, or never, failed to malign those who befriended him."

In his Literati essay on Briggs, a frequent contributor to Clark's *Knickerbocker*, Poe disparaged his work, his person and his character. "The author of *Harry Franco*," Poe wrote, "carries the simplicity of Smollett to insipidity, and his picturesque low-life is made to degenerate into sheer vulgarity." Poe also stated that his "personal appearance is not prepossessing" and (with good reason) that Briggs was "very apt to irritate and annoy."

On May 26 the New York *Evening Mirror*, edited by Hiram Fuller, who had been business manager of the paper when Poe had been assistant editor in 1844, published a scathing attack by Briggs. Disgusted by Poe's articles, Briggs repeated the rumor (started by Poe himself) that he had been confined to an Insane Retreat and claimed that students at Columbia University had "made a pilgrimage to Bloomingdale to gaze upon the asylum where Mr. Poe was reported to be confined." Briggs maintained that Poe's mental and physical illness, his defects of character and his desperate poverty, all rendered him quite unsuitable to evaluate his fellow authors. He concluded by reducing Poe's height by six inches, and (like Alexander Pope's enemies) by wittily mocking Poe's physical appearance and grotesquely exaggerating his personal idiosyncrasies:

> His face is pale and rather thin; eyes gray, watery and always dull; nose rather prominent, pointed and sharp; nostrils wide; hair thin and cropped short; mouth not very well chiseled, nor very sweet; his tongue shows itself unpleasantly when he speaks earnestly, and seems too large for his mouth . . . chin narrow and pointed, which gives his head, upon the whole, a balloonish appearance . . . his walk is quick and jerking, sometimes waving . . . his hands are singularly small, resembling bird claws.[6]

In a sympathetic letter of July 1846, the South Carolina novelist William Gilmore Simms sagely advised Poe to avoid the irritation, distraction and scandal of public quarrels: "These broils do you no good—vex your temper, destroy your peace of mind, and hurt your reputation." But Poe ignored this well-intentioned advice, and seemed to thrive on the publicity and excitement of unrestrained literary combat. Despite his keen sensitivity to criticism, he was eager to stir up controversy and willing to risk public mockery. He believed it was always desirable to know his enemies and the nature of their attacks, and to use them to *enhance* his reputation. "You should regard," he wrote in 1844, imitating the disdainful superiority of Swift and Pope, "the animosities of small men—of the literary animalculae (who have their uses, beyond doubt)—as so many tokens of your ascent—or, rather, as so many stepping stones to your ambition. I have never yet been able to make up my mind whether I regard as the higher compliment, the approbation of a man of honor and talent, or the abuse of an ass or a blackguard."

After his attacks on the Literati had provoked Briggs' caustic reply, Poe returned to the arena by attacking another enemy, Thomas Dunn

English. But English's volcanic vituperation, more abusive than that of Briggs, led to a protracted libel suit. Though Poe and English had occasionally been on good terms after their first meeting in 1839, their antithetical personalities soon led to frequent clashes and mutual contempt. During his trip to Washington in March 1843 to seek a place in the Tyler administration, Poe became drunk and publicly mocked the physical appearance of English, who was extremely sensitive to ridicule and unwilling to endure it. A powerful supporter of the Tyler faction in Philadelphia, English may have used his influence to keep Poe out of the soft job in the Custom House.

He certainly retaliated by portraying Poe as a drunken literary critic in his temperance novel, *The Doom of the Drinker* (1843). In this work, English rated Poe's criticism superior to his creative work, accused him of plagiarism (always a sensitive point) and maligned his battered character:

> Next to him sat a pale, gentlemanly looking personage, with a quick, piercing, restless eye, and a very broad and peculiarly shaped forehead. He would occasionally under the excitement of the wine utter some brilliant jests. . . . He was an extraordinary being, one of the few who arise among us with a power to steal judiciously. He was a writer of tact, which is of a higher order than ordinary genius. But he was better known as a critic, than as any thing else. His fine analytical powers, together with his bitter and apparently candid style, made him the terror of dunces and the evil spirit of wealthy blockheads, who create books without possessing brains. He made no ceremony though, in appropriating the ideas of others when it suited his turn; and as a man, was the very incarnation of treachery and falsehood.[7]

Though they were superficially reconciled in 1845, when English reviewed Poe's *Tales* and *The Raven*, they soon lapsed into habitual hostility. The immediate provocation for Poe's attack on English in the Literati essays had been his refusal to assist Poe during his quarrel with Ellet and their brief but degrading fistfight. On June 20, after returning the now-familiar accusation of plagiarism, Poe counterattacked English (who had graduated from the University of Pennsylvania Medical School) for his lack of education and ignorance of grammar. Poe also maladroitly claimed that he was not personally acquainted with English, the man who had punched his face with a seal ring: "No spectacle can be more pitiable than that of a man

without the commonest school education busying himself in attempting to instruct mankind on topics of polite literature. The absurdity in such cases does not lie merely in the ignorance displayed by
the would-be instructor, but in the transparency of the shifts by which
he endeavors to keep this ignorance concealed."

English's prompt "Reply to Mr. Poe," which appeared only three
days later in the New York *Morning Telegraph* as well as in Hiram
Fuller's *Evening Mirror*, was more damaging than Poe's inaccurate
assertions. English maintained that he had known Poe through a long
succession of disreputable acts and proceeded to recount them. He
rejected Poe's absurd statement that they were unacquainted, said
Poe had fraudulently obtained money from English for the *Broadway
Journal* and that Edward Thomas, a New York merchant, had accused
Poe of committing forgery. English emphasized Poe's chronic alcoholism, mocked his ridiculous performance at the Boston Lyceum
and gave his own version of the quarrel with Elizabeth Ellet. He
exposed Poe's pretension to knowledge and habitual plagiarism, and
concluded with a resounding condemnation of his character:

> That he does not know me is not a matter of wonder. The
> severe treatment he received at my hands for brutal and das-
> tardly conduct, rendered it necessary for him, if possible, to
> forget my existence. . . .
>
> He said that though his friendship was of little service, his
> enmity might be dangerous. To this I rejoined that I shunned
> his friendship and despised his enmity. . . .
>
> He told me that he had vilified a certain well known and
> esteemed authoress, of the South, then on a visit to New
> York; that he had accused her of having written letters to him
> which compromised her reputation; and that her brother (her
> husband being absent) had threatened his life unless he pro-
> duced the letters he named. . . . He then begged the loan of
> a pistol to defend himself against attack. . . . He sent a letter
> to the brother of the lady he had so vilely slandered, denying
> all recollection of having made any charges of the kind al-
> leged, and stating that, if he had made them, he was laboring
> under a fit of insanity to which he was periodically sub-
> ject. . . .
>
> His review of my style and manner is only amusing when
> contrasted with his former laudation, almost to sycophancy,
> of my works. . . . He professes to know every language and

to be proficient in every art and science under the sun—when
. . . he is ignorant of all. . . .

He mistakes coarse abuse for polished invective, and vulgar
insinuation for sly satire. He is not alone thoroughly unprincipled, base and depraved, but silly, vain and ignorant.[8]

Battered but still feisty, Poe replied to English's reply two and a
half weeks later in the Philadelphia *Spirit of the Times*, where he
had published occasional pieces since 1840. Poe accused English of
cowardice by failing to appear for a duel and, citing as witness the
man who had paid him to prepare *The Conchologist's First Book*,
claimed victory for himself in their fistfight: "[I] bestowed upon Mr.
E. the 'fisticuffing' of which he speaks, and [was] dragged from
his prostrate and rascally carcase by Professor Thomas Wyatt, who,
perhaps with good reason, had fears for the vagabond's life."

Clearly getting the worst of the mud-slinging battle, Poe now
descended to feeble puns on the name "Thomas Done Brown," to
name-calling and to scurrilous language. He called English "a blackguard of the lowest order—[and] it would be a silly truism, if not
unpardonable flattery, to term him either a coward or a liar." He
noted "the family resemblance between the whole visage of Mr.
English and that of the best-looking but most unprincipled of Mr.
Barnum's baboons." Finally, he asked: "Does he really conceive that
there exists a deeper depth of either moral or physical degradation
than that of the hog-puddles in which he has wallowed from his
infancy . . . among the dock-loafers and wharf-rats, his cronies?"

Poe also seriously defended himself in earnest against the charge
of intoxication by poignantly explaining that "the irregularities so
profoundly lamented were the *effect* of a terrible evil [Virginia's illness]
rather than its cause." And—having secured the denial of the merchant Edward Thomas—he defiantly rejected the base accusations of
fraud and forgery: "The charges are criminal, and with the aid of *The
Mirror* I can have them investigated before a criminal tribunal."[9]

English—having been called a baboon, a hog and a rat—still
thirsted for Poe's blood. His "Reply to Mr. Poe's Rejoinder," which
appeared in the New York *Evening Mirror* three days later, on July
13, emphasized Poe's moral defects and confidently challenged him
to bring the case to court. Poe was "profligate in habits and depraved
in mind. . . . It is not a week since he was intoxicated in the streets
of New York. . . . His attempt to excuse his drunkenness and meanness on the ground of insanity [is absurd]. . . . Let him institute a

suit, if he dare, and I pledge myself to make my charges good by the most ample and satisfactory evidence."

A formidable adversary, English renewed his assault on Poe in his satirical novel, *1844*, which was serialized in the *Evening Mirror* in September and October. He portrayed Poe as Marmaduke Hammerhead—the harsh critic of Longfellow, the friend of Monsieur Dupin and the author of "The Black Crow"—"Him with the broad, low, receding and deformed forehead, and peculiar expression of conceit on his face." In one chapter English stated: "He never gets drunk more than five days out of the seven; tells the truth sometimes by mistake; has moral courage sufficient to flog his wife." In another he described, with clinical precision and frightening accuracy, the alcoholic deterioration and ravaged condition that would destroy Poe at the very end of his life: "The bloated face—blood-shotten eyes—trembling figure and attenuated frame, showed how rapidly he was sinking into a drunkard's grave; and the drivelling smile, and meaningless nonsense he constantly uttered, showed the approaching wreck of his fine abilities. [Delirium tremens], under which he had nearly sunk, [was rapidly followed] by confirmed insanity, or rather mono-mania."

During his war with the Literati in 1846 Poe had lost most of his friends and had been attacked by his enemies. He was ill, dreadfully poor and deeply depressed. But on July 23 he took the offensive, challenged English's assertions, carried out his threat and sued him for libel. Poe's suit was based on the charges that Poe had committed forgery and that he had taken money from English under false pretenses. English had gone too far—even at a time when the law allowed the most outrageous public defamations—and for the accusation that he had committed criminal acts, Poe asked damages of five thousand dollars.

Though English had told the editors of the *Evening Mirror* that every word he had written was true and had promised to appear for the defense in court, he fled to Washington shortly before the case finally came to trial on February 17, 1847. Despite the frequent attacks on Poe and the intense animosity he had aroused, the defense, with English in hiding, could not produce any witnesses to testify against Poe's character. Poe's lawyer, however, called three effective witnesses. Edward Thomas swore (as Poe knew he would) that the charge of forgery was false. And two others, Judge Mordecai Noah and Freeman Hunt, testified that they never "heard anything against him except that he is occasionally addicted to intoxication."[10] Though this revelation hurt Poe, he easily won his suit and was publicly vindicated. He was awarded $225.06 for damages and $101.42 for costs. With this money, he immediately bought a new black suit for himself and some "sumptuous delicacies,"·a new rag carpet, a large table and a silver-plated urn for the cottage at Fordham.

III ===

In November 1846, while engaged in his bitter quarrel with English, Poe published in *Godey's Lady's Book* one of his finest stories, "The Cask of Amontillado." This tale—in which the narrator Montresor lures his enemy Fortunato into the catacombs with an offer of rare Sherry and then buries him alive—may have expressed his own desire for revenge against the troublesome enemies who had also insulted and injured him.

Poe's choice of Amontillado as the death bait was significant. There were five kinds of Spanish Sherry from the region of Jerez to choose from: Fino, Manzanilla, Amoroso, Oloroso and Amontillado. "The most Sherry-like of all Sherries," named after the mountain village of Montilla, "Amontillado starts out as Fino, but then the *flor* (the floating layer of yeasts) mysteriously subsides and stops feeding on the wine. The result is a darker-colored, more complex Sherry with a pronounced nutty taste. In its natural state it is quite dry, but it is usually sweetened for export." This quintessential Sherry is used ironically in the story. Its "dryness" contrasts to the damp catacombs, its sweetness to Fortunato's bitter experiences and its mountain name to the depths of the crypt where he is buried. And the victim, like the Sherry, is carefully sealed up in a deep cave.

"The Black-Cat" and "The Tell-Tale Heart" also describe the confession of an insane and malignant murderer. But in "The Cask of Amontillado," Montresor commits the perfect crime—avenging himself with impunity—and manages to escape detection. He encounters Fortunato, drunk and in motley during the carnival season. He tempts him by appealing to his vanity, inciting his jealousy of a rival connoisseur, and soliciting his expert opinion about whether or not the rare Sherry is genuine.

They pause on their way through the pernicious catacombs, where Fortunato (like Virginia Poe) cannot stop coughing, drink some Medoc (a claret) as the bells of his costume jingle, and toast the pile of bones that surround them. Montresor meaningfully tells his victim that his Latin family motto means "No one insults me with impunity." After polishing off a flagon of Graves (another Bordeaux wine),

Fortunato makes a secret Masonic sign and Montresor miraculously produces a symbolic trowel from beneath his cape.

When they reach the most remote end of the crypt, Montresor quickly chains up his besotted, unsuspecting victim and begins to wall him in with the aid of his Masonic trowel. The increasingly constricted enclosure recalls the claustrophobic cell of the prisoner in "The Pit and the Pendulum." As the eleven tiers (which may correspond to the hieratic ranks of the Freemasons) of the homemade wall rise, Fortunato's low moaning cries turn to shrill screams. And as he loses energy and gasps for air, the furious vibrations of his chain turn into a feeble jingling of his bells. Not only is he buried alive (like so many of Poe's fictional characters), but he is never permitted to taste the precious Amontillado. An expert in revenge as well as in wine, Montresor now has two *"tresors"* in his catacombs—his Sherry and his victim—and has used the former to lure the latter to his doom. Though he expresses his hatred and is coldly methodical in exacting his revenge, Montresor is still, half a century later, tormented by a guilty conscience ("My heart grew sick"), which mars his premeditated and otherwise perfect revenge.

Even a story as taut and brilliant as "The Cask of Amontillado" did not alleviate Poe's poverty. Disturbed by his lawsuit and his wife's illness, and writing much less than usual, he continued to beg his friends for money and to reproach them for seeking repayment of his debts. Nathaniel Willis and a few others offered to help him out of his misery. On December 30, 1846 some well-intentioned friends publicized Virginia's grave illness and his own humiliating poverty in an announcement that must have reminded Poe, in the most painful way, of a similar notice that had foreshadowed the death of his mother. In November 1811 the Richmond *Enquirer* had stated: "On this night, Mrs. Poe, lingering on the bed of disease and surrounded by her children, asks your assistance and *asks it perhaps for the last time.*" Thirty-five years later, the New York *Morning Express* announced:

ILLNESS OF EDGAR A. POE.—We regret to learn that this gentleman and his wife are both dangerously ill with the consumption, and that the hand of misfortune lies heavily upon their temporal affairs. We are sorry to mention the fact that they are so far reduced as to be barely able to obtain the necessaries of life. That is, indeed, a hard lot, and we do hope that the friends and admirers of Mr. Poe will come promptly to his assistance in his bitterest hour of need.

This notice was immediately picked up by the Philadelphia *Saturday Evening Post*, which maliciously asserted, during his bitterest controversy, that Virginia was in a hopeless condition (as his mother had been) and that Poe had no friends: "It is said that Edgar A. Poe is lying dangerously ill with brain fever, and that his wife is in the last stages of consumption—they are without money and without friends."[11]

IV ═══

Virginia was all the more precious to Poe because she was so fragile, so delicate and so doomed. In the only surviving letter to his wife, written on June 12, 1846, Poe alluded to the optimistic *sursum corda* of Lamentations 3:41, expressed his dependence upon Virginia and urged her to hold on to her life for *his* sake, if not for her own: "Keep up your heart in all hopefulness, and trust yet a little longer.—In my last great disappointment [the loss of the *Broadway Journal*], I should have lost my courage *but for you*—my little darling wife you are my *greatest* and *only* stimulus now to battle with this uncongenial, unsatisfactory and ungrateful life."

Toward the end of the year a friend reported that Virginia was wasting away, but "wearing on her beautiful countenance the smile of resignation, and the warm, even cheerful look with which she ever greeted her friends." But her attempt to remain sanguine and her struggle to survive could not halt the inexorable progress of her disease. In the course of her pulmonary tuberculosis, bacilli had infected and damaged her lungs. As her body tissues were attacked and destroyed, tubercules formed that contained bacteria and caused lesions in her lungs. Her wasting disease slowly progressed from lesions, necrosis and cavities to erosion of the blood vessels and bleeding into the lungs. She was always in danger of a massive hemorrhage, which would drown her in her own blood.

Virginia had the classic symptoms of tuberculosis: irregular appetite, facial pallor, flushed cheeks, unstable pulse, night sweats, high fever, sudden chills, shortness of breath, chest pains, severe coughing and spitting of blood. Each day, as the microscopic organisms gnawed through her tissue and destroyed a bit more of her lung, she found it increasingly difficult to breathe. The consumptive Katherine Mansfield described this agonizing condition toward the end of her short life: "I cough and cough and at each breath a dragging, boiling, bubbling sound is heard. I feel that my whole chest is boiling. I sip water, spit, sip, spit. I feel I must break my heart. And I can't expand my chest [because the lung tissue has been destroyed]; it's as though the chest had collapsed. Life is—getting a new breath: nothing else counts."[12]

During the terminal phase of Virginia's illness, when she was constantly struggling for breath, Mary Gove became a frequent visitor to the depressing household. In the Literati essays Poe categorized the mystical minor novelist and crankish health reformer as "a Mesmerist, a Swedenborgian, a phrenologist, a homeopathist, a disciple of [the water-cure charlatan] Priessnitz" and, he wittily added, "what more I am not prepared to say." Despite her crackpot ideas, he was fond of the sympathetic, kindhearted lady, whom he went on to describe as "rather below the medium height, somewhat thin, with dark hair and keen, intelligent black eyes. She converses well and with enthusiasm. In many respects a very interesting woman"—and one who (like Fanny Osgood) could provide much more intellectual stimulation than Maria or Virginia.

Mary Gove has left the most vivid and moving accounts of the shabby-genteel Poes at the very nadir of their existence. During her first visit in 1846, she thought the careworn Maria looked much older than her fifty-six years and contrasted the "snow-white hair" of the large mother to the "raven hair" of her tiny, ethereal daughter:

> On this occasion I was introduced to the young wife of the poet, and to the mother, then more than sixty years of age. She was a tall, dignified old lady, with a most ladylike manner, and her black dress, though old and much worn, looked really elegant on her. She wore a widow's cap of the genuine pattern, and it suited exquisitely with her snow-white hair. Her features were large, and corresponded with her stature, and it seemed strange how such a stalwart and queenly woman could be the mother of her almost petite daughter. Mrs. Poe looked very young; she had large black eyes, and a pearly whiteness of complexion, which was a perfect pallor. Her pale face, her brilliant eyes, and her raven hair gave her an unearthly look. One felt that she was almost a disrobed [pure] spirit, and when she coughed it was made certain that she was rapidly passing away. The mother seemed hale and strong, and appeared to be a sort of universal Providence for her strange children.

The cottage had an air of taste and gentility that must have

been lent to it by the presence of its inmates. So neat, so
poor, so unfurnished, and yet so charming a dwelling I never
saw. . . . There were pretty presentation copies of books on
the little shelves, and the Brownings had posts of honour on
the stand.

Once the cold weather set in, Virginia's health deteriorated alarm-
ingly and their heartrending poverty became much worse. Tormented
by the alternating chills and fever of tuberculosis, she had neither
blankets nor fire to warm her frail body. Only their cat (who sat on
Poe's shoulders when he composed his works) and his thick gray
overcoat, with long buttonholes, wide lapels and a high collar—which
Poe had saved from his army service and wore in the "Whitman"
daguerreotype of November 1848—covered the dying Virginia. Only
the human warmth and emotional strength of her husband and mother
kept her alive:

> The autumn came and Mrs. Poe sank rapidly in consumption,
> and I saw her in her bed chamber. Everything here was so
> neat, so purely clean, so scant and poverty-stricken, that I
> saw the sufferer with such a heartache as the poor feel for the
> poor. There was no clothing on the bed, which was only
> straw, but a snow white spread and sheets. The weather was
> cold, and the sick lady had the dreadful chills that accompany
> the hectic fever of consumption. She lay on the straw bed,
> wrapped in her husband's great-coat, with a large tortoise-
> shell cat on her bosom. The wonderful cat seemed conscious
> of her great usefulness. The coat and the cat were the sufferer's
> only means of warmth, except as her husband held her hands,
> and her mother her feet.
>
> Mrs. Clemm was passionately fond of her daughter, and
> her distress on account of her illness and poverty and misery,
> was dreadful to see.

Unable to provide proper food, housing and warmth, the lack of
which undoubtedly hastened the death of his beloved wife, Poe felt
humiliated, tormented and racked with guilt. Regretting, in a discussion with Mary Gove, that he had been forced to compromise his
critical standards in order to earn a bit of money, he turned fiercely
upon her, his fine eyes flashing, and cried: "Would you blame a man
for not allowing his sick wife to starve?"[13]
Virginia's final thoughts were of her husband. Knowing he would

be devastated by her death, she begged her mother, on her deathbed, to look after him: "Darling, darling Muddy, you will console and take care of my poor Eddie—you will *never, never* leave him? Promise me, my dear Muddy, and then I can die in peace." At the very end Virginia was so weak that she could only speak with her large black eyes. On January 29, 1847, Poe told Marie Louise Shew, who had been nursing his wife: "My poor Virginia still lives, although failing fast and now suffering much pain." The following day, five years after she had ruptured a blood vessel while singing, Poe's twenty-four-year-old wife died, at the same age and of the same disease as his mother and brother.

A few hours later, when Poe realized he had no image of Virginia, he commissioned a watercolor portrait. "The hair, neatly coifed, is painted brown, while the sweeping eyebrows are of a slightly darker shade. The complexion is pale, the eyes are hazel colored, and the entire image has been crisply silhouetted by an opaque black background. The vacant expression of the face and listless tilt of the head betray the grim circumstances under which the portrait was painted." Yet Virginia had not, apparently, suffered from the characteristic emaciation of tuberculosis. Her youth is revealed in her surprisingly full face and in the hint of a double chin. "The white, shawllike garment encircling her shoulders," as the critic Michael Deas observes, "is almost certainly made of the 'fine linen sheets' in which Virginia was laid to rest on February 2, 1847."[14]

V

The physical and psychological strain of Virginia's illness radically changed Poe's attitude toward his tubercular fictional heroines. In a passage deleted from his early story "Metzengerstein" (1832), Poe, following the Romantic death wish expressed in Keats' "Ode to a Nightingale," idealized his sick heroines and *wanted* them to die. It would be more glorious, he felt, to avoid "the weariness, the fever and the fret," to "cease upon the midnight with no pain" and to become extinguished in the full blaze of youth: "How *could* she die?— and of consumption! But it is a path I have prayed to follow. I would wish all I love to perish of that gentle disease. How glorious! to depart in the heyday of the young blood—the heart all passion—the imagination all fire—amid the remembrances of happier days—in the fall of the year—and so be buried up forever in the gorgeous autumn leaves!" By December 1844, however, when Virginia was seriously ill, he completely rejected this "gentle" Romantic transformation and adopted, in *Marginalia*, a more harshly realistic attitude: "Who ever *really* saw anything but horror in the smile of the dead? We so earnestly *desire* to fancy it 'sweet'—this is the source of the mistake."

Poe's health also began to deteriorate. Just as Egaeus, as Berenice moved toward "positive dissolution," experienced a sympathetic intensification of his own mysterious disease—it "grew rapidly upon me . . . hourly and momently gaining vigor, and at length obtaining over me the most incomprehensible ascendency"—so Poe's chronic fever of 1846 intensified after Virginia's death. He was unable to appear in court for his libel suit, two weeks later, on February 17, and suffered a rapid physical decline during the last years of his life.

Marie Shew—the daughter of a doctor, who nursed Poe during his physical and mental breakdown—attributed his irregular heartbeat to a vaguely diagnosed "lesion of the brain" rather than to a cardiac condition. This diagnosis (which seemed to account for his confinement in an Insane Retreat) was frequently cited, after his death, to explain Poe's bizarre behavior. Shew also said that alcohol instantly turned Poe into a madman, and despaired of his life: "At best, when Mr. Poe was well, his pulse beat only ten regular beats, after which it suspended, or intermitted (as doctors say). I decided that in his best health he had lesion of one side of the brain, and as he could not bear stimulants or tonics, without producing insanity, I did not feel much hope that he could be raised up from brain fever brought on by extreme suffering of mind and body." In "The Beloved Physician," his fragmentary poem of 1847, Poe mentioned his alarming physical condition and paid tribute to the devoted care of Marie Shew:

> The pulse beats ten and intermits.
> God nerve the soul that ne'er forgets
> In calm or storm, by night or day,
> Its steady toil, its loyalty.[15]

In the months following Virginia's death, Poe also fell into a deep depression that was not far from insanity. One friend recalled that "the loss of his wife was a sad blow to him. He did not seem to care, after she was gone, whether he lived an hour, a day, a week or a year; she was his all." Attempting to forget his anguished memories, he often eluded Maria's watchful eye and became terribly drunk. In a revealing letter of January 1848, Poe explained how Virginia's continuous oscillation between relapse and remission forced him to *imagine* her death. This fearful anticipation tormented his nervous sensibility,

and drove him to madness and to drink. Stressing a crucial but frequently ignored point, he said that he drank to escape this madness,
and that he was finally released from the intolerable wavering between
optimism and despondency—though not from grief and guilt—by
the long-expected death of his wife:

> Each time I felt all the agonies of her death—and at each
> accession of the disorder [tuberculosis] I loved her more dearly
> & clung to her life with more desperate pertinacity. But I am
> constitutionally sensitive—nervous in a very unusual degree.
> I became insane, with long intervals of horrible sanity. During
> these fits of absolute unconsciousness I drank, God only
> knows how often or how much. As a matter of course my
> enemies referred the insanity to the drink rather than the drink
> to the insanity. I had indeed, nearly abandoned all hope of a
> permanent cure when I found one in the *death* of my wife.
> This I can & do endure as becomes a man—it was the horrible
> never-ending oscillation between hope & despair which I
> could *not* longer have endured without the total loss of reason.
> In the death of what was my life, then, I receive a new but—
> oh God! how melancholy an existence.

During the emotional turmoil following Virginia's death, Poe
turned once again to Fanny Osgood for sustenance, solace and hope.
Since he was now free to marry Fanny, their relations became less
poetic and more intensely personal. But Fanny, though separated
from her husband, was still married. The respectable matron could
not possibly respond to Poe's wild, theatrical, partly insincere, possibly drunken and finally embarrassing pleas to abandon her two daughters and run off with him. According to her brother-in-law, the
Reverend Henry Harrington, who lived in Albany:

> While I had been gone Poe had sought an interview with her
> alone in my parlor, and in passionate terms had besought
> her to elope with him. She described his attitudes as well as
> reported his words—how he went down on his knee and
> clasped his hands, and pleaded for her consent; how she met
> him with mingled ridicule and reproof, appealing to his better
> nature, and striving to stimulate a resolution to abandon his
> vicious courses; and how finally he took his leave, baffled and
> humiliated, if not ashamed.[16]

A final, bitterly ironic twist to this episode was that Rufus Griswold, who had succeeded Poe as editor of *Graham's* in 1842, replaced Poe, six years later, in the affections of Fanny Osgood. In 1845, three years after the death of his first wife, Griswold had married a woman from Charleston. But this second marriage was unhappy and he was later granted a divorce. He had an epileptic fit in the autumn of 1848 and told his publisher, James Fields, of his pathetic state: "I am in a terrible condition, physically and mentally. I do not know what the end will be. . . . I am exhausted—betwixt life and death—and heaven and hell."

At precisely this time, Griswold also fell under the spell of Fanny Osgood and used his literary influence to win her affection: "Eagerly he took over the pleasant occupation of escorting her to the salons of the city [from which Poe had been excluded], criticizing her poems, and acting as her personal sponsor. . . . Griswold made no secret of his admiration for Fanny," and told Fields: "She is in all things the most admirable woman I ever knew." The following year Fanny warmly responded by dedicating her *Poems* to Griswold "as a souvenir of admiration for his genius, of regard for his generous character, and of gratitude for his valuable literary counsels."[17] Fanny's trust in her admirer may have helped persuade Poe to make Griswold his literary executor.

Though Virginia's death reduced Poe's medical and domestic expenses, his own illness and inability to work left him permanently impoverished. In February 1847 he apologized to Horace Greeley for his inability to repay the money Greeley had advanced to save the *Broadway Journal*. But—always sensitive to any slur that impugned his honor as a gentleman—he claimed, with considerable exaggeration, that the charge that he did not pay his debts "is *horribly* false— I have a hundred times left myself destitute of bread for myself and my family that I might discharge debts."

Poe—who had once defended himself by asking Mary Gove: "Would you blame a man for not allowing a sick wife to starve?"— also had to compromise *after* her death in order to stave off his own hunger. During 1847 Sarah Anna Lewis, an ambitious but mediocre poetess, became a frequent visitor to the Fordham cottage. Late that year, when Poe was financially *in extremis*, Lewis paid Poe one hundred dollars to write a favorable review of her book. Poe dutifully kept his side of the bargain by hyperbolically praising her person as well as her poetry and by attributing to her a melancholy persona that was similar to his own:

In character, Mrs. Lewis is everything which can be thought desirable in woman—generous, sensitive, impulsive; enthusiastic in her admiration of Beauty and Virtue, but ardent in her scorn of wrong. The predominant trait of her disposition, as before hinted, is a certain romantic sensibility, bordering upon melancholy, or even gloom. In person, she is distinguished by the grace and dignity of her form, and the nobility of her manner. She has auburn hair, naturally curling, and expressive eyes of dark hazel. . . .

All critical opinion must agree in assigning her a high, if not the very highest rank among the poetesses of her land. . . .

She is quite accomplished, a good classical scholar, young, and beautiful in face and form.[18]

Marie Shew, who resented Sarah Lewis, described in a letter of uncharacteristic astringency Poe's feeling of humiliation and his subsequent rejection of that far-from-beautiful lady: "She paid Mrs. Clemm in advance, when they were needy, and poor Poe *had to notice* her writings, and praise them. He expressed to me the *great mortification it was to him* and I hated the fat gaudily dressed woman whom I often found sitting in Mrs. Clemm's little kitchen, waiting to see the man of genius, who had rushed out to escape her." Poe later expressed his true feelings by confessing: "She is really commonplace, but her husband was kind to me." Henry James' comment on Hawthorne, in similarly degrading circumstances, applies equally to Poe: "There is . . . something really touching in the sight of a delicate and superior genius obliged to concern himself with such paltry undertakings."[19]

Poe's degrading poverty—and his friends' embarrassed response to it—was vividly described by Mary Gove. While walking with friends in the countryside in November 1847 Poe, who had been a great jumper in his youth, proposed a game of leaping and outdistanced all the other literary men who accompanied him. "But alas!," wrote Mary Gove,

> his gaiters [shoes with elastic insertions], long worn and carefully kept, were both burst in the grand leap that made him victor. . . . I pitied Poe more now. I was certain he had no other shoes, boots, or gaiters. Who amongst us could offer him money to buy a new pair? . . . When we reached the cottage, I think all felt that we must not go in, to see the shoeless unfortunate sitting or standing in our midst.

Then Maria Clemm, awkwardly seizing what she thought was an opportune moment, exclaimed that if the editor who had witnessed this fiasco would only accept the poem Poe had just written, "Eddie can have a pair of shoes."

The new poem, "Ulalume"—whose title suggests ululation, or wailing—was published in December 1847 and is one of Poe's finest works. Inspired by the death of Virginia, this tormented tribute was an appropriate memorial to his wife. When Poe read this work aloud to guests before publication, "he remarked that he feared that it might not be intelligible to us, as it was scarcely clear to himself."[20] But its meaning is not quite as obscure as he suggested. The poem concerns the conflict between the soul (symbolized by Psyche), who urges him to remain loyal to the memory of his dead wife, and sensual love (represented by Astarte, the Phoenician moon goddess associated with Venus) who suggests the possibility of a new love.

The rhythmic and hypnotic opening stanza describes the late season and spectral setting (reminiscent of the opening paragraph of "The Fall of the House of Usher"). It alludes to the French operatic composer Daniel François Auber and to Robert Weir—Poe's former teacher—who taught drawing at West Point for more than forty years:

> The skies they were ashen and sober;
>   The leaves they were crispéd and sere—
>   The leaves they were withering and sere:
> It was night, in the lonesome October
>   Of my most immemorial year:
> It was hard by the dim lake of Auber,
>   In the misty mid region of Weir:—
> It was down by the dank tarn of Auber,
>   In the ghoul-haunted woodland of Weir.

Roaming, restless and alone, in this fantastic landscape, which he compares to Mount Yaanek (or Erebus), a recently discovered volcano in Antarctica, the narrator engages in serious discourse with his Soul. As the night advances, he describes—in exquisitely delicate lines—a new moon and associates it with Astarte:

> At the end of our path a liquescent
> And nebulous lustre was born,

Out of which a miraculous crescent
Arose with a duplicate horn.

Then, remembering the satanic torments of "the worm [who] never
dies" in Isaiah 66:24, he seeks in the flickering stars the forgetful,
"Lethean peace of the skies." Though Psyche warns him against those
stars, he replies that they are merely part of a dream which promises
"Hope and Beauty" and poses no danger to him. After pacifying
Psyche, he reaches the door of a tomb which, she tells him, " 'Tis
the vault of thy lost Ulalume!" Suddenly, he realizes that he has
unconsciously returned to the grave of his beloved on the first anniversary of her death. *She* has shaped his vision of the weird landscape
that contains her "dread burden." Realizing that he is tormented by
an inextinguishable grief, he knows he will always remain in her
thrall:

Then my heart it grew ashen and sober
    As the leaves that were crispéd and sere—
    As the leaves that were withering and sere—
And I cried—"It was surely October,
    On *this* very night of last year,
    That I journeyed—I journeyed down here!—
    That I brought a dread burden down here—
    On this night, of all nights in the year,
    Ah, what demon has tempted me here?
Well I know, now, this dim lake of Auber—
    This misty mid region of Weir:—
Well I know, now, this dank tarn of Auber—
    This ghoul-haunted woodland of Weir."

Chapter 12

FORDHAM: *EUREKA* AND HOPELESS LOVE, 1848

I ═══

Having survived his literary quarrels, recovered from his bereavement and temporarily regained his health, Poe started the new year with renewed vigor. He had been working on a long prose book, *Eureka*, in 1847 and completed it in January of 1848. Poe not only wrote indoors with the tortoiseshell cat draped around his shoulders, but also composed outdoors while walking in the garden. Maria, his only remaining connection to Virginia, now replaced both his mother and his wife, providing both physical and emotional support:

> He never liked to be alone [Maria wrote], and I used to sit up with him, often until four o'clock in the morning, he at his desk, writing, and I dozing in my chair. When he was composing *Eureka*, we used to walk up and down the garden, his arm around me, mine around him, until I was so tired I could not walk. He would stop every few minutes and explain his ideas to me, and ask if I understood him. I always sat with him when he was writing, and gave him a cup of hot coffee every hour or two. At home he was simple and affectionate as a child, and during all the years he lived with me I do not

remember a single night that he failed to come and kiss his "mother," as he called me, before going to bed.

It was extremely doubtful that Maria, or anyone else, understood Poe's ideas, for *Eureka* returned to the murky style and specious reasoning of "Al Aaraaf," and to an equally vague theme: man's relation to God and to the universe. This work seemed to justify Thomas Dunn English's criticism of Poe's pretentious claim to abstruse knowledge. As a reviewer noted in July 1848, *Eureka* "ingeniously smatters of astronomical systems, concentric circles, centrifugal forces, planetary distances, the Nebular theory and the star Alpha Lyrae."

Eureka was (to borrow Kierkegaard's title) Poe's *Concluding Unscientific Postscript*, his equivalent to Yeats' mystical book, *A Vision*. Poe, the archrationalist, had frequently criticized the Transcendentalists for their lack of intellectual rigor and called them "mystics for mysticism's sake." But in *Eureka* he became more mystical than any of them and outdid the fuzziness of the Frogpondians. Filled with erroneous "facts" and fantastic speculations, the book has no scientific merit. Its poetic value is severely limited by its opacity and incoherence. Confused by the contents of his own mind, Poe could not—as Byron said of Coleridge—explain his explanation.

Poe's "Sonnet—To Science" (1829) was a defiant protest against cold reason. *Eureka*—which rejected analytic logic and emphasized intuition and inspiration (Poe incorrectly asserts: "these vital laws Kepler *guessed*—that is to say, he *imagined* them")[1]—followed in the pseudo-scientific tradition of stories like "Hans Pfaall," "MS. Found in a Bottle," "A Descent into the Maelström" and "The Facts in the Case of M. Valdemar."

Eureka is based on the untenable nebular hypothesis of the French astronomer and mathematician, Marquis de Laplace, who explained the genesis of the heavenly bodies by the gradual coalescence of a thin, luminous substance diffused through space. It is dedicated to the German naturalist Alexander von Humboldt, whose massive *Cosmos* attempted to harmonize a knowledge of the physical environment with a classical ideal of humanity. But it was actually much closer (as Daniel Hoffman points out) to the dubious revelations of his contemporaries, Joseph Smith and Mary Baker Eddy, the founders of Mormonism and of Christian Science. Unlike most of Poe's major works, *Eureka* fell stillborn from the press, was ignored by the general public and had absolutely no influence on scientific or philosophical thought.

Exceeding Francis Bacon's vast intellectual ambition to take all knowledge for his province, Poe chose a rather broad subject: the essence, origin, creation, condition and destiny of the universe. Never one to make modest claims about his own work, Poe megalomaniacally declared, in a letter of January 1848 to his young admirer from Maine, George Eveleth: "What I have propounded will (in good time) revolutionize the world of Physical & Metaphysical Science. I say this calmly—but I say it." Expounding his paradoxical and pseudo-logical "General Proposition," he told Eveleth, "Because Nothing was, therefore All Things Are." Poe also explained, in a handwritten note in Griswold's copy of *Eureka*, that in his philosophical system the individual finds transcendental unity by finally merging with God: "The pain of the consideration that we shall lose our individual identity [in death] ceases at once when we further reflect that the process, as above described, is neither more nor less than that of the absorption, by each individual intelligence, of all other intelligences (that is, of the Universe) into its own. That God may be all in all, *each* must become God."[2]

Though presented as a scientific treatise, Poe wanted the book to be read as a work of art, as a romance, even as a poem. In his Preface, he offered *Eureka* to his few intimate friends, and emphasized emotion rather than reason, dreams rather than reality, as a key to its meaning: "To the few who love me and whom I love—to those who feel rather than to those who think—to the dreamers and those who put their faith in dreams as the only realities—I offer this Book of Truths, not in its character of Truth-Teller, but for the Beauty that abounds in its Truth, constituting it true."

The seriousness of *Eureka* was undermined not only by the Preface, which demanded that the book be read without recourse to reason or reality, but also by the peculiar opening, which offered a burlesque on the Aristotelian and Baconian methods of ascertaining the truth, and made porcine puns on the names of Bacon and Hogg. Poe thought the artist must free himself from the empirical quest for knowledge and admitted that "according to the schools, I *prove* nothing. So be it:—I design but to suggest—and to *convince* through suggestion." Though he expressed fears "of being taken for a madman,"[3] he tried to prove the unprovable and presented his speculative ideas as if they were scientific fact.

Poe saw the infinite universe as a process of contracting and expanding forces, as "a shadowy and fluctuating domain, now shrinking, now swelling, in accordance with the vacillating energies of the imagination"—rather than with the laws of physics and astronomy.

He believed that man was a mere extension of the Deity; that as the cosmos shrinks back into spatial nothingness he will regain his lost harmony by surrendering his self (as well as his earthly sorrows) and becoming absorbed into a perfect, mystical unity with "the Spirit Divine": "the final globe of globes will instantaneously disappear, and God will remain in all."[4] But Poe did not offer any explanation of why, when and how this would happen.

Several critics have tried to make sense of Poe's wild speculations. Edward Davidson makes *Eureka* seem much more rational than it actually is: "The book is concerned with three scientific problems relating to the physical universe: first, the concept of creation (or, how did matter become what it appears to be?); second, the nature of matter (or, what is matter and how is the observed physical universe energized?); and third, the prospect for the natural world (or, toward what end is the ever-changing universe moving?)."

Eric Carlson gives a clear summary of Poe's principal ideas:

> The overriding question is the Unity of the "Universe"— embracing its origin, its expansion, and its ultimate destiny. From the initial act of creation, when God as spirit was individualized in the Primordial Particle, the universe has expanded by radiation and then by gravitation and attraction. Eventually all matter, all creation, will return to Unity or Nothingness, at which point, by another act of creative will, the process will repeat itself in a continuous rhythm of diastole and systole. In this grand design, man, God, and nature are inseparable ingredients of an organic whole.

Richard Wilbur sees this work as a Blakean attempt to achieve unity by transcending self-enclosed isolation. He usefully connects *Eureka* to the central themes in Poe's poetry and fiction: "the war between the poetic soul and the external world; the war between the poetic soul and the earthly self to which it is bound." Wilbur explains that "the planet Earth, according to Poe's myth of the cosmos . . . has fallen away from God by exalting the scientific reason above poetic intuition, and by putting its trust in material fact rather than in visionary knowledge."[5]

Critics have been as sharply divided about the merit and value of *Eureka* as about *The Narrative of Arthur Gordon Pym*. *Eureka* has been taken as seriously by Poe's admirers as by Poe himself. Allen Tate has tried to relate the book to the quest for unity—from unity with the beloved dead to unity with the cosmos—in Poe's works. And

Paul Valéry, in keeping with the French exaltation of Poe, has praised both its scientific and its poetical qualities: "The reader of *Eureka* will see how Poe has extended the application both of the nebular hypothesis and the law of gravity. On these mathematical foundations he has built an abstract poem, one of the rare modern examples of a total explanation of the material and spiritual universe, a *cosmogeny*." Poe's biographer Arthur Quinn evaded evaluation by seeking the opinion of an eminent English astronomer and physicist. In September 1940 Sir Arthur Eddington tactfully replied: "It is the work of a man trying to reconcile the science of his time with the more philosophical and spiritual cravings of the mind"; and another scientist suggested its limitations by concluding: "That *Eureka* produced little effect upon the science of its own day is not surprising."[6]

In 1885 George Woodberry—with impressive force and considerable irritation—made the most negative judgment of *Eureka*. Refusing to treat Poe's metaphysical speculations with respect and commenting on the density of his ignorance in this department of knowledge ("he had not advanced farther in science than the elements of physics, mathematics, and astronomy, as he had learned them at school or from popular works, such as Dr. Nichol's *Architecture of the Heavens*"), Woodberry thought it pointless "to illustrate the worthlessness of Poe's thought in this field, and to indicate the depth of delusion under which he labored in believing himself a discoverer of new truth." He explained that Poe's theory was "built out of Cartesian notions, crudely apprehended, and rendered ridiculous by the effort to yoke them with thoroughly materialistic ideas." He felt the undoubted power of the work lay "in its exposition of Laplace's nebular theory and its vivid and popular presentation of astronomical phenomena," and by the tireless imagination that "gave his confused dogmatism the semblance of a reasoned system." Woodberry confidently concluded that Poe had been "tempted by an overweening pride to an Icarian flight and betrayed, notwithstanding its merely specious knowledge, into an ignoble exposure of its own presumption and ignorance."

In 1926 Joseph Wood Krutch supported Woodberry's views with his own convincing condemnation. He first gave a useful summary of Poe's eclectic sources: "The materialist's theory of the atoms he mingled with [German] transcendental ideas, borrowed probably from Coleridge, concerning the individual's intuitive knowledge of God; to this he added a pantheistic conception of an all-pervasive deity, part of whom is resident in every object, and then attempted to support the whole by vague references to Gravity . . . to the nebular hypothesis, and to the laws of Kepler concerning which he knew practically nothing." Krutch also revealed Poe's scientific errors, adding that he was wrong not only in his "statement, which violates Newtonian principles, concerning the manner in which the planets rotate in elliptical orbits but in such easily obtainable data as the density of the planets." He concluded that "Poe's speculations [are] so confused and so self-contradictory as to be well nigh incomprehensible. . . . As science, the intrinsic worth of the work in question is absolutely nil."[7] Despite recent efforts to explain, justify and revive *Eureka*, it remains a rambling, incoherent and excruciatingly boring book.

After completing *Eureka*, his longest nonfiction work, Poe used this unpromising material to return to the lecture circuit. He wanted to try out his ideas before publication, to reestablish himself in the literary world and to raise money to bring out his long-cherished magazine, the *Stylus*. In 1845 Poe had been terribly disappointed when forced to cancel a lecture after only twelve people had shown up, and appeared drunk the next morning at the office of the *Broadway Journal*. But he now took up public speaking with renewed confidence.

In New York, on the stormy evening of February 3, 1848, about sixty people assembled to hear Poe give, in a slight Southern accent, an extremely protracted account of *Eureka*. Though one newspaper reporter called the lecture "hyperbolic nonsense," a second said it was "characterized by strong analytical powers and intense capacity of imagination." A third rather surprisingly noted "the conclusion of this brilliant effort was greeted with warm applause by the audience, who had listened with enchained attention throughout." Another enthusiastic listener suggested that Poe had influenced his audience more by the force of his personality than by the power of his arguments:

> I have seen no portrait of Poe that does justice to his pale, delicate, intellectual face and magnificent eyes. His lecture was a rhapsody of the most intense brilliancy. He appeared inspired, and his inspiration affected the scant audience almost painfully. He wore his coat tightly buttoned across his slender chest; his eyes seemed to glow like those of his own raven, and he kept us entranced for two hours and a half.

Yet Poe's sympathetic friend Evert Duyckinck, who had also attended the lecture, contradicted this account. He told his brother that he had been bored to death and considered the performance a disaster: "Poe delivered a lecture last evening on the Universe—full of a ludicrous dryness of scientific phrase—a mountainous piece of absurdity for a popular lecture and moreover an introduction to his projected magazine—the *Stylus*: for which it was to furnish funds. It drove people from the room, instead of calling in subscribers."[8]

Encouraged, nevertheless, by the public response to his abstract ideas, Poe tried to persuade George Putnam—who had brought out the English edition of *The Narrative of Arthur Gordon Pym*, as well as the *Tales* and *The Raven* in 1845—to publish a gigantic edition of the work Poe considered more momentous than Newton's discovery of gravity. Though Putnam published only one one-hundredth of the edition demanded, Poe actually managed to extract a miniscule advance of fourteen dollars, after solemnly promising not to ask for any other loans or advance from Putnam.

Putnam later recalled his dramatic interview with Poe:

A gentleman with a somewhat nervous and excited manner claimed attention on a subject which he said was of the highest importance. Seated at my desk, and looking at me a full minute with his "glittering eye," he at length said: "I am Mr. Poe." I was "all ear," of course, and sincerely interested. It was the author of "The Raven" and "The Gold-Bug"! "I hardly know," said the poet, after a pause, "how to begin what I have to say. It is a matter of profound importance." After another pause, the poet seeming to be in a tremor of excitement, he at length went on to say that the publication he had to propose was of momentous interest. Newton's discovery of gravitation was a mere incident compared to the discoveries revealed in this book. It would at once command such universal and intense attention that the publisher might give up all other enterprises, and make this one book the business of his lifetime. An edition of fifty thousand copies might be sufficient to begin with, but it would be but a small beginning. No other scientific event in the history of the world approached in importance the original developments of this book. All this and more, not in irony or in jest, but in *intense* earnest. . . . I was really impressed—but not overcome, promising a decision on Monday. . . . The poet had to rest so long in uncertainty about the *extent* of the edition— partly reconciled, by a small loan, meanwhile. We *did* venture,

not upon fifty thousand, but five hundred. . . . It has never,
apparently, caused any profound interest either to popular or
scientific readers.

Difficult to review because impossible to understand, *Eureka* re-
ceived confused, hesitant yet generally respectful notices. Some critics
suspected another hoax. Others traced its sources to the mysticism of
Emanuel Swedenborg and to Robert Chambers' *Vestiges of Creation*.
Still others—like George Bush, Professor of Hebrew at New York
University—criticized its pantheistic tendencies.

In January 1848, just before the lecture on *Eureka*, Poe's literary
reputation was enhanced when the Virginia poet and critic James
Pendleton Cooke wrote a sequel to Lowell's memoir in the *Southern
Literary Messenger*. Ignoring Poe's controversial criticism—"With
tomahawk upraised for deadly blow, / Behold our literary Mohawk,
Poe!" (as one magazine put it)—Cooke analyzed "The Raven" and
"The Facts in the Case of M. Valdemar"; praised his invention, imagination and style; and observed that Poe was less popular than he
deserved to be because he "deals in mysteries of 'life in death,' dissects
monomania, exhibits convulsions of soul—in a word, wholly leaves
beneath and behind him the wide and happy realm of the common
cheerful life of man."[9]

II ⎓

Poe's irrational thought and unbalanced behavior were revealed not
only in the obfuscations of *Eureka* and the delusional conversation
with George Putnam, but also in his dangerous drinking bouts and
his simultaneous, frantic and ultimately disastrous courtship of three
different women: Marie Louise Shew, Annie Richmond and Sarah
Helen Whitman.

Poe, the penniless orphan, had two principal aims in marriage: to
find a woman who would rescue and take care of him, prevent his
drinking and prolong his life, and who would also have the money
to finance the *Stylus*. Like D. H. Lawrence, Poe could say: "I daren't
sit in the world without a woman behind me." Like George Orwell,
who desperately wanted to remarry after the death of his first wife,
Poe precipitously proposed to several ladies who rejected him. One
acquaintance observed that Poe was extremely attractive to women:
"His remarkable personal beauty, the fascination of his manners and
conversation, and his chivalrous deference and devotion to women,

gave him a dangerous power over the sex."[10] He might have added that Poe was both a talented poet and a physical wreck—irresistible to the intellectual and aesthetic as well as the sentimental and maternal impulses of his lady friends.

Students of Poe, attempting to fathom his bizarre mode of courtship, have seized upon Lambert Wilmer's statement: "Of all men that I ever knew, he was the most *passionless*." But both his letters to and his behavior with women seemed, despite the theatrical element, to be excessively passionate. W. H. Auden, inexperienced in heterosexual love, wittily but harshly characterized the emotional life of Poe— who was an athlete, soldier and fistfighter—as effeminate, regressive and infantile: he was "an unmanly sort of man whose love-life seems to have been largely confined to crying in laps and playing house." But if Poe had been impotent, as Krutch, Auden and others have suggested, then he would surely have courted innocent virgins— emotional and physical replicas of Virginia—rather than experienced wives and worldly widows.

H. L. Mencken, with his usual exaggeration, believed that Poe deliberately sought out unattractive women who disqualified themselves from serious consideration: "most of them were fantastic bluestockings, as devoid of sexual charm as so many lady embalmers."[11] In fact, photographs of these women explode Mencken's theory and reveal that Fanny Osgood, Sarah Helen Whitman and Elmira Royster Shelton (if not Marie Louise Shew and Annie Richmond) were rather good-looking. It is true, however, that various problems—ill-health, nervous temperament, difference in age, financial considerations, family responsibilities, parental opposition, religious beliefs or married state, not to mention horror at Poe's outrageous behavior—made all the women Poe courted quite unattainable. And his multiple suits naturally precluded absolute commitment to any one woman. Poe's loyalty to the memory of Virginia and guilt about remarrying—a conflict poignantly expressed in both "Eleonora" and "Ulalume"— destroyed all hope of a successful courtship.

Poe liked to worship women from afar, in letters and in verse. When he drew dangerously close to them, he became overwrought and insecure, and deliberately—if unconsciously—ruined his chances of marriage. There was a strong contrast between Poe's highly disciplined writing and the emotional eruptions of his love letters. In his volatile confrontations with women, Poe invariably lapsed into the romantic clichés and operatic gestures he had employed with Fanny Osgood: falling on his knees, clasping his hands and hopelessly pleading for their consent.

Poe seemed to think the occasion required soppy and often embarrassing emotions. "I cannot *write* to you," he told Helen Whitman, in "the calm, cold language of a world which I loathe"; and he constantly recycled the feelings, if not the actual words of his love letters, just as he had recycled his love poems. It is rather surprising that his excessive flattery, adoration and self-abasement effectively engaged the emotions of the ladies he wished to marry. Despite the unfortunate outcome of all his suits, Poe's friendships with Osgood, Shew, Richmond, Whitman and Shelton all "met the supreme test of separation under high emotional tension or even the embittered tongues of slander." All these women remained loyal to his memory and staunchly defended his reputation after his death.

Marie Louise Shew—who had devotedly nursed both Virginia and Poe—became, after the death of his wife, an object of Poe's affections. Unlike Fanny Osgood, Mrs. Shew—then married to and later divorced from a water-cure physician—was an unsophisticated lady with no interest in literature. Plain-looking, kindhearted and deeply religious, she generously devoted her life to nursing the poor and the suffering.

Imitating the pattern of his courtship with Fanny, Poe began by writing valentine poems to Marie Louise and followed them with passionate letters. In his description of an ideal landscape in "The Domain of Arnheim" (1847), Poe also paid tribute to Marie Louise by writing of "the sympathy of a woman, not unwomanly, whose loveliness and love enveloped his existence in the purple atmosphere of Paradise." "To M. L. S——" (February 1847) conventionally praised her soft words, seraphic glance, fervent devotion and angelic spirit, and expressed gratitude "For the resurrection of deep-buried faith / In Truth—in Virtue—in Humanity." "To [Marie Louise]," published exactly a year later, described the difficulty of expressing his love for her in "Unthought-like thoughts that are the souls of thought"; and echoed the words and images of Keats' sonnet "When I Have Fears" in his homage to her:

> for 'tis not feeling,
> This standing motionless upon the golden
> Threshold of the wide-open gate of dreams,
> Gazing, entranced, adown the gorgeous vista,
> And thrilling as I see . . .
> Amid empurpled vapors, far away
> To where the prospect terminates—*thee only*.

While Poe was visiting her home in early May 1847, Marie Louise briefly assumed the role of Muse and—just as Maria Clemm had encouraged Poe when he was writing *Eureka*—helped him, when inspiration was flagging, complete the first draft of "The Bells":

> He came in and said, "Marie Louise, I have to write a poem. I have no feeling, no sentiment, no inspiration—." I answered we will have supper and I will help you. So after tea had been served in a conservatory with windows open, near a church— I playfully said, here is paper. A Bell (very jolly and sharp) rang at the corner of the street. He said "I so dislike the noise of bells tonight. I cannot write. I have no subject. I am exhausted." So I took his pen and wrote "The Bells. By E. A. Poe," and I mimicked his style, and wrote "the Bells, the little silver Bells, &c. &c." he finishing each line.

"The Bells," once a popular favorite at public recitations, is a somewhat mechanical, onomatopoeic, forced tour de force, in which the four resonant stanzas describe both the positive and negative sensations suggested by the various sounds of bells. The silver sledge bells tinkle merrily

> In the icy air of night!
> While the stars that oversprinkle
> All the Heavens, seem to twinkle
> With a crystalline delight.

The melodious golden wedding bells foretell a world of happiness and harmony. The brazen "alarum" bells inspire terror as they clang and clash to announce the danger of a frantic fire:

> In the startled ear of Night
> How they scream out their affright!
> Too much horrified to speak,
> They can only shriek, shriek.

Finally, the climactic, solemn tolling of iron bells, influenced by some unknown demonic power, suggests the groaning and sobbing of mourners in a funeral:

> In the silence of the night
> How we shiver with affright
> At the melancholy meaning of the tone!

In June 1848 Marie Louise, who described herself as "a mere coun-
trywoman," became alarmed at Poe's demands for affection and his
increasingly eccentric behavior. At the same time, her friend Reverend
John Hopkins denounced the pantheistic ideas in *Eureka* and convinced
her that she was endangering her religious beliefs by continuing her
friendship with Poe. Marie Louise, who had deep sympathy and
affection for Poe but did not want to marry him, was finally forced
to sever their relations. The bitterly wounded Poe then expressed the
same self-pity as he had in his cringing letters to John Allan and
begged her not to desert him. Using a cliché of sentimental fiction,
he appealed to the pure, self-sacrificing woman to rescue her "unfortunate patient" from a life of debauchery and damnation:

> Are you to vanish like all I love, or desire, from my darkened
> and "lost Soul"?—I have read over your letter again, and
> again, and can not make it possible with any degree of cer-
> tainty, that you wrote it in your right mind (*I know you did
> not without tears of anguish and regret*). . . . Unless some true
> and tender and pure womanly love saves me, I shall hardly
> last a year longer, alone! . . . Was it not you who renewed
> my hopes and faith in God—and in humanity? . . . I say I am
> a coward, to wound your loyal, unselfish and womanly heart,
> but you must know *and be assured*, of my *regret*, my *sorrow*, if
> aught I have ever written [*Eureka*] has hurt you! My *heart* has
> never *wronged you*. I place you *in my esteem* in all *solemnity* . . .
> as the truest, tenderest, of this world's most womanly souls,
> and an angel to my forlorn and darkened nature.[12]

Deeply hurt, depressed and unbalanced by Marie Louise's unexpected rejection and by her refusal to listen to his desperate pleas, Poe
began to drink heavily and become extremely belligerent. In August
1848 he challenged John Daniel, the acerbic editor of the Richmond
Semi-Weekly Examiner, to a duel—which never took place. After Poe's
death, Daniel praised "the complexity of his intellect, its incalculable
resources, and his masterly control." But he also criticized Poe's
"Ishmaelite" character: "His proud reserve, his profound melancholy,
his unworldliness—may we not say *unearthliness*—of nature [that]
made his character very difficult of comprehension." Daniel repeated

the rumor, started by the Baltimore journalist John Hewitt, that
Poe had made improper advances to John Allan's second wife and
condemned his barbarous drinking habits in Richmond: "Thousands
have seen him drunk in the streets of this city. In all his visits save
the last, he was in a state approaching mania. Whenever he tasted
alcohol, he seldom stopped drinking it so long as he was able. . . .
His taste for drink was a simple disease—no source of pleasure or
excitement."[13]

III ===

Poe met Nancy "Annie" Richmond—eleven years younger, happily
married to a prosperous paper manufacturer and the mother of one
daughter—by indirect means. Early in 1847 (just after Virginia's
death) Jane Locke, who was in her forties and lived with her large
family in Lowell, Massachusetts, sent a poem to Poe and began corresponding with him. He hoped to remarry and assumed she was a
widow. When she finally visited him in Fordham in June 1848 (the
month Marie Louise severed their relations), he was dismayed to
discover that Jane was a middle-aged housewife with five children.
On July 10, Jane arranged Poe's lecture in Lowell on "The Poets and
Poetry of America" and invited him to stay at her house. When he
returned for a second visit in October, he infuriated Jane by courting
her young neighbor Annie Richmond and, with her husband's permission, moving into her house on Ames Street.

Annie was a kind and simple lady, more like Marie Louise than
Fanny Osgood, and her letters to Maria Clemm (who lived with her
after Poe's death) are rather gushing and poorly written. A photograph portrays Annie, with chin in hand, gazing stiffly but placidly
away from the camera. She is laced into an elaborately embroidered
black satin dress, with lace cuffs and collar, and has her hair tortured
into a curled, waved, parted, braided and dangling coiffure. Her eyes
are deep set and widely spaced, her nose short and blunt, her lips thin
and mouth small. Though she lacked intellectual and literary interests,
Poe and Annie's strong mutual attraction quickly developed into a
passionate but platonic romance. Poe seemed to love her more deeply
than any of the women he was involved with at the end of his life.

As usual, Poe wrote a story and poems about Annie, and sent
her intensely emotional love letters. In "Landor's Cottage" (1849), a
description of an ideal house in a charming setting and complement
to "The Domain of Arnheim," Annie makes a cameo appearance as

Marie Louise had done in the earlier story. Poe emphasizes their immediate and intuitive sympathy as well as her grace, enthusiasm, romantic expression and gleaming eyes:

> Instantly a figure advanced to the threshold—that of a young woman about twenty-eight years of age—slender, or rather slight, and somewhat above the medium height. As she approached, with a certain *modest decision* of step altogether indescribable, I said to myself, "Surely here I have found the perfection of natural, in contradistinction from artificial *grace*." The second impression which she made on me, but by far the more vivid of the two, was that of *enthusiasm*. So intense an expression of *romance*, perhaps I should call it, or of unworldliness, as that which gleamed from her deep-set eyes, had never so sunk into my heart of hearts before. I know not how it is, but this peculiar expression of the eye, wreathing itself occasionally into the lips, is the most powerful, if not absolutely the *sole* spell, which rivets my interest in woman. . . . The eyes of Annie . . . were "spiritual gray"; her hair, a light chestnut.

At the same time that he was emotionally involved with Annie, who was of course unobtainable and for that reason, perhaps, more desirable, Poe also began to court a far more complex and sophisticated woman, Sarah Helen Whitman. Yet Poe's letters to Annie, with whom he had a purely platonic relationship, were more passionate than those written to the woman he could have actually married. Though Helen was unaware of Annie, Annie knew all about Poe's quest for Helen, and actually advised him to marry her. Poe's divided loyalty to Annie and Helen expressed the antithetical claims—portrayed in "Ulalume"—of Psyche and Astarte, of spiritual and sensual love.

Helen Whitman, who had the same birthday (January 19) as Poe, was six years older and lived in Providence, Rhode Island. She became fascinated with Poe's works in the early 1840s, and learned many details about his personal life through correspondence with her close literary friends, Fanny Osgood and Anne Lynch, who had once lived in Providence. Poe's romance with Helen began, as with Fanny, as a sentimental poetic flirtation. "To Edgar A. Poe," the first of sixteen poems (all strongly influenced by Poe) with which she "besieged" him, was read aloud at Anne Lynch's valentine party on February 14, 1848:

> Oh, thou grim and ancient Raven,
>   From the Night's Plutonian shore,
> Oft, in dreams, thy ghostly pinions
>   Wave and flutter round my door. . . .
>
> While these warbling "guests of summer"
>   Prate of "Progress" evermore,
> And, by dint of *iron foundries*,
>   Would this golden age restore,
> Still, methinks, I hear thee croaking,
>   Hoarsely croaking, "Nevermore."

When this poem appeared in print, Fanny sent a friendly warning, which was more likely to tempt than to discourage Helen: "I see by the *Home Journal* that your beautiful invocation has reached the Raven in his eyrie and I suppose, ere this, he has *swooped* upon your little *dove cote* in Providence. May Providence protect you if he has!—for his croak [is] the most eloquent imaginable. He is in truth 'A glorious devil, with large heart & brain.' "

Poe responded to this effusion with his second "To Helen." Compared to his poems to Marie Louise and to Annie, which thank them for saving him during his illnesses, the more conventional poem to Helen Whitman (whom he had not yet met) was appropriately vague and ethereal. It opens with his recollection of the first time he saw (but did not speak to) her, when he was visiting Providence in July 1845 with Fanny Osgood. Helen, on that fateful midnight, was dressed in white and taking a breath of air in her enchanted rose garden:

> Their odorous souls in an ecstatic death—
> Fell on the upturn'd faces of these roses
> That smiled and died in this parterre, enchanted
> By thee, and by the poetry of thy presence.

The divine light in Helen's eyes inspires Poe with the hope of future love; he wishes "*to be saved* by their bright light, / And purified in their electric fire."

Helen's sad life, peculiar habits and mystical strain made her extremely responsive to a poem that not only flattered, idealized and exalted her, but also portrayed her as Poe's potential savior. In 1815, when she was twelve, her father went to sea and did not return to his family for nineteen years. At the age of twenty-five she married a Boston lawyer. But she was left a childless widow at thirty and had remained in that state for the past fifteen years—living with her eccentric younger sister and her dominating mother, Anna Power.

Helen's portrait reveals an intense, determined and attractive woman. Wearing a white diaphanous dress and bonnet, and sharply set off against a black background, her dark hair is charmingly curled and hangs down the sides of her high forehead. She has clear eyes, a broad pointed nose, full lips, handsomely wide jaws and a nicely rounded chin.

Romantic in temperament and interested in spiritualism, the poetical Helen provided a strong contrast to the uneducated and uncultured Maria and Virginia. Helen shaded her eyes with a fan and lived in the same crepuscular light that pervaded Poe's stories. She clothed her fragile beauty in silken draperies, lace scarves, floating veils and trailing shawls. And, like one of Poe's fictional invalids, she frequently sniffed strong-smelling ether as a stimulant for her weak heart.

In late July Poe was visiting his old cronies in Richmond, drinking heavily and about to depart on a tour of the South that would publicize and promote the *Stylus*. But when he received two stanzas of poetry from Helen, which had been delayed in the post, he suddenly abandoned the tour and left immediately for New York in order to meet her. After writing a pseudonymous letter to find out if she were in Providence, Poe appeared there on September 21 and immediately began their romance. In his first, eight-page love letter of October 1, Poe described, in high-flown diction, his ecstatic impression of and intuitive attraction to her: "As you entered the room, pale, timid, hesitating, and evidently oppressed at heart; as your eyes rested appealingly, for one brief moment, upon mine, I felt, for the first time in my life, and tremblingly acknowledged, the existence of spiritual influences altogether out of the reach of reason. I saw that you were *Helen—my* Helen—the Helen of a thousand dreams—she whose visionary lips had so often lingered upon my own in the divine trance of passion."[14]

On September 22 Poe was introduced to some of Helen's friends. One of them recalled that the lovers were behaving strangely and that (just after their first meeting) Poe impulsively kissed her in public: "Of a sudden the company perceived that Poe and Helen were greatly agitated. Simultaneously both arose from their chairs and walked toward the center of the room. Meeting, he held her in his arms, kissed her; they stood for a moment, then he led her to his seat. There was a dead silence through all this strange proceeding."

The following day they visited (appropriately enough) the secluded Swan Point Cemetery on the outskirts of Providence. While "bitter, bitter tears" sprang into Poe's eyes, he nervously put his arm around her waist and exclaimed: "Helen, I love now—now—for the first and only time," and proposed marriage to her. Helen later said that Poe had asked her to rescue and inspire him, that he endeavored "to persuade me that my influence and my presence would have the power to lift his life out of the torpor of despair which had weighed upon him, and give an inspiration to his genius, of which he had as yet given no token."[15] Helen demurred, and promised to answer him by letter.

In late September, aware of nasty rumors about Poe, Helen rejected his proposal. She claimed as insurmountable impediments to marriage her age, her weak heart and her nervous temperament as well as her financial dependence on and responsibility for her mother and sister. On October 1 he responded from Fordham with a long, emotionally turbulent and extremely flattering letter (far removed from our current language of courtship), which tried to change her mind:

> I have pressed your letter again and again to my lips, sweetest Helen—bathing it in tears of joy, or of a "divine despair." . . .
>
> All thoughts—all passions now seem merged in that one consuming desire—the mere wish to make you comprehend—to make you see *that* for which there is no human voice—the unutterable fervor of my love for you. . . .
>
> If, throughout some long, dark summer night, I could but have held you close, close to my heart and whispered to you the strange secrets of its passionate history, then indeed you would have seen. . . . [Only you could] surround and bathe me in this electric light, illumining and enkindling my whole nature—filling my soul with glory, with wonder, and with awe.

He mentioned that he had heard about her eccentricities and sorrows from Anne Lynch and Fanny Osgood, and "the merest whisper that concerned you awoke in me a shuddering sixth sense, vaguely compounded of fear, ecstatic happiness, and a wild, inexplicable sentiment that resembled nothing so nearly as the consciousness of guilt." He compared her to Jane Stanard, "the first, purely ideal love of my soul," who had inspired the first "To Helen," and told her that their destinies were interwoven. He described the overpowering impression she had made on him: "I would have fallen at your feet in as

pure—in as real a *worship* as was ever offered to Idol or to God. . . .
I grew faint with the luxury of your voice and blind with the volup-
tuous lustre of your eyes."

Poe sympathized with her sorrows and illness, minimized their
difference in age, honestly admitted his "late errors and reckless ex-
cesses." As if all this were not sufficient, he reached the heights of
passion (and depths of style) with a self-abasing confession: "how
proud would I be to persevere—to sue—to plead—to kneel—to
pray—to beseech you for your love—in the deepest humility—at
your feet—at your feet, Helen, and with floods of passionate tears."
Finally, Poe promised to "comfort you—soothe you—tranquilize
you," when, in fact, he distressed, upset and excited her. He concluded with the characteristically perverse suggestion that she would
be as attractive to him when dead as when alive: "if you *died*—then
at least would I clasp your dear hand in death, and willingly—*oh,
joyfully—joyfully—joyfully*—go down *with* you into the night of the
Grave."[16]

In a second, six-page letter of October 18, almost as long and
equally hyperbolic, Poe continued his emotional onslaught. The
opening sentence resumed the mystical strain and reads like an operatic libretto: "In pressing my last letter between your dear hands,
there passed into your spirit a sense of the *Love* that glowed within
those pages." Poe then reproached Helen for lack of feeling, mentioned the devastating effect her refusal had upon him and declared
his undying passion: "Alas! you do *not* love me. . . . *My heart is
broken.* . . . I have no farther object in life—I have absolutely no wish
but to die. . . . [But] I *still* kneel—in deeper worship than ever man
offered to God." His most forceful—and most dishonest—argument
was to promote his present suit by denying that he had ever loved
Virginia and claiming that with Helen he truly loved a woman for
the first time in his life: "I did violence to my own heart, and married,
for another's happiness, where I knew that no possibility of my own
existed."

Emphasizing, as always, the passionate throbbings of his heart, he
denied (as she strongly suspected) that he would ever marry her for
money. He begged her, once again, to be the inspiration of his creative
work and renewed his offer of marriage: "It was then only—then
when I thought of *you*—that I dwelt exultingly upon what I felt that
I could accomplish in Letters and in Literary Influence—in the widest
and noblest field of human ambition . . . [and] ask you—*again* ask
you—to become my wife."[17] These volatile letters, though filled with
romantic clichés, had a powerful impact on the respectable widow,

who had led a quiet life for the past fifteen years. Though she began the descent into an emotional maelström, she would still not agree to marry him; and Poe was driven to more desperate measures to win her heart and gain her consent.

IV

As Helen wavered between acceptance and rejection, and Poe remained torn between his love for Annie and for Helen, he returned to Providence on November 4—impoverished, anguished and severely depressed. In a hysterical letter to Annie, written on November 16, Poe repeatedly expressed his exalted love for her: "But oh, *my darling, my* Annie, my own sweet *sister* Annie, my *pure* beautiful angel—*wife* of my soul—to be mine hereafter & *forever in the Heavens*. . . . I opened my whole heart to you—to *you*—my Annie, whom I so madly, so distractedly love." He tested Annie's love against Helen's and was excited by the thought that she was jealous of his affection for another woman: "*Can* you, *my* Annie, *bear* to think I am another's? *It would give me supreme—infinite bliss* to hear you say that you could *not* bear it."

More significantly than this playacting, Poe told Annie that on November 5 he had bought two ounces of laudanum and taken a train from Providence (where he had not seen Helen) to Boston. After writing to Annie and reminding her that she had promised to come to his deathbed, he swallowed half the drug. His halfhearted suicide attempt was meant to arouse compassion in both women and to convince Helen of the depths of his love. But, Poe explained:

> I had not calculated on the strength of the laudanum, for, before I reached the Post Office my reason was entirely gone, & the letter was never put in. Let me pass over, my darling *sister*, the awful horrors which succeeded.—A friend was at hand, who aided & (if it can be called saving) saved me—but it is only within the last three days that I have been able to remember what occurred in that dreary interval.

Poe emerged from his delirium after vomiting the potion, and became pitifully sick. He concluded his pathetic letter by regressing to infantile dependence, telling Annie that he could not survive without her maternal support: "I am so *ill*—so terribly, hopelessly ILL in body and mind, that I feel I CANNOT live, unless I can feel your sweet, gentle, loving hand pressed upon my forehead—oh my *pure, virtuous, generous, beautiful, beautiful* sister Annie!"

A similar incident, which occurred fifteen years earlier, illuminates Poe's motives and behavior in this episode. In 1833, the French composer Hector Berlioz had also taken a near-fatal dose of opium in order to punish and persuade the woman who had refused to marry him. Regaining his desire to live after she had declared her love, he swallowed a powerful emetic and survived to describe the experience:

> There have been the beginnings of a marriage process, a civil act which her loathsome sister promptly tore up. Terrible scenes of despair on her part, and reproaches for not loving her, to which I replied with passive resistance by poisoning myself in front of her. Dreadful cries from Henriette (her despair was sublime)—fiendish laughter on my part—desire to live again on seeing her protestations of love—emetics (ipecacuanha)—vomiting for two hours, only two grains of opium were left: I was ill for three days but I survived. In her frantic state she offered to do anything I chose, but now she begins to hesitate again.

Though Poe, like Berlioz, recovered, Maria Clemm emphasized his suffering by telling Annie: "I thought he would die several times. God knows I wish we were both in our graves. It would, I am sure, be far better."[18]

Poe immediately returned to Providence and on November 9, only four days after this episode, had a dimly lit daguerreotype taken by Edwin Manchester. It makes him look much older than thirty-nine and reveals the ravaging effects of his suicide attempt. It also bears an uncanny resemblance—especially in the massive forehead and gloomy, devastated expression—to Nadar's famous photograph of the syphilitic Baudelaire. This tragic "Ultima Thule" image portrayed Poe with a slightly tilted head, an asymmetrical face and a contorted expression of the mouth that curls into a contemptuous sneer. Baudelaire, who strongly identified with Poe and perceived his vulnerability, wrote that in this daguerreotype "he is very French: moustache; no sideburns; collar folded down. His brow is enormous both in breadth and height; he looks very pensive. . . . Despite the immense masculine force of the upper part of his head, it is, all in all, a very feminine face. The eyes are vast, very beautiful and abstracted." Edmund Wilson, who had great respect for Poe and was himself a heavy drinker, emphasized the effects of alcohol that would kill Poe within a year: "[He is] a pasty and dilapidated personage with untrimmed, untidy hair [high on one side, flat on the other], an uneven toothbrush moustache and large pouches under the eyes; the eyes themselves have a sad unfocused stare; one eyelid is drooping. . . . [His] visible disintegration unpleasantly suggests an alcoholic patient."[19]

Poe's suicide attempt and pathetic condition succeeded where all his letters and personal pleas had failed, and helped persuade Helen to marry him. In February 1848 Poe had described his daily routine, with woefully misplaced confidence, as if he were training for the Olympics: "My *habits* are rigorously abstemious and I omit nothing of the natural regimen requisite for health:—i.e., I rise early, eat moderately, drink nothing but water, and take abundant and regular exercise in the open air." But John Thompson, the editor of the *Southern Literary Messenger*, who saw him in Richmond that summer, painted an entirely different picture that stressed Poe's ludicrous, uncontrolled behavior: "Once I found him in a saloon called 'The Alhambra,' frequented by gamblers and sporting men. He was mounted on a marble-top table, declaiming passages from . . . *Eureka* to a motley crowd to whom it was as unintelligible as so much Hebrew."

In Providence on November 9, while attempting to win Helen's consent, Poe got madly drunk and appeared at her house in a frightening condition. She later told his biographer John Henry Ingram that Poe had said he was doomed and begged for her help:

> He came alone to my mother's house in a state of wild & delirious excitement, calling upon me to save him from some terrible impending doom. The tones of his voice were appalling & rang through the house. Never have I heard anything so awful. . . .
>
> It was long before I could nerve myself to see him. My mother was with him more than two hours before I entered the room. He hailed me as an angel sent to save him from perdition. When my mother requested me to have a cup of strong coffee prepared for him, he clung to me so frantically as to tear away a piece of the muslin dress I wore.
>
> In the afternoon he grew more composed, & my mother sent for Dr. A. H. Oakie, who, finding symptoms of cerebral congestion, advised his being taken to the house of his friend Wm. J. Pabodie, where he was kindly cared for.[20]

When confronted for the first time with concrete evidence of Poe's legendary drunkenness, Helen paradoxically and perversely agreed to marry him. Though she had many misgivings, she believed that she loved him and wanted to be the wife of a great poet. She also felt sorry for Poe and thought she could save him from alcoholic destruction. They entered into a conditional engagement in which Poe agreed to abstain completely from drink and Helen promised to obtain the consent of her implacable mother. Her mother naturally wondered how Poe—who was still as poor as ever and lived from hand to mouth on lecture money and occasional journalism—could support a wife. She said "more than once in his presence that [Helen's] death would not be regarded by her as so great an evil as marriage under circumstances of such ominous import."

On November 24 Poe wrote Helen, at the very same time that he was still sending passionate declarations to Annie, that he had passed through his crises, had been strengthened by them and could now deal effectively with his enemies: "An agony known only to my God and to myself—seems to have passed my soul through fire and purified it from all that is weak. Henceforward I am strong:—this those who love me shall see—as well as those who have so relentlessly endeavored to ruin me."

But fate was against him, and greater "enemies" than Helen's mother were strongly opposed to the marriage. Fanny Osgood, still smarting from her humiliating role in Poe's fiasco with Elizabeth Ellet and jealous of his love for Helen, visited Helen in Providence during the winter and advised her not to marry Poe. William Pabodie, the neighbor who had chaperoned Helen and nursed Poe after his alcoholic collapse, wanted to marry Helen himself and counseled her to reject his rival. Even Maria Clemm was against the marriage, since she preferred Annie (like herself, a simpler sort of woman) and was jealous of the more intellectual Helen. As she confided to Annie: "I so much fear *she* is not calculated to make him happy. I fear I will not love her. I *know* I shall never love her as I do *you*, my own darling."

On December 15 Helen's mother, realizing that her daughter seriously intended to marry Poe, obtained sole control of the family estate, thus putting it out of reach of the potential fortune hunter and son-in-law. Poe agreed to this arrangement and endorsed copies of the documents, and Helen risked destitution by agreeing to marry him. When Poe lectured on "The Poetic Principle" before an audience of 1,800 people on the evening of December 20, Helen sat in the front row, intently watching every change of expression on his face.

Impressed by Poe's great success, she finally agreed to prepare for an immediate marriage.

Two evenings later, no doubt nervous about the impending event, Poe had a drink before going to a party at Helen's house. But he was very quiet, and promised to abstain from alcohol. Fortifying himself with yet another glass of wine the next morning, Poe apologized for drinking the previous evening, promised once again to amend his habits and insisted that the marriage take place before he left Providence. He wrote to the minister of the local Episcopal church, asking him to post the banns, and directed Pabodie to carry the note in person. But Pabodie, still hoping the marriage could be prevented, did not deliver it. With the last apparent obstacles now removed, Poe announced to Maria on Saturday December 23: "My own dear Mother—We shall be married on Monday, and will be at Fordham on Tuesday on the first train."[21] But this marriage never took place.

In January 1849 Horace Greeley, hearing rumors that Poe was going to marry Helen Whitman, expressed concern for her welfare and told Griswold: "She seemed to me a good girl, and—you know what Poe is. Now I know a widow of doubtful age [forty-five] will marry almost any sort of a white man, but this seems to me a terrible conjunction. Has Mrs. Whitman no friend within your knowledge that can faithfully *explain* Poe to her?" In fact, Pabodie—who had seen Poe at his worst and was determined to prevent the marriage— later told Griswold that "Many of Mrs. W.'s friends deprecated this hasty and *imprudent marriage*, and it was their urgent solicitations and certain representations which were that afternoon made by them to Mrs. W. and her family, that led to the postponement of the marriage, and eventually to the dissolution of the engagement."

Helen later recalled that while she and Poe were in a circulating library on the afternoon of December 23, "a communication was handed me cautioning me against this *imprudent marriage* & informing me of many things in Mr. Poe's recent career with which I was previously unacquainted. I was at the same time informed that he had [that very morning] *already* violated the solemn promises that he had made to me & my friends on the preceding evening." Shocked by this letter and convinced that neither she nor Poe could do anything to stop his drinking, Helen immediately canceled the preparations for the wedding. Poe tried to persuade her that she had been misinformed and begged for one more chance, but her mother intervened and terminated the anguished interview. "Mr. Poe then started up," Helen said, "and left the house with an expression of bitter resentment at what he termed 'the intolerable insults' of my family. I never saw him any more."[22]

Just after Poe's death, Helen explained to Griswold that she had been well aware of the dangers involved in marrying him and had intended to keep her promise—until she heard that he had broken his pledge:

> I knew from the first that our engagement was a most imprudent one.—I clearly foresaw all the perils & penalties to which it would expose us.—But having consented to it (under circumstances which seemed to make life or death, happiness or misery alike indifferent to me) I resolved not to retract my promise.—Nor would I have done so.—The union to which I was so rashly urged, & to which I so rashly consented, was in the end prevented by circumstances over which I had no control—by a fatality which no act of mine could have averted.

In "Our Island of Dreams," one of her many poems about Poe, Helen concluded:

> Tell him I lingered alone on the shore,
> Where we parted, in sorrow, to meet nevermore;
> The night wind blew cold on my desolate heart
> But colder those wild words of doom, "Ye must part!"[23]

Helen's motives and behavior were much clearer than Poe's, and we can only speculate on why he ruined his chance to marry her. He may have wanted to reveal the darker side of his character and make a final test of Helen's fidelity and love. He may have wanted to break off the marriage because he could not (at the last moment) completely commit himself to another woman or because he felt he loved the unattainable Annie more than the available Helen. He may have wanted to punish himself for being "unfaithful" to Virginia. He may have been completely out of control and unable to stop drinking— even if he wanted to—despite the dire consequences.

Whatever his reasons, the morbidly sensitive Poe was deeply wounded by Helen's rejection. In his final letters to her of January 21 and 25, 1849, he blamed her ogreish mother and her addiction to ether ("from the effects of those terrible stimulants you lay prostrate without even the power to bid me farewell"). Ignoring his previous declaration that he would never marry her for financial "interest," he condemned "the suspicious & grossly insulting parsimony of the [financial] arrangements into which you suffered yourself to be forced by your Mother." Poe, who had been both nourished and betrayed by the bluestockings, also swore that "from this day forth I shun the pestilential society of *literary women*. They are a heartless, unnatural, venomous, dishonorable *set*, with no guiding principle but inordinate self-esteem."

The warmhearted Helen, also devastated by this emotional upheaval, sympathized with Poe but could not bring herself to answer him: "I was utterly hopeless of my power to sustain or console him. I longed to assure him of my unalterable sympathy, and my continued interest in his welfare and happiness, but I dared not incur the consequences of further direct communication."[24] Like Fanny Osgood, Helen broke off relations with Poe but later defended him against his detractors. She remained strangely devoted to the memory of their love and, like Poe, may have preferred the idea to the actuality of marriage.

After Helen had rejected him, Poe naturally turned for consolation to Annie. Making the best of a humiliating situation, he told her, with feigned relief: "how great a burden is taken off my heart by my rupture with Mrs W.; for I have fully made up my mind to break the engagement." Poe had, as if hedging his bets, continued to write love letters to Annie throughout his courtship of Helen. And in January 1849, contrasting his spiritual love for Annie with his earthly love for Helen, he declared: "there is *nothing* in this world worth living for except love—love *not* such as I once thought I felt for Mrs. [Whitman] but such as burns in my very soul for *you*—so pure—so unworldly— a love which would make *all* sacrifices for your sake."

But by mid-February Jane Locke—who had been jealous of Poe's love for Annie—used the scandalous rupture with Helen to spread vicious rumors about him. Jane turned Annie's tolerant and deferential husband against Poe by distorting the nature of Poe's spiritual love for his wife. For this reason Poe felt, with uncharacteristic docility and the deepest regret, that he would have to sacrifice the friendship that had meant so much to him:

> It only remains for me, beloved Annie, to consult *your* happiness—which under all circumstances, will be & must be mine.—Not only must I *not* visit you at Lowell, but I must discontinue my letters & you yours.—I cannot & *will* not have

it on my conscience that I have interfered with the domestic
happiness of the only being in the whole world, whom I have
loved, at the same time with truth & with *purity*.[25]

Jane Locke had vindictively ruined Poe's friendship with Annie just
as Elizabeth Ellet had done with Fanny Osgood. He was devastated
that he had lost Annie, as he had lost Marie Louise and Helen, that
he no longer had the friendship and love, the inspiration and support,
of a redemptive woman.

Poe's idealized portrait of Annie in "Landor's Cottage" was followed in March 1849 by his long love offering, "For Annie." This
was the best as well as the most tender and melodious poem that Poe
had written to a woman since he had composed "To Helen" for
Jane Stanard in 1831. "For Annie" describes Poe's recovery from his
suicide attempt with laudanum the previous November and alludes
to the "holy promise" he had extracted from Annie: "that, under all
circumstances, you will come to me on my bed of death." It opens
with a dramatic, throbbing rhythm which expresses Poe's gratitude
for recovery from his dangerous illness:

> Thank Heaven! the crisis—
> The danger is past,
> And the lingering illness
> Is over at last—
> And the fever called "Living"
> Is conquered at last. . . .
>
> The sickness—the nausea—
> The pitiless pain—
> Have ceased, with the fever
> That maddened my brain.

Freed at last from the torments of passion, his tantalized spirit, in a
deathlike but fully conscious state, finds repose amidst the myrtle,
rose, rosemary, pansies and rue that symbolize—in the contemporary
"language-of-flowers" books—love, beauty, fidelity, thought and
grace.

Halfway through the poem the focus shifts to the true and beautiful
Annie, whom he sees in a dream that suggests their maternal-filial
relations. Annie now protects him and shields him from harm:

> She tenderly kissed me,
> She fondly caressed,

> And then I fell gently
> To sleep on her breast.

The final stanza, which ends on an unusually positive note, provides a gentle contrast to the suffering suggested in the opening one. Poe attributes his recovery to the devoted care, loyalty and love that are expressed in the luminous eyes of the kind but passive Annie:

> But my heart it is brighter
> Than all of the many
> Stars in the sky,
> For it sparkles with Annie—
> It glows with the light
> Of the love of my Annie.

V ═══

In December 1848, just before his break with Helen, Poe published in John Thompson's *Southern Literary Messenger* one of his most important aesthetic statements, "The Poetic Principle," which he read at his impressive public lecture in Providence that month. Poe defined poetry as "*The Rhythmical Creation of Beauty*" and illustrated his ideas with excerpts from some of his favorite authors: Moore, Hood, Byron, Shelley and Tennyson, as well as from Bryant and Longfellow.

Arguing strongly against "epic mania" and prolixity in poetry, Poe declared that

> A long poem does not exist. I maintain that the phrase, "a long poem," is simply a flat contradiction in terms. . . .
>
> The degree of excitement which would entitle a poem to be so called at all, cannot be sustained throughout a composition of any great length. After the lapse of half an hour, at the very utmost, it flags—fails—a revulsion ensures—and then the poem is, in effect, and in fact, no longer such . . . [because it has lost] that vital requisite in all works of Art, Unity.

Long works like *Paradise Lost*, Poe maintained, were "merely a series of minor poems." This theory explained the failure of his only long poem, "Al Aaraaf," and his inability to finish any of his other long works.

Poe also criticized poetry written for didactic or moral purposes and expressed his belief in "pure" poetry—a concept that was adapted by the art-for-art's-sake aesthetes of the late nineteenth century: "There neither exists nor *can* exist any work more thoroughly dignified—more supremely noble than this very poem—this poem *per se*— this poem which is a poem and nothing more—this poem written solely for the poem's sake."

At the end of "The Poetic Principle," Poe attempted to give a clear idea of true poetry by referring to a few of "the simple elements which induce in the Poet himself the true poetical effect." The list of natural elements that inspire a poet end with the water in brooks, rivers, lakes and wells; and bears a striking stylistic and thematic resemblance to the earlier list of natural elements that were endued by morphine with an intensity of interest during Bedloe's walk in "A Tale of the Ragged Mountains":

> [The Poet] recognises the ambrosia which nourishes his soul,
> in the bright orbs that shine in Heaven—in the volutes of the
> flower—in the clustering of low shrubberies—in the waving
> of the grain-fields—in the slanting of tall, Eastern trees—in
> the blue distance of mountains—in the grouping of clouds—
> in the twinkling of half-hidden brooks—in the gleaming of
> silver rivers—in the repose of sequestered lakes—in the star-
> mirroring depths of lonely wells.[26]

In his early essays as well as in "The Poetic Principle" Poe created the foundations of serious criticism in America. His ideas "on brevity, originality, and unity of effect; his rejection of didacticism in poetry; his insistence upon the values of sound and rhythm; and his concept of the poetic sentiment, [have become] bywords in literary criticism." Edmund Wilson, the preeminent modern American critic, maintained that Poe wrote the "only first-rate classical prose of this period"; that "his literary articles and lectures, in fact, surely constitute the most remarkable body of criticism ever produced in the United States."[27] The poet-critic of our own time who comes closest to Poe is Randall Jarrell. Both Poe and Jarrell have a similar Southern conservatism, impressive learning, wide range of interests, shrewd insight, sound judgment, unusual severity and slashing wit. Though emotionally exhausted, Poe was still at the height of his critical powers.

Chapter 13

DRINK, DELIRIUM AND DEATH, 1849

I

Despite his emotional upheavals, Poe continued to write creative as well as critical work. In 1849 he published the minor revenge tale, "Hop-Frog," the descriptive "Landor's Cottage" and the love poem "For Annie" in the popular, trashy but comparatively well-paying Boston weekly, *The Flag of Our Union*. He also brought out the hoax story "Von Kempelen and His Discovery," the brief lyric "Eldorado" (both works about the current craze for gold) and the sonnet for Maria Clemm, "To My Mother."

His most important work, which appeared in February, was "Mellonta Tauta" (Greek for "These things are in the near future"). This futuristic story has significant connections with *Eureka*, whose title is mentioned in the text. Like *Eureka*, "Mellonta Tauta" refers to the star Alpha Lyrae, offers many "astronomical amusements," repeats the awful puns on "Bacon" and "Hogg," reaffirms Poe's belief that "Kepler guessed—that is to say *imagined*," and is, in the words of the pedantic narrator, "as tedious, as discursive, as incoherent, and as unsatisfactory as possible." Like the cyclical theory of expansion and contraction in *Eureka*, it opposes the contemporary exaltation of material progress.

"Mellonta Tauta," like "Hans Pfaall," describes a balloon voyage that begins on April Fool's Day; but it is set in 2848, a thousand years in the future. A parody of philosophy, pronounced by a muddled female pundit, this dogmatic tract, disguised as a story, also allows Poe to rail against beliefs he considered naive: the innate goodness of man and the merits of democracy. He continued to hold the views he had expressed to the liberal and progressive Lowell in July 1844: "I have no faith in human perfectibility. I think that human exertion will have no appreciable effect upon humanity." The aristocratic Poe, fearing that individual rights would be lost in government by the masses, echoed in "Some Words with a Mummy" (1845), the King of Brobdingnag's speech to Lemuel Gulliver by calling mob rule "the most odious and insupportable despotism that was ever heard of upon the face of the Earth."[1]

Poe had expressed a milder form of his antidemocratic views as early as "Hans Pfaall" (1835), where he doubted the political capacity of ordinary men and wrote: "we soon began to feel the [negative] effects of liberty and long speeches, and radicalism. . . . [People] had as much as they could do to read about the revolutions, and keep up with the march of intellect and the spirit of the age." His Swiftian disdain for the mob had intensified by 1849. In "Mellonta Tauta" he mocked "the queerest idea conceivable, viz: that all men are born free and equal—this in the very teeth of the laws of *gradation* so vividly impressed upon all things both in the moral and physical universe." And he bitterly called democracy "a very admirable form of government—for dogs." If Poe had lived until the Civil War, he would surely have been one of the most forceful and effective advocates of the Southern cause.

Poe's hopes for the *Stylus*, which would provide a desperately needed outlet for his own work, were suddenly revived in December 1848. Edward Patterson, whose father owned a weekly newspaper in Oquawka, Illinois (on the Mississippi River, across from Iowa), offered to publish a national magazine, with Poe as half owner and sole editor. Though only twenty-one years old, Patterson had inherited substantial funds and owned a printing shop. In late April 1849, when Patterson's letter finally caught up with him, Poe described the kind of quality magazine he envisioned and his method of securing a thousand subscribers, who would be needed before publication could commence:

We must aim high—address the intellect—the higher classes—of the country . . . and put the work at $5:—giving about 112 pp. (or perhaps 128) with occasional wood-engrav-

ings in the first style of art, but only in obvious illustration
of the text. . . .

My plan, in getting up such a work as I propose, would be
to take a tour through the principal States—especially West
& South—visiting the small towns more particularly than the
large ones—lecturing as I went, to pay expenses—and staying
sufficiently long in each place to interest my personal friends
(old College & West Point acquaintances scattered all over the
land) in the success of the enterprize.

This project—his final hope for his own magazine—eventually failed.
They could neither find the necessary subscribers nor agree about the
kind of magazine they planned to publish. And—though Patterson
sent fifty dollars for travel expenses—Poe's drinking bouts and subsequent illness prevented them from meeting, as planned, in St. Louis.
Poe continued to have difficulty placing his work and frequently
borrowed from friends. In June he asked a Richmond editor to send
him ten dollars, "if you can possibly spare it."

After the publication of *The Raven and Other Poems* in 1845, Poe
wrote only one or two important poems each year. Marie Louise
Shew's account of the genesis of "The Bells" seems to confirm Susan
Archer Talley's statement about Poe's difficulty in composing during
the final lustrum of his life: "Mr. Poe seems to have been incapable
of writing poetry with sustained effort. Impulsive, erratic, he would
soon weary of the task and lay aside the sketchy outlines of his poem,
to be filled up, touched and retouched."[2]

In May Poe completed his last poem, "Annabel Lee." Though early
poems—like "Tamerlane" and "Al Aaraaf"—were allegorical, his
later works, especially those about women, became increasingly autobiographical. His favorite theme, grieving for the death of a beautiful
woman, had been the subject of "Lenore," "The Sleeper," "To One
in Paradise," "The Raven" and "Ulalume," and recurred in "Annabel
Lee." But in the last poem, as in the story "Eleonora," young love
transcends death and survives in spiritual union.

This mournful dirge on ideal love achieves its effects through subtle
variations and ballad-like repetition. The slightly archaic, fairy-tale
opening describes the idyllic setting:

> It was many and many a year ago,
>   In a kingdom by the sea,
> That a maiden there lived whom you may know
>   By the name of Annabel Lee;—

And this maiden she lived with no other thought
Than to love and be loved by me.

But even the angels became jealous of this innocent child-love. They
sent down a chilling wind that carried Annabel away and "shut her
up, in a sepulchre / In this kingdom by the sea." Their souls remained
linked however, and the narrator continues to dream of Annabel and
to feel her presence in his life. At night he demonstrates his morbid
devotion to her memory by sleeping next to her grave:

And so, all the night-tide, I lie down by the side
Of my darling—my darling—my life and my bride,
    In her sepulchre there by the sea—
    In her tomb by the sounding sea.

Annie Richmond, whose name resembled the heroine's, was the
first to see the manuscript. Sarah Anna Lewis (whose poems Poe had
been bribed to review), Helen Whitman and Elmira Shelton (whom
he would soon court in Richmond) each believed that *she* was the
subject of the poem. But Fanny Osgood was surely right in thinking
that this poem—like "The Raven" and "Ulalume"—was really about
Virginia Poe. Virginia was the only one of these women he had loved
when she was a child, who had loved him exclusively, who had been
his bride, who had shivered during a fatal illness and who had died.

The posthumous publication of Poe's last poem was unusually
complex. To make certain that it would appear in print, Poe gave a
copy to Griswold, sold the manuscript to John Thompson to repay a
five-dollar debt and also sold it for publication to *Sartain's Union
Magazine*. After Poe's unexpected death, Griswold and Thompson
both jumped the gun: the former included it in his obituary of October
9, the latter in the November issue of his *Southern Literary Messenger*.
It did not appear in *Sartain's* until January 1850.

II ═══

Contrary to his habit of remaining in one city for several years, Poe
was extremely restless during the last year of his life. While courting,
lecturing, fund-raising, visiting and drinking, he frequently moved up
and down the East Coast between New York, Lowell, Philadelphia,
Richmond, Norfolk and Baltimore—hesitating not only about the
day of departure but also about the next destination. Poe's health and

moods were also subject to wild fluctuations. Writing from Fordham in mid-February, he exuberantly told his friend Frederick Thomas: "living buried in the country makes a man savage—wolfish. I'm just in the humor for a fight. You will be pleased to hear that I am in better health than I ever knew myself to be—full of energy and bent on success." But by late April, just before he received Patterson's letter and still troubled by the heart disease that had been noted by Marie Louise Shew, he complained to Annie Richmond of an almost Kafkaesque *Angst*: "My sadness is *unaccountable*, and this makes me the more sad. I am full of dark forebodings. *Nothing* cheers or comforts me. My life seems wasted—the future looks a dreary blank."[3]

On June 29 Poe bid a tearful farewell to Maria Clemm and left New York for Richmond to lecture in the South and raise money for the *Stylus*. The next day he stopped in Philadelphia, began to drink heavily, lost his suitcase (containing the Richmond lecture), was arrested for drunken behavior and briefly confined in Moyamensing prison. In the epigraph to "Al Aaraaf," borrowed from the Renaissance poet John Cleveland, Poe had joyfully boasted: "Who drinks the deepest?—here's to him." But his habit of throwing drinks down his throat as fast as he could made him an ugly and abusive alcoholic—until he passed out.

In prison, after his sudden and total withdrawal from alcohol, Poe suffered his first attack of delirium tremens. He was terrified by weird and fantastic hallucinations, which seemed to come straight out of his own horror stories and promised retribution for his drinking. In one of them, he barely escaped being plunged up to his lips in a cauldron of boiling spirits. In another, he watched Maria being methodically cut up and dismembered: "As a means to torture me and wring my heart, they brought out my mother, Mrs. Clemm, to blast my sight by seeing them first saw off her feet at the ankles, then her legs to the knees, her thighs at the hips, and so on." After the hallucinations had finally stopped, he was brought before the mayor with a miserable group of derelicts and criminals. When his turn came and he stepped forward, someone recognized him as "Poe, the poet" and he was dismissed without the customary fine.

Poe tried to return to New York, to the care of Maria and the security of his home. But his hallucinations were followed by paranoid fears of persecution. On the northbound train he heard some men, sitting a few seats behind him, plotting to kill him and throw him off the platform of the car. He quickly got off at the next station and returned to Philadelphia. Seeking refuge in the studio of his artist friend John Sartain, who had worked with Poe at *Burton's* and

Graham's, "he suddenly entered [the] engraving room, looking pale and haggard, with a wild and frightened expression in his eyes." Explaining that he was in danger of being murdered, he asked Sartain to lend him a razor so he could shave off his mustache and avoid recognition. Sartain eased his fears by taking him into the bathroom and cutting off his Chaplinesque mustache with a scissors.

That evening Poe said he was going for a walk near the Schuylkill River, and Sartain thought it prudent to stay with him. Since Poe's shoes were worn out, he put on Sartain's slippers. They took a bus to the river and in the dark climbed up a long flight of stairs to the top of the reservoir. As Poe described his recent hallucinations, "the horror of the imagined scene threw him into a sort of convulsion" and Sartain feared that his deranged friend (like Professor Moriarty with Sherlock Holmes at Reichenbach Falls) "might possibly in a sudden fit of frenzy leap freely forth with me in his arms into the black depth below." But they returned home safely. After two days of rest and regular meals, Poe's mind began to clear. He finally agreed that "the whole thing had been a delusion and a scare caused by his own excited imagination."

On July 7, while still recuperating at Sartain's, he wrote to Maria, to whom he clung even more desperately after losing Marie Louise, Sarah and Annie. Attributing his symptoms to the cholera epidemic then raging in the city, he expressed a powerful death wish and once again admitted that he had been temporarily insane:

> I have been *so* ill—have had the cholera, or spasms quite as bad, and can now hardly hold the pen.
>
> The very instant you get this, *come* to me. The joy of seeing you will almost compensate for our sorrows. We can but die together. It is no use to reason with me *now*; I must die. I have no desire to live since I have done *Eureka.* I could accomplish nothing more. . . .
>
> I was never *really* insane, except on occasions where my heart was touched. I have been taken to prison once since I came here for getting drunk.[4]

On about July 10, having recovered from the delirium tremens that had disabled him for the past ten days, Poe found his missing suitcase at the train station. He spent the next two days trying to borrow money for his trip to Richmond, but the danger of cholera and the heat of summer had driven many people out of town. On July 12, poorly dressed and wearing only one shoe, Poe climbed up four flights of stairs to the office of his young admirer George Lippard, editor of the *Quaker City*, confessing that he had "no bread to eat—no place to sleep." Lippard had no money himself, but borrowed it from several other journalists. When Poe finally reached Richmond on July 14, wearing ragged clothes and feeling desperately ill, he discovered that the lecture he planned to give was missing from his suitcase.

III ═══

Poe put up at the Swan Tavern, a cheap two-story hotel with high chimneys and a covered, eight-columned front porch. The native son was met with great kindness and entered the comfortable social life that would have been his if he had inherited John Allan's fortune. He saw his embarrassingly doting and backward sister Rosalie, and visited her adopted family, the Mackenzies, whom he had known since childhood. The hot Richmond summer made him discard his tattered black clothing; and his handsome, slender and erect figure—dressed in a white suit and Panama hat—was frequently seen in the fashionable parts of the city.

Susan Archer Talley—a young Richmond author who, Poe encouragingly said, "ranks already with *the best* of American poetesses, and in time will surpass them all"—met him that summer and was struck by his aristocratic, poetic and perfectly controlled demeanor:

> As I entered the parlor, Poe was seated near an open window, quietly conversing. His attitude was easy and graceful, with one arm lightly resting upon the back of his chair. His dark curling hair was thrown back from his broad forehead—a style in which he habitually wore it. At the sight of him, the impression produced upon me was of a refined, high-bred, and chivalrous gentleman. . . . He rose on my entrance, and, other visitors being present, stood with one hand resting on the back of his chair, awaiting my greeting. So dignified was his manner, so reserved his expression, that I experienced an involuntary recoil, until I turned to him and saw his eyes suddenly brighten as I offered my hand.

Poe managed to reconstruct his lost lecture on "The Poetic Principle" and delivered it in Richmond on August 17 and September 24, and in Norfolk on September 14. A master of poetic recitation, he had by now perfected his style of delivery, knew exactly how to please a large audience and always concluded the evening by reading one of his popular poems. Susan Talley noticed that Poe "had no manuscript, and that, though he stood like a statue, he held his audience as motionless as himself—fascinated by his voice and expression."

The Virginia newspapers were equally enthusiastic. The Richmond *Daily Republican* reported: "The lecture of this talented gentleman, at the Exchange Concert Room on Friday evening, was one of the richest intellectual treats we have ever had the good fortune to hear. . . . Mr. Poe was honored with the presence of a large, respectable, and intelligent audience. . . . All present must have highly appreciated the entertainment, and we trust that Mr. Poe will give us another illustration of his fine literary acquirements." The Norfolk *Southern Argus* agreed that Poe's talk, "chaste and classic in its style of composition, smooth and graceful in its delivery, had the happiest effect upon the fashionable audience."[5]

Poe's visit naturally brought back memories of his early years in Richmond and turned his thoughts to his youthful love, Elmira Royster Shelton. The mother of four children (two of whom survived infancy), she had been, since the death of her husband in 1844, a wealthy widow. Poe had renewed his acquaintance with Elmira when visiting Richmond in July 1848. But his complicated involvements with Marie Louise, Annie and Helen, as well as his drunken "debauch, in one of the lowest haunts of vice upon the wharves in this City," had precluded anything more than an exploratory visit.

Nor had Elmira forgotten Poe. As she followed his career and saw his fame increase, she must have wondered how different her life would have been if she had married the fiery poet instead of the successful businessman. In September 1849 she vividly remembered seeing and being tempted by Poe, who was with the "lovely" Virginia, just after their marriage in Richmond in May 1836. Elmira later gave Maria Clemm her own version of Poe's early song, "I saw thee on thy bridal day": "I met them.—I shall never forget my feelings at the time.—They were indescribable, almost agonizing. However in an instant, I remembered that I was a married woman, and banished them from me, as I would a poisonous reptile." Poe's poignant reunion with Elmira, who had inspired his youthful lyrics, revived his love.

A daguerreotype portrayed Elmira (who was a year younger than Poe) in an elaborately decorated dress. She is wearing a high lace collar, fixed by a brooch, and dangling earrings. Her dark hair, parted in the middle, is cut rather short and spread down from her cheeks.

She has an oval forehead, clear eyes, pert nose and downward-sloping mouth. Despite her stiff pose and severe expression, she is an extremely attractive woman. Susan Talley, who clearly disliked Elmira and thought her unsuited to be the wife of a poet, has left a rather condescending description of her appearance and character:

> [She] was a tall, rather masculine looking woman, with good features, hollow cheeks, thin lips and large blue eyes with purplish shadows about them, which had once probably been handsome. She was richly dressed, but had not a particle of grace or *style*, and her countenance was wholly expressionless. She impressed me as being hard and cold—the type of a thoroughly respectable, sensible, matter-of-fact woman, with whom no one could associate an idea of romance or poetry.

But Edward Alfriend, another member of their Richmond circle, formed a much more favorable impression, and suggested the feminine qualities that Poe found attractive in Elmira:

> Her eyes were a deep blue, her hair brown, touched with grey, her nose thin and patrician, her forehead high and well developed, her chin finely modeled, projecting and firm, and her cheeks round and full. Her voice was very low, soft and sweet, her manners exquisitely refined, and intellectually she was a woman of education and force of character. Her distinguishing qualities were gentleness and womanliness.[6]

Poe's courtship of Elmira—his fifth and final attempt to remarry—was driven by the same impetuous emotions as his earlier suits. Elmira recalled that in mid-July, soon after Poe's arrival in Richmond:

> I was ready to go to church and a servant told me that a gentleman in the parlour wanted to see me. I went down and was amazed to see him—but knew him instantly.—He came up to me in the most enthusiastic manner and said: "Oh! Elmira, is this you?" That very morning, I told him, I was going to church, that I never let anything interfere with that, that he must call again, and when he did call again he renewed his addresses. I laughed at it; he looked very serious and said he was in earnest and had been thinking about it for a long time. Then I found out that he was very serious and I became serious.

Elmira sat in the front row during his Richmond lecture, as Helen had done in Providence, and was equally impressed by his performance. Wasting no more time than he had with Helen, Poe proposed to Elmira in late July. Though he tried (as usual) to rush her into an engagement, she managed to postpone her response. As she later wrote: "I told him if he would not take a positive denial he must give me time to consider of it. And he said a love that hesitated was not a love for him. But he sat there a long time and was very pleasant and cheerful. He continued to visit me frequently but I never engaged myself to him. He begged me when he was going away to marry him. Promised he would be everything I could desire."

Despite the stirring of youthful memories, there were several obstacles to the marriage. Elmira, much more practical and down-to-earth than Helen (who closely followed Poe's affairs and continued to crank out poems about him), realized that her habits, interests and religious beliefs were very different from Poe's. Her two children were opposed to the marriage. There were also (as with Helen) complicated financial considerations. Her late husband had left her an estate of more than $100,000. But his will also stipulated that if she remarried, she would have to make a substantial sacrifice and receive only one-quarter of the estate.

Unsure of himself, despite his impatient pleas, Poe had also resumed relations with Annie. After Annie's husband discovered that Jane Locke had indeed spread malicious rumors about Poe, Poe had spent a week with them in early June. But on August 29 he wrote Maria: "Do not tell me anything about Annie.—I cannot bear to hear it now—unless you can tell me that Mr. R[ichmond] is dead.—I have got the wedding ring—and shall have no difficulty, I think, in getting a dress-coat." As in his courtship with Helen, Poe remained strongly attached to Annie—even while buying the ring for Elmira. He expressed doubts, hesitated, made preparations. Then, at the last moment, he took refuge from emotional commitment in drink.

On August 27, to show his good faith and clamp on some external restraints, Poe joined the Richmond chapter of the Sons of Temperance. Three weeks later, after telling Maria that the local newspapers had praised him to death and that he had been received with enthusiasm everywhere, he explained his feelings for Elmira and the characteristically unsettled state of his affairs: "I think she loves me more devotedly than any one I ever knew & I cannot help loving her in return. Nothing is yet definitely settled and it will not do to hurry matters. . . . On Tuesday [September 25] I will start for Phila to attend to Mrs. Loud's Poems. . . . *If possible* I will get married before

I start—but there is no telling."[7] Poe had now become a more passive recipient of a woman's affection, and seemed to love Elmira because she loved him. He still did not know if he wanted to—or if she was willing to—get married immediately, and was driven by extreme, almost manic-depressive swings of mood.

Remembering how Poe's life had ended, Elmira later maintained that though there was a partial understanding between them, she would not "have married him under any circumstances." But in her letter of September 22 to Maria, she had already assumed the role of prospective daughter-in-law:

> I am fully prepared to *love* you, and I do sincerely hope that our spirits may be congenial.—There shall be nothing wanting on my part to make them so.—I have just spent a very happy evening with your dear Edgar, and I know it will be gratifying to you, to know, that he is all that you could desire him to be, sober, temperate, moral, & much be- loved. . . . "I trust a kind Providence" will protect him, and guide him in the way of truth, so that his feet slip not.

And her emotional account of their last evening together also suggests that Elmira planned to marry Poe:

> He came up to my house on the evening of the 26th Sept. to take leave of me.—He was very sad, and complained of being quite sick; I felt his pulse, and found he had considerable fever, and did not think it probable that he would be able to start the next morning, as he anticipated.—I felt so wretched about him all of that night, that I went up early the next morning to enquire after him, when, much to my regret, he had left in the boat for Baltimore.

Susan Talley did not mention Poe's sadness (appropriate for a part- ing lover) and said that he left in a positive mood. She thought he expected to return to Richmond and marry Elmira: "He declared that the last few weeks in the society of his old and new friends had been the happiest that he had known for many years, and that when he again left New York he should there leave behind all the trouble and vexation of his past life."[8] Mistaking an old friend's malacca cane when saying good-bye, Poe exchanged it for his own and took it with him when he left Richmond.

IV ═══

Poe set off for New York on September 27, planning to settle his affairs there and return to Richmond with Maria. He also intended to stop in Philadelphia on his way up the coast, for he had accepted one hundred dollars (seven times more than he had received for *Eureka*) from a wealthy piano manufacturer, St. Leon Loud, to prepare his wife's poems for publication. But his boat went from Norfolk to Baltimore. Just as he had stopped to drink in Philadelphia on the way down to Richmond in late June, so he now stopped to drink in Baltimore on the way up to New York.

Trapped in self-destructive drinking, Poe repeated his Philadelphia experience in Baltimore. In both places he drank himself into oblivion, collapsed into unconsciousness and suffered hallucinations. He had survived the debauch in Philadelphia, but his health had been undermined by it. The newly enrolled Son of Temperance had prayed that his first experience with delirium tremens would provide a warning to him for the rest of his days. He now saw himself "as the victim of a preordained damnation, *une âme perdue*, a soul lost beyond all hope of redemption." Separated from Maria and from his friends in Richmond, and with no one to rescue him as Sartain had done, Poe surrendered once again to his suicidal impulses and drank himself to death.

Disembarking from the Norfolk steamer on September 28, Poe met several old Baltimore friends who insisted they all drink a sociable glass of whiskey. Poe, who had not touched alcohol in three months, eagerly agreed to their suggestion. Following his usual manic practice, he swallowed a great many drinks as quickly as possible and soon became unconscious. Poe's cousin Neilson, who was living in Baltimore, told Maria that no one knew what had happened to Poe during the six days between his arrival on September 28 and his discovery on October 3: "At what time he arrived in the city, where he spent the time he was here, or under what circumstances, I have been unable to ascertain." We do know, however, that he died under exceptionally ugly, wretched and pitiful conditions.

Poe's last week probably resembled not only his experiences in Philadelphia, but also the events that followed his attempted suicide with laudanum in November 1848. At that time, after experiencing "awful horrors," he could not remember, for an entire week, what had just happened to him. While in some disreputable flophouse, Poe most likely remained drunk, semiconscious and tormented by frightful visions. Six days later, he staggered into the street and collapsed in the gutter. Finally—in Hart Crane's words—"they dragged [his] retching flesh, / [His] trembling hands that night through Baltimore."[9]

On that afternoon, Wednesday October 3, during a local election, a young printer found Poe, semiconscious and in desperate condition, outside Gunner's Hall, an Irish tavern run by Cornelius Ryan. He at once sent an urgent note to Poe's old friend Joseph Snodgrass: "There is a gentleman, rather the worse for wear, at Ryan's 4th ward polls, who goes under the cognomen of Edgar A. Poe, and who appears in great distress, & he says he is acquainted with you, and I assure you, he is in need of immediate assistance." Though delirious, Poe was still clutching his malacca cane—as if it were his last connection to respectable life.

Snodgrass, a Virginia-born doctor and editor, was (like Poe's other medical friends, Thomas Holley Chivers and George Eveleth) also a literary man. In April 1846 he had reprinted the rumor that Poe was mentally deranged and had been confined in the Insane Retreat at Utica. Snodgrass found Poe, usually so fastidious about his attire, dressed in ragged clothing that was obviously not his own. He thought Poe's clothes might have been stolen when he was insensible, though Poe might also have sold his good clothes, bought cheap ones and used the money for drink:

> His hat—or rather the hat of somebody else, for he had evidently been robbed of his clothing, or cheated in an exchange—was a cheap palm-leaf one, without a band, and soiled; his coat, of commonest alpaca, and evidently "secondhand"; his pants of gray-mixed cassimere, dingy and badly fitting. He wore neither vest nor neckcloth, if I remember aright, while his shirt was sadly crumpled and soiled.

Snodgrass also noted that Poe's "face was haggard, not to say bloated, and unwashed, his hair unkempt, and his whole physique repulsive." As a strict temperance advocate, he could not resist using the sad example of Poe to emphasize, with clinical precision, the evils of alcohol:

> The intellectual flash of his eye had vanished, or rather had been quenched in the bowl. . . .
> He was so utterly stupefied with liquor that I thought it best not to seek recognition or conversation. . . . So insensible was he, that we had to carry him to the carriage as if

a corpse. The muscles of articulation seemed paralyzed to speechlessness, and mere incoherent mutterings were all that were heard.[10]

Realizing that Poe's life was in danger, Snodgrass sent him directly to Washington College Hospital.

Poe was cared for there by John Moran, the resident physician. He was confined in a prison-like room with barred windows that resembled the grim cells, chambers, vaults and tombs of his most lurid stories, and placed in the turret of the building with the other alcoholic patients. According to Dr. Moran, "when brought to the Hospital [Poe] was unconscious of his condition—who brought him or with whom he had been associating"—and remained in that state for the next ten hours. After that, he suffered the same hallucinations he had encountered in Philadelphia. He experienced a "tremor of the limbs, and at first a busy, but not violent or active delirium—constant talking—and vacant converse with spectral and imaginary objects on the walls. His face was pale and his whole person drenched in perspiration."[11] The doctor could not calm him down until Friday, October 5, two days later.

Upon regaining consciousness, Poe again became confused and incoherent. He thought Virginia was still alive, did not know when he had left Richmond or what had happened to his trunk of clothing. (He had, in fact, left it behind at the Swan Tavern and it was recovered after his death.) Moran tried to convince him that he would recover but, horrified by his degradation, Poe exclaimed that "the best thing his best friend could do would be to blow out his brains with a pistol." "He was in a sinking condition," wrote Moran, "yet perfectly conscious. I had his body sponged with warm water, to which spirits were added, sinapisms [mustard plaster] applied to his stomach and feet, cold applications to his head, and then administered a stimulating cordial." Another doctor at the hospital believed that Poe was about to die "from excessive nervous prostration and loss of nerve power, resulting from exposure, affecting the encephalon, a sensitive and delicate membrane of the brain."

When describing his last days, Moran attributed to Poe some uncharacteristic religious last words, supposedly spoken before "the fever called 'Living' was conquered at last":

When I returned [later that Friday] I found him in a violent delirium, resisting the efforts of two nurses to keep him in bed. This state continued until Saturday evening (he was ad-

mitted on Wednesday) when he commenced calling for one
"Reynolds," which he did through the night up to *three* on
Sunday morning. At this time a very decided change began
to affect him. Having become enfeebled from exertion he
became quiet and seemed to rest for a short time, then gently
moving his head he said, *"Lord help my poor Soul"* and ex-
pired.[12]

Poe died on Sunday, October 7 at 5 A.M., at the age of forty.

Poe had reviewed Jeremiah Reynolds' *Address on the Subject of a
Surveying and Exploring Expedition to the Pacific Ocean and South Seas*
in January 1837 and had used it as a source for *The Narrative of Arthur
Gordon Pym.* While persistently crying out for Reynolds during the
final hours of his life, Poe may have imagined the spectral figure near
the black hole of death, which he had magnificently described at the
end of *Pym*: "And now we rushed into the embraces of the cataract,
where a chasm threw itself open to receive us. But there arose in our
pathway a shrouded human figure, very far larger in its proportions
than any dweller among men. And the hue of the skin of the figure
was of the perfect whiteness of the snow."

Poe's last days were strikingly similar to those of another *poète
maudit*, Dylan Thomas, who died in a New York hospital, a century
later, at the age of thirty-nine. Both suicidal poets took an alcoholic
overdose, became unconscious, suffered delirium tremens, fell into a
coma and died four days later. John Malcolm Brinnin has described
Thomas' last Poe-like hours: "His fever had subsided; his breathing
had become so slight as to be almost inaudible; and now and then
there would be little gasps and long breathless intervals that threatened
to last forever. His face was wan and expressionless, his eyes half-
opening for moments at a time, his body inert." The poet John
Berryman, himself a suicidal alcoholic, was with Thomas at the time
of his death and described his hopeless, corpse-like condition:

> Tubes all over, useless versus coma,
> on the third day his principal physician
> told me to pray he'd die, brain damage such.
> His bare stub feet stuck out.[13]

Dylan Thomas' autopsy dramatically described the cause of his
death, from acute alcoholic poisoning, as "insult to the brain."
Though Poe had advocated dissection as "the surest and truest basis
. . . of all medical knowledge," he did not have an autopsy. The cause

of his death, therefore, has been as mysterious as the circumstances surrounding it. A great many explanations have been suggested: exposure, nervous prostration, alcoholic poisoning, delirium tremens, heart disease, brain congestion, brain fever, brain lesion, brain tumor, meningeal inflammation, cerebral epilepsy, apoplexy and syphilis.

Poe most probably suffered from hypoglycemia, or low blood sugar—possibly brought on by chronic liver disease, which can also induce altered states of consciousness. Hypoglycemia made it difficult for him to metabolize and tolerate alcohol, which always had an immediate and disastrous effect on his system. The symptoms of this disease, which interferes with the supply of glucose to the brain, are extreme anxiety and excitement, followed by delirium, hallucinations and coma. Mild confusion and sluggish but occasionally wild and aggressive speech are followed by "visual blurring, a feeling of uncertainty . . . and then increasing ignorance of [what is happening] . . . a feeling of impending doom, fine muscular tremor . . . and, lastly, excessive sweating." Poe experienced all these symptoms and probably died in a diabetic coma.

George Eveleth, surprised by the news of Poe's death, thought he "was perpetrating one of his hoaxes upon the public by pretending he had died." But Poe was buried in the Presbyterian Cemetery in Baltimore on October 8 at four in the afternoon. The pitifully few mourners included Neilson Poe, Joseph Snodgrass, Henry Herring (married to Poe's aunt) and Z. Collins Lee (a Baltimore lawyer and classmate of Poe at the University of Virginia). The brief three-minute ceremony, conducted by Virginia Poe's cousin, Reverend William Clemm of the Methodist Episcopal Church, was described by one observer as "cold-blooded and unchristianlike."

Poe's cheap and austere coffin—very different from the elaborate caskets of his fictional heroines—lacked handles, a nameplate, a cloth lining and even a cushion for his head. He was buried in the Poe family plot with unseemly haste and indelicacy. As Snodgrass wrote: "Into this [grave] the plainly coffined body was speedily lowered, and then the earth was shoveled directly upon the coffin-lid. This was so unusual, even in the burials of the poor, that I could not help noticing the absence of not only the customary box, as the inclosure for the coffin itself, but even of the commonest boards to prevent direct contact of the decomposing earth with it."[14] A few years later, Neilson Poe finally ordered a tombstone. But it was destroyed, before it could be erected, when a freight train jumped the track and crashed into the mason's yard.

Poe's closest surviving relations had no better luck than he did.

Maria Clemm had not seen Poe since he left New York on June 29. The woman who had served and suffered with Poe, who had visited newspaper offices to find work for him and tried to sell his manuscripts to various editors, was denied the solace of a final farewell and the chance to express her grief at his funeral. After his death, she lived with several friends, including Annie Richmond, until admitted in 1863 to a charity home for the poor in Baltimore, where she died a pauper, at the age of eighty-one, in 1871. Rosalie Poe, after leaving the Mackenzies, was forced to support herself by selling photographs of her brother in the streets of Richmond and Baltimore. Admitted in 1870 to a home for the indigent in Washington, she died there four years later at the age of sixty-four.

Chapter 14

REPUTATION

I

Poe was the first major American writer whose personal reputation influenced the reception of his work. He was also the only nineteenth-century American writer whose poems and stories were valued more highly in Europe than in his homeland. These two facts were closely related. The scandalous reputation that began in Poe's lifetime was fostered by his literary executor and editor Rufus Griswold, who insisted that Poe was a vicious man and lacked moral principle in his writing. At the same time, he argued, confusing the man with the work, the creator of hallucinating murderers must himself be evil, to have so evil an imagination. In midcentury America this was, unfortunately, a powerful argument and it has proved an enduring one.

In France, however, Poe found an ardent translator and follower in the great poet and critic, Charles Baudelaire. He saw Poe's self-destructive life as a fitting response to a stultifying, philistine society, and rejoiced in the music of his verse as well as in his lack of moral purpose. In England, John Henry Ingram's two-volume biography of 1880 cleared away many of Griswold's lies. The English poets of the 1890s followed Baudelaire in emphasizing the very qualities that American critics had sought to denounce.

Though Poe was as unhappy as Strindberg or Van Gogh, he received more condemnation than sympathy from the moralistic critics of his age. In this he was partly to blame, for he helped to create his own negative persona. Like Tennessee Williams and Truman Capote in our own time, Poe seemed to court bad publicity. He initiated the rumor of his own insanity, engaged in vituperative literary quarrels, started fistfights and took part in drunken binges. As Virginia Poe lay dying, the newspapers baldly announced his degrading poverty. Enemies like Thomas Dunn English and Lewis Gaylord Clark eagerly circulated malicious gossip in magazines and novels, and gloated over his wretched death.

Susan Talley, who defended Poe after his death, shrewdly noted that "in knowledge of human nature he was, for a man of his genius, strangely deficient." Nothing illustrated this more clearly than his choice of Rufus Griswold as his literary executor. Just as Poe had mistakenly underestimated a foe's hostility and asked Thomas Dunn English, whom he disliked and had insulted, to assist him in the quarrel with Elizabeth Ellet, so he also named Griswold, who had often been the target of his critical tomahawk, to superintend the posthumous publication of his collected works. Poe's greatest hoax, with himself as victim, was appointing to this task the vengeful and unrelenting Griswold.

On October 9, 1849, two days after Poe's death, Griswold, an evangelical moralist, published under the pseudonym "Ludwig" an extremely hostile obituary in Horace Greeley's New York *Daily Tribune*. He began by announcing Poe's sudden death; then stated, as if it were an undeniable fact, that "*few will be grieved by it*" because "*he had few or no friends.*" Griswold adopted the second phrase, without justification, from the public announcement of Virginia's illness in December 1846, which had stated they were "without money and without friends." Griswold, so often the butt of Poe's satire, maintained that Poe was worthless as a critic: always biased and "*little better than a carping grammarian.*" Comparing Poe to a damned Byronic character in Bulwer-Lytton's novel *The Caxtons*, he claimed that Poe was cynical, envious and arrogant; that he "walked the streets, in madness or melancholy, with lips moving in indistinct curses." He concluded by declaring that Poe had "no moral susceptibility; and what was more remarkable in a proud nature, little or nothing of the true point of honor."[1] This obituary, reprinted in the *Weekly Tribune* on October 20, did incalculable damage.

During the next six months, several of Poe's friends—Lambert Wilmer, Nathaniel Willis, Henry Hirst, George Lippard, George Graham and John Neal—attempted to defend him against Griswold's attacks and vindicate his memory. But, as Wilmer noted, "the whole press of the country seemed desirous of giving circulation and authenticity to the slanders." In November 1849, for example, John Thompson reported that "the untimely death of Mr. Poe occasioned a very general feeling of regret, although little genuine sorrow."[2] The views of Griswold—Baptist minister, respected anthologist and official editor—were regarded as authoritative, and those who challenged him were ignored.

In the years following Poe's death, his character and work were accorded the treatment frequently applied since then to literary and political figures in America. In life he had been briefly lionized as the creator of original forms of poetry and fiction. In death he was vilified in the press and despised by the public.

Since Poe died intestate, Rosalie Poe, his sister and closest surviving relative, was his natural heir. But the mentally defective woman was in no position to dispute the strong claims of Maria Clemm, who soon took control of the literary estate. Maria had had some previous dealings with Griswold. Only a month before Poe's death she had tried to persuade him to bring out an unspecified piece by Poe with a coy but barefaced bribe: "I wish you to publish it exactly as he has written it. If you will do so I will promise you a favorable review of your books as they appear. You know the influence I have with Mr. Poe."

Though Maria had devotedly cared for Poe during his lifetime, she was naive about literary matters. Now that Poe was dead, she was especially eager to see his work published and desperate to get money for her own survival. Knowing that Griswold was an efficient and influential editor, she minimized Poe's previous quarrels with Griswold, exaggerated his admiration for him and gave her *imprimatur* in the Preface to the first volume of Griswold's 1850 edition: "[Poe] decidedly and unequivocally certified his respect for the literary judgment and integrity of Mr. Griswold, with whom his personal relations, on account of some unhappy misunderstanding, had for years been interrupted."

By mid-December 1849, however, Griswold had already lost patience with Maria, whom he considered ignorant and meddlesome. Maria had also dared to criticize the behavior in the Ellet affair of his beloved Fanny Osgood. After Helen Whitman had criticized his obituary of Poe, Griswold warned her, in his most sanctimonious biblical style, that Maria "has no element of goodness or kindness in her nature, [and her] heart and understanding are full of malice and wickedness."[3]

With his usual industry, Griswold compiled the first two volumes of his edition of Poe's works, for which he received no payment, in only six weeks. (Maria got a few free sets, which she tried to sell to Longfellow and others.) This extremely popular collection sold 1,500 sets a year for many years, and by 1858 had reached its seventeenth edition. Ironically, however, Griswold's thirty-five page "Memoir of the Author," expanded from his obituary and prefixed to the third volume in September 1850, equated Poe with his depraved fictional characters and firmly established him, in the minds of his readers, as quintessentially dissolute and immoral.

Griswold employed lies, plagiarism and forgery to denigrate Poe. Though he adopted some of the factual errors from Poe's romanticized account of himself, Griswold added a great many falsehoods of his own. He maliciously claimed that Poe had been expelled from the University of Virginia, had deserted from the army, had tried to seduce the second Mrs. Allan and had been addicted to drugs. He removed the quotation marks in the passage from Bulwer-Lytton's novel, which he had quoted in the obituary, and used it to describe Poe directly. He forged many of Poe's letters to suggest that Poe had admired Griswold and had adopted a servile attitude toward him. Though it was difficult to exaggerate Poe's "morbid and insatiable" appetite for alcohol, Griswold asserted that on the very evening before his projected marriage to Helen Whitman, "in his drunkenness he committed at her house such outrages as made necessary a summons of the police." Helen denied this lie and told Poe's first American biographer, William Gill, that her Intended "was essentially and instinctively a gentleman, utterly incapable, even in moments of excitement and delirium, of such an outrage as Dr. Griswold has ascribed to him."

Griswold concluded by thoroughly condemning Poe's character, declaring that he "exhibits scarcely any virtue in either his life or his writings. Probably there is not another instance in the literature of our language in which so much has been accomplished without a recognition or a manifestation of conscience. . . . Irascible, envious— bad enough, but not the worst, for these salient angles were all varnished over with a cold repellent cynicism, his passions vented themselves in sneers." Not content with publishing these vindictive libels, Griswold generated more gossip by telling William Pabodie (who, though hostile to Poe, had objected to Griswold's distorted account of Poe's relations with Helen) that Poe was mercenary, lascivious and even incestuous. According to Griswold, Poe had had sexual relations with Maria Clemm; and if he had married Elmira Shelton, "to whom he was engaged, in Richmond, for her money, he must still manage to live so near [Annie Richmond], a creature whom he *loved* in Lowell, as to have intercourse with her as his mistress."[4]

Griswold minimized his undying hatred when he told Helen: "I was not his friend, nor was he mine." Hypersensitive to Poe's criticism of his anthologies, both in reviews and public lectures, and jealous of Poe's romantic relations with Fanny Osgood, Griswold was slow to retaliate in Poe's lifetime. Gnawed by envy of a far greater talent, he quietly stored up his venom and waited until after Poe's death to strike and to wound. When criticized for his transparently malign memoir, Griswold, believing that his portrait was accurate, while the views of Poe's defenders were sanitized, told James Fields: "These attacks on me for the life of Poe are certainly undeserved. Everybody who knows anything about Poe's life, understands perfectly well that I've suppressed much worse than I have printed against him, and [my] preface to 'The Literati' shows that I was absolutely compelled to write what I have written by the assaults of Graham and Neal."[5]

Some of the women who had known Poe well did their best to counter Griswold's assertions. Helen Whitman, jostling with the others for first place among the beloved, staunchly defended Poe in *Edgar Poe and His Critics* (1860). In this book she stressed his gentler side and undeniable virtues: "his devotion to his wife, his courtesy, his rare gifts as a conversationalist, his social charm, and his innate rectitude." Between 1874 and 1878 she engaged in an extensive correspondence with Poe's biographer, John Henry Ingram, which was published in 1979 as *Poe's Helen Remembers*.

Annie Richmond, eager to get control of Poe's papers, urged Maria to give up the Fordham cottage and live with her. After her husband died in 1873, she legally changed her name from Nancy to Annie to match Poe's name for her. Three years later, she too began to correspond with the industrious Ingram and sent him copies of Poe's letters. Ingram enraged her by publishing them without her consent. Annie outlived Poe by nearly half a century, dying at the age of seventy-five in 1898. Elmira Shelton remained silent about Poe, except for a single interview in 1875. She died ten years before Annie, at the age of seventy-eight.

Griswold's purpose had been not only to pay off old scores against Poe by attacking his character, but also to impose his own conventionally pious literary taste. But his damning portrait eventually had the opposite effect. By emphasizing Poe's wicked and scandalous behavior, he ensured that Poe's work would continue to attract attention. The efforts of loyal friends and sensible critics initially did little to dispel Griswold's negative image. But readers who followed Griswold not only enjoyed Poe's poems and stories for their own sake, but also experienced the extra thrill of reading the works of an evil man. The serious discussion of Poe and his writings has always coexisted alongside a morbid Poe cult. Though this cult originated in Poe's poetic recitals during his lifetime, it was largely created by Griswold's grotesque exaggerations.

Even Virginia, identified with his tubercular heroines, became involved in the public's creepy delight in stories about Poe. According to Philip Lindsay, "in 1875 when the [New York] cemetery in which she lay was destroyed, her bones were tossed aside. Poe's early biographer, William F. Gill, reverently gathered them together and placed them in a box which he kept under his bed and opened to those guests who wished to fondle the bones of the great man's beloved."[6] Virginia was eventually removed from Gill's private ossuary and reunited with Poe in the Presbyterian cemetery in Baltimore.

II

In 1820 the English critic Sydney Smith had suggested the low status of United States' authors by asking the awkward question: "Who reads an American book?" Griswold's memoir reinforced this prejudice while defaming Poe in England. A few moralistic English critics, knowing nothing of Poe, simply repeated Griswold's accusations. Two years after the memoir was reprinted in England, George Gilfillan, a British clergyman, caustically condemned Poe's character in the London *Critic* of March 1854: "His heart was as rotten as his conduct was infamous. He knew not what the terms honour and honourable meant. He had absolutely no virtue or good quality. . . . He showed himself, in many instances, a cool, calculating, deliberate blackguard. . . . Poe was a habitual drunkard, licentious, false, treacherous, and capable of everything that was mean, base, and malignant." And the anonymous critic in the *Edinburgh Review* of April 1858 took great pleasure, as Gilfillan had, in denouncing Poe in properly Pecksniffian fashion:

> Edgar Allan Poe was incontestably one of the most worthless persons of whom we have any record in the world of let-

ters. . . . He outraged his benefactor, he deceived his friends, he sacrificed his love, he became a beggar, a vagabond, the slanderer of a woman, the delirious drunken pauper of a common hospital, hated by some, despised by others, and avoided by all respectable men.[7]

Despite these pernicious essays, Poe's reputation in England did not sink as low as it did in America. In England there were no personal enemies, and no one with a direct knowledge of his savage controversies and unseemly behavior. We have seen that three of Poe's greatest English contemporaries—Dickens, Elizabeth Barrett and Tennyson—returned his admiration. Dickens took a liking to Poe, tried to find him an English publisher and later helped Maria Clemm. Barrett, though disturbed and puzzled by Poe's work, perceived the penetration of his criticism and the unaccountable power of his poems and stories. And Tennyson praised his "original genius" as well as the technical mastery of his verse.

Soon after his death, Poe's friends and supporters in America began the long process of restoring his personal and literary reputation. John Henry Ingram published the first significant life of Poe in 1874, which he expanded to two volumes in 1880. A civil servant who worked in the post office by day and wrote his voluminous works at night, Ingram devoted years of his life to corresponding with everyone he could find who had known Poe (especially Helen and Annie) or who had reliable information about him.

Ingram also edited a four-volume edition of Poe's works and wrote nearly fifty articles about him. Though his work was useful, Ingram's attempt to rescue Poe frequently went too far in the other direction and was eventually balanced by George Woodberry's life in 1885. But Ingram's biography, and the memorial ceremony organized in Baltimore in 1875 by Sara Sigourney Rice, effected a turning point in Poe's reputation.

Of all the major American writers of the mid-nineteenth century, only Hawthorne, who had praised the "force and originality" of Poe's stories, had recognized his merit. Other writers, whose disapproval of Poe's conduct was reinforced by Griswold's memoir, tended to ignore his best work and dismiss Poe as insignificant. Emerson, the most prominent Frogpondian, had never, like Longfellow, been directly attacked by Poe, but he shared the New England disdain for him. When William Dean Howells, conversing with Emerson, said he would now be ashamed of enjoying, as he once did, the cruel and spiteful aspects of Poe's criticism, Emerson, alluding to the onomatopoeic effects of "The Bells," dismissively replied: "Oh . . . you mean that jingle man!" Ignoring Poe's technical virtuosity and echoing Lowell's criticism of his prosody, Emerson disparaged *all* Poe's verse as mere jingles.

Sara Sigourney Rice organized the memorial ceremony by soliciting statements about Poe's work from eminent writers in America and abroad. She then included these letters in her volume of reminiscences and speeches. Words of praise arrived not only from Whittier, Bryant, Longfellow and Holmes, but also from Tennyson and Swinburne. Rice's volume was the first opportunity for Americans to see how highly Poe was regarded in Europe.

When corresponding with Ingram in 1875, Swinburne—who admired Poe's rebellious qualities and saw him as a literary martyr—had insisted that "America should do something to shew public reverence for the only one (as yet) among her men of genius who has won not merely English but European fame." Writing that year to Rice, he took care to emphasize the best part of Poe's uneven work and praised "the special quality of his strong and delicate genius, so sure of aim and faultless of touch in all the better and finer part of work he has left us."

Walt Whitman had briefly met Poe at the office of the *Broadway Journal* in November 1845, and paid homage to him by attending the memorial ceremony. Later, in *Specimen Days*, Whitman praised the virtuosity that Emerson had ignored, but, like Griswold, criticized the lack of didactic elements, which Poe had deliberately excluded from his poetry: "Almost without the first sign of moral principle, or of the concrete or its heroisms, or the simpler affections of the human heart, Poe's verses illustrate an intense faculty for technical and abstract beauty." Although, in his final judgment, he thought Poe belonged "among the electric lights of imaginative literature, brilliant and dazzling, but with no heat," Whitman acknowledged the "indescribable magnetism about the poet's life and reminiscences, as well as the poems."[8]

In contrast to Emerson and Whitman, the English poets who followed Swinburne in the Decadent, Aesthetic and fin-de-siècle tradition—Dowson, Wilde and (to a lesser extent) Yeats—emphasized the beauty of Poe's lyrics and were not concerned with the absence of "moral principle." Ernest Dowson said the euphonious "The viol, the violet, and the vine" from "The City in the Sea" was his favorite line of poetry. In 1886 Wilde too praised Poe as "this marvellous lord of rhythmic expression."[9] When appreciation of Poe in his native land was at best lukewarm, he was greatly admired in England. Between

1880 and 1930 his genius was proclaimed in books and essays by Andrew Lang, Francis Thompson, George Saintsbury, Arthur Symons, Norman Douglas, Edmond Gosse, Arthur Ransome, Holbrook Jackson and A. J. A. Symons. Following the success of Ingram's life, which turned the tide in Poe's favor, British publishers brought out, during the last two decades of the nineteenth century, about thirty-five editions of his works.

III ═══

The French felt most strongly the "indescribable magnetism" of Poe's life that Whitman had mentioned. Stéphane Mallarmé's dense and difficult sonnet, "Le Tombeau d'Edgar Poe," written in 1876 for the memorial volume, is a tribute to the master. It celebrates a Poe transformed by death into a triumphant angel who has made his native language purer. His conflicts are now ended; his tomb, having fallen from the sky, will protect him against blasphemy in the years to come. Inspired rather than influenced by Poe, the poem shows how by this date he had become in France an icon of the doomed, self-sacrificial poet, whose poverty and sordid death signified not degradation, but greatness.

Mallarmé's poem sums up the view of Poe largely created by Baudelaire. Though the first French translation, an adaptation of "William Wilson," appeared in December 1844 and the first essay on Poe was published by Émile Forgues in October 1846, his reputation in France was primarily established by Baudelaire. His translations of Poe's fiction, published over a period of sixteen years between 1848 (when Poe was still alive) and 1864, comprise five of the twelve volumes in the standard edition of Baudelaire's works. In addition to sacrificing his own creative work in order to translate Poe, Baudelaire published three essays about him in the 1850s—the first of which was a translation of John Daniel's article in the *Southern Literary Messenger* of March 1850. John Weightman has noted that "no other major figure has ever been known to perform such a sustained act of piety towards a fellow author." Baudelaire's translations are still considered among the best in any language.

The negative aspects of Poe's personality, so vividly portrayed by Griswold, were positively *attractive* to Baudelaire. Instead of defending Poe's character, as Ingram chose to do, Baudelaire exalted it. Baudelaire, who had so many traits in common with Poe, identified with him and wrote about Poe as if he were writing about himself.

To Baudelaire, *"le pauvre Eddie"* was *"mon semblable, mon frère,"* and he himself was the double of William Wilson.

Both Poe and Baudelaire (who was twelve years younger), as their photographic images reveal, had a prominent curved forehead and a head that seemed too large for the body. Baudelaire falsely claimed that he had traveled on from Mauritius to India just as Poe claimed he had made a journey to Greece and Russia. Baudelaire's plan to lecture and give poetry readings was probably inspired by the example of Poe. Both had, as Alex de Jonge writes of Baudelaire, "a profound strain of masochism, and a taste for self-destruction provoked in part by parental rejection." Baudelaire's revolt against his stepfather, General Aupick, resembled Poe's rebellion against his adopted father, John Allan. Both lived in a perpetual state of insecurity and anguish, and compulsively changed their addresses. Both made many enemies through their savage criticism. As Jacques Crépet said of Baudelaire: "Many of the writers of the age—and still more the hacks—loathed him . . . because he delighted in making them look foolish."

Both were great chroniclers of boredom and restlessness, "and of the savage lengths to which man would go to alleviate [them]"; both were driven by a complementary and equally urgent quest for serenity and fulfillment. Both had a sexual nature more cerebral than physical. Both were despairing personalities; and Poe, like Baudelaire, was called "the saddest and greatest alcoholic of the age." Both led desperate and violent lives that careened from one disaster to another and ended in degradation and squalor. The author of "The Facts in the Case of M. Valdemar," who deceived and despised the masses, could say with his French *confrère*: "When I shall have inspired universal disgust and horror I shall have achieved solitude."[10]

It is scarcely surprising, considering the striking physical, psychological and biographical similarities, that Baudelaire became "possessed" by Poe. He could think and talk of nothing else, drove his friends mad with endless questions about Poe and was more concerned with Poe's literary reputation than with his own. During his first reading of Poe, Baudelaire was amazed to discover that works he himself had but vaguely conceived had already been composed and published by Poe:

> In 1846 or 1847 I became acquainted with certain fragments by Edgar Poe. I felt a singular excitement. Since his complete works were not collected in one volume until after his death, I took the trouble of looking up Americans who were living in Paris so that I might borrow files of the magazines which

Poe had edited. And then—believe me or not as you like—I found poems and stories which I had thought about, but in a confused, vague, and disordered way, and which Poe had been able to treat perfectly. . . .

The first time I opened one of his books I saw, to my amazement and delight, not simply certain subjects which I had dreamed of, but *sentences* which I had thought out, written by him twenty years before.

To improve his English, Baudelaire would frequent a wineshop on the rue de Rivoli where British grooms and servants gathered to drink whiskey. His biographer records that Baudelaire would go to comical extremes to track down his American quarry: "Once, hearing that a famous American writer had arrived at a hotel in Paris, he forced his way into his presence and found him trying on a new suit of clothes. In spite of this, he insisted on asking him, as he stood there, an incongruous figure in [his underwear], whether he had ever known Poe personally, and how his reputation now stood in the United States."[11]

Baudelaire told the painter Édouard Manet: "People accuse me of imitating Edgar Poe! Do you know why I translate Poe so patiently? Because he resembled me." And he rightly believed that their fraternal affinities enabled him to comprehend Poe better than anyone else: "In the midst of the terrible solitude that surrounds me I was able to understand so well the genius of Edgar Poe, and wrote such an excellent [biographical essay] on his abominable life."

Baudelaire saw Poe not only as a precursor of Decadence, who anticipated his own political and poetical ideas, but also as a *poète maudit*, an alienated modern artist, destroyed by the crass industrialism of mid-nineteenth-century America. Baudelaire was especially eager, as Patrick Quinn remarks, "to inscribe Poe's name in the roll of literary martyrs," along with the classic cases of two suicides: Thomas Chatterton and Gérard de Nerval. "Edgar Poe, who isn't much in America," Baudelaire wrote, "*must* become a great man in France— at least that is what I want." In his third essay on Poe, published as a Preface to *Nouvelles histoires extraordinaires* in 1857, Baudelaire explored the secret chambers of Poe's mind, and analyzed the dual and distinctive aspects of his character—the primitive, irresistible and perverse force that "makes man constantly and simultaneously a murderer and a suicide, an assassin and a hangman."[12]

Later French writers, when evaluating Poe, followed the path so brilliantly explored by Baudelaire. In 1856 the Goncourt brothers,

having read Baudelaire's translations, perceived the startling originality of his science fiction, his pathological decadence, his analytic and
intellectual powers, which foreshadowed the literature of the next
century:

> After reading Edgar Allan Poe. Something critics have not
> noticed: a new literary world, pointing to the literature of the
> future twentieth century. Scientific miracles, fables on the
> pattern A + B; a clear-sighted, sickly literature. No more
> poetry, but analytic fantasy. Something monomaniacal.
> Things playing a more important part than people; love giv-
> ing way to deductions and other sources of ideas, style, sub-
> ject, and interest; the basis of the novel transferred from the
> heart to the head, from the passion to the idea, from the drama
> to the dénouement.

In contrast to the Americans, whose appreciation of Poe was always
grudging and hedged with reservations, his French followers valued
all his writings. Paul Valéry particularly admired *Eureka*, which to
English-language readers never seemed more than a tedious mixture
of pseudoscience and metaphysical fantasy. In 1892 and again in 1903
both Paul Valéry and Paul Claudel praised Poe's genius in letters to
the young André Gide. Valéry, oddly enough, stressed the perfection
of Poe (an extremely uneven writer) and, comparing him to the God
of Genesis, called him "the only writer—without any fault. He never
makes a false move—he is not guided by instinct—but with lucidity
and to advantage, he creates form out of the void." Claudel, crediting
Baudelaire with drawing his attention to Poe, also singled out *Eureka*
as his favorite work. Setting aside the great Sainte-Beuve, Claudel
exclaimed: "I only know two critics who really deserve the name—
Baudelaire and Poe. Speaking of Poe, do you know his *Eureka*? It's
magnificent." By 1922 Gide had learned his lesson and "credited Poe
with being one of the inventors of *le monologue intérieur*."[13]
    Finally, in his essay of 1930 on Baudelaire, Valéry echoed the ideas
originally stated by the Goncourts seventy-five years earlier, and
praised the originality and intelligence in Poe's science fiction, *Eureka*,
detective stories and tales of horror:

> It is not astonishing that Poe, possessing so effective and sure
> a method, should be the inventor of several different varieties,
> should have offered the first and most striking example of the
> scientific tale, of the modern cosmogenic poem, of the novel

of criminal investigation, of the introduction into literature
of morbid psychological states, and that all his work should
manifest on every page an intelligence which is to be observed
to the same degree in no other literary career.[14]

Poe's reputation in Germany (which had no equivalent of Baudelaire) was not as high as in France. But he still attracted the admiration
of three of its greatest writers. Like Baudelaire, Nietzsche—in *Beyond
Good and Evil* (1886)—identified with Poe. Nietzsche saw him as one
of the damned poets, as a tortured and tormented soul, who tried to
escape bitter reality and sought uneasy refuge in his own imaginative
world:

> Those great poets . . . men like Byron, Musset, Poe . . . are
> and perhaps must be men of fleeting moments, enthusiastic,
> sensual, childish, frivolous and sudden in mistrust and trust;
> with souls in which they usually try to conceal some fracture;
> often taking revenge with their works for some inner contam-
> ination, often seeking with their high flights to escape into
> forgetfulness from an all-too-faithful memory; often lost in
> the mud and almost in love with it, until they become like
> the will-o'-the-wisps around swamps and *pose* as stars . . .
> often fighting against a long nausea. . . . What *torture* are these
> great artists and all the so-called higher men for anyone who
> has once guessed their true nature.

In his last work, *The Will to Power* (1901), Nietzsche placed Poe with
Baudelaire and with Nietzsche's sometime hero Wagner as an idealist
in conflict with himself as well as with society: "A certain catholicity
of the ideal above all is almost sufficient proof in the case of the artist
of self-contempt, of 'Morass': the case of Baudelaire in France, the case
of Edgar Allan Poe in America, the case of Wagner in Germany."[15]

Three years later, in 1904, Rilke, who had read and admired Poe,
told his wife of a vital and excellent conversation he had had about
Poe. During that year Rilke also reflected on the similarities between
the daring creative artist, who leaves his comfortable room to explore
dangerous new worlds, and the introspective heroes in Poe's stories,
who scrutinize the nature of their fearful prisons:

> Most people learn to know only a corner of their room, a
> place by the window, a strip of floor on which they walk up

and down. Thus they have a certain security. And yet that dangerous insecurity is so much more human which drives the prisoners in Poe's stories to feel out the shapes of their horrible dungeons and not be strangers to the unspeakable terror of their abode.

Like Nietzsche, Kafka sympathized with Poe's personal weaknesses and believed that he had fled from an intolerable reality into the world of the imagination. And, like Rilke, Kafka was concerned with how the extraordinary artist comes to terms with the world: "Poe was ill. He was a poor devil who had no defences against the world. So he fled into drunkenness. Imagination only served him as a crutch. He wrote tales of mystery to make himself at home in the world. That's perfectly natural. Imagination has fewer pitfalls than reality has. . . . I know his way of escape and his dreamer's face."[16]

IV ═══

American writers were puzzled by the French exaltation of Poe. In his 1876 essay on Baudelaire, Henry James first defined the contradiction in Poe that later critics have also pondered: the impressive literary tricks and glittering surface, but lack of considered ideas and profound meaning. Like Elizabeth Barrett, James had at first dismissed Poe, and then wondered, in conscientious afterthoughts, if there were not some significance in Poe's work that he had somehow failed to perceive. In his 1876 essay, James (like Lowell) both acknowledged Poe's achievement and dismissed it as puerile. But he also paid Poe the high compliment of calling him a greater genius than Baudelaire: "With all due respect to the very original genius of the author of the 'Tales of Mystery,' it seems to us that to take him with more than a certain degree of seriousness is to lack seriousness one's self. An enthusiasm for Poe is the mark of a decidedly primitive stage of reflection. . . . Nevertheless, Poe was much the greater charlatan of the two, as well as the greater genius."

James' nagging sense of Poe's merit, despite his defects of character and lack of substance, made him return to the subject several times during the next thirty-five years. In his book on Hawthorne, published in 1879, James once more both praised and condemned Poe's role in the intellectual life of America in the 1840s: "He had the advantage of being a man of genius, and his intelligence was frequently great." But his critical sketches of American writers, "The

Literati," was "the most complete and exquisite specimen of *provincialism* ever prepared for the edification of men. Poe's judgments were pretentious, spiteful, vulgar; but they contained a great deal of sense and discrimination as well."[17]

Though James acknowledged Poe's talent, he blamed him for succumbing to the limitations of his provincial environment. In fact, as his reviews and essays show, Poe was unusually cosmopolitan and free from conventional thought. James' own independent means enabled him to escape to Europe; he never had to engage in the desperate struggle to support himself by writing. James condemned Poe as a charlatan and vulgarian, but gave him no credit for transcending the narrow literary culture of his time.

In his autobiography, *A Small Boy and Others* (1913), James described how as a child he had been thrilled and delighted by reading Poe's elegiac poems and mystery stories. However, in his Preface to *The Altar of the Dead* (a Poe-like title), in the New York edition of 1909, James discussed the ending of *The Narrative of Arthur Gordon Pym* as a way of explaining his own artistic principles. Floating on a white, milky sea, faced with a rolling white curtain of mist and about to descend into a cataract, Pym is confronted by "a shrouded human figure" far larger than life-size, whose skin is "of the perfect whiteness of the snow." James felt that Poe had sacrificed moral content (an American obsession) for terrifying effects: "Intrinsic values [his works] have none—as we feel for instance in such a matter as the would-be portentous climax of Edgar Poe's *Arthur Gordon Pym*, where the phenomena evoked, the moving accidents, coming straight, as I say, are immediate and flat, and the attempt is all at the horrific in itself."

In his own ghost tales, James declared, he had registered the presence of the mysterious and horrific only through their effect on the characters, "from the sense that in art economy is always beauty." To James, the climax of *Pym* "fails because it stops short, and stops short for want of connexions. There *are* no connexions; not only, I mean, in the sense of further statement, but of our own further relation to the elements, which hang in the void; whereby we see the effect lost, the imaginative effort wasted."

Though James found this passage lacking in meaning, he was able to use it to moving and resonant effect in his late masterpiece, *The Golden Bowl* (1904). When Prince Amerigo, the impoverished Italian nobleman "collected" by the wealthy American Adam Verver as a husband for his lovely daughter Maggie, is pondering the complexities of his situation before his wedding, he

remembered to have read, as a boy, a wonderful tale by Allan
Poe, his prospective wife's countryman—which was a thing
to show, by the way, what imagination Americans *could* have:
the story of the shipwrecked Gordon Pym, who, drifting in
a small boat further toward the North Pole—or was it the
South?—than anyone had ever done, found at a given moment before him, a thickness of white air that was like a
dazzling curtain of light, concealing as darkness conceals, yet
of the colour of milk or of snow.

The "imagination Americans *could* have" suggests the ability to
grasp the evil in man, which the Prince possesses but which his future
wife in her ignorance or innocence does not. The Prince had known
only black curtains that always hid what lay behind them. In his
attempt to understand "the quantity of confidence reposed in him"
by his bride and her father, to know if they value him or are merely
using him, the Prince identifies with Pym's bafflement: "There were
moments when he felt his own boat move upon one such mystery.
The state of mind of his new friends . . . had resemblances to a great
white curtain."[18]

In the Prince's mind Poe's white curtain, which confusingly equates
whiteness with evil, suggests that the Ververs' apparent innocence
hides their evil attempt to exploit him. James uses Poe's image to
suggest one of his persistent themes: that American ignorance or
innocence can itself be evil. James believed that Poe was a wasted
talent, a genius manqué whose crimes had been committed against
art rather than against decency. But James paid tribute to Poe by
incorporating this passage into his own work of art.

V ===

English and American criticism of Poe after James has echoed the
disparity between Poe's talent and his achievement, and expressed
bafflement or irritation about his popularity in France. Acknowledging the gift of an illustrated edition of Poe in September 1899, Yeats
mentioned Poe's minor virtues and then attacked the vulgar, insincere
and (like James) the horrific elements in a characteristic story and
poem:

His fame always puzzles me. . . . I admire a few lyrics of his
extremely and a few pages of his prose, chiefly in his critical

essays, which are sometimes profound. The rest of him seems to me vulgar and commonplace and the Pit and the Pendulum and the Raven do not seem to me to have permanent literary value of any kind. Analyse the Raven and you find that its subject is a commonplace and its execution a rhythmical trick. Its rhythm never lives for a moment, never once moves with an emotional life. The whole thing seems to me insincere and vulgar. Analyse the Pit and the Pendulum and you find an appeal to the nerves by tawdry physical affrightments.

Two years later, called upon for a statement to mark the centenary of Poe's birth, held at the University of Virginia in 1909, Yeats contributed the much more positive comment that Poe "is so certainly the greatest of American poets, and always and for all lands a great lyric poet."

Thomas Hardy and George Bernard Shaw found different formulas for responding to Poe's centenary. Hardy praised Poe for being "the first to realise to the full the possibilities of the English language in thought and rhyme." Shaw chose to emphasize other aspects of his multifaceted work, calling him "this finest of fine artists, this born aristocrat of Letters . . . the greatest journalistic critic of his time . . . [and] the most legitimate, the most classical, of modern writers."[19]

Poe's verse remained an essential part of the literary experience of most modern American writers. But the radical changes in poetic thought and diction made his language of little use to those who were trying to forge a distinctively modern idiom. Pound, who followed in the unconventional tradition of Whitman, reacted against the traditional verse of the nineteenth century. Like James, Pound thought Poe was talented, but flawed. Poe could not help Pound "make it new" and no one, Pound felt, had been able to follow him successfully. In 1915 Pound wrote: "Poe is a good enough poet, and after Whitman the best America has produced." But, he added, "he is a damn bad model. . . . A damned bad rhetorician half the time. . . . One condemns a fault in Poe, [but not only] because it is in Poe. It is all right for Poe if you like, but it is damn bad for the person who is trying uncritically to write like Poe. (Incidentally no one who has tried to write like Poe (verse: leave his prose out of it for the present) has done anything good. Personally I think an ambition to write as well as Poe is a low one.)"

Robert Frost similarly discounted Poe because his poetic style was so alien to the kind of language Frost created. He attacked Poe's obsession with the dead (though Frost himself had his pathological side) and told a friend: "Poe was not truly great, his chief feeling was that derived from throwing stones at a tomb."[20]

Poe's prose similarly came under attack. Writing to William Dean Howells in 1909, Mark Twain displayed some provincialism of his own. Failing to distinguish between Poe's major achievements and his inferior work—a trait common in all Poe's negative critics—Twain (like Emerson) was casually dismissive: "To me his prose is unreadable—like Jane Austen's. No, there is a difference. I could read his prose on salary, but not Jane's." Ernest Hemingway, making a similar point in one of the ex cathedra pronouncements in *Green Hills of Africa* (1935), said Poe had technical expertise—but nothing else: "Poe is a skillful writer. It is skillful, marvellously constructed, and it is dead." Thirteen years later, when comparing Faulkner's drinking to Poe's, Hemingway was a bit more positive and told Malcolm Cowley: "He is almost as much of a prick as Poe. But thank God for Poe and thank God for Faulkner." The rhythms of Poe's prose, his repetition, his embroidered diction, were useless to the idiomatic language of Twain and of Hemingway.

William Carlos Williams' essay of 1925 was the notable exception to the generally negative view of Poe in America during the first half of the twentieth century. A classmate and friend of Pound, Williams insisted that Poe was a distinctively American writer, who had rejected the European tradition and turned inland to his native locale: "Poe gives the sense for the first time in America, that literature is *serious*."[21]

VI ==

The question of Poe's high status in France continued to preoccupy modern authors. In two essays written during the Great War, Pound argued that Baudelaire had uncritically adopted Poe's fuzziest ideas: "Poe was his metaphysician, and his devotion sustained him through a translation of *Eureka*." Pound traced the origins of Poe's foreign reputation to Stéphane Mallarmé's famous sonnet of 1876 and to Arthur Symons' four essays on Poe. After distinguishing between the value of Poe's prose and verse, he condemned Mallarmé's translation of "The Raven": "The cult of Poe is an exotic introduced via Mallarmé and Arthur Symons. Poe's glory as an inventor of macabre subjects has been shifted into a reputation for verse. The absurdity of the cult is well gauged by Mallarmé's French translation—*Et le corbeau dit: jamais plus*." To Pound, Poe remained Emerson's "jingle man," whose vulgar poems had been unaccountably praised by great French poets.

Pound's contemporary Aldous Huxley also reacted against the French adoration of Poe. Adopting the essential point of Yeats' early critique, Huxley cited Poe as the prime example of vulgarity in literature—of rhythmical tricks and horrific effects. He roundly declared that "Baudelaire, Mallarmé and Valéry are wrong and Poe is not one of our major poets," and illustrated his belief that Poe was "unhappily cursed with incorrigible bad taste" by mercilessly mocking "the walloping dactylic metre" of "Ulalume."[22]

The iconoclastic poet Kenneth Rexroth attempted to explain the discrepancy between Poe's reputation in America and in France, and particularly Valéry's admiration for *Eureka*, by echoing Pound's dismissal of Mallarmé's translation and running down Poe's achievement. Rexroth argued that the French interpret Poe before they start to read him and invest him with their own cultural apparatus:

> All sensible men to whom English is native are distressed at the French enthusiasm for M. Poe, the author of *Jamais Plus*. Nobody in France seems to be able to learn, ever, that his verse is dreadful doggerel and his ratiocinative fiction absurd and his aesthetics the standard lucubrations that go over in Young Ladies' Study Circles and on the Chatauqua Circuit. The reason is, of course, that the French translate their whole culture into Poe before they even start to read him. They think his formalism is their formalism and his scientific speculation the speculation of d'Alembert. They think the giddy early nineteenth century misses in Baltimore who swooned over the architectonics of *Eureka* are the same over-civilized courtesans who once bestowed their favors on the brocaded inventors of ingenious mathematical machines.

The French critic Roger Asselineau also attempted to reconcile Valéry's praise of *Eureka* with Huxley's condemnation of Poe's vulgarity. Though the leading poets of three successive generations—Baudelaire, Mallarmé and Valéry—all had a good command of English, Asselineau wrote that "because of linguistic differences [they] have not felt the vulgarities of Poe's manner. They have been sensitive only to the high seriousness of his poetic quest and been filled with admiration for the boldness of his attempt to express the inexpressible by means of words."[23]

Fortunately for Poe's reputation, two of the greatest writers of the twentieth century, D. H. Lawrence and T. S. Eliot, sought to define what was most significant and worthy, rather than reprehensible, in his art. In 1923 Lawrence—who, unlike his friend Huxley, understood the psychological depths of Poe's work—composed the most penetrating, original and influential essay ever written on Poe, and explained for the first time why the French Symbolists praised him.

Analyzing two ghastly "love stories," "Ligeia" and "The Fall of the House of Usher," he praised Poe for unveiling "the disintegration-processes of his own psyche" and of modern neurotic man. Love in Poe, as in Lawrence, was often equated with neurosis and disease. "The best tales," Lawrence observed, "all have the same burden. Hate is as inordinate as love, and as slowly consuming, as secret, as underground, as subtle. . . . He sounded the horror and the warning of his own doom."

Eliot, at first, adopted Henry James' magisterial condescension and emphasized Poe's American provincialism. Forgetting Poe's five years of education in London and his wide knowledge of Continental literature, Eliot claimed, in a radio broadcast of 1943, that "he was a European who knew Europe only in his imagination." But he also acknowledged the memorable aspects of poems like "For Annie" ("The sickness—the nausea—/ The pitiless pain—/ Have ceased, with the fever / That maddened my brain"): "Only after you find that it goes on throbbing in your head, do you begin to suspect that perhaps you will never forget it." Five years later, in his Introduction to Charles Williams' All Hallows' Eve, Eliot connected Poe's stories to his life and recognized their artistic significance. The tales of Poe, he wrote, are "woven out of morbid psychology . . . [and] the symbolism of nightmare has its reference in the psychological ailment of Poe, which is itself a serious matter."[24]

In 1949, on the centenary of Poe's death, Eliot recognized that "this French [Symbolist] movement itself owed a great deal to an American of Irish extraction: Edgar Allan Poe." As Pound had done, he examined the impact of Poe's poetic theory and practice on Baudelaire, Mallarmé and Valéry, and tried to explain the enormous esteem he enjoyed in their country. Eliot began by contrasting Poe's literary defects with his extensive influence: "If we examine his work in detail, we seem to find in it nothing but slipshod writing, puerile thinking unsupported by wide reading or profound scholarship, haphazard experiments in various types of writing, chiefly under pressure of financial need, without perfection in any detail." Eliot conceded "that Poe had a powerful intellect is undeniable," but, following Henry James, he also called it "the intellect of a highly gifted young person

before puberty." Like James, Eliot found it improper, almost embarrassing, to admire Poe. Despite his reservations, he finally admitted
that "by trying to look at Poe through the eyes of Baudelaire, Mallarmé, and Valéry, I become more thoroughly convinced of his importance, of the importance of his *work* as a whole."[25]

VII ===

It took one hundred years for Poe's artistic reputation to be finally
established in America. Eliot's essay was followed by praise from
three leading poets of the next generation: "Our Cousin, Mr. Poe"
(1949) by Allen Tate (who, like Baudelaire, had the same domelike
forehead as Poe), the favorable Introduction to Poe's works (1950) by
W. H. Auden (who had by then settled in America) and "The House
of Poe" (1959) by Richard Wilbur (who would write a brilliant series
of essays about him).

Ironically, Griswold's early portrait of Poe as an arrogant, inde-
cent drunkard helped to create the romantic idea of the visionary
artist sacrificed to a philistine society. Modern novelists have absorbed Poe and the romantic myth of the ruined artist into their
portrayals of the writer in America. The would-be author in Lionel
Trilling's story "Impediments" (1979), thinking Poe used alcohol to
inspire his writing (though he could never, in fact, compose while
drunk) admits: "I bought this [bottle of gin] to see if I couldn't get
inspiration for the writing of a story . . . but all I got was a thick
head. I suppose if I can't seduce the Muse in the E. A. Poe style,
I'll have to follow DeQuincey and try opium." In *Humboldt's Gift*,
a novel partly based on the wretched life of the poet Delmore
Schwartz, Saul Bellow used Poe to represent the first American artist to be destroyed by a brutal society: "Edgar Allan Poe, picked
out of the Baltimore gutter. And Hart Crane over the side of a ship.
And poor John Berryman jumping from a bridge. . . . The country
is proud of its dead poets. It takes terrific satisfaction in the poets'
testimony that the USA is too tough, too big, too much, too rug-
ged, that American reality is overpowering."

Nevertheless, with all his imperfections, "Poe has been, and remains, the best known and most widely read American writer, both
in the United States and abroad."[26] His popular reputation for ratiocination and for horror attracted the attention of political leaders as
antithetical as Abraham Lincoln and Joseph Stalin. The presidential
campaign biography by William Dean Howells (who would later

hear Emerson's and Twain's opinions of Poe) revealed that Lincoln habitually used the analytical method in Poe's detective stories to sharpen and test his own powers of logical thought:

> The bent of [Lincoln's] mind, however, is mathematical and metaphysical, and he is therefore pleased with the absolute and logical method of Poe's tales and sketches, in which the problem of mystery is given, and wrought out into every-day facts by processes of cunning analysis. It is said that he suffers no year to pass without the perusal of this author.

Stalin was attracted to Poe for very different reasons. He was probably drawn to the elements of terror, torture and revenge in tales like "The Tell-Tale Heart," "The Pit and the Pendulum" and "The Cask of Amontillado," and Poe was "reported to be one of [his] favorite authors."[27]

Chapter 15

INFLUENCE

I ⬜

In his provocative introduction to Poe's works, W. H. Auden suggested the wide range of his influence and mentioned the three literary genres he had virtually invented—the story of horror, of detection and of science fiction: "His portraits of abnormal or self-destructive states contributed much to Dostoevski, his ratiocinating hero is the ancestor of Sherlock Holmes and his many successors, his tales of the future lead to H. G. Wells, his adventure stories to Jules Verne and Stevenson." But to Auden in 1950, Poe's influence on other poets appeared negligible and he seemed "in danger of becoming the life study of a few professors."

In fact, Poe's influence on European and American art has been extraordinarily wide. Poe had a short life and a limited number of finished works. But he possessed great originality and imagination. His poems and literary theories influenced the French Symbolists and English Aesthetes. His concern with guilt, anxiety and the divided personality inspired Dostoyevsky's great fiction. His pessimistic view of the human condition and fascination with death appealed to writers as diverse as Joseph Conrad and James Joyce. The Goncourts were right to declare that Poe—more than any other writer of the nineteenth century—had foreshadowed the literature of the future and would become a major figure in Western culture.[1]

For most readers Poe is a byword for horror, and his work has spawned innumerable imitations. But his memorable phrases and frightening images so permeate our culture that we now simply take him for granted. During the battle of Verdun in 1916, for example, a French soldier wrote that the night bombardment made him think of "The Pit and the Pendulum," "of that nightmare room of Edgar Allan Poe, in which the walls closed in one after the other." For one hundred and fifty years Poe has provided images of suffocation, fear, morbidity and the horror of life.

Poe was such a remarkable innovator, so far ahead of his own time, that he often seems like our contemporary. His realistic use of science fiction to deceive the gullible public, in stories like "The Balloon-Hoax," foreshadowed the H. G. Wells–Orson Welles *War of the Worlds* broadcast in October 1938, which convinced many uneasy Americans that their country was being invaded by Martians. Poe's "The Philosophy of Composition," the first essay to give a detailed account of how a work of art was conceived and composed, antici-pated the contemporary fascination with the creative process and modern books like Thomas Mann's *The Making of "Doctor Faustus"* (1949) and Stephen Spender's *The Making of a Poem* (1955).

Poe was also unusually modern in his description of narcotic visions and portrayal of mental illness. His belief that opium heightened the imagination and intensified perception, expressed in "The Fall of the House of Usher" and "A Tale of the Ragged Mountains," preceded by more than a century writings on drug-inspired visionary experi-ence, like Aldous Huxley's *The Doors of Perception* (1954) and Allen Ginsberg's *The Yage Letters* (1964).

Poe's story "The System of Doctor Tarr and Professor Fether," in which the director of a madhouse goes mad and inspires the patients to mutiny against their nurses, explores the thin borderline between the lunatic and the sane, suggests that crazy people may have superior insight and condemns the tendency to call insane those people whose ideas and behavior differ from the norm. Poe's ironic statement— "When a madman appears *thoroughly* sane, indeed, it is high time to put him in a strait-jacket"—prefigures the ideas of iconoclastic think-ers like R. D. Laing and Thomas Szasz, and the theme of Ken Kesey's novel *One Flew Over the Cuckoo's Nest* (1962).

When Henry James wrote that "the American writer seemed des-tined to follow a pattern of 'broken careers, orphaned children, early disasters, violent deaths,' " he was surely thinking of the notorious example of Poe. But by the end of the nineteenth century, these characteristics had become distinguishing marks of the writer of genius, with whom sensitive readers and aspiring authors could identify.

The Swedish writer Ola Hansson, following Baudelaire's and Nietzsche's glorification of Poe as a *poète maudit*, saw him as "one of the great *malades* of mankind. His sickness is the sickness of beauty at its most sublime. . . . Like most princes of culture, he is in *one* person the cloven trunk of madness and genius." Eugene O'Neill, for one, "had a special feeling for Poe; he not only respected him as one of the authentic geniuses of American literature, but felt a personal identification with the haunted author."

Poe's adversarial relationship with his public and with other writers prefigured Hemingway's propensity to slug it out with critics and rivals, and Mailer's notorious attacks on his fellow writers in *Advertisements for Myself* (1959). Poe's savage literary criticism suggests the severe strictures of an Edmund Wilson or a Randall Jarrell. His role as a satirist and a visionary of doom inspired the stories and novels of Scott Fitzgerald and Tom Wolfe. His bitterly disappointed and self-destructive life anticipated the modern pattern of alcoholic and suicidal American writers from Hart Crane to Sylvia Plath.

Allen Tate, in a persuasive essay that developed the ideas of D. H. Lawrence, saw the unstable Poe, in his life and in his works, as a quintessentially modern writer: "Poe is the transitional figure in modern literature because he discovered our great subject, the disintegration of personality."[2] This great subject gradually made its way into American literature. But writers in France, Russia and England seized upon Poe's work more eagerly. They appreciated his complexity, developed his themes and genres, adopted his imagery and ideas.

II ═══

Poe's employer George Graham said that "Literature to him was religion; and he, its high-priest." It was this aspect of Poe that most appealed to the French. He was the catalyst who inspired the high art of Symbolist poetry, which (like most of Poe's verse) did not narrate events, but described psychological states. Like Poe in "The Poetic Principle," the French Symbolists believed that poetry should create beauty, should never be moral or didactic, and should be "written solely for the poem's sake." It should convey the indefiniteness of music and a sense of mystery, and suggest a superior—even divine—reality.

Baudelaire had identified with Poe's tragic life and spent years translating his works.[3] He was attracted to Poe's emphasis on artistic purity, his love of the exotic, his obsession with morbid subjects and his concern with rationality and conscious method. Most significant for Baudelaire—who exclaimed: "I have cultivated my hysteria with pleasure and terror"—was Poe's portrayal of extreme mental states. Nightmare and insanity, inspired by drugs and drink, allowed past sensations, dream sequences and subconscious fears to float to the surface and become transformed into art. Valéry's essay summarized the impact of Poe's extraordinary qualities on his young contemporary and disciple, Baudelaire:

> [Poe] determined his opinion on a quantity of subjects: philosophy of composition, theory of the artificial, comprehension and condemnation of the modern [world], importance of the exceptional and of a certain strangeness, an aristocratic attitude, mysticism, a taste for elegance and precision, even politics. . . .
>
> A demon of lucidity, a genius of analysis and an inventor of the newest, most seductive combinations of logic and imagination, of mysticism and calculation, a psychologist of the exceptional, a literary engineer who studied and utilized all the resources of art—this Poe appeared to [Baudelaire].[4]

Poe's words and ideas echoed throughout Baudelaire's works. In the last entry of his journal, Baudelaire included Poe in his earthly trinity and beseeched him for sustenance and inspiration: "Every morning I will pray to God, the reservoir of all strength and justice, to my father, to Mariette and to Poe, as intercessors." In *Marginalia* Poe noted that all a writer had to do to achieve fame was "to write and publish a very little book. Its title should be simple—a few plain words—'My Heart Laid Bare.' But—this little book must be *true to its title*." Baudelaire precisely fulfilled Poe's injunction in his confessional *Mon coeur mis à nu*.

Baudelaire's projected play, *The Drunkard*, a study of delirium and violence in which an alcoholic jubilantly succumbs to the temptation to kill his wife, seemed inspired by "The Black Cat." One of the six banned poems from *The Flowers of Evil* (1857), "To She Who Is Too Gay," also described "the psychology of a perverse and despairing man who yields to a surge of temptation" and portrayed several of the themes of "Ligeia." In this work, the impact of a woman "upon the violent and broken personality of the poet, who finds such beauty and health arouse a sadistic thirst for destruction . . . is both disturbing and beautiful in the sheer intensity and control of its vertigo, its rendering of a heady and sick imagination."[5]

Baudelaire paraphrased the conclusion of Poe's second "To Helen" in "The Living Flame." The gloomy opening sentence of "The Fall of the House of Usher"—"During the whole of a dull, dark, and soundless day in the autumn of the year, when the clouds hung oppressively low in the heavens . . ."—reappeared in "Spleen":

> When the low heavy sky weighs like a lid
> Upon the spirit aching for the light
> And all the wide horizon's line is hid
> By a black day sadder than any night.

And Poe's grim description in *The Narrative of Arthur Gordon Pym* of seabirds devouring human flesh:

> On his back, from which a portion of the shirt had been torn, leaving it bare, there sat a huge sea-gull, busily gorging itself with horrible flesh, its bill and talons deep buried. . . . The eyes were gone, and the whole flesh around the mouth, leaving the teeth utterly naked,

recurred in "Voyage to Cythera," where guilty men are hanged and fed to birds of prey as punishment for their sexual crimes:

> Ravenous birds, perched on their prey
> Were ferociously demolishing a ripe body that had been hanged,
> Each one planting, like an instrument, its impure beak
> In all the bleeding parts of the rotting flesh;
>
> The eyes were two holes, and from the collapsed belly
> The heavy intestines flowed over the thighs,
> And its tormentors, gorged with hideous food,
> Had totally castrated it with their sharp beaks.

In "The Painter of Modern Life" (1863), Baudelaire paid tribute to one of Poe's best stories and noted the obsessive connection between the impulsive narrator and the decrepit old man: "Do you remember a picture (it is really a picture!), painted—or rather written—by the

most powerful pen of our age, and entitled *The Man of the Crowd*? . . .
He hurls himself headlong into the midst of the throng, in pursuit
of an unknown, half-glimpsed countenance that has, on an instant,
bewitched him. Curiosity has become a fatal, irresistible passion!"
Baudelaire is the poet par excellence of the modern city. In *Paris Spleen*
and *Little Poems in Prose* as well as in *The Flowers of Evil* he immerses
himself in the crowd and makes fertile use of the interchangeable
themes of multitude and solitude.

One of Baudelaire's finest poems, "The Seven Old Men," was
directly inspired by "The Man of the Crowd." In the "Ant-seething
city, city full of dreams, / Where ghosts by daylight tug the passer's
sleeve. . . . I coaxed my weary soul with me to pace / The backstreets
shaken by each lumbering cart." There the narrator encounters a
loathsome, malevolent wretch in tattered yellow clothing:

> He plunged his soles into the slush as though
> To crush the dead; and to the world around
> Seemed less of an indifferent than a foe.

The old man spawns seven of his own images, which follow him,
and all the "spectres steered / With the same gait to the same unknown
goal." The narrator returns to his room,

> sick, fevered, chilled with fright:
> With all my spirit sorely hurt and troubled
> By so ridiculous yet strange a sight.[6]

But, unable to free himself from the impression of horror, he falls
into a state of complete nervous collapse and is left in loneliness and
despair—precisely like the wretched and disgusting man, his alter
ego, whom he has been following.

Joris-Karl Huysmans's *Against Nature* (1884) illustrates how Baudelaire's work had transformed Poe into a French Decadent artist, whose
revulsion from the modern world results in an exaltation of the senses
and a retreat from reality. Huysmans suggests numerous parallels
between Roderick Usher and his own hero, Des Esseintes, when he
invokes "that master of induction, the wise and wonderful Edgar
Allan Poe," who "better perhaps than anyone else, possessed those
intimate affinities that could satisfy the requirements of Des Esseintes'
mind." Usher's weird library and fantastic paintings are reflected in
Des Esseintes' collection of corrupt Latin literature and in his evocation of Gustave Moreau's Decadent portrayals of Salome. Like Roder-

ick Usher, Des Esseintes systematically exploits every possible sensation, yet is hypersensitive and erethic. Usher "suffered much from a morbid acuteness of the senses; the most insipid food was alone endurable; he could only wear garments of a certain texture; the odors of all flowers were oppressive; his eyes were tortured by even a faint light; and there were but peculiar sounds, and these from stringed instruments, which did not inspire him with horror."

In a similar fashion, Des Esseintes seeks to escape from the intolerable vulgarity and materialism of the contemporary world into "the tumultuous spaces of nightmares and dreams." In the Preface, Huysmans remarks that his cultured, refined and wealthy hero, "has discovered in artificiality a specific for the disgust inspired by the worries of life and the American manners of his time. I imagined him winging his way to the land of dreams, seeking refuge in extravagant illusions, living alone and apart, far from the present-day world, in an atmosphere suggestive of more cordial epochs and less odious surroundings."[7] Des Esseintes is attracted to the unsexed women of Edgar Poe; and the primary purpose of his hermetic phantasmagoria is to create through artifice and imagination an aesthetic and sexual substitute for the hackneyed luxury of commonplace caresses.

The poet Arthur Rimbaud also assimilated Poe through Baudelaire's essays and translations. Rimbaud's famous statement about the divided self, "*Je est un autre*" (I is another), reflects Poe's concept of the double self. Rimbaud's bold declaration in *A Season in Hell* (1873)—"I am going to unveil all the mysteries: religious mysteries, or natural mysteries, death, birth, the future, the past, cosmogyny, nothingness. I am master of phantasmagoria"—sounds remarkably like the wild claims of *Eureka*.

Rimbaud's use of synesthesia in his sonnet "Vowels" (1871), in which each vowel of the alphabet (placed out of order to suggest an apparent lack of logical meaning) corresponds to a different color, derives from E. T. A. Hoffmann, Poe and Baudelaire. In "The Salon of 1846" Baudelaire quoted a passage from Hoffmann that perfectly expressed his own idea: " 'It is not only in dreams, or in that mild delirium which precedes sleep, but it is even awakened when I hear music—that perception of an analogy and an intimate connection between colours, sounds and perfumes." Baudelaire himself portrayed this concept in "Correspondences":

> Like long echoes which in a distance are mingled
> In a dark and profound vision

Vast as night is and light
Perfumes, colors, and sounds answer one another.[8]

But Poe also flowed into this stream of influence. In "The Masque of
the Red Death" each of the seven rooms in Prince Prospero's secluded
abbey is dominated by a different color; and five of them—purple,
white, scarlet, green and blue—correspond almost exactly to the
colors associated with Rimbaud's vowels: "*A noir, E blanc, I rouge, U
vert, O bleu, voyelles.*"[9]

III ==

Just as Poe's imagery and morbid themes influenced Baudelaire's life
and poetry, so his fictional ideas and narrative methods had a great
impact on Dostoyevsky. The theme of the double—the existence of
a second self who haunts the protagonist and drives him insane, or is
even an expression of his insanity—preoccupied Dostoyevsky for
years. Poe's "William Wilson" provided a fictional example of how
this theme could be successfully developed. Thomas Mann, discussing
the influence of this story on Dostoyevsky's *The Double* (1846),
thought Poe's tale was a superior work of art: "Certainly he by no
means improved on Edgar Allan Poe's 'William Wilson,' a tale that
deals with the same old romantic motiv in a way far more profound
on the moral side and more successfully resolving the clinical [theme]
in the poetic." This crucial theme was expressed not only in Poe's
self-divided characters, but also in stories like "The Fall of the House
of Usher," "The Murders in the Rue Morgue," "The Purloined
Letter" and "The Man of the Crowd," where the hero and narrator
are complementary aspects of a split personality.

In *The Insulted and Injured* (1861) Dostoyevsky's hero becomes not
so much divided in himself as alienated from the society around him.
The pathological narrator describes his extraordinary and ineluctable
state of dread that not only recalls Poe's "The Man of the Crowd,"
but also anticipates the anguish of Kierkegaard and Kafka. The very
inability to define the cause of his obsession is exactly what makes it
so unbearable: "I gradually began at dusk to sink into that condition
which is so common with me now at night in my illness, and which
I call *mysterious horror*. It is a most oppressive and agonising state of
terror of something which I don't know how to define, something
passing all understanding and outside the natural order of things. . . .

In my distress the indefiniteness of the apprehension makes my suffering even more acute."

Notes from Underground (1864) reveals Poe's influence on both subject and style. Like "The Man of the Crowd," the pathetic anti-hero is reduced to insignificance when he merges into an anonymous mass of people. But he decides to assert his identity by crashing into a huge officer on Nevsky Prospect in St. Petersburg. Though he suffers more than the officer does from this brusque encounter, he ironically considers himself the equal of the other man of the crowd: "Suddenly I decided. I closed my eyes and we banged hard against each other, shoulder against shoulder, I didn't yield an inch and walked past him as an equal!"

Dostoyevsky not only expanded Poe's evocation of the helpless individual lost in the swarming city mob, he also more directly imitated the deeply disturbing opening sentences and colloquial but manic voice of the narrator of "The Tell-Tale Heart." Poe's narrator states:

> True—nervous—very, very dreadfully nervous I had been and am; but why *will* you say that I am mad?

And Dostoyevsky's narrator declares:

> I'm a sick man . . . a mean man. There's nothing attractive about me. I think there's something wrong with my liver.

Dostoyevsky used Poe's technique to create an extended confession of self-loathing, of physical and psychological illness, of pathological despair.

Like Poe, Dostoyevsky—nearly always desperately in debt, prone to drink heavily and with a personal life as emotionally wrenching as any of his fictions—dedicated a great deal of effort to establishing and maintaining a literary journal. In 1861, four years after Baudelaire's last essay on Poe, Dostoyevsky introduced Russian readers to three of Poe's stories in his journal *Wremia* (*Time*). His comments show what he had learned from Poe about narrative technique. He called Poe an "enormously talented writer"; praised his vivid realism, powerful imagination and psychological insight; and explained his method of persuading the reader, by the use of realistic details, to believe in the most extraordinary events: "Poe merely supposes the outward possibility of an unnatural event, though he always demonstrates logically that possibility and does it sometimes even with astounding skill; and this premise once granted, he in all the rest proceeds quite realistically."[10]

Dostoyevsky developed Poe's method of putting characters with absurd and bizarre feelings into realistic settings in order to create poignant and dramatic situations. In this way, Poe's concentrated tales of horror, like "The Black Cat" and "The Tell-Tale Heart," inspired the lengthy psychological studies of guilt, fear and repentance in *Crime and Punishment* and *The Brothers Karamazov*.

Dostoyevsky's pioneering essay and exploration of Poe's themes helped to arouse great interest in his work. He eventually became an extremely popular writer; and between 1918 and 1959, 900,000 copies of Poe's books were printed in the Soviet Union.

IV ═══

Poe fed several streams of English writers: the Pre-Raphaelite poets and Aesthetes—Rossetti, Pater and Wilde—who valued his theories of poetry and art; the writers of masculine adventure stories—Stevenson and Kipling—who imitated his plots and techniques; novelists as different as Conrad and Joyce, who echoed Poe's religious scepticism and fundamental pessimism; and Conan Doyle, the first writer of the modern detective story.

The Pre-Raphaelite Brotherhood, a group of painters who first came together in 1848, included Poe in their list of "Immortals," which, they said, constituted "the whole of their creed." They kept his reputation alive in the dark days between his death and the memorial ceremony in 1875. The poet and painter Dante Gabriel Rossetti, who dominated the group, mentioned near the end of his life that one of his major poems, "The Blessed Damozel" (1847), written when he was only eighteen, had been influenced by Poe's "The Raven": "I saw that Poe had done the utmost it was possible to do with the grief of the lover on earth, and so I determined to reverse the condition, and give utterance to the yearning of the loved one in heaven."[11]

The story of Rossetti's protracted love affair and brief, unhappy marriage to his model, Elizabeth Siddal, seems to come straight out of Poe's tales. Though Elizabeth had been his ideal of beauty, she became ill with tuberculosis and by the time of their marriage Rossetti no longer loved her. Depressed and ill, she attempted to kill herself with an overdose of sleeping potion and died shortly after. Overcome by grief and guilt, Rossetti buried the manuscript of his poems with her, and many years later had her exhumed so he could retrieve and publish them.

Poe was important to the late Victorians as a theoretician of poetry. Walter Pater, whose aesthetic ideas influenced many late nineteenth-century writers, took over Poe's concept, expressed in his early "Letter to B——," that music—which produced pleasurable sensations and stirred man's deepest feelings—intensified the effect of poetry. Poe believed that "music is an *essential*, since the comprehension of sweet sound is our most indefinite conception. Music, when combined with a pleasurable idea, is poetry." Following Poe's emphasis, Pater exalted music as the most abstract and therefore the purest art. In *The Renaissance* (1888), he decisively stated: "to the condition of [music's] perfect moments, all the arts may be supposed constantly to tend and aspire." And in *Appreciations* (1889) he called music "the ideal of all art whatever, precisely because in music it is impossible to distinguish the form from the substance, the subject from the expression."

In 1886 Wilde, a disciple of Pater, had praised Poe's marvelous rhythmical expression. Five years later, he adapted the ideas in Poe's story "The Oval Portrait" in his novel *The Picture of Dorian Gray*. Poe had suggested that a painting could reveal evil and guilt, and that the artist feeds on—and sometimes destroys—the life he has transformed into art. In Poe's tale the artist, maniacally absorbed in executing the portrait, neglects his beloved subject and allows her to wither away and die. Wilde varied this theme by having the portrait gradually change to reveal the evil of its subject (rather than of its artist), and added the idea of the double from "William Wilson." Threatened with exposure of his crime, Dorian Gray becomes convinced that if he destroys the painting with the same knife he used to kill the painter, "It would kill the past, and when that was dead he would be free." But, as Wilde explained in 1890, the year the book was serialized, "In his attempt to kill conscience, Dorian Gray kills himself."[12]

Reviewing Ingram's edition of Poe's works in 1875, Robert Louis Stevenson commended Poe's "brilliant and often solid workmanship," "true story-teller's instinct" and "important contribution to morbid psychology." Though Stevenson deplored the calumnies of Griswold, "who makes so repulsive a figure in literary history," he still found Poe an unsympathetic figure and wrote a generally negative evaluation of his work. Stevenson condemned the fustian and imposture in the stories, and the lack of "such scrupulous honesty as guides and restrains the finished artist." Repelled by the subject matter, he exclaimed: "He who could write 'King Pest' [a grotesque story of drunkenness during a plague] had ceased to be a human being."

In a letter to a friend Stevenson planned a comically composite "Ode by Ben Jonson, Edgar Allan Poe, and a bungler." Though he disapproved of Poe's imperfections as a man and an artist, Stevenson nevertheless borrowed extensively from his work. Stevenson's special talent lay in making plots and themes suitable for a popular audience. Providing just enough horror to make a story enjoyable, he used Poe as a source for themes of his own fiction, simplifying Poe's ideas and making them more easily comprehensible. He transformed the theme of the destructive double in "William Wilson" into the highly successful *Dr. Jekyll and Mr. Hyde* (1886). The hunt for buried treasure in Poe's most popular story, "The Gold-Bug," inspired *Treasure Island* (1883). In his Preface Stevenson acknowledged his indebtedness: "I broke into the gallery of Mr. Poe. . . . No doubt the skeleton [in my novel] is conveyed from Poe."[13] Johnny Tremaine, the hero of Stevenson's popular book, is named after the birthplace of a heroine in "Ligeia."

Rudyard Kipling, a far greater writer than Stevenson, who wrote in many of the same genres and sometimes for a juvenile audience, also acknowledged: "My own personal debt to Poe is a heavy one." Poe's extensive influence on Kipling ranged from the use of technical details to make stories more realistic and the device of including poems within tales (as in "Ligeia" and "The Fall of the House of Usher"), to the reworking of Poe's tales of revenge and the supernatural. In Poe's "Metzengerstein" and Kipling's "The Phantom Rickshaw," the hero is pursued and punished by the horse or rickshaw of the person he has murdered. In "The Murders in the Rue Morgue" and in Kipling's "Bimi," a pet orang-outang commits a murder.

Kipling admired Poe's ability to evoke terror. In "In the House of Suddhoo" he draws on the reader's knowledge of "The Facts in the Case of M. Valdemar" to suggest the terrifying effects of sorcery. Old Suddhoo pays for spells to save his sick son's life, and one of them involves the "dried shrivelled black head of a native baby," which appears to speak. Kipling's narrator says: "Read Poe's account of the voice that came from the mesmerised dying man, and you will realise less than one half of the horror of that head's voice."

In his stories of shell shock and war psychosis, Kipling refined Poe's habit of describing certain horrors and then hinting at other things too horrible to be described. In Kipling's "The Miracle of St. Jubanus," the returned French soldier was one of those who "entered hells of whose existence they had not dreamed—of whose terrors they lacked words to tell." In his story "In the Same Boat" the hero, "while he lay between sleep and wake, would be overtaken by a long shuddering sigh, which he learned to know was the sign that his brain had once more conceived its horror, and in time—in due time— would bring it forth."[14]

Many of Kipling's stories have supernatural plots. He frequently employed Poe's ideas, most forcefully expressed in "A Tale of the Ragged Mountains," that the same experience could persist through time, and that a person living in the present could reenact past events or reincarnate the dead. In Poe's tale and in Kipling's "The Finest Story in the World" the characters have knowledge of previous incarnations. In "By Word of Mouth" the death of a living man is predicted by a ghost. In "The Tomb of His Ancestors" Young Chinn bears the mark of his forebears, and inevitably repeats their actions. In "In the Same Boat" a man and a woman reexperience in dreams things that had happened to their parents. In "Wireless" a young shop clerk almost repeats the experience of Keats and "The Eve of St. Agnes."

Kipling was capable of infinite variations on Poe's imaginative ideas. But Poe's Gothic elements also attracted other writers whose art tended to the weightier realistic and moral tradition of the English novel. In an early story, "The Lifted Veil" (1859), George Eliot rather surprisingly used Poe-like plot devices to develop her theme. Her biographer writes: "Bertha's inadequately motivated plan to poison Latimer is exposed through the revival of a dying maid by means of blood transfusion, a melodramatic expedient worthy of Poe, whose tales 'The Lifted Veil' occasionally reminds one of with the abnormally heightened consciousness of its hero, its foreign setting . . . and its pseudo-scientific climax."

When Joseph Conrad, as eager for financial reward as Poe or Stevenson, tried his hand at a popular mystery story, he imitated the horrific effect of Poe's "The Pit and the Pendulum" in a Spanish-Gothic tale, "The Inn of the Two Witches" (1913). During the Peninsular War an English naval officer, searching on land for a trusty seaman, discovers that he has been murdered for his money and crushed to death by a heavy four-poster bed at a sinister inn. When given the same room as the missing sailor, he realizes what must have happened when he observes the top of the bed descending upon him. Conrad's story was a failure. The narrative is clumsy, the plot mechanical, the style arch (he says of the two old women who keep the inn, "there was something grotesque in their decrepitude"). Though Conrad did not repeat this experiment, it may have increased his respect for Poe, whose "MS. Found in a Bottle" he praised for its authentic detail and called "a very fine piece of work."

Conrad was mainly interested in Poe's ideas about art and his tragic view of life. His belief that literature must approximate the quality of music was very close to Poe's. In *Marginalia* Poe wrote: "The *indefinitiveness* which is, at least, *one* of the essentials of true music, must, of course, be kept in view." Conrad echoed this in the Preface to *The Nigger of the "Narcissus,"* his major aesthetic statement: "[Art] must strenuously aspire to the plasticity of sculpture, to the colour of painting, and to the magic suggestiveness of music—which is the art of arts."[15]

When discussing suicide (which, like Poe, he himself had attempted), Conrad alluded to Poe and wrote: "Men are always cowards. They are frightened by the expression 'nevermore.' " Like Poe, Conrad did not believe in the idea of progress. In "The Man of the Crowd" Poe mourned the loss of social community and the alienation of the solitary individual who experienced loneliness, self-doubt, loss of identity and a sense of estrangement. Conrad, also obsessed with the theme of isolation, defined the human condition when he wrote in *Heart of Darkness* (1899): "We live, as we dream—alone." In 1844 Poe had despairingly told Chivers: "I disagree with you in what you say of man's advance toward perfection. Man is now only more active, not wiser, nor more happy, than he was 6,000 years ago." Fifty years later, Conrad was even gloomier than Poe. He believed that faith was an illusion, that life was meaningless suffering, that there were no moral absolutes: "In this world—as I have known it— we are made to suffer without the shadow of a reason, of a cause or of guilt. . . . There is no morality, no knowledge and no hope. . . . A moment, a twinkling of an eye, and nothing remains—but a clot of mud, of cold mud, of dead mud cast into black space, rolling around an extinguished sun."[16]

Since Poe's themes and ideas found their way into so many literary works of the nineteenth and twentieth centuries, it is not surprising that a central Poe motif appears in James Joyce's *Ulysses* (1922). Joyce was well acquainted with the works of Poe, who had experienced a revival in England at the turn of the century and had been praised by the leading Irish writers: Wilde, Shaw, Yeats and George Moore.[17] Joyce probably knew that Poe had been the subject of a study, published in 1901, by a Colonel John A. Joyce. In his essay on James Clarence Mangan (1902), Joyce calls Poe "the high priest of most modern schools," and he alludes to Poe's works a dozen times in *Dubliners, Ulysses* and *Finnegans Wake*.

In *Ulysses* Joyce's hero shares Poe's sceptical, rationalistic attitude toward life, but is also fascinated and disgusted by the physical facts of death. Leopold Bloom's thoughts during Paddy Dignam's funeral in the "Hades" chapter of the novel reveal Joyce's knowledge of the "life-preserving" coffins that Poe had described in "The Premature Burial."

Bloom—obsessed with the deaths of his father and his son, and cut off from the natural cycle of regeneration—ponders, at Dignam's funeral, the mysteries of conception, marriage, paternity and death. Emotionally, intellectually and spiritually isolated, the ever-solitary son of a suicide is taunted and rejected by his fellow Dubliners. Denied the consolation of religious belief and the promise of an afterlife ("Once you are dead you are dead"), Bloom perceives the emptiness of ritual and dogma, mocks the Catholic clergy and burial service, and adopts a cynically defensive attitude to hide his terror of the grave.

When the gravediggers take up their spades and sling the heavy clods of clay on to the coffin, Bloom is suddenly confronted with one of his deepest fears: "And if he was alive all the time? Whew! By jingo, that would be awful!" But he immediately tries to reassure himself and suggests pragmatic remedies to make certain the body is really dead, to alert the living if it is still alive and unable to breathe, and to prevent the disaster of a Poe-like premature burial: "No, no: he is dead, of course. Of course he is dead. Monday he died. They ought to have some law to pierce the heart and make sure or an electric clock or a telephone in the coffin or some kind of a canvas airhole. Flag of distress. [Wait] three days."

The ingenious coffins and escape devices invented in the nineteenth century to prevent premature burial included all the features imagined by Leopold Bloom: the speaking tube (or prototypal telephone), the air opening, the electrical alarm and the flag of distress. On the way to Dignam's funeral, when Martin Cunningham mentions a hearse that capsized round Dunphy's and upset the coffin on to the road, Bloom vividly imagines what must have occurred—"Bom! Upset. A coffin bumped out on to the road. Burst open. Paddy Dignam shot out and rolling over stiff in the dust in a brown habit too large for him. Red face: grey now. Mouth fallen open. Asking what's up now"[18]—and describes an escape from a "life-preserving" coffin. Joyce's use of Poe's idea achieved the same grisly mixture of humor and horror that had appeared in the original.

Conan Doyle was always very generous in publicly acknowledging, over a period of nearly forty years, his immense debt to Poe.[19] He also paid tribute to Poe in his fiction. In *A Study in Scarlet* (1887), it is the critical Sherlock Holmes—rather than the admiring Conan Doyle—who speaks when, after analyzing and adopting Dupin's methods, Holmes attempts, ironically, to denigrate his extraordinary achievement. After Dr. Watson says:

"You remind me of Edgar Allan Poe's Dupin. I had no idea that such individuals did exist outside of stories."

Sherlock Holmes rose and lit a pipe. "No doubt you think that you are complimenting me in comparing me to Dupin," he observed. "Now, in my opinion, Dupin was a very inferior fellow. That trick of his of breaking in on his friends' thoughts with an apropos remark after a quarter of an hour's silence is really very showy and superficial. He had some analytical genius, no doubt; but he was by no means such a phenomenon as Poe appeared to imagine."

Six years later, however, in "The Cardboard Box" (1893), Holmes acknowledged the impact of Dupin and compared his own methods to those of his predecessor:

You remember that some little time ago when I read you the passage in one of Poe's sketches in which a close reasoner follows the unspoken thoughts of his companion, you were inclined to treat the matter as a mere *tour-de-force* of the author. On my remarking that I was constantly in the habit of doing the same thing you expressed incredulity.

The famous passage to which Holmes refers occurs in "The Murders in the Rue Morgue" when the narrator and Dupin are strolling at night through a long street near the Palais Royal:

Being both, apparently, occupied with thought, neither of us had spoken a syllable for fifteen minutes at least. All at once Dupin broke forth with these words:

"He is a very little fellow, that's true, and would do better for the *Théâtre des Variétés*."

"There can be no doubt of that," I replied, unwittingly, and not at first observing . . . the extraordinary manner in which the speaker had chimed in with my meditations."

Doyle copies this exactly in "The Dancing Men" when Holmes unaccountably reads Watson's secret thoughts:

"So, Watson," said he, suddenly, "you do not propose to invest in South African securities?"

I gave a start of astonishment. Accustomed as I was to Holmes' curious faculties, this sudden intrusion into my most intimate thoughts was utterly inexplicable.[20]

Poe's pervasive influence on Doyle extends from minor details to major themes. Both "The Purloined Letter" and "The Sign of the Four" end with a quotation in a foreign language. The cipher theme in "The Gold-Bug" reappears in "The Musgrave Ritual" and "The Dancing Men." In "The Murders in the Rue Morgue" Dupin discovers, by a process of ratiocination, that the brutal murderer is an orang-outang; in "The Sign of the Four" Holmes deduces that the assassin—larger than a child and as agile as a monkey—is, in fact, a pygmy. Doyle's description of the approach to moldering Baskerville Hall is strikingly similar to Poe's account of the approach to the House of Usher. Both stories have fearful, decadent characters and a heroine who expires in the arms of her twin.

In *Memories and Adventures* (1924) Doyle wrote that "M. Dupin had from boyhood been one of my heroes"; and Dupin was, in fact, the literary model for Holmes. Like Holmes, Dupin "is fond of enigmas, of conundrums, hieroglyphics, exhibiting in his solutions of each a degree of *acumen* which appears to the ordinary apprehension praeternatural."

Both Dupin and Holmes recur in several stories and like to recall their success in solving previous cases. Both are portrayed through the eyes of a dim but devoted friend, who (like the reader) remains in the dark until the final startling revelation. Both detectives reside with the narrator in seclusion, exclude sunlight from their chambers and tend to venture outside after nightfall. Both are sexless bachelors and casual dilettantes (Holmes' violin descends from Usher's guitar), with erudite tastes and arcane learning. Both are experts in ciphers and much superior to the plodding police, and attract suspects to their rooms through advertisements in newspapers. Both indulge in abstract reflection before their logical analysis leads to a solution of the crime, exhibit virtuoso displays of knowledge, identify their reasoning intellect with that of the criminal, have uncanny powers of observation and can deduce occupations from physical appearance.

Like Dupin, the perceptive narrator in "The Man of the Crowd" notes that "the right ears [of clerks], long used to pen-holding, stand off on end" and that gamblers have "a more than ordinary extension of the thumb." Holmes acutely remarks, after observing a client:

"From South Africa, sir, I perceive."

"Yes, sir," he answered, with some surprise.

"Imperial Yeomanry, I fancy."

"Exactly."

"Middlesex Corps, no doubt."

"That is so. Mr. Holmes, you are a wizard."

The opening paragraph of "The Purloined Letter" had a powerful impact on Conan Doyle. The two friends are silently smoking pipes in Dupin's study when the door is suddenly thrown open and the ignorant prefect of police arrives to seek the detective's help. A great many of Doyle's stories—"A Case of Identity," "The Blue Carbuncle," "The Beryl Coronet," "The Copper Beeches," "The Bruce-Partington Plans," "The Mazarin Stone" and "The Three Gables"— begin in a similar fashion. In "The Six Napoleons" Doyle notes that "It was no very unusual thing for Mr. Lestrade, of Scotland Yard, to look in upon us of an evening, and his visits were welcome to Sherlock Holmes, for they enabled him to keep in touch with all that was going on at the police headquarters"—and, incidentally, to make a fool of their chief official.

During a grand banquet at the Hotel Metropole to celebrate the centenary of Poe's birth, Doyle truly observed: "These tales have been so pregnant with suggestion, so stimulating to the minds of others, that it may be said of many of them that each is a root from which a whole literature has developed."[21] As modern writers learned to appreciate Poe's complexity and to take him more seriously, they explored and mined his fascinating and farsighted works. George Eliot, Wilde and Stevenson borrowed his plots; Rossetti, Kipling and Joyce adopted his themes; Pater and Conrad utilized his theories; Conan Doyle recreated his characters.

V ═

Poe's influence on American literature was deep and pervasive. His Gothic mystery tales had supplied European authors with new themes, images and genres, which they freely adapted to their own cultural contexts and literary forms. To Americans, Poe was an originator. With Hawthorne and Melville, he created the ambiguous opposition of good and evil that has dominated American literature. His *Narrative of Arthur Gordon Pym* was, in this context, an allegory of the American's search for dominion over himself as well as a new geographic territory, a struggle to achieve an individual and a national identity. Poe was one of the first satirists of this potentially rich society, ambitiously seeking wealth and power; and the first artist who attempted—and failed—to support himself by writing. Poe's controversial life eventually became part of the symbolic meaning of his work.

Though Melville never mentioned *Pym* and there is no concrete evidence that he had read it, there are, as Patrick Quinn has pointed out, striking similarities that suggest the influence of Poe's book on *Moby-Dick* (1851). Both writers used the works of Jeremiah Reynolds as a common source. Poe's opening sentence: "My name is Arthur Gordon Pym" becomes more dramatic, immediate and familiar in Melville's "Call me Ishmael." Pym and Ishmael each have a ferocious, exotic, half-savage comrade who saves his life. Both are narrators of as well as participants in a dangerous sea voyage. Pym's journey culminates in a confrontation with an enigmatic evil, a menacing white being in a strange white sea. While the purpose of Pym's journey is not defined, Melville's Ahab seeks a definite goal—the destruction of Moby-Dick, the white whale that represents both un-tamed nature and the evil in Ahab himself. Pym risks his life, nearly dying of dehydration, suffocation, ambush or capture; but he pursues his journey, like the crew of the *Pequod*, toward the white blankness of the end. Melville's comment on the sinister atmosphere of *Moby-Dick* applies with equal force to Poe's *Pym*: "A polar wind blows through it, & birds of prey hover over it."[22] Just as Poe's stories of revenge, murder and remorse influenced the more elaborate novels of Dostoyevsky, so his incomplete tale of an imaginary voyage doubtless helped Melville create his American masterpiece.

In this century American novelists have used Poe's satiric as well as symbolic elements. Scott Fitzgerald, casting his moral fable of youthful obsession with the rich and disillusion with money in the form of a fantasy, deliberately imitated and parodied Poe's most famous story, "The Fall of the House of Usher" in "The Diamond as Big as the Ritz" (1922). Fitzgerald was not only influenced by Poe's literary works, but was also acutely aware of the parallels between Poe's life and his own.

Both had eminent ancestors (Poe's grandfather was a Quartermas-ter in the Revolutionary Army, Fitzgerald was descended from the patriotic poet Francis Scott Key), but since Poe's parents were impov-erished actors and Fitzgerald's father a pathetic failure, each writer, uneasy about his social status, was powerfully attracted to old families and envied solid wealth. Though Poe was born in Boston and Fitzgerald in St. Paul, they associated themselves with the Southern gentility and courtly manners of Virginia (where Poe grew up) and of Maryland (where Fitzgerald's father was raised). Poe left the University of Virginia, as Fitzgerald left Princeton, without graduating. After serving as an enlisted man, Poe was expelled from West Point; Fitzgerald had an equally undistinguished career in American military camps and never crossed the ocean to fight in the European war. He strongly identified with and even imitated Poe's life, and spoke for both of them when he said: "I talk with the authority of failure."

Both men had tragic marriages. Virginia Poe died of tuberculosis at the age of twenty-four; Zelda Fitzgerald became insane when she was twenty-nine. Both men wasted their artistic talents as hack writers for popular magazines, yet were desperately short of money and frequently had to borrow from their friends. Alcoholics who became intoxicated after one or two glasses, they often lost control of themselves, behaved in an abject and humiliating manner, and remained drunk for a week at a time. Poe ruined his career by offending literary editors just as Fitzgerald did with powerful film producers. Both authors died from the effects of drink and were buried in the state of Maryland. Their reckless personal behavior seriously damaged their literary reputations, which were not revived until many years after their deaths.

It is not surprising, then, given Fitzgerald's lifelong identification with Poe, that he should have sought in Poe's well-known story a Gothic setting and a fantastic form that would express his own ambivalent feelings about the rich. Though Poe characteristically emphasizes the decay and horror, Fitzgerald the glamour and luxury of the house; Poe's heroine is diseased and moribund, Fitzgerald's "the incarnation of physical perfection"; Poe has a tragic, Fitzgerald an apparently happy ending, the numerous parallels, once perceived, are unmistakable.

Fitzgerald echoes the name of Poe's Usher by calling his hero Unger. In both stories a young man, Poe's narrator and Fitzgerald's naive schoolboy, is invited to visit an "intimate" boyhood friend. The neurasthenic Roderick Usher comes from an ancient family, and Percy Washington boasts to the provincial Unger that his father is the richest man in the world. Both visitors represent a conventional ordinariness, a certain norm of behavior that helps to define the bizarre nature of the events they observe.

The narrator in Poe and the naive hero in Fitzgerald see their friends as part of a doomed family in a cursed house. Both mansions have intricate subterranean passages and are remote, isolated and fantastically unreal. Situated near a tarn or lake, each monstrous house contains an oppressive secret, and reflects the fearful mood of its inhabitants.

Poe's hothouse rhetoric: "What was it—I paused to think—what was it that so unnerved me in the contemplation of the House of Usher?" is echoed in John Unger's troubled questions when he first arrives at the mountain house: "What desperate transaction lay hidden here? What moral expedient of a bizarre Croesus? What terrible and golden mystery?" Poe mentions the sentience of vegetable matter—the proliferating fungi that overspread and the decayed trees that surround the house—which reflects the doom of the family. Fitzgerald imitates the idea of the house as prison by describing an old family trapped, stupefied and corrupted by its selfish accumulation of useless wealth and by the enormous diamond that cannot be sold lest it destroy the economic foundations of the world.

Roderick Usher's dissipated artistic endeavors—his dreary dirges, phantasmagoric paintings and morbid poetry—are reflected in Fitzgerald by a kidnapped "landscape gardener, an architect, a designer of stage settings, and a French decadent poet" who fail to create as expected, go mad and are confined to a mental asylum. Only a crude "moving picture fella" from Hollywood succeeds in designing the lavish reception rooms and luxurious baths.

Both visitors briefly glimpse their host's sister as she passes through the house. Madeline Usher is cursed by a secret sexual guilt she shares with her brother. Kismine Washington (Unger's girlfriend and *kismet*, or fate) is cursed by the murder of the friends who had visited her in the past, could not be permitted to betray the secret wealth to the outside world and were sacrificed after they had provided distraction and pleasure for the family.

Fitzgerald echoes the premature entombment of Madeline in one of the numerous vaults beneath the House of Usher in Braddock Washington's incarceration of the captured aviators in a deep, Poe-like pit, covered by an iron grating. Both young men are suddenly awakened in the middle of the night by a strange, frightening noise. Poe's familiar physiological description of fear when Usher realizes he has entombed the living Madeline:

> there came a strong shudder over his whole person; a sickly smile quivered about his lips; and I saw that he spoke in a low, hurried, and gibbering manner,

is equaled by Fitzgerald's fantastic simile when Unger perceives that
the Washingtons have murdered their guests:

> Stunned with the horror of this revelation, John sat there
> open-mouthed, feeling the nerves of his body twitter like so
> many sparrows perched upon his spinal column.[23]

In Poe, Usher throws back the ebony jaws of the huge antique
panels to reveal his vengeful, bloodstained sister. In Fitzgerald, the
ebony panel of one wall slides aside to reveal a uniformed manservant
who assists Unger with his bath. Madeline murders her brother; Percy
Washington's grandfather was also compelled to murder his brother,
who had the unfortunate Poe-and-Fitzgerald-like habit "of drinking
himself into an indiscreet stupor." At the end of both stories the evil
houses are completely destroyed, but the visitors escape disaster.

Both stories are moral fables that offer a purely external portrayal
of the characters and express the quintessential theme of illusion and
reality. In "The Fall of the House of Usher," the decaying mansion
symbolizes the perhaps unconscious incestuous and necrophilic de-
sires of the Usher twins, Roderick and Madeline, who are finally rent
asunder (like the house itself), after "he had to kill something inside
himself" and she had to commit retributive murder. If the Ushers'
sin is incest, the Washingtons' is greed; and both sins lead to the final
destruction of their family, dynasty and class. Poe's narrator, who
never reveals why Roderick entombed Madeline or why she murdered
him, merely records the events and expresses his abstract horror.
Fitzgerald, building on Poe's story, shows his hero moving from
sheer enjoyment of the overwhelming luxury to an awareness of
evil in the House of Washington, to a condemnation of its perverse
corruption. Fitzgerald indicates, by the name of the family, that his
purpose is allegorical and satiric. The House of Washington represents
a vulgar, venal, greedy America where everything—freedom, human
values, art and culture—is sacrificed to gross wealth. Just as Melville
developed many of the themes of *Pym*, so Fitzgerald expressed the
latent symbolism of "The Fall of the House of Usher."

The personality and ideas of Poe made a deep impression on Vladimir Nabokov soon after he came to America. His story, "A Forgotten
Poet" (1944), was directly inspired by Poe. In this wry tale, "a Russian
poet, supposed drowned at twenty-four in 1849, turns up as a seventy-
four-year-old at a memorial gathering in 1899 on the fiftieth anniversary of his death, and demands the money that had been raised for a
monument in his name." The noun in the title and the name of the

main character, the talented poet Perov, both include the letters of
Poe's name. The dates are important to Nabokov, who was as keen
as Poe on puzzles, coincidences and codes. Poe also died impoverished
in 1849; and the fiftieth anniversary of his death was the year of
Nabokov's birth. Like Perov, Poe's reputation plunged immediately
after his death, and *his* tomb was dedicated at a memorial gathering
in 1875.

Like Poe, Nabokov knew what it was like to struggle with poverty
during the years following his exile from Russia, when he lived from
hand to mouth in Berlin and Paris. He no doubt sympathized with
Poe's shabby dignity as he went the rounds of editors and offices
trying to get work. Like Perov, Poe would have preferred some cash
in his lifetime to a marble monument after his death.

Nabokov admired Poe's doctrine of pure art, detached from moral
freight. He translated Poe's story "Silence—A Fable" into Russian,
and echoed the phrase "the ghoul-haunted woodland of Weir" from
"Ulalume" in *Bend Sinister*'s "the ghoul-haunted Province of Perm."
Considering his professional interest in entomology, it is a pity that
Nabokov did not carefully investigate the taxonomy of Poe's Gold-
Bug as he had of Kafka's monstrous dung beetle.

Nabokov's best novel, *Lolita* (1955), shows Poe's influence most
strongly. He originally called it *The Kingdom by the Sea*, an allusion
to "Annabel Lee," and made dozens of references to Poe throughout
the novel. Humbert's obsession with the pubescent nymphet Lolita—
revealed first in a small town and then, as they travel by car, in
the vast transcontinental landscape—is an ironic recreation of Poe's
strange marriage to his adolescent cousin. "Did she have a precursor?"
Humbert remarks. "She did, indeed, she did. In point of fact there
might have been no Lolita at all had I not loved, one summer, a
certain initial girl-child. In a princedom by the sea."[24] The strange
metamorphosis of the slim, Southern Edgar into another awkward
outsider, the middle-aged European Humbert, and of the childish,
dying Virginia into the naive yet knowing Lolita, is as brilliantly
original as anything in Poe. Nabokov's novel uses Poe's life and
works to satirize the meaningless conventions and philistine values of
bourgeois American society.

Just as Fitzgerald had used Poe's story to portray the corruption in
American life, so Tom Wolfe, in his novel *The Bonfire of the Vanities*
(1987), called one chapter "The Masque of the Red Death" to suggest
the rottenness of the New York rich. Instead of a masked ball, the
scene is a dinner party at the Bavardages, where Lord Buffing, an
elderly English poet, rises to address the guests. Invoking the memory

of Poe and his poetry, he states that our art is finished and that we can no longer write: "we poets no longer even have the vitality to write epics. We don't even have the courage to make rhymes, and the American epic should have rhymes, rhyme on top of rhyme in a shameless cascade, rhymes of the sort that Edgar Allan Poe gave us." In Buffing's view, Poe is the archetype of the fevered visionary, the prophet despised in his own land:

> Poe, who lived his last years just north of here, I believe, in a part of New York called the Bronx . . . in a little cottage with lilacs and a cherry tree . . . and a wife dying of tuberculosis. A drunk he was, of course, perhaps a psychotic—but with the madness of prophetic vision. He wrote a story that tells all we need to know about the moment we live in now.

Lord Buffing, who knows he is dying of AIDS, represents the masqued figure in Poe's story who enters disguised as death and whose touch is fatal. Like Prince Prospero and his revelers, these New Yorkers are cut off from the poverty that surrounds them. But AIDS, the spectral curse and modern plague, is among them. Lord Buffing narrates Poe's story, emphasizing how the guests are irresistibly drawn toward the room where Death awaits them, for

> families, homes, children, the great chain of being, the eternal tide of chromosomes mean nothing to them any longer. . . . So Poe was kind enough to write the ending for us more than a hundred years ago. Knowing that, who can possibly write all the sunnier passages that should come before? Not I, not I. The sickness—the nausea—the pitiless pain—have ceased with the fever that maddened my brain—with the fever called "Living"—those were among the last words he wrote.[25]

Wolfe uses Poe's story and his lyric "For Annie" to create an atmosphere of hysteria and fear, a sense of impending doom. This contrasts in the novel with the blind narcissism of the characters, who react to the old man's speech with embarrassed silence. Poe's pathological imagery of sickness, nausea and maddening fever, based on his observation of the ravages of tuberculosis, poignantly suggests the symptoms of AIDS.

Wolfe used "The Masque of the Red Death" to stress the meaningless pursuit of wealth, the self-destruction of the most talented artists and the doom-laden quality of American society. Just as Poe remains the quintessential example of the struggling American writer, so his suggestive stories remain an inexhaustible repository of meaning for his American followers.[26]

Neither Poe's mannered Latinate style nor his highly idiosyncratic content became a *direct* model for subsequent poetry or prose (as Pound said: "no one who has tried to write like Poe . . . has done anything good"). Yet his extensive influence on later writers has been quite out of proportion to the extremely uneven quality of his hundred poems and seventy stories. Though Poe has always appealed to popular taste, his originality and imagination have also had a considerable impact on the most advanced thinkers and most serious writers. Poe has overcome his notorious reputation (which today makes him interesting rather than repulsive), survived the vicissitudes of art during the last hundred and fifty years and remained contemporary because he has always appealed to basic human feelings and expressed universal themes common to all men in all languages: dreams, love, loss; grief, mourning, alienation; terror, revenge, murder; insanity, disease and death.[27]

CHAPTER ONE. AN INAUSPICIOUS BIRTH

1. Thomas Scharf, *The Chronicles of Baltimore* (Baltimore, 1874), p. 415.
2. Arthur Hobson Quinn, *Edgar Allan Poe: A Critical Biography* (New York, 1941), p. 6.
3. Geddeth Smith, *The Brief Career of Eliza Poe* (Rutherford, New Jersey, 1988), p. 27.
4. *Ibid.*, p. 70.
5. Richard Henry Stoddard, "Edgar Allan Poe," *Harper's Magazine*, 45 (September 1872), 557.
6. Dwight Thomas and David Jackson, *The Poe Log: A Documentary Life* (Boston, 1987), p. 9.
7. Quinn, *Poe*, p. 36.
8. *Ibid.*, p. 35.
9. *Ibid.*, pp. 32–33.
10. Susan Archer Weiss, "The Sister of Edgar A. Poe," *Continent*, 3 (June 27, 1883), 817.
11. Thomas, *Poe Log*, p. 13.
12. Quinn, *Poe*, pp. 44–45.
13. James Harrison, *The Life and Letters of Edgar Allan Poe* (New York, 1902), p. 10.
14. Edgar Allan Poe, "The Drama," *The Complete Works*, ed. James Harrison (New York, 1902), 12:186.

CHAPTER TWO. CHILDHOOD: JOHN ALLAN AND ENGLAND

1. Agnes Bondurant, *Poe's Richmond* (Richmond, 1942), pp. 199–200; Susan Archer Weiss, "Reminiscences of Edgar Allan Poe," *Independent*, 57 (August 25, 1904), 443–444.
2. Thomas, *Poe Log*, p. 834; Eugene Didier, "Life of Edgar Poe," *The Life and Poems of Edgar Allan Poe* (New York, 1877), p. 28.
3. Quinn, *Poe*, p. 66; *Works*, 8:169–170.
4. Brian Simon, *Studies in the History of Education, 1780–1870* (London, 1960), p. 98; Walter Jackson Bate, *John Keats* (New York, 1966), pp. 9–10.
5. William Elijah Hunter, "Poe and His English Schoolmaster," *Athenaeum*, 2660 (October 19, 1878), 496–497; Thomas, *Poe Log*, pp. 36, 42.
6. Quinn, *Poe*, pp. 82–83; Edgar Allan Poe, *Letters*, ed. John Ostrom (1948; New York, 1966), p. 57.
7. Colonel J. T. Preston, "Some Reminiscences of Edgar A. Poe as a Schoolboy," *Edgar Allan Poe; A Memorial Volume*, ed. Sara Sigourney Rice (Baltimore, 1877), pp. 36, 40–41.
8. Susan Archer Weiss, *The Home Life of Poe* (New York, 1907), pp. 219–220; *Works*, 17:437.
9. Poe, *Letters*, p. 385. Both the Marchesa Aphrodite in "The Assignation" and Ligeia have hyacinthine hair.
   For a modern comparison of a woman to a ship, see Hemingway's description of Brett Ashley in *The Sun Also Rises* (New York, 1926), p. 22: "She was built with curves like the hull of a racing yacht."
10. Quinn, *Poe*, p. 91; Edward Alfriend, "Unpublished Recollections of Edgar Allan Poe," *Literary Era*, 8 (August 1901), 489; *Works*, 10:85.
11. Weiss, *Home Life*, p. 86; Thomas, *Poe Log*, pp. 61–62.

CHAPTER THREE. THE UNIVERSITY OF VIRGINIA

1. Herbert Adams, *Thomas Jefferson and the University of Virginia* (Washington, 1888), p. 89; Dumas Malone, *Jefferson and His Time: The Sage of Monticello* (Boston, 1981), p. 42.
2. See John Lewis, *Tables of Comparative Etymology and Analogous Formations in the Greek, Latin, Spanish, Italian, French, English, and German Languages*. The Greek by George Long, the German by George Blaetterman (Philadelphia, 1828), and H. J. Mathews, *In Memoriam: George Long* (Brighton, 1879).

3. Thomas, *Poe Log*, p. 70; William Wertenbaker, "Edgar A. Poe," *Virginia University Magazine*, 7 (November–December 1868), 115; James Southall Wilson, "Poe at the University of Virginia," *Alumni Bulletin, University of Virginia*, 16 (April 1923), 167; William Burwell, "Edgar A. Poe and His College Contemporaries," *Alumni Bulletin, University of Virginia*, 16 (April 1923), 168; Thomas, *Poe Log*, p. 75.

4. Thomas, *Poe Log*, p. 75; Wilson, "Poe at the University of Virginia," pp. 166–167.

5. Poe, *Letters*, pp. 5–6.

6. Thomas Holley Chivers, *Life of Poe* (1852), ed. Richard Davis (New York, 1952), p. 57; Charles Kent, "Poe's Student Days at the University of Virginia," *Bookman* (New York), 44 (January 1917), 523; Douglass Sherley, "Edgar Allan Poe While a Student at the University of Virginia," *Virginia University Magazine*, 19 (April 1880), 428–429; Charles Baudelaire, "Edgar Allan Poe: His Life and Works," *The Painter of Modern Life and Other Essays*, trans. Jonathan Mayne (London, 1965), p. 88.

7. Wertenbaker, "Edgar A. Poe," p. 115. During his army career, when promoted to sergeant major, Poe replaced R. L. Glenndening.

8. Floyd Stovall, *Edgar Poe the Poet* (Charlottesville, 1969), p. 18; Poe, *Letters*, pp. 39–41.

9. Alfriend, "Unpublished Recollections," p. 490; Poe, *Letters*, pp. 7–9; Mary Newton Stanard, *Edgar Allan Poe Letters Till Now Unpublished, in the Valentine Museum, Richmond, Virginia* (Philadelphia, 1925), p. 67.

10. Edward Davidson, *Poe: A Critical Study* (Cambridge, Mass., 1957), p. 208; Richard Davis, *Intellectual Life in Jefferson's Virginia* (Chapel Hill, 1964), p. 259.

CHAPTER FOUR. THE ARMY AND WEST POINT

1. T. E. Lawrence, *Seven Pillars of Wisdom* (London, 1935), p. 564.

2. Edgar Allan Poe, *Poems*, ed. Thomas Ollive Mabbott (Cambridge, Mass., 1969), p. 21; David Randall, *The J. K. Lilly Collection of Edgar Allan Poe* (Bloomington, 1964), p. 3; Poe, *Poems*, p. 31.

3. Poe, *Letters*, pp. 9–10, 12. Poe's behavior is similar to that of Wyndham Lewis, who would take a taxi to his patron's house, abuse the generous man and then demand the fare for the waiting cab.

4. Poe, *Letters*, p. 14.

5. See Rufus Griswold, "Edgar Allan Poe" (1850), *The Poets and Poetry of America*, 11th edition (Philadelphia, 1852), p. 417 and

Alexandre Dumas, "[Account of a Visit by Poe to Paris]," *Saturday Review of Literature*, 6 (December 21, 1929), 594–595.

6. Poe, *Letters*, pp. 24, 26, 30, 32.

7. Thomas, *Poe Log*, pp. 91–93.

8. Poe, *Letters*, pp. 20–21; Stovall, *Edgar Poe the Poet*, p. 205; Poe, *Letters*, pp. 18–19.

9. Stovall, *Edgar Poe the Poet*, p. 70; Quinn, *Poe*, p. 165; Thomas, *Poe Log*, p. 103.

10. Stephen Ambrose, *Duty, Honor, Country: A History of West Point* (Baltimore, 1966), pp. 147, 150, 163, 93.

11. Stoddard, "Edgar Allan Poe," p. 561; T. W. Gibson, "Poe at West Point," *Harper's Magazine*, 35 (November 1867), 754–756; George Woodberry, *The Life of Edgar Allan Poe*, 2 vols. (New York, 1909), 1:170, 1:369–372.

12. E. R. and J. Pennell, *The Life of James McNeill Whistler*, 2 vols. (London, 1908), 1:37; Roy McMullen, *Victorian Outsider: A Biography of J. A. M. Whistler* (New York, 1973), p. 46.

13. Poe, *Letters*, pp. 39–42, 36, 471.

14. Poe, *Letters*, p. 43; Stanard, *Poe Letters Till Now Unpublished*, p. 268; Poe, *Letters*, p. 44.

15. Woodberry, *Life of Edgar Allan Poe*, 1:372; Poe, *Poems*, p. 151; Gibson, "Poe at West Point," p. 755.

16. David Halliburton, *Edgar Allan Poe: A Phenomenological View* (Princeton, 1973), p. 41.

17. Gibson, "Poe at West Point," p. 756; *Works*, 7:xxxix, xlii; 8:284; 9:51.

18. Samuel Taylor Coleridge, *Biographia Literaria*, ed. J. Shawcross, 2 vols. (Oxford, 1907), 2:10, and *Works*, 7:xliii; Floyd Stovall, "Poe's Debt to Coleridge," *University of Texas Studies in English*, 10 (1930), 174, 137.

19. John Hewitt, *Recollections of Poe*, ed. Richard Harwell (Atlanta, 1949), p. 20; Augustus Van Cleef, "Poe's Mary," *Harper's Monthly*, 78 (March 1889), 636; Weiss, "Reminiscences of Poe," p. 1011.

20. Harrison, *Life and Letters of Poe*, p. 113; John Carl Miller, *Building Poe Biography* (Baton Rouge, 1977), p. 116; *Works*, 1:344–345.

CHAPTER FIVE. BALTIMORE: MARIA CLEMM AND EARLY STORIES

1. Richard Wilbur, "Poe," *Major Writers of America*, ed. Perry Miller (New York, 1962), p. 373.

2. Thomas, *Poe Log*, p. x; Daniel Hoffman, *Poe Poe Poe Poe Poe Poe Poe* (Garden City, New York, 1972), p. xii.

3. Thomas, *Poe Log*, p. 731; Lambert Wilmer, *Merlin, Baltimore, 1827*, ed. T. O. Mabbott (New York, 1941), p. 27; Edgar Allan Poe, *Marginalia*, Introduction by John Carl Miller (Charlottesville, 1981), p. 199.

4. *Works*, 17:28; 17:258; Poe, *Marginalia*, p. 196.

5. Mayne Reid, *Edgar Allan Poe* (Isleta, Texas, 1933), pp. [3–4]; Poe, *Letters*, p. 29; Susan Weiss, "The Last Days of Edgar Allan Poe," *Scribner's Monthly*, 15 (March 1878), 713. Poe's "To My Mother" echoes the last lines of Coleridge's "To A Friend Who Asked": "So for the mother's sake the child was dear, / And dearer was the mother for the child."

6. Miller, *Building Poe Biography*, p. 95; Poe, *Letters*, pp. 46–49; Stanard, *Poe Letters Till Now Unpublished*, p. 304.

  For a cheeky modern attempt by an improvident son to extract money from a prosperous but tightfisted father, see D. H. Lawrence's *Mr. Noon* (1921; Cambridge, England, 1984), p. 59:

  "You see father, I want a few quid to start off with."
  "Save 'em then, my boy."
  "I haven't saved them, Dad, and you have. So you give me a few."
  "Tha does talk."
  "Ay—what else should I do!"
  "Save thy wind."
  "Like you save your money?"
  "Ay—t'same."
  "And you won't give me any?"
  "Tha'lt get th' lot when I'm gone."
  "But I don't want you gone, and I want a little money."

7. Poe, *Letters*, p. 84; Wilmer, *Merlin*, pp. 29–31; J. H. Whitty, "Memoir," *The Complete Poems of Edgar Allan Poe* (Boston, 1911), p. xxi.

8. Quinn, *Poe*, p. 203; Hewitt, *Recollections of Poe*, p. 19; John Livingston Lowes, *The Road to Xanadu* (1927; New York, 1964), p. 518.

9. Jay Hubbell, "Edgar Allan Poe," *Eight American Authors*, ed. James Woodress, revised edition (New York, 1971), p. 14; Poe, *Letters*, pp. 257–258.

10. Henry Tuckerman, *The Life of John Pendleton Kennedy* (New

York, 1871), p. 376; Thomas, *Poe Log*, p. 135; Rice, *Poe: Memorial Volume*, p. 60.

11. Poe, *Letters*, p. 50; Thomas, *Poe Log*, p. 137. Poe may have felt that St. Valentine's Day, which would have reminded Allan of his first wife's maiden name, would be propitious for this visit.

CHAPTER SIX. RICHMOND: *THE SOUTHERN LITERARY MESSENGER* AND MARRIAGE

1. Poe, *Letters*, pp. 56–57; George Woodberry, *Edgar Allan Poe* (Boston, 1885), pp. 70–71; Tuckerman, *Life of Kennedy*, pp. 376–377.
2. David Jackson, *Poe and the Southern Literary Messenger* (Richmond, 1934), p. 21; Poe, *Letters*, pp. 69–71; 73.
3. Jackson, *Poe and the Southern Literary Messenger*, pp. 98, 100; Poe, *Letters*, p. 81.
4. Poe, *Marginalia*, p. 3; *Works*, 10:47–48; Woodberry, *Edgar Allan Poe* (1909), 2:2–3.

    The manuscript of another American oddball, Jack Kerouac, resembled Poe's and was also used for theatrical effect. After completing *On the Road*, and wishing to emphasize its continuous narrative, "he appeared at [Robert] Giroux's office with a huge roll of paper under his arm and threw it across the floor shouting, 'Here's your novel!' Jack had pasted the sheets of teletype paper together . . . to make one big roll." Ann Charters, *Kerouac: A Biography* (New York, 1974), p. 128.
5. Poe, *Letters*, pp. 327–328; 256.
6. N. Bryllion Fagin, *The Histrionic Mr. Poe* (Baltimore, 1949), p. 78; Edward Wagenknecht, *Edgar Allan Poe: The Man Behind the Legend* (New York, 1963), p. 108; Poe, *Poems*, p. 259.
7. The obsession in "Berenice" recurs in the tortured soul of Kafka, with whom Poe had so much in common. Kafka told his fiancée Felice Bauer that "my letters to you are not so much letters as whimpers and baring of teeth." And he described her teeth with all the fascination and horror of Egaeus: "This gleaming gold (a really hellish luster for this inappropriate spot) so scared me at first that I had to lower my eyes at the sight of Felice's teeth and the grayish yellow porcelain." Franz Kafka, *Letters to Felice*, ed. Erich Heller and Jürgen Born, trans. James Stern and Elizabeth Duckworth (London, 1974), pp. 391, 406. For an interesting account of this theme in literature, see Theodore Ziolkowski, "The Telltale Teeth: Psychodontia to Sociodontia," *PMLA*, 91 (1976), 9–22.

8. F. L. Mott, *History of American Magazines* (New York, 1930), 1:633; Poe, *Letters*, pp. 57–58; Rice, *Poe: A Memorial Volume*, p. 61; John Henry Ingram, *Edgar Allan Poe: His Life, Letters and Opinions* (London, 1880), 1:120.

9. W. H. Auden, "Edgar Allan Poe" (1950), *Forewords and Afterwords*, ed. Edward Mendelson (New York, 1974), p. 216; René Wellek, "Edgar Allan Poe," *A History of Modern Criticism, 1750–1950* (New Haven, 1955), 3:153; George Orwell, *Collected Essays, Journalism and Letters*, ed. Sonia Orwell and Ian Angus (New York, 1968), 4:183.

10. Poe, *Marginalia*, pp. 207–208; *Works*, 9:185; 9:24, 9:33; 8:178–179, 8:205.

11. Poe, *Letters* p. 102n; Quinn, *Poe*, p. 484; Jackson, *Poe and the Southern Literary Messenger*, p. 115; Thomas, *Poe Log*, p. 180.

12. *Works*, 11:175; Chivers, *Life of Poe*, p. 40; Rice, *Poe: A Memorial Volume*, p. 67; Wagenknecht, *Edgar Allan Poe*, p. 4.

13. Wilmer, *Merlin*, p. 32; Quinn, *Poe*, p. 497; Mrs. A. B. Harris, in Ingram, *Edgar Allan Poe*, 1:221; Frances Osgood, in Griswold, "Memoir of the Author" (1850), pp. xxxvi–xxxvii.

14. Frederick Coburn, "Poe as Seen by the Brother of 'Annie' [Richmond]," *New England Quarterly*, 16 (1943), 471; Joseph Wood Krutch, *Edgar Allan Poe: A Study in Genius* (New York, 1926), p. 53.

15. Ernest Hemingway, *Green Hills of Africa* (New York, 1935), p. 28; John Ostrom, "Fourth Supplement to the *Letters of Poe*," *American Literature*, 45 (January 1974), 517; I. M. Walker, *Edgar Allan Poe: The Critical Heritage* (London, 1986), p. 364.

16. Donald Goodwin, *Alcoholism: The Facts* (New York, 1981), p. 63.

    This self-destructive lineage, which associated heavy drinking with masculinity, included: Twain, Bierce, Dreiser, Jack London, Stevens, Lewis, Lardner, O'Neill, Chandler, Aiken, Parker, Marquand, Hammett, Edmund Wilson, Fitzgerald, Faulkner, Hemingway, Hart Crane, Wolfe, Steinbeck, Caldwell, Charles Jackson, O'Hara, Roethke, Saroyan, Agee, Tennessee Williams, Cheever, Irwin Shaw, Berryman, Ruark, James Jones, Kerouac and Capote. Though British and Irish alcoholic writers were much rarer than American, there were a few notorious examples: Waugh, Lowry, Dylan Thomas and Brendan Behan.

17. Ernest Hemingway, *Selected Letters, 1917–1961*, ed. Carlos Baker (New York, 1981), p. 877; *Works*, 14:190; Ingram, *Edgar Allan Poe*, 1:216.

18. Poe, "For Annie," *Poems*, p. 457. Two provocative remarks about Poe's drinking are worth quoting to show how he inspired perverse judgments. H. L. Mencken, in "The Mystery of Poe," *Nation*, 122 (March 17, 1926), 289, ignores the fact that alcoholism had permeated Poe's being and remarks: "Strapped to the water-wagon, with a ton of Bibles to hold him down, he would have been precisely the same Poe." And Laura Riding, in "The Facts in the Case of Monsieur Poe," *Contemporaries and Snobs* (London, 1928), p. 232, ignores the tragedy of his addiction and expresses her personal hostility by noting: "The more we learn about Poe, the more grateful we are for his alcoholism. It was apparently the one thing that could restrain Poe from himself: the idea of a sober Poe is intolerable."

19. Woodberry, *Edgar Allan Poe* (1909), 2:443; Poe, *Letters*, p. 141; Samuel Johnson, *Lives of the Poets: Congreve to Gray* (Garden City, New York, n.d.), pp. 100–101.

20. Jackson, *Poe and the Southern Literary Messenger*, pp. 14, 109–110; Quinn, *Poe*, p. 260.

CHAPTER SEVEN. PHILADELPHIA: *BURTON'S GENTLEMAN'S MAGAZINE*

1. Quinn, *Poe*, p. 267; John Sartain, *Reminiscences of a Very Old Man* (New York, 1889), p. 215; Thomas Dunn English, "Reminiscences," *Independent*, 48 (October 22, 1896), 1415.

2. *Works*, 8:255; 4:281; Edgar Allan Poe, "Instinct vs. Reason—A Black Cat," in Clarence Brigham, "Edgar Allan Poe's Contributions to *Alexander's Weekly Messenger*," *Proceedings of the American Antiquarian Society*, 52 (April 1942), 73; Poe, *Letters*, p. 681.

3. *The Letters of James Kirke Paulding*, ed. Ralph Aderman (Madison, 1962), p. 174; George Putnam, "Leaves from a Publisher's Letter-Book," *Putnam's Magazine*, 4 (October 1869), 471.

4. *Works*, 10:200–201; Evert and George Duyckinck, *Cyclopaedia of American Literature* (New York, 1855), 1:158; Poe, *Letters*, p. 130; Walker, *Critical Heritage*, pp. 96, 93, 98.

5. Leslie Fiedler, *Love and Death in the American Novel*, new, revised edition (1966; New York, 1969), p. 392; see Patrick Quinn, *The French Face of Edgar Poe* (1957; Carbondale, Illinois, 1971), pp. 169–215, and Richard Wilbur, "*The Narrative of Arthur Gordon Pym*," *Responses* (New York, 1976), pp. 190–214; Ernest Hemingway, Introduction to *Men at War* (New York, 1942), p. xxvii.

6. *Works*, 10:62; Orwell, *Collected Essays, Journalism and Letters*,

1:249; Joris-Karl Huysmans, *Against the Grain*, trans. Robert Baldick (1884; London, 1959), p. 191.

7. See William Feaver, *The Art of John Martin* (Oxford, 1975).

8. Quinn, *Poe*, p. 678; *Works*, 14:177; 11:72; 14:201; Dylan Thomas, *Collected Letters*, ed. Paul Ferris (New York, 1985), p. 92.

9. *Works*, 11:128; Davidson, *Poe: A Critical Study*, p. 111; Poe, *Letters*, p. 118.

10. Thomas, *Poe Log*, p. 259; *Works*, 10:26; 14:95; Quinn, *Poe*, p. 427.

11. Thomas, *Poe Log*, p. 304; Quinn, *Poe*, pp. 278; 283; Woodberry, *Edgar Allan Poe* (1885), p. 129. For more on Burton, see William Keese, *William Burton: Actor, Author, and Manager* (New York, 1885).

12. Poe, *Letters*, pp. 115–116; 120.

13. See Jonathan Swift, *Collected Poems*, ed. Joseph Horrell (Cambridge, Mass., 1958), 1:248–249:

> Then, seated on a three-leg'd Chair,
> Takes off her artificial Hair:
> Now, picking out a Crystal Eye,
> She wipes it clean, and lays it by.
> Her Eye-brows from a Mouse's Hyde,
> Stuck on with Art on either Side,
> Pulls off with Care, and first displays 'em,
> Then in a Play-book smoothly lays 'em.
> Now dext'rously her Plumpers draws,
> That serve to fill her hollow Jaws.
> Untwists a Wire; and from her Gums
> A Set of Teeth compleatly comes.
> Pulls out the Rags, contriv'd to prop
> Her flabby Dugs, and down they drop.
> Proceeding on, the lovely Goddess,
> Unlaces next her Steel-ribb'd Bodice;
> Which by the Operator's Skill,
> Press down the Lumps, the Hollows fill.
> Up goes her Hand, and off she slips
> The Bolsters that supply her Hips. . . .
> The Nymph, though in this mangled
> Plight,
> Must ev'ry Morn her Limbs unite;
> But, how shall I describe her Arts
> To recollect the scatter'd Parts?

> Or, shew the Anguish, Toyl, and Pain,
> Of gathering up her self again.

Poe's description in "The Spectacles" of the hideous old hag, with whom the hero imagines himself to be in love, is another virulent Swiftian revelation of a vain attempt to disguise the ravages of old age: "Was that—was that—was that *rouge*? And were those—were those—were those *wrinkles*, upon the visage of Eugénie Lalande? And oh! Jupiter, and every one of the gods and goddesses, little and big!—what—what—what—*what* had become of her teeth?"

14. Poe, *Letters*, p. 161; A. E. Housman, "The Name and Nature of Poetry" (1933), *Selected Prose*, ed. John Carter (Cambridge, England, 1961), p. 187; *Works*, 10:65; D. H. Lawrence, *Studies in Classic American Literature* (London, 1924), p. 84.

     For a decadent modern story on this theme, in which strange narcissistic twins shut themselves off from the outside world and, inspired by music, behave atavistically and commit incest when the brother is threatened by a sexual rival, see Thomas Mann's "The Blood of the Walsungs" (1905).

15. Walker, *Critical Heritage*, pp. 115–116; Thomas, *Poe Log*, p. 282; Walker, *Critical Heritage*, pp. 125, 127; Thomas, *Poe Log*, p. 281; Woodberry, *Edgar Allan Poe* (1885), p. 165.

16. Edgar Allan Poe, *The Journal of Julius Rodman*, ed. Burton Pollin (Boston, 1981), pp. 551, 522, 557. Poe may have borrowed his hero's name from the middle name of the respected American poet Joseph Rodman Drake, whose works he had reviewed at some length in April 1836.

17. Ingram, *Edgar Allan Poe*, 1:181. See Jean de La Bruyère, *Characters*, trans. Jean Stewart (London, 1970), p. 204: "All our troubles spring from our inability to endure solitude." This epigraph applies even more forcefully to Conrad's *Victory* (1915).

18. Poe, *Letters*, pp. 156, 132, 130; Thomas, *Poe Log*, p. 300.

19. Thomas, *Poe Log*, p. 307; Poe, *Letters*, pp. 155–156; English, "Reminiscences," p. 1415.

     This humiliating scenario would recur with modern alcoholic authors. Hemingway, who frequently had to carry James Joyce home after an evening's drinking, recalled that his wife Nora would open the door and angrily exclaim: "Well, here comes James Joyce the writer, drunk again with Ernest Hemingway." Jeffrey Meyers, *Hemingway: A Biography* (New York, 1985), p. 83.

CHAPTER EIGHT. PHILADELPHIA: *GRAHAM'S MAGAZINE*

1. *Works*, 14:119–120; 14:116; Poe, *Letters*, p. 236.
2. Jacob Neu, "Rufus Wilmot Griswold," *University of Texas Studies in English*, 5 (1925), 164–165. See also *Passages from the Correspondence and Other Papers of R. W. Griswold*, ed. E. M. Griswold (Cambridge, Mass., 1898), and Joy Bayless, *Rufus Wilmot Griswold: Poe's Literary Executor* (Nashville, 1943).
3. *Works*, 17:197; Walker, *Critical Heritage*, pp. 182–183; Thomas, *Poe Log*, p. 444.
4. *Works*, 15:215; 11:124; 11:221–222, 11:239, 11:242–243.
5. Mrs. A. B. Harris, "Edgar A. Poe," *Hearth and Home*, 8 (January 9, 1875), 24; Walker, *Critical Heritage*, p. 381; Whitty, "Memoir," p. xliii; Chivers, *Life of Poe*, p. 42.
6. *Works*, 10:96; 10:109; Thomas, *Poe Log*, p. 324; *Works*, 11:53.
7. *The Letters of Charles Dickens. Volume Three, 1842–1843*, ed. Madeline House, Graham Storey and Kathleen Tillotson (Oxford, 1974), pp. 106, 194, 388.
8. *Works*, 11:106, 11:110, 11:104, 11:106–108.
9. *Works*, 13:142, 13:155; Nathaniel Hawthorne, *Letters, 1843–1853*, ed. Thomas Woodson *et al.* (Colombus, 1985), p. 168.
10. Both Truman Capote's *In Cold Blood* (1965) and Norman Mailer's *The Executioner's Song* (1979) follow the tradition of Poe by using fictional techniques to write about actual murder cases.
11. John Walsh, *Poe the Detective* (New Brunswick, New Jersey, 1968), pp. 69, 52.
12. Thomas, *Poe Log*, p. 434.
13. Johnson, *Lives of the Poets*, p. 351; *Works*, 14:160, 14:162; 17:430.
14. Walker, *Critical Heritage*, p. 12; Poe, *Letters*, p. 226; *Works*, 13:15; 8:230. For an excellent discussion of this subject, see John Ostrom, "Edgar A. Poe: His Income as a Literary Entrepreneur," *Poe Studies*, 15 (June 1982), 1–7.
15. *Works*, 17:171; Poe, *Letters*, p. 154; *Works*, 10:208.
16. Poe, *Letters*, p. 197; *Works*, 11:222; Quinn, *Poe*, p. 682; Walker, *Critical Heritage*, p. 379.
17. Howard Paul, "Recollections of Edgar Allan Poe," *Munsey's Magazine*, 7 (August 1892), 555–556; Reid, *Edgar Allan Poe*, pp. [5–6].
18. Wilmer, *Merlin*, p. 37; Poe, *Letters*, pp. 698–699.
19. *Works*, 17:85; Poe, *Letters*, p. 700; Hewitt, *Recollections of Poe*, p. 19.
20. Quinn, *Poe*, p. 378; Poe, *Letters*, pp. 230; 229; 247; William Gill,

Life of Edgar Allan Poe (1877), 3rd edition, revised and enlarged (London, 1878), pp. 117–118.

21. Quinn, *Poe*, p. 374; Poe, *Letters*, p. 223; *Works*, 12:166; 13:213. The 1843 woodcut is reproduced in Michael Deas' *The Portraits and Daguerreotypes of Edgar Allan Poe* (Charlottesville, 1989), p. 17.

22. Weiss, *Home Life of Poe*, pp. 96–97; *Works*, 10:145; Ingram, *Edgar Allan Poe*, 2:189; Thomas, *Poe Log*, pp. 441–443.

CHAPTER NINE. A LION IN NEW YORK

1. Poe, *Letters*, pp. 251–253.

2. Thomas, *Poe Log*, p. 473; *Works*, 10:27; 15:18; Quinn, *Poe*, p. 434.

3. Charles Baudelaire, "Eugène Delacroix," *The Mirror of Art*, trans. and ed. Jonathan Mayne (Garden City, New York, 1956), p. 218; Edgar Allan Poe, *Doings of Gotham*, ed. T. O. Mabbott and J. E. Spannuth (Pottsville, Pa., 1929), p. 33; Poe, *Letters*, p. 260.

4. Quoted in J. Gerald Kennedy, *Poe, Death, and the Life of Writing* (New Haven, 1987), pp. 38–39; Philippe Ariès, *The Hour of Our Death*, trans. Helen Weaver (New York, 1981), p. 396; Joseph Taylor, *The Danger of Premature Interment* (London, 1816), p. 5.

5. *Works*, 17:225; "The Buried Alive," *Blackwood's Magazine*, 10 (October 1821), 262–263.

6. Robert Louis Stevenson, *The Body-Snatcher and Other Stories*, edited with an Introduction by Jeffrey Meyers (New York, 1988), pp. 6, 15. In "The Fall of the House of Usher," Madeline is buried in a vault inside the house because of "certain obtrusive and eager inquiries on the part of her medical men, and of the remote and exposed situation of the burial-ground of the family."

    In Julian Hawthorne's story, "My Adventures with Edgar Allan Poe," *Lippincott's Magazine*, 43 (1891), 240–246, Poe returns to life after a premature burial.

7. Quoted in Clarence Brigham, "Edgar Poe's Contribution to *Alexander's Weekly Messenger*," *Proceedings of the American Antiquarian Society*, 52 (April 1942), 107.

    A social historian and a literary critic vaguely refer to "Rube Goldberg contraptions called 'life signals'—complicated arrangements of wires and bells designed to set off an alarm if the occupant of the coffin should have been inadvertently buried alive"; of "charnal houses equipped with alarm systems so that the 'dead' could signal for help, and luxury coffins fitted with ventilators and speaking tubes." T. O. Mabbott suggests that an 1843 article by Nathaniel Willis on a "life-preserving" coffin was a source for Poe's story and mentions a report that year by Thomas Hood of a "corpse" who came to life, pulled the bell in the coffin and caused a terrified caretaker to die of a heart attack. W. T. Bandy suggests another source in the 1844 account of Christian Eisenbrandt's "life-preserving" coffin, which preceded a feeble poem on that subject by Mrs. Seba Smith. This poem concludes:

> And there they saw their daughter,
> As the moonbeams on her fell,
> In her narrow coffin sitting,
> Ringing that solemn bell.

But none of these writers gives a complete history and description of these increasingly sophisticated coffins, which were invented by German immigrants to protect people from premature burial and allow living corpses to communicate from the grave. Eisenbrandt's coffin, invented (during Poe's lifetime) in Baltimore in 1843, "was designed, by an arrangement of wires and pins and a spring lid to enable the occupant of the coffin by the slightest movement of hand or head to cause the coffin lid to spring open."

Since Eisenbrandt's coffin was only effective *before* the coffin was buried in the earth, the next four ingenious devices were designed to operate *after* the body was interred. In 1868 Franz Vester of Newark invented "a square tube, containing a ladder and a cord, one end of which was to be placed in the hand of the person laid in the coffin, while the other extended up to a bell on the top of the tube which was attached to the head of the coffin." In 1871 Theodore Schroeder and Hermann Wuest of Hoboken patented an "Improvement in Life-Detectors for Coffins": "a narrow round tube, similar to a *speaking tube*, was to be attached to the head end of the coffin in such manner that the rope within it might be pulled by the buried person, releasing an *air opening* in the mouth of the tube and simultaneously setting off an *electrical alarm*."

In 1882 Albert Fearnaught of Indianapolis, whose very name implied protection, invented "a rather elaborate device to release a *flag* through the end of a tube which projected up from the foot of the grave, if its occupant were to move a hand." Finally, that same year John Krichbaum of Youngstown patented a "device for Indicating Life in Buried Persons," which consisted of "a rather formidable arrangement of pipes, bars, tubes and cross-pins, which would, upon a movement of the hands of 'persons being buried in a trance,' open an air vent and at the same time give indication that there was life in the coffin below." The invention during the Civil War of modern embalming, in which the blood was drained from the corpse, formaldehyde and other chemicals were pumped into the body cavities and vascular system, and its widespread practice in America (though not in Europe) toward the end of the nineteenth century, began to dispel the widespread fears of premature burial.

But the dangers of body-snatchers, who specialized in premature resurrection, and of medical dissection, mentioned by *Blackwood's*, Poe and Stevenson, remained a serious threat. Coffins were therefore invented not only to allow people to get out, but also—like "mort-cages"—to prevent them from getting in. In 1878 a company in Toledo marketed a coffin-torpedo, "made of iron, about an inch in diameter and six inches long, which contained a charge of explosive and a mechanism set to go off with the tampering of any coffin which had properly been prepared."

Jessica Mitford, *The American Way of Death* (New York, 1963), p. 157; David Galloway, Introduction to Poe's *Comedies and Satires* (London, 1983), p. 13; See also James Farrell, "The Container for the Body," *Inventing the American Way of Death* (Philadelphia, 1980), pp. 169–172; Edgar Allan Poe, *Tales: 1843–1844*, ed. T. O. Mabbott (Cambridge, Mass., 1978), p. 971; W. T. Bandy, "A Source for Poe's 'Premature Burial,' " *American Literature*, 19 (April 1947), 167–168; Robert Habenstein and William Lamers, "Coffins, Burial Cases and Caskets," *The History of American Funeral Directing* (Milwaukee, 1955), pp. 180, 183.

8. *Works*, 12:34; 14:182; 17:385–386; Quinn, *Poe*, p. 451.
9. *Works*, 17:229; *The Letters of Robert Browning and Elizabeth Barrett Browning*, ed. Elvan Kintner, 2 vols. (Cambridge, Mass., 1969), pp. 297–298, 373, 416.
10. Gerald Grubb, "The Personal and Literary Relationships of Dickens and Poe," *Nineteenth Century Fiction*, 5 (December 1950), 210–211; *Works*, 14:206; 14:208; 14:201; 14:204; 14:202.
11. Joel Benton, "Poe's Opinion of 'The Raven,' " *Forum*, 22 (February 1897), 733; Krutch, *Edgar Allan Poe*, p. 154; Alfriend, "Unpublished Recollections of Poe," p. 490.
12. Thomas, *Poe Log*, p. 484; Poe, *Letters*, p. 287.
13. *Works*, 11:125; 11:249; *Letters of James Russell Lowell*, ed. Charles

Eliot Norton (Cambridge, Mass., 1904), 1:108; Walker, *Critical Heritage*, pp. 158, 163, 167.

14. Chivers, *Life of Poe*, p. 45; Quinn, *Poe*, pp. 462, 461; Thomas, *Poe Log*, p. 536.

15. *Works*, 17:388; Martin Duberman, *James Russell Lowell* (Boston, 1966), p. 83.

16. James Russell Lowell, *Complete Poetical Works* (Cambridge, Mass., 1897), p. 183; *Works*, 13:168, 13:174–175, 13:173, 13:171.

CHAPTER TEN. NEW YORK: THE *BROADWAY JOURNAL*

1. Quinn, *Poe*, pp. 455–456; Stoddard, "Edgar Allan Poe," p. 565.

2. Howard Paul, "Recollections of Edgar Allan Poe," p. 554; *Works*, 12:161; 12:134; 12:136.

3. Poe, *Letters*, p. 159; *Works*, 11:223; *The Letters of Henry Wadsworth Longfellow*, ed. Andrew Hilen (Cambridge, Mass., 1966), 2:302.

4. *Works*, 15:4; 10:80; Poe, *Letters*, p. 161; *Works*, 11:75; 11:71–72, 11:84.
   See Shelley's "One Word is Too Often Profaned" (1821):

> The desire of the moth for the star,
>   Of the night for the morrow,
> The devotion to something afar
>   From the sphere of our sorrow.

5. Samuel Longfellow, *Life of Henry Wadsworth Longfellow* (London, 1886), 2:150.

6. Margaret Fuller, *Letters*, ed. Robert Hudspeth (Ithaca, New York, 1988), 5:289; *Works*, 13:192; Griswold, "Memoir of the Author" (1850), p. xxxvii.

7. Griswold, "Memoir of the Author" (1850), pp. xxxvi–xxxvii; English, "Reminiscences," *Independent*, p. 1448.

8. Thomas, *Poe Log*, p. 518; *Works*, 13:18, 13:125; Poe, *Marginalia*, p. 176; Griswold, "Memoir of the Author" (1850), p. xxxvii. The article on Fanny *was* longer than the others.

9. *Works*, 15:241; 12:206; Chivers, *Life of Poe*, pp. 56–57, 53, 62, 59.

10. *Works*, 17:279; Poe, *Letters*, p. 326.

11. *Works*, 15:60; Walker, *Critical Heritage*, pp. 179, 180, 177.

12. *Works*, 9:166; 17:225; 17:263–264.

13. Thomas, *Poe Log*, p. 509; *Works*, 15:260; Poe, *Letters*, p. 427.

14. Quinn, *Poe*, p. 489; *Works*, 13:5–12.

15. *Works*, 7:xlvii; 7:xlix.

16. *Works*, 13:28; Walker, *Critical Heritage*, pp. 263, 232, 234, 255; Thomas, *Poe Log*, p. 594.
17. Woodberry, *Edgar Allan Poe*, p. 226; 234; Poe, *Letters*, p. 290.
18. Mott, *History of American Magazines*, p. 761; Woodberry, *Edgar Allan Poe*, pp. 237–239; Walt Whitman, *Specimen Days* (1882; New York, 1961), p. 31.
19. Ostrom, "Poe: His Income as a Literary Entrepreneur," p. 7; Poe, *Letters*, pp. 304–305; 300–301.
20. *Works*, 17:214; Chivers, *Life of Poe*, pp. 60–61; Quinn, *Poe*, p. 494.
21. Walker, *Critical Heritage*, pp. 382; 381; Quinn, *Poe*, p. 32; Poe, *Letters*, p. 303.

CHAPTER ELEVEN. FORDHAM AND LITERARY QUARRELS

1. *Works*, 8:140; Francis Desmond, "Poe's Libel Suit Against T. D. English," *Boston Public Library Quarterly*, 5 (1953), 31; Poe, *Letters*, p. 322.
2. Thomas, *Poe Log*, pp. 633–634; *Works*, 13:214; Poe, *Letters*, pp. 393, 407–408.
3. Thomas, *Poe Log*, p. 651; Griswold, *Correspondence*, pp. 256–257.
4. Quinn, *Poe*, p. 520; Thomas, *Poe Log*, p. 644; Griswold, "Memoir of the Author," p. xxxvii.

   Stephen Crane had the same remarkable fluency—and the same unevenness in the quality of his work. As Joseph Conrad wrote in his article on Crane in *Last Essays* (1926; London, [1957]), p. 319: "I have seen him sit down before a blank sheet of paper, dip his pen, write the first line at once and go on without haste and without pause for a couple of hours."
5. Thomas, *Poe Log*, p. 505; Mott, *History of American Magazines*, p. 586; *Works*, 15:121; Alexander Pope, "Epilogue to the Satires: Dialogue II" (1738), *Poems*, ed. John Butt (New York, 1963), p. 701.
6. Sidney Moss, "Poe's Infamous Reputation: A Crux in the Biography," *American Book Collector*, 9 (November 1958), 7; *Works*, 15:21–23; Thomas, *Poe Log*, pp. 642–643.
7. *Works*, 17:262; Poe, *Letters*, p. 243; William Gravely, Jr., "Poe and Thomas Dunn English: More Light on a Probable Reason for Poe's Failure to Receive a Custom-House Appointment," *Papers on Poe: Essays in Honor of J. Ward Ostrom*, ed. Richard Veler (Springfield, Ohio, 1972), pp. 182–183.

8. *Works*, 15:65; 17:234–237.
9. *Works*, 17:242; 17:239–240; 17:241; 17:248–249; 17:242; 17:250.
10. *Works*, 17:254; Thomas, *Poe Log*, pp. 663, 668; Sidney Moss, *Poe's Literary Battles* (1963; Carbondale, Illinois, 1969), p. 238.
11. Alexis Bespaloff, *The Signet Book of Wine* (New York, 1971), p. 158; Terry Robards, *The New York Times Book of Wine* (New York, 1976), p. 379; Poe, *Letters*, p. 339; Quinn, *Poe*, p. 525.
12. Poe, *Letters*, p. 318; Woodberry, *Edgar Allan Poe*, p. 188; Katherine Mansfield, *Journal*, ed. John Middleton Murry (London, 1954), p. 207.
13. *Works*, 15:61; Mary Gove Nichols, *Reminiscences of Edgar Allan Poe* (1863; New York, 1931), pp. 8–9, 12, 11.
14. *Works*, 17:394; Poe, *Letters*, p. 340; Deas, *Portraits of Poe*, p. 168. The "Whitman" daguerreotype is reproduced on p. 43.
15. Ingram, *Edgar Allan Poe*, 1:131–132; Poe, *Marginalia*, p. 46; Quinn, *Poe*, p. 528; Poe, *Poems*, ed. Mabbott, p. 403.
16. Quinn, *Poe*, p. 506; Poe, *Letters*, p. 356; Henry Harrington, "Poe Not To Be Apotheosized," New York *Critic*, October 3, 1885, p. 158.
17. Bayless, *Rufus Wilmot Griswold*, pp. 148, 144; Neu, "Rufus Wilmot Griswold," p. 141.
18. Poe, *Letters*, p. 345; *Works*, 13:216, 13:224, 13:226.
19. Thomas, *Poe Log*, p. 711; Phillips, *Edgar Allan Poe*, 2:1378–1379; Henry James, *Hawthorne* (1879; New York, 1966), p. 43.
20. Gove, *Reminiscences*, pp. 9–10; Quinn, *Poe*, p. 630.

CHAPTER TWELVE. FORDHAM: *EUREKA* AND HOPELESS LOVE

1. Woodberry, *Edgar Allan Poe*, pp. 301–302; Walker, *Critical Heritage*, p. 280; *Works*, 16:197.
2. Poe, *Letters*, pp. 362–363; Stoddard, "Edgar Allan Poe," p. 567.
3. *Works*, 16:183; 16:221; 16:224.
4. *Works*, 16:204; 16:311.
5. Davidson, *Poe: A Critical Study*, p. 224; Eric Carlson, ed., *Introduction to Poe* (Glenview, Illinois, 1967), p. 598; Richard Wilbur, "The House of Poe" (1959), *Literary Lectures* (Washington, D.C., 1973), pp. 333–334.
6. Paul Valéry, "On Poe's *Eureka*," *Variety*, trans. Malcolm Cowley (New York, 1927), p. 110; Quinn, *Poe*, pp. 555, 557.
7. Woodberry, *Edgar Allan Poe*, pp. 290–300; Krutch, *Edgar Allan Poe*, pp. 184–185, 91, 181–182. Recent books, most notably Joan

Dayan's *Fables of Mind: An Inquiry into Poe's Fiction* (New York, 1987), have taken *Eureka* quite seriously and even used it as a key to Poe's stories.

8. Thomas, *Poe Log*, pp. 720–722.
9. Putnam, "Leaves from a Publisher's Letter-Box," p. 471; Thomas, *Poe Log*, p. 784; Walker, *Critical Heritage*, p. 274.
10. D. H. Lawrence, *Letters*, ed. James Boulton (Cambridge, England, 1979), p. 503; Miller, *Building Poe Biography*, p. 75.
11. Lambert Wilmer, *Our Press Gang* (Philadelphia, 1859), p. 284; Auden, "Edgar Allan Poe," p. 218; Mencken, "The Mystery of Poe," p. 290.
12. Poe, *Letters*, p. 392; Quinn, *Poe*, p. 694.
13. Thomas, *Poe Log*, p. 732; Poe, *Letters*, pp. 372–374; Krutch, *Edgar Allan Poe*, p. 166; Walker, *Critical Heritage*, p. 364.
14. Thomas, *Poe Log*, pp. 729–730; Poe, *Letters*, p. 387.
15. Phillips, *Edgar Allan Poe*, 2:1316; Poe, *Letters*, p. 383; Richard Henry Stoddard, "Life of Poe," in *Works of Edgar Allan Poe* (New York, 1884), 1:156.
16. Poe, *Letters*, pp. 382, 383, 385, 387, 389–390.
17. Poe, *Letters*, pp. 391–393, 395–397.
18. Poe, *Letters*, pp. 401–403; Hector Berlioz, *A Selection from His Letters*, ed. Humphrey Searle (New York, 1966), p. 54; Woodberry, *Edgar Allan Poe*, p. 322.
19. Charles Baudelaire, *Selected Letters*, translated and edited by Rosemary Lloyd (Chicago, 1986), p. 156; Edmund Wilson, "Poe at Home and Abroad" (1926), *The Shores of Light* (New York, 1952), p. 181.
20. Poe, *Letters*, p. 360; Thomas Dimmock, "Notes on Poe," *Century Magazine*, 28 (June 1895), 316; Sarah Helen Whitman, *Poe's Helen Remembers*, ed. John Miller (Charlottesville, 1979), p. 348.
21. Thomas, *Poe Log*, p. 767; Poe, *Letters*, pp. 406–407; Thomas, *Poe Log*, p. 773; Poe, *Letters*, p. 412.
22. Thomas, *Poe Log*, p. 788; *Works*, 17:414; Stanley Williams, "New Letters about Poe," *Yale Review*, 14 (July 1925), 762–763.
23. Quinn, *Poe*, p. 650; Harrison, *Life and Letters of Edgar Allan Poe*, p. 291.
24. Poe, *Letters*, pp. 421, 419; Richard Henry Stoddard, "Life of Edgar Allan Poe," *Select Works of Edgar Allan Poe* (New York, 1880), p. cxxxviii.
25. Poe, *Letters*, p. 414, 431.
26. Poe, *Letters*, p. 402; *Works*, 14:266–267; 14:272; 14:290–291.

27. Richard Cary, "Poe and the Literary Ladies," *Texas Studies in Literature and Language*, 9 (1967), 101; Edmund Wilson, "Poe's Criticism," *The Shock of Recognition* (New York, 1943), p. 80; Edmund Wilson, "Poe as a Literary Critic," *Nation*, 155 (October 31, 1942), 452.

CHAPTER THIRTEEN. DRINK, DELIRIUM AND DEATH

1. Poe, *Letters*, p. 256; See Jonathan Swift, *Gulliver's Travels and Other Writings*, ed. Ricardo Quintana (New York, 1958), p. 101: The English were "the most pernicious Race of little odious Vermin that Nature ever suffered to crawl upon the surface of the Earth."
2. Poe, *Letters*, p. 440; Weiss, "Reminiscences of Edgar Allan Poe," p. 1013.
3. Poe, *Letters*, pp. 428, 438.
4. Sartain, *The Reminiscences of a Very Old Man*, pp. 210, 206, 210, 212; Poe, *Letters*, p. 452.
5. *Works*, 11:158; Weiss, "The Last Days of Edgar A. Poe," p. 708; Weiss, *The Home Life of Poe*, pp. 199–200; Thomas, *Poe Log*, pp. 826, 836.
6. Quinn, *Poe*, p. 569; Thomas, *Poe Log*, p. 208; Weiss, "Reminiscences of Edgar Allan Poe," p. 446; Alfriend, "Unpublished Recollections of Edgar Allan Poe," p. 490.
7. Quinn, *Poe*, p. 628; Poe, *Letters*, pp. 459, 461.
8. Quinn, *Poe*, p. 634; Thomas, *Poe Log*, p. 843; Weiss, "The Last Days of Edgar A. Poe," pp. 713–714.
9. *Works*, 17:404; Quinn, *Poe*, p. 642; Hart Crane, "The Bridge," *Complete Poems*, ed. Brom Weber (Garden City, New York, 1966), p. 107.
10. Thomas, *Poe Log*, pp. 844–845; Joseph Snodgrass, "The Facts of Poe's Death and Burial," *Beadle's*, 3 (March 1867), 284; Joseph Snodgrass, "Death and Burial of Edgar A. Poe," *Life Illustrated*, 2 (May 17, 1856), 24.
11. Dr. John Moran, *A Defense of Edgar Allan Poe* (Washington, D.C., 1885), pp. 65, 60; Woodberry, *Edgar Allan Poe*, pp. 344–345.
12. Thomas, *Poe Log*, p. 846; Moran, *Defense*, pp. 66, 71; Thomas, *Poe Log*, p. 846.
13. John Malcolm Brinnin, *Dylan Thomas in America* (Boston, 1955), pp. 291–292; John Berryman, "In Memoriam (1914–1953)," *Delusions, Etc.* (1972; New York, 1974), p. 28.

14. *The Oxford Textbook of Medicine*, ed. D. J. Weatherall *et al.* (Oxford, 1987), 9:95; Bayless, *Rufus Wilmot Griswold*, p. 194; Snodgrass, "The Facts of Poe's Death and Burial," p. 285.

CHAPTER FOURTEEN. REPUTATION

1. Weiss, "The Last Days of Edgar A. Poe," p. 709; Walker, *Critical Heritage*, pp. 294, 301, 299, 300.
2. Wilmer, *Merlin*, p. 26; Walker, *Critical Heritage*, p. 328.
3. *Works*, 17:395; Maria Clemm, in *Works*, 1:348; *Works*, 17:406.
4. Griswold, "Memoir of the Author," p. xxx; *Works*, 17:435; Griswold, "Memoir," pp. xxxi, xxxix; Quinn, *Poe*, p. 680.
5. Quinn, *Poe*, p. 651; Griswold, *Correspondence*, p. 267.
6. Oral Coad, Introduction to Sarah Helen Whitman, *Edgar Poe and His Critics* (1860; New Brunswick, New Jersey, 1949), p. 18; Philip Lindsay, *The Haunted Man: A Portrait of Edgar Allan Poe* (London, 1953), p. 194.
7. George Gilfillan, "Edgar Poe," *A Third Gallery of Portraits* (New York, 1855), pp. 327–328; Walker, *Critical Heritage*, p. 51.
8. William Dean Howells, *Literary Friends and Acquaintances* (New York, 1901), p. 65; Algernon Charles Swinburne, *Letters*, ed. Cecil Lang (New Haven, 1959–62), 3:34, 3:84; Walt Whitman, "Edgar Poe's Significance," *Specimen Days*, p. 212.
9. Thomas Swann, *Ernest Dowson* (New York, 1964), p. 57; Oscar Wilde, *Selected Letters*, ed. Rupert Hart-Davis (Oxford, 1979), p. 65.
10. John Weightman, "Poe in France: A Myth Revisited," *Edgar Allan Poe: The Design of Order*, ed. Robert Lee (New York, 1987), p. 202; Alex de Jonge, *Baudelaire: Prince of Clouds* (New York, 1976), pp. 62, 170, 45, 87, 29.
11. Quinn, *French Face of Poe*, pp. 70, 15; Enid Starkie, *Baudelaire* (Norfolk, Conn., 1958), p. 214.
12. William Bandy, *The Influence and Reputation of Edgar Allan Poe in Europe* (Baltimore, 1962), p. 9; Baudelaire, *Selected Letters*, p. 56; Patrick Quinn, *French Face of Poe*, pp. 17, 9; *Baudelaire on Poe*, trans. and ed. Lois and Francis Hyslop (State College, Penna., 1952), p. 125.
13. Edmond and Jules Goncourt, *The Goncourt Journal*, ed. Robert Baldick (Oxford, 1978), pp. 19–20; Eric Carlson, ed., *The Recognition of Edgar Allan Poe* (Ann Arbor, 1966), p. 102; *Correspondence Between Paul Claudel and André Gide*, trans. John Russell (Boston, 1952), p. 38; Carlson, *Introduction to Poe*, p. xxxiii.

14. Paul Valéry, "The Position of Baudelaire," *Variety: Second Series*, trans. William Bradley (New York, 1938), p. 87.

15. Friedrich Nietzsche, *Beyond Good and Evil*, trans. and ed. Walter Kaufmann (1886; New York, 1966), pp. 218–219; Friedrich Nietzsche, *The Will to Power*, trans. and ed. Walter Kaufmann and R. J. Hollingdale (1901; New York, 1968), p. 555.

16. *Letters of Rainer Maria Rilke, 1892–1910*, trans. Jane Greene and M. D. Herter Norton (New York, 1945), p. 171; Rainer Maria Rilke, *Letters to a Young Poet*, trans. M. D. Herter Norton (1904; New York, 1963), p. 68; Gustav Janouch, *Conversations with Kafka*, trans. Goronwy Rees (New York, 1971), p. 42.

17. Henry James, "Baudelaire" (1876), *French Poets and Novelists* (London, 1878), p. 76; Henry James, *Hawthorne* (1879; New York, 1966), p. 63.

18. Henry James, Preface to *The Altar of the Dead, The Art of the Novel: Critical Prefaces*, Introduction by Richard Blackmur (New York, 1962), pp. 256–257; Henry James, *The Golden Bowl*, Introduction by Richard Brett (New York, 1975), pp. 22–23.

19. W. B. Yeats, *Letters*, ed. Alan Wade (New York, 1955), p. 325; Carlson, *Recognition of Poe*, p. 76; Charles Kent and John Patton, eds., *The Book of the Poe Centenary* (Charlottesville, 1909), p. 197; George Bernard Shaw, "Edgar Allan Poe" (1909), *Pen Portraits and Reviews*, in *Collected Works* (New York, 1932), 29: 231, 235, 238.

20. Ezra Pound, *Selected Letters, 1907–1941*, ed. D. D. Paige (New York, 1950), pp. 50, 55; William Evans, *Robert Frost and Sidney Cox: Forty Years of Friendship* (Hanover, New Hampshire, 1981), p. 111.

21. *The Mark Twain-Howells Letters: The Correspondence of Samuel Langhorne Clemens and William Dean Howells, 1872–1910*, ed. Henry Nash Smith and William Gibson (Cambridge, Mass., 1960), 2:841; Ernest Hemingway, *Green Hills of Africa* (New York, 1935), p. 20; Hemingway, quoted in Tom Dardis, *The Thirsty Muse* (New York, 1989), p. 204; William Carlos Williams, "Edgar Allan Poe," *In the American Grain* (New York, 1925), p. 216.

22. Ezra Pound, *Literary Essays*, Introduction by T. S. Eliot (New York, 1948), pp. 308, 218; Aldous Huxley, *Vulgarity in Literature* (London, 1930), pp. 67, 82, 84.

23. Kenneth Rexroth, "The Poet as Translator," *The Craft and Context of Translation*, ed. William Arrowsmith and Roger Shattuck

(Garden City, New York, 1964), p. 48; Roger Asselineau, "Edgar Allan Poe," *Seven American Stylists*, ed. George Wright (Minneapolis, 1973), p. 45.

24. D. H. Lawrence, *Studies in Classic American Literature*, pp. 67, 82, 84; T. S. Eliot, "A Dream Within a Dream," *Listener*, 29 (February 25, 1943), 243–244; T. S. Eliot, Introduction to Charles Williams, *All Hallows' Eve* (New York, 1948), p. xv.

25. T. S. Eliot, *Notes Toward a Definition of Culture* (New York, 1949), p. 115; T. S. Eliot, "From Poe to Valéry" (1948), *To Criticize the Critic* (New York, 1965), pp. 27, 35, 42.

    In her Preface to *The American Genius* (London, 1951), p. xiii, Edith Sitwell wrote that Poe, "now derided by stupid persons," was the only American poet before Whitman whose work was not "bad and imitative of English poetry."

26. Lionel Trilling, "Impediments," *Of This Time, Of That Place* (New York, 1979), p. 6; Saul Bellow, *Humboldt's Gift* (1975; New York, 1984), p. 118; Thomas, *Poe Log*, p. ix.

27. William Dean Howells, *Life of Abraham Lincoln* (1860; Bloomington, Indiana, 1960), pp. 31–32; Wagenknecht, *Edgar Allan Poe*, p. 6.

CHAPTER FIFTEEN. INFLUENCE

1. Auden, "Edgar Allan Poe," *Forewords and Afterwords*, pp. 212, 210.

    For a discussion of Poe's influence on European literature, art and music, see:

    Célestin Cambiare, *The Influence of Edgar Allan Poe in France* (New York, 1927);

    Léon Lemonnier, *Edgar Poe et la critique française de 1845 à 1875* (Paris, 1928);

    Arthur Miller, "The Influence of Edgar A. Poe on Ambrose Bierce," *American Literature*, 4 (1932), 130–150;

    John Engelkirk, *Edgar Allan Poe in Hispanic Literature* (New York, 1934);

    May Evans, *Music and Edgar Allan Poe* (Baltimore, 1939);

    John French, ed., *Poe in Foreign Lands and Tongues* (Baltimore, 1941);

    Elizabeth Bishop, "Miss Moore and Edgar Allan Poe," *Quarterly Review of Literature*, 4 (1948), 132–134;

    Francis Dedmond, "Poe in Drama, Fiction and Poetry: A Bibliography," *Bulletin of Bibliography*, 21 (1954), 107–114;

Norman Suckling, "The Adaptation of Edgar Poe," *Paul Valéry and the Civilised Mind* (London, 1954), pp. 58–95;

Robert Falk, ed., "The Decline and Fall of the House of Usher," *American Literature in Parody* (New York, 1955), pp. 93–113;

Patrick Quinn, *The French Face of Edgar Poe* (Carbondale, Illinois, 1957);

H. F. Peters, "Ernst Jünger's Concern with Edgar Allan Poe," *Comparative Literature*, 10 (1958), 144–149;

Ada Giaccari, *La fortuna di Edgar Poe in Italia* (Roma, 1959);

Saul Moskowitz, ed., *The Man Who Called Himself Poe* (Garden City, New York, 1959);

Paul Ramsey, "Poe and Modern Art," *College Art Journal*, 18 (1959), 210–215;

Laura Hofrichter, "From Poe to Kafka," *University of Toronto Quarterly*, 29 (1960), 405–419;

M. E. Kronegger, "Joyce's Debt to Poe and the French Symbolists," *Revue de littérature comparée*, 39 (1965), 243–254;

Monique Sprout, "The Influence of Poe on Jules Verne," *Revue de littérature comparée*, 41 (1967), 37–53;

Thomas Inge, "Miguel de Unamuno's *Canciones* on American Literature," *Arlington Quarterly*, 2 (1969), 83–97;

George Clark, "A Further Word on Poe and *Lolita*," *Poe Newsletter*, 3 (1970), 39;

Larry Rubin, "An Echo of Poe in *Of Time and the River*," *Poe Newsletter*, 3 (1970), 38–39;

Michel Fabre, "Black and White Cat: Richard Wright's Debt to Edgar Allan Poe," *Poe Studies*, 4 (1971), 17–19;

André Karátson, *Edgar Allan Poe et le groupe des écrivains "Nyugat" en Hongrie* (Paris, 1971);

John Tytell, "Anais Nin and 'The Fall of the House of Usher,' " *Under the Sign of Pisces: Anais Nin and Her Circle*, 2 (1971), 5–11;

Carl Anderson, *Poe in Northlight* (Durham, North Carolina, 1973);

Joan Grossman, *Edgar Allan Poe in Russia* (Würzburg, 1973);

Burton Pollin, "Poe and Kipling: A 'Heavy Debt' Acknowledged," *Kipling Journal*, 47 (1980), 13–25;

Burton Pollin, *Images of Poe's Works* (Westport, Conn., 1989);

Ronald Smith, *Poe in the Media* (New York, 1990);

John Irwin, "The Journey to the South: Poe, Borges, and Faulkner," *Virginia Quarterly Review*, 67 (1991), 416–432.

2. Alistair Horne, *The Price of Glory: Verdun 1916* (1962; London, 1986), p. 190; Henry James, quoted in William Goldhurst, *F.*

Scott Fitzgerald and His Contemporaries (New York, 1963), p. 204;
Ola Hansson, "Edgar Allan Poe" (1889), *Poe in Northlight*, p. 168;
Louis Schaeffer, *O'Neill: Son and Playwright* (New York, 1968),
p. 304; Allen Tate, "The Angelic Imagination" (1952), *The Man
of Letters in the Modern World* (New York, 1955), p. 118.

3. Walker, *Critical Heritage*, p. 379. The poet Guillaume Apollinaire
also called Poe "the marvellous drunkard of Baltimore" (quoted
in André Breton, *Anthology of Black Humor* (1940), in *The Unknown Poe*, ed. Raymond Foye (San Francisco, 1980), p. 117).

4. Charles Baudelaire, *Flowers of Evil and Other Works*, trans. and
ed. Wallace Fowlie (New York, 1964), p. 263; Valéry, "The
Position of Baudelaire," pp. 88, 73.

5. Baudelaire, *Flowers of Evil*, p. 263; Poe, *Marginalia*, p. 150; de
Jonge, *Baudelaire*, p. 124.

6. Baudelaire, "Spleen," *Flowers of Evil*, ed. Marthiel and Jackson
Matthews (New York, 1955), p. 63; Baudelaire, "Voyage to
Cythera," *Flowers of Evil*, ed. Fowlie, p. 91; Baudelaire, *The
Painter of Modern Life*, p. 7; Baudelaire, "The Seven Old Men,"
Flowers of Evil, ed. Matthews, trans. Roy Campbell, pp. 83–87.

7. Cambiare, *The Influence of Poe in France*, p. 247; Huysmans,
Against Nature, p. 190; Joris-Karl Huysmans, "Preface d'*A Re-
bours*," *En marge*, ed. Lucian Descaves (Paris, 1927), p. 126. For
more on Huysmans, see Jeffrey Meyers, "Gustave Moreau and
Against Nature," *Painting and the Novel* (Manchester, 1975), pp.
84–95.

8. Arthur Rimbaud, *A Season in Hell*, trans. Louise Varese (1873;
New York, 1961), p. 31; Baudelaire, *The Mirror of Art*, p. 49;
Baudelaire, "Correspondences," *Flowers of Evil*, ed. Fowlie, p.
27.

9. In *Through the Magic Door* (London, 1907), p. 115, Arthur Conan
Doyle suggested a very different sort of influence, on a different
genre: "all pseudo-science Verne-and-Wells stories have their
prototypes in the *Voyage to the Moon* ["Hans Pfaall"]." In his long
essay "Poe et ses oeuvres" (1864), Verne analyzed the stories and
praised them enthusiastically. He was influenced by Poe's use of
cryptograms, hypnotism and catalepsy. His *Journey to the Center
of the Earth* (1864) revealed the impact of *The Narrative of Arthur
Gordon Pym*, *Around the World in Eighty Days* (1869) of "The
Balloon-Hoax" and *Twenty Thousand Leagues Under the Sea* (1873)
of "A Descent into the Maelström." Most importantly, Verne
continued and completed the unfinished *Pym* in *The Sphinx of the
Ice-Fields* (1897), which was dedicated "A la mémoire d'Edgar

Poe." At the end of this novel, "the '*Sphinx des Glaces*' appears; and attached to the side of the monster, which as an irresistible magnet attracts every piece of steel, is the frozen body of A. G. Pym, with his gun strapped on his shoulder. Dirk Peters kneels beside his old friend and dies."

Wells' *The Time Machine* (1895), *The War of the Worlds* (1898) and *The First Men in the Moon* (1901) were influenced by Poe's application of scientific thought to fiction. In his *Experiment in Autobiography* (New York, 1934), p. 71, Wells wrote that "Poe's *Narrative of A. Gordon Pym* tells what a very intelligent mind could imagine about the [virtually unknown] south polar regions a century ago."

It is worth noting two other French figures who were influenced by Poe. The famous actor and director Aurélien-François Lugné felt a close affinity to, conceived an imaginary blood relationship with and even adopted the name of Poe, finally calling himself Lugné-Poe. And the Surrealist poet André Breton reacted against the French adoration with his Griswold-like declaration: "let us spit in passing on Edgar Poe." Breton later praised Poe for emphasizing the rational element in the process of creation and for making "the accomplishment of the work of art depend upon a prior methodic organization of its elements in view of the effect to be produced" (quoted in Maurice Nadeau, *History of Surrealism*, trans. Richard Howard [New York, 1965], p. 159, and in *The Unknown Poe*, p. 117).

10. Thomas Mann, "Dostoyevsky—Within Limits," *The Thomas Mann Reader*, ed. Joseph Angell, trans. H. T. Lowe-Porter (New York, 1960), pp. 445–446; Fyodor Dostoyevsky, *The Insulted and Injured*, trans. Constance Garnett (1981; New York, 1962), pp. 47–48; Fyodor Dostoyevsky, *Notes from Underground*, trans. Andrew MacAndrew (1864; New York, 1961), pp. 135, 90; Carlson, *Recognition of Poe*, p. 61.

In Mann's *Buddenbrooks*, trans. H. T. Lowe-Porter (1901; New York, 1946), p. 576, Kai tells Hans: "This Roderick Usher is the most remarkable character ever conceived."

In 1938 Valentin Bulgakov (a friend of Tolstoy, who later wrote *The Master and Margarita*) completed *Edgar Poe: Drama in Five Acts and Seven Scenes*, and published it two years later in Tientsin, China, where he was living in exile during Stalin's purge trials. It has not been translated.

11. Lionel Stevenson, *The Pre-Raphaelite Poets* (New York, 1974), pp. 26–27.

12. *Works*, 7:xliii; Walter Pater, "The School of Giorgione," *The Renaissance* (1888; New York, 1959), p. 98; Walter Pater, "Style," *Appreciations* (1889; New York, 1967), p. 37; Jeffrey Meyers, "*The Picture of Dorian Gray*," *Homosexuality and Literature, 1890–1930* (London, 1977), p. 31.

13. Robert Louis Stevenson, "The Works of Edgar Allan Poe" (1875), *Works*, ed. Charles Bigelow (New York, 1906), 9:255–262; Robert Louis Stevenson, *Letters to Charles Baxter*, ed. DeLancey Ferguson and Marshall Waingrow (New Haven, 1956), p. 96; Robert Louis Stevenson, Preface to *Treasure Island* (1883; New York, 1941), pp. xv, xii.

14. Kipling, quoted in Frederick Hopkins, "Shall We Preserve the Poe Cottage at Fordham?" *Review of Reviews*, 13 (April 1896), 459; Rudyard Kipling, "In the House of Suddhoo," *Plain Tales from the Hills* (New York, 1907), p. 167; Rudyard Kipling, "The Miracle of St. Jubanus," *Limits and Renewals* (London, 1932), pp. 326–327; Rudyard Kipling, "In the Same Boat," *A Diversity of Creatures* (London, 1917), p. 73.

    Hemingway perfected this technique in "The Snows of Kilimanjaro" (1936), *Short Stories* (New York, 1953), p. 66, when he wrote: "Later he had seen the things he could never think of and later still he had seen much worse."

15. Gordon Haight, *George Eliot: A Biography* (Oxford, 1968), p. 296; Poe, *Marginalia*, p. 169; Joseph Conrad, Preface to *The Nigger of the "Narcissus"*, *Three Great Tales* (New York, n.d.), p. ix.

16. Joseph Conrad, *Collected Letters*, ed. Frederick Karl and Laurence Davies (Cambridge, England, 1983–88), 1:191; Conrad, "*Heart of Darkness*," *Three Great Tales*, p. 246; Poe, *Letters*, p. 260; Conrad, *Collected Letters*, 2:427, 2:30, 2:70.

17. In *Conversations on Ebury Street* (London, 1930), pp. 201–204, George Moore discusses Poe's poetry with Walter De la Mare. In De la Mare's story "A Revenant," *The Wind Blows Over* (London, 1936), pp. 185–234, Poe attends and later criticizes a lecture about himself.

18. James Joyce, "James Clarence Mangan," *Critical Writings*, ed. Ellsworth Mason and Richard Ellmann (New York, 1964), p. 80; James Joyce, *Ulysses*, ed. Hans Gabler (New York, 1986), pp. 87, 91, 81.

    Poe's theme of premature burial is brilliantly portrayed in the Dutch film, *The Vanishing* (1990).

19. For Conan Doyle on Poe, see: Pierre Nordon, *Conan Doyle: A Biography* (New York, 1967), p. 79; Charles Higham, *The*

Adventures of Conan Doyle (New York, 1976), p. 133; Conan Doyle, *Through the Magic Door*, pp. 114–115; Arthur Conan Doyle, *Our American Adventure* (New York, 1923), p. 157; Brander Matthews, "Poe and the Detective Story," *Scribner's Magazine*, 42 (September 1907), 291.

20. Arthur Conan Doyle, *A Study in Scarlet* in *Sherlock Holmes: The Complete Novels and Stories* (New York, 1986), 1:16. In a draft monologue by Holmes for *A Study in Scarlet*, Doyle wrote: "Dupin was decidedly smart. His trick of following a train of thought was more sensational than clever, but still . . ." (Nordon, *Conan Doyle*, p. 212). Doyle, "The Cardboard Box," *Complete Novels*, 2:322; Doyle, "The Dancing Men," *Complete Novels*, 1:704.

21. Arthur Conan Doyle, *Memories and Adventures* (London, 1924), p. 74; Doyle, "The Blanched Soldier," *Complete Novels*, 2:486; Doyle, "The Six Napoleons," *Complete Novels*, 1:806; Arthur Conan Doyle, "The Poe Centenary," *Times* (London), March 2, 1909, p. 10.

The leading detective novelist in Japan today writes under the pen name of Edogawa Rampo—the Japanese form of Edgar Allan Poe.

Poe's influence on English authors has continued until the present time. In Evelyn Waugh's *The Loved One* (1948), Denis Barlow courts Aimée by passing off Poe's great lyric "To Helen" as one of his own works. At the end of the novella, Denis quotes the poem three times, identifies with Poe's love-stricken narrator and (paraphrasing Poe's "The weary way-worn wanderer bore / To his own native shore") bears his own experience "home to his ancient and comfortless shore"—England (New York, 1970), pp. 189–190. Poe's sentimental longing for his childhood sweetheart in "Annabel Lee" influenced not only *Lolita* but also the poem by Waugh's friend John Betjeman, "Indoor Games near Newberry." Most recently, Bruce Chatwin's *In Patagonia* (1977) discusses, as he nears the South Pole, *The Narrative of Arthur Gordon Pym*. And Angela Carter's "The Cabinet of Edgar Allan Poe," in *Saints and Strangers* (1986), is a fictionalized biography that emphasizes his relations with his mother and his wife.

22. Herman Melville, *Letters*, ed. Merrell Davis and William Gilman (New Haven, 1960), p. 138.

23. F. Scott Fitzgerald, *Notebooks*, ed. Matthew Bruccoli (New York, 1980), p. 318; F. Scott Fitzgerald, *Short Stories*, ed. Matthew Bruccoli (New York, 1989), pp. 188, 203, 204. For a more thor-

ough discussion of this subject, see Jeffrey Meyers, "Poe and Fitzgerald," *London Magazine*, 31 (August–September 1991), 67–73.

24. Brian Boyd, *Vladimir Nabokov: The American Years* (Princeton, 1991), p. 70; Vladimir Nabokov, *Bend Sinister* (1947; New York, 1964), p. 34; Vladimir Nabokov, *Lolita* (1955; New York, 1968), p. 11.

Poe had a genius for inventing memorable phrases and suggested a number of other book titles, from André Salmon's *Le Manuscrit trouvé dans un chapeau*, 1919, to Barbara Tuchman's *The Proud Tower*, 1966 (from "The City in the Sea"), Paul Theroux's *The Kingdom by the Sea*, 1983, and Richard Powers' *The Gold Bug Variations*, 1991.

25. Tom Wolfe, *The Bonfire of the Vanities* (New York, 1987), pp. 355–356.

26. Poe also had an impact, lasting until the present time, on several other American writers, who continued to borrow what they found useful in his prose style, his poetic rhythms and even his scholarly apparatus. Gertrude Stein's definition of her literary genealogy—"The natural line of descent is the big four: Poe to Whitman to James to myself"—could easily be dismissed as characteristically megalomaniacal and self-serving. But a keen observer like William Carlos Williams has confirmed the connection between the innovative and irrational elements in Poe's style and the humorous insouciance of Stein's experimental prose: "Sometimes he used words playfully, his sentences seem to fly away from sense, the destructive! with the conserving abandon, foreshadowed, of a Gertrude Stein."

Poe's influence on Marianne Moore and on T. S. Eliot was more specific than on Stein. Moore "said in conversation that she has been influenced by Poe's prose." And at the end of her poem "The Steeple-Jack," in which each stanza ends with a short, three-syllable phrase, Moore's friend and disciple Elizabeth Bishop wrote next to the final phrase, "stands for hope," the word " 'NEVERMORE,' a glance at Poe's rhythmic effect." Poe's use of multilingual epigraphs in his work and of learned explanatory notes for "Tamerlane" and "Al Aaraaf" provided a pedantic precedent for *The Waste Land* (1922). His bold theft and cunning transformation of other poets' work seemed to justify Eliot's pronouncement: "Immature poets imitate, mature poets steal."

Wambly Bald, *On the Left Bank, 1929–1933*, ed. Benjamin Franklin V (Athens, Ohio, 1987), p. 58; Williams, "Poe," *In the*

American Grain, p. 221; Elizabeth Bishop, "Miss Moore and Edgar Allan Poe," p. 132; David Kalstone, *Becoming a Poet* (New York, 1989), p. 39; T. S. Eliot, "Philip Massenger," *The Sacred Wood* (1920; London, 1966), p. 125.

The next generation of American authors were attracted to and identified with the grotesque, Gothic and ghoulish elements in Poe's works and life. The dismantling, bit by bit, of the hero in "The Man That Was Used Up" was adopted in Nathanael West's bizarre satire *A Cool Million* (1934). Flannery O'Connor, whose weirdly funny Southern Gothic stories were also affected by Poe's works, told a friend that her "Edgar Allan Poe period lasted for years and consisted of a volume called *The Humorous Tales of E. A. Poe*." Richard Stern's story "Teeth" (1964), about an anxious visit to a dentist, is a comic inversion of "Berenice."

The ghoulish, sacrificial, Poe-like artist in Robert Lowell's "The Severed Head" writes with his own blood and "dripped / a red ink dribble on us, as he pressed / the little strip of plastic tubing clipped / to feed it from his heart." The narrator of Philip Levine's "On the Edge" (1963) identifies, like O'Neill and Fitzgerald, with the self-destructive Poe and credits him with vast knowledge, despite his chaotic life:

> I did not write for I am Edgar Poe,
> Edgar the mad one, silly, drunk, unwise,
> But Edgar waiting on the edge of laughter,
> And there is nothing that he does not know
> Whose page is blanker than the raining skies.

Flannery O'Connor, *The Habit of Being: Letters*, ed. Sally Fitzgerald (New York, 1979), p. 98; Robert Lowell, "The Severed Head," *For the Union Dead* (1964; New York, 1967), p. 53; Philip Levine, "On the Edge" (1963), *The Contemporary American Poets*, ed. Mark Strand (New York, 1969), p. 201.

27. Poe also had a significant impact on art and music. Major painters who illustrated or were inspired by Poe's works include John Martin, Sir John Tenniel, Édouard Manet, Gustave Doré, Odilon Redon, Albert Pinkham Ryder, Paul Gauguin, James Ensor, Aubrey Beardsley, Henri Matisse and René Magritte. Manet, a close friend of Baudelaire, executed three studies of Poe in the mid-1870s, the last of which was reproduced as the frontispiece to Mallarmé's translation of *Les Poèmes d'Edgar Poe* (1888). Beardsley drew striking illustrations for several of Poe's best stories: "The Fall of the House of Usher," "The Murders in the Rue Morgue,"

"The Masque of the Red Death" and "The Black Cat." Gauguin used Poe's life as a salutary warning and in *The Writings of a Savage* (New York, 1978), p. 28, told a friend: "Remember the life of Edgar Poe, whose troubles and state of nerves led him to become an alcoholic." Gauguin's great Tahitian painting *Nevermore* (1897) alluded to Paul Verlaine's poem of that title, which was written in 1866. ("Nevermore" was later used by Marianne Moore and mentioned in a letter by Conrad.) In 1932 Matisse executed a simple but magnificently effective etching, *Le Tombeau d'Edgar Poe*, that portrayed his disturbing asymmetrical face, uneven eyes, long curving nose and anguished mouth (see Deas, *Portraits of Poe*, p. 129). When the Belgian Surrealist painter René Magritte came to New York in 1966, he visited the Fordham cottage to pay homage to the author who had had a great influence on his career as an artist.

Inspired by Poe's poetry, Edward MacDowell composed *Eldorado* and Sergei Rachmaninoff created a choral symphony, *The Bells* (1913). But Claude Debussy was the great Poe enthusiast among musicians. He believed Poe "possessed the most original fantasy among the literature of all lands; he found a note absolutely new and different" (Evans, *Music and Poe*, p. 26). Debussy wrote two unfinished operas based on *La Chute de la maison Usher* and on *Le Diable dans le beffroi* (The Devil in the Belfry); and, like so many artists, was strongly attracted to Poe's strange, abnormal characters:

I have recently been living in the House of Usher which is not exactly the place where one can look after one's nerves—just the opposite. One develops the curious habit of listening to the [sentient] stones as if they were in conversation with each other and of expecting houses to crumble to pieces as if this were not only natural but inevitable. Moreover, if you were to presume, I should confess that I like these people more than many others. . . . I have no confidence in the normal, well-balanced type of persons.

I. WORKS

Tamerlane and Other Poems. Boston: Calvin Thomas, 1827.

Al Aaraaf, Tamerlane and Minor Poems. Baltimore: Hatch & Dunning, 1829.

Poems. New York: Elam Bliss, 1831.

The Narrative of Arthur Gordon Pym. New York: Harper, 1838.

The Conchologist's First Book. Philadelphia: Haswell, Barrington and Haswell, 1839.

Tales of the Grotesque and Arabesque. Philadelphia: Lea & Blanchard, 1840.

Prose Romances. Philadelphia: William Graham, 1843.

The Raven and Other Poems. New York: Wiley & Putnam, 1845.

Tales. New York: Wiley & Putnam, 1845.

Eureka: A Prose Poem. New York: Putnam, 1848.

II. BIOGRAPHY

Rufus Griswold, "The 'Ludwig' Article," *New York Daily Tribune*, October 9, 1849, p. 2.

Rufus Griswold. "Memoir of the Author." *The Literati . . . by Edgar Allan Poe*. New York, 1850. Pp. v–xxxix.

Thomas Holley Chivers. *Life of Poe* (1852). Ed. Richard Davis. New York, 1952.

William Gill. *Life of Edgar Allan Poe* (1877). 3rd ed., revised & enlarged. London, 1878.

Eugene Didier. "Life of Edgar Poe." *The Life and Poems of Edgar Allan Poe*. New York, 1877. Pp. 19–129.

John Henry Ingram. *Edgar Allan Poe: His Life, Letters and Opinions*. 2 vols. London, 1880.

Richard Henry Stoddard. "Life of Edgar Allan Poe." *Select Works of Edgar Allan Poe*. New York, 1880. Pp. xv–clxx.

Edmund Clarence Stedman. "Memoir." *Edgar Allan Poe*. Boston, 1881. Pp. xix–xcix.

George Woodberry. *Edgar Allan Poe*. Boston, 1885. 2nd ed. 2 vols. Boston, 1909.

James Harrison. *Life and Letters of Edgar Allan Poe*. New York, 1902.

Émile Lauvrière. *Edgar Poe, sa vie et son oeuvre: Étude de psychologie pathologique*. Paris, 1904.

J. H. Whitty. "Memoir." *The Complete Poems of Edgar Allan Poe*. Boston, 1911. Pp. xix–lxxxvi.

John Robertson. *Edgar A. Poe: A Psychopathic Study*. New York, 1923.

Joseph Wood Krutch. *Edgar Allan Poe: A Study in Genius*. New York, 1926.

Hervey Allen. *Israfel: The Life and Times of Edgar Allan Poe*. New York, 1926.

Mary Elizabeth Phillips. *Edgar Allan Poe: The Man*. 2 vols. New York, 1926.

Marie Bonaparte. *The Life and Works of Edgar Allan Poe: A Psychoanalytic Interpretation*. Foreword by Sigmund Freud. (1933). Trans. John Rodker. London, 1949.

Una Pope-Hennessy. *Edgar Allan Poe: A Critical Biography*. London, 1934.

Edward Shanks. *Edgar Allan Poe*. London, 1937.

Arthur Hobson Quinn. *Edgar Allan Poe: A Critical Biography*. New York, 1941.

Philip Lindsay. *The Haunted Man: A Portrait of Edgar Allan Poe*. London, 1953.

Frances Winwar. *The Haunted Palace: The Life of Edgar Allan Poe*. New York, 1959.

William Bittner. *Poe: A Biography*. Boston, 1962.

Edward Wagenknecht. *Edgar Allan Poe: The Man Behind the Legend*. New York, 1963.

David Sinclair. *Edgar Allan Poe*. London, 1977.

Wolf Mankowitz. *The Extraordinary Mr. Poe*. New York, 1978.

Julian Symons. *The Tell-Tale Heart: The Life and Works of Edgar Allan Poe*. London, 1978.

Dwight Thomas and David Jackson. *The Poe Log: A Documentary Life of Edgar Allan Poe*. Boston, 1987.

Georges Walter. *Edgar Poe*. Paris, 1991.

Note: I completed my biography before the publication of Kenneth Silverman's *Edgar A. Poe: Mournful and Never-ending Remembrance* (New York, 1991), and reviewed his book in the *Virginia Quarterly Review*, summer 1992.

III. CRITICISM

Campbell, Killis. *The Mind of Poe and Other Studies*. Cambridge, Mass., 1933.

Carlson, Eric, ed. *The Recognition of Edgar Allan Poe*. Ann Arbor, 1966.

Dameron, J. Lasley and Irby Cauthen, eds. *Edgar Allan Poe: A Bibliography of Criticism, 1827–1967*. Charlottesville, 1974.

Davidson, Edward. *Poe: A Critical Study*. Cambridge, Mass., 1957.

Deas, Michael. *The Portraits and Daguerreotypes of Edgar Allan Poe*. Charlottesville, 1989.

Fagin, N. Bryllion. *The Histrionic Mr. Poe*. Baltimore, 1949.

Hoffman, Daniel. *Poe Poe Poe Poe Poe Poe Poe*. Garden City, New York, 1972.

Jackson, David. *Poe and the Southern Literary Messenger*. Richmond, 1934.

Jacobs, Robert. *Poe, Journalist and Critic*. Baton Rouge, 1969.

Kennedy, J. Gerald. *Poe, Death, and the Life of Writing*. New Haven, 1987.

Moss, Sidney. *Poe's Literary Battles*. Carbondale, Illinois, 1963.

Quinn, Patrick. *The French Face of Edgar Poe*. Carbondale, Illinois, 1957.

Stovall, Floyd. *Edgar Poe the Poet*. Charlottesville, 1969.

Tate, Allen. *The Man of Letters in the Modern World*. New York, 1955.

Thompson, G. R. *Poe's Fiction: Romantic Irony in the Gothic Tale*. Madison, 1973.

Walker, I. M. *Edgar Allan Poe: The Critical Heritage*. London, 1986.

Walsh, John. *Poe the Detective*. New Brunswick, New Jersey, 1968.

Wilbur, Richard. *Responses: Prose Pieces, 1953–1976*. New York, 1976.

—Compiled by Valerie Meyers